Also By Morse Peckham

*Art and Pornography:*
*An Experiment in Explanation*

*Beyond the Tragic Vision:*
*The Quest for Identity in the Nineteenth Century*

*Explanation and Power:*
*The Control of Human Behavior*

*Humanistic Education for Business Executives*

*Man's Rage for Chaos:*
*Biology, Behavior, and the Arts*

*The Romantic Virtuoso*

*Victorian Revolutionaries:*
*Speculations on Some Heroes of a Culture Crisis*

\*

*The Triumph of Romanticism:*
*Collected Essays*

*Romanticism and Behavior:*
*Collected Essays II*

\*

*Charles Darwin's* Origin of Species:
*A Variorum Text*

# ROMANTICISM
# AND
# IDEOLOGY

## Morse Peckham

Wesleyan University Press

Published by University Press of New England

Hanover and London

Wesleyan University Press
Published by University Press of New England, Hanover, NH 03755
© 1995 by Robert S. Peckham
All rights reserved
Printed in the United States of America     5   4   3   2   1
CIP data appear at the end of the book

To

HENRY WILLIAM MATALENE

AND

CAROLYN BURROWS MATALENE

# Contents

## III. THEORY OF ART AND CRITICISM

# Preface

The present volume continues the series of papers published in *The Triumph of Romanticism* (1970) and *Romanticism and Behavior* (1976). Of the nineteen papers in this volume, six have not been previously published. The papers were written from 1971 to 1981, and the writing of most of them was contemporary with work on *Explanation and Power: The Control of Human Behavior* (completed February 1978, published January 1979). Most of the papers written after the completion of the first draft of that book in 1976 use ideas briefly stated in the papers themselves but derived from and dependent upon more elaborate exposition in that book. It has been suggested to me that it would be fitting to present in an introduction a summary of the ideas in *Explanation and Power* in order to make a number of the papers more comprehensible and also to eliminate certain repetitions.

A word of caution may be helpful in understanding my use of "behavior." A good many readers have jumped to the conclusion that I am a behaviorist in the sense of academic behaviorist psychology. I am not. But I see no reason why a group of social scientists should have exclusive control over so useful a term.

All the papers in this volume were commissioned. This volume will probably be the last of this series. The principal reason is that the first of the papers here presents a position on Romanticism with which at last I feel reasonably satisfied; and in the last I have succeeded, at least to my satisfaction, in solving a problem which I set myself twenty-five years ago: "How can the philosophy of science be applied to the study of literature?"

*Columbia, South Carolina*                                                     M.P.
*March 1983*

# Acknowledgments

Chapters in this book previously were presented or published in the following places:

Chapter 1, "Cultural Transcendence: The Task of the Romantics," was presented at the Conference on English and German Romanticism, the University of Houston, February 1981.

Chapter 2, "Romanticism, Science and Gossip," was presented at the annual meeting of the Modern Language Association, December 1971. Reprinted by permission from *Shenandoah* 23, no. 4 (Summer 1972): 81–89. Copyright © by *Shenandoah.*

Chapter 3, "Romantic Historicism in Italy: Opera, Painting, Fiction," appeared in *Concept, The Texas Arts Journal,* 2–4 (Dallas, Texas: New London Press, 1978).

Chapter 4, "Frederick the Great," is reprinted by permission from *Carlyle Past and Present,* ed. K. J. Fielding and Rodger L. Tarr (London: Vision Press, 1976), pp. 198–215. Copyright © 1976 by Vision Press Ltd.

Chapter 5, "Browning and Romanticism," is reprinted by permission from *Robert Browning,* ed. Isobel Armstrong (London: G. Bell & Sons, 1974), pp. 47–76. © G. Bell & Sons, Ltd., 1974.

Chapter 6, "An Explanation of 'Realism,'" is reprinted by permission from *Denver Quarterly* 13, no. 2 (Summer 1978): 3–10. Copyright © 1978 by the University of Denver.

Chapter 7, "Victorian Counterculture," was presented at an interdisciplinary conference, "The Victorian Counterculture," at the University of South Florida, February 27–March 2, 1974. Reprinted by permission from *Victorian Studies* 18, no. 3 (March 1975): 257–276. © The Trustees of Indiana University, 1975.

Chapter 8, "Edgar Saltus and the Heroic Decadence," is reprinted by permission from *Essays in American Literature in Memory of Richard P. Adams, Tulane Studies in English* 23 (1978): 61–69. © 1978 by Tulane University.

Chapter 9, "Romanticism, Surrealism, *Terra Nostra*," was presented at a conference on Carlos Fuentes, the University of South Carolina, April 1978.

Chapter 10, "Philosophy and Art as Related and Unrelated Modes of Behavior," was presented at a conference of the State University of New York, Albany, held at Saratoga, New York, November 1973.

Chapter 11, "Man's Use of Nature," was presented at James Madison University, October 1974.

Chapter 12, "Two Ways of Using 'Creativity,'" was presented at the annual meeting of the Modern Language Association, December 1979.

Chapter 13, "Truth in Art? Why Not?" is reprinted by permission from *The Structurist*, no. 19/20 (1979/1980), pp. 15–20. © Copyrighted in Canada and the United States of America.

Chapter 14, "Psychology and Literature," is reprinted by permission from *Literary Criticism and Psychology*, ed. Joseph P. Strelka, *Yearbook of Comparative Criticism*, vol. 7, pp. 48–68. Copyright © The Pennsylvania State University.

Chapter 15, "Perceptual and Semiotic Discontinuity in Art," is reprinted by permission from *Poetics* 6 (1978): 217–230. © North-Holland Publishing Company.

Chapter 16, "Literature: Disjunction and Redundancy," is reprinted by permission from *What Is Literature?* ed. Paul Hernadi (Bloomington and London: Indiana University Press, 1978), pp. 219–230. Copyright © 1978 by Indiana University Press.

Chapter 17, "Three Notions about Criticism," is reprinted by permission from *What Is Criticism?* ed. Paul Hernadi (Bloomington and London: Indiana University Press, 1980). Copyright © Indiana University Press.

Chapter 18, "The Problem of Interpretation," is reprinted by permission from *College Literature*, vol. 6 (1979–1980), pp. 1–17. Copyright © by *College Literature*.

Chapter 19, "Literature and Behavior," was presented at the Center for the Study of Art and Symbolic Action, University of Pennsylvania, April 3, 1980.

# Introduction

The basic proposition on which the essays in this book are based is that the only generally useful comprehension of "meaning" is a behavioral comprehension, the place of meaning in the rest of human behavior. Such a notion of "meaning" yields the proposition that the meaning of an utterance is the response to that utterance, *any* response to that utterance. Since successful verbal interaction does take place, meaning behavior is controlled, but not completely nor with full success. The primary means of controlling verbal meaning behavior is verbal behavior, which is thus best conceived as instructions for verbal and nonverbal behavior. A behavioral analysis of such words as "cause," "logic," "mind," "intention," shows that their use is normative and that, in fact, all utterance is normative. Examined behaviorally, descriptive sentences are prescriptive sentences. Such a word as "truth" indicates that if an utterance is said to be "true," that statement amounts to a recommendation that the utterance in question be used as a control over behavior. Behaviorally, one can only say that a response to an utterance is appropriate—more precisely, that it is appropriate only in the judgment of someone. Thus all utterance is normative.

A behavioral analysis of categorization provides the basis for understanding explanation. Behaviorally, a category in subsuming two or more words or propositions amounts to the assertion that it is appropriate to respond to such words or propositions in the same way, a response made possible only by neglecting some attributes of the items subsumed. Thus all utterance is revealed as fictive, since all terms are categorial. One acts "as if" two or more items were appropriately responded to in the same way. Categorial subsumption is itself subsumed by more inclusive categories. Explanation is built up by a hierarchy of such subsumptive levels. The hierarchy or explanatory regress can be terminated only arbitrarily. Furthermore, since meaning is not immanent in utterance, there is no necessary subsumptive relation between any two levels of an explanatory regress. Thus, given an initial act of categorization, behavior can move in any subsuming direction, terminating, for example, equally well with theistic statements or naturalistic statements. Moreover, the higher the level of regress the more instances that can be subsumed, but at the same time the less specific are the instructions to respond to any given instance. Validation and justification are behaviorally specialized modes of explanation. All verbal behavior is both normative and fictive, and there is no position which can transcend verbal behavior, such as a meta-verbal position.

What applies to responses to utterance applies also to responses to the nonverbal. The other aspect of linguistic behavior is intonation, which is used to control response to the verbal factor of linguistic behavior. An intonation of an utterance can be considered as a sign of how the utterance ought to be responded to. Hence both the verbal factor and the intonation factor of an utterance are signs. "Sign" subsumes both word and intonation. Hence "sign" can be applied as well to the nonverbal world, not only signs produced by human beings, such as gestures, but any configuration in the non-human-made world. When a configuration, or figure, is perceptually distinguished from its ground, it is then a sign. What is true of verbal signs is also true of nonverbal signs; responses to signs are both fictive and normative, for response depends upon categorial subsumption and response transfer from familiar signs to an unfamiliar sign. As the world comes into our perceptual field, the world turns into signs. Our relation to the world is a semiotic relation. From the evolutionary point of view, the puzzle is how the leap from nonverbal to verbal behavior was accomplished, that is, the leap from categorization dependent upon continuity of attributes from one sign to another (nonverbal semiotic response) to categorization not so dependent, except for the attribute of sound (verbal semiotic response). That the human brain is capable of random response accounts for this leap. From the perspective of nonverbal behavior, all verbal response is thus random. The result of the imposition of verbal semiosis on nonverbal semiosis is the enormous increase of the possibilities of randomness of response, of destabilization of behavior, and consequently for the necessity of control of verbal behavior if interaction is to take place, as it must for economic reasons. The complete form of that verbal control over behavior is explanation, built up initially by verbal subsumption of nonverbal signs.

The defining attribute of human semiotic behavior, then, is that response to signs entails the production of signs. Thus the most precise definition of human behavior is "semiotic transformation." Explanation controls behavior, and the recognition that semiotic behavior must be controlled is complemented by the recognition that all behavior is aggressive, in that the organism has no choice but to struggle to control and exploit the environment, including, for human beings, the centrally important verbal environment. Two basic categories of signs can be distinguished, both most easily identified in linguistic behavior: "performatory signs," which give instructions on what is to be done, and "regulatory signs," which give instructions concerning the appropriate level of aggression. Semiotic behavior, including verbal behavior, thus controls both "meaning" and "aggression." In linguistic behavior, words are performatory signs and intonational signs are regulatory. Any configuration for which the response has been established can be a performatory sign; regulatory signs are such matters as pitch, rhythm, volume, tempo, color, verticality, horizontality, shallowness, depth, and so on. Regulatory signs are interpreted to signify either guidance or hindrance to aggression. Interpretation has the same structure as explanation, is hierarchical, and is historical, depending upon response transfer and semiotic transformation. Interpretation is a perceptual disengagement of an analogically determined recurrent semiotic pattern from an analogically determined series of semiotic matrices.

Mythology and science are both modes of interpretation, for both are derived not from empirical data (the world of semiotic configurations) but from preceding and less developed explanatory regresses. Science differs from mythology in not resting on a judgment of an explanatory regress as a stable guidance, but in exploiting the instability and nonimmanency of all levels of explanation from sign configurations in the natural world to that termination of explanation known as scientific theory. Thus experiment modifies explanation by generating semiotic material (or data) which the current explanation cannot successfully subsume. This is feedback. Science is merely the most complete model of the semiotic hierarchy from configuration to the termination of an explanatory regress, inasmuch as it depends upon the capacity for randomness of response.

Man, then, is best understood as *homo scientificus*. But he is not so as an individual organism. Rather, the behavior that controls explanation is the kind of behavior subsumed under "society" and "culture." "Sciencing" brings out the universality of "scientific" behavior, which is of course primarily a verbal mode of behavior, and therefore both normative and fictive. The exploitation of the brain's capacity for randomness makes scientific innovation possible, but this is the model for all learning, since the acquisition of a behavior pattern is, for that organism, an innovation. Thus the factors in learning are the production of any response, the production of random responses, and the selection or validation of one of those random responses. (The brain's capacity to produce random responses is the termination of the explanatory construct of human behavior here proposed.)

To be controlled, behavior must be channelled, which is the task of any learning situation. Left to itself, the brain will produce random responses. Channelling depends first upon unreliable remembering, which must be supplemented by the constant reiteration in various semiotic modalities of the same instructions, that is, by cultural redundancy, and redundancy is supplemented by policing, the use of force. Thus meaning is ultimately stabilized by the ultimate sanctions of economic deprivation, imprisonment, the infliction of pain, and execution. In modern societies the first three are constantly used in the socialization of children, and in the past the fourth was available, as it still is in certain less developed societies. But if force fails, there is no recourse; therefore culture (or civilization) has as its principal task the maintenance of behavioral stability by circumventing the use of force. The modes of circumvention are the two basic rhetorical modes of seduction and intimidation. Thus "culture" may be defined as those semiotic, directive redundancy systems in response to which behavior is controlled, and patterns of behavior are maintained through time. But culture by itself cannot successfully channel behavior. Because culture depends upon the nonimmanence of meaning and the consequent instability of meaning, it is constantly threatened with disintegration, with undermining, and with impoverishment. Culture not only channels behavior; it is also responsible for the spread of deviance into a behavior delta configuration. Controls, therefore, are set over culture. These controls are social institutions, of which five may be distinguished: teaching-learning institutions (the family is the initial institution), value institutions (which maintain the individual's self-ascription of value, which subsumes judgments of his competence, but these judgments are necessarily, by reason of subsumption, unstable), economic institutions, governmental institutions, and ideological institutions (sciences, the arts, philosophy, scholarship). The structure of the interaction among institutional levels is the structure of explanation, for the verbal behavior within an institution is that of an explanatory regress. An institution is an explanatory regress. An ideology itself consists of the high and terminating levels of an institution. Behavior within government institutions is either of governance (the resolution of ideological incoherence) or of politics (concerned with stabilizing or destabilizing governmental institutions). The tasks of ideological institutions are those of maintaining ideological redundancies, exemplifying them (a particular task of the arts, though not unique to them), and criticizing them, either by evaluative criticism or by the critique, which is the ideological mode of undermining ideologies. The importance of ideological institutions is indicated by the fact that a revolutionary government aims as soon as it possibly can at complete ideological control over ideological institutions. Cultural levels are the levels of explanatory regress in ideological institutions. The higher the cultural level the greater the exploitation of behavioral instability, and the lower the cultural level the greater the behavioral stabilization. These five kinds of institutions are, in a sense, analytical abstractions, for every institution carries on all five institutional functions. Cultural history is the gradual emergence of institutions which specialize in one particular kind of institutional control over culture, using the other kinds as subsidiary and subordinate modes of control.

The argument so far can be summarized in the following rather melancholy conclusions. Culture controls behavior; culture consists of performatory and regulatory semiotic redundancy systems; words control redundancy systems; the defining attribute of verbal behavior is explanation; explanation is hierarchical, behavioral control is thus hierarchical, and all institutions are hierarchically organized; behavioral control is a matter of learning socially validated performances; performances consist of responses appropriate to the presentation of particular signs; behavior control depends upon the meaning of those signs; and smooth behavioral interaction of any kind depends upon the illusion that meaning is immanent, but since meaning is not immanent, appropriate response can ultimately be maintained only by the application of force in the forms of economic deprivation, imprisonment, torture, and execution. The brightest spot in this picture is the capacity of science to exploit ideological instability, which is particularly noticeable in the culture of the West. In Western countries is to be found the greatest proportion of the population which experiences the life enhancement of the negative inversions of the ultimate sanctions: economic ease, the privileges of freedom and pleasure, and the enhancement of the individual's own value (i.e., human dignity). But that very individual is the cyclonic center of disturbance in the structure of human behavior, the Catch-22.

The individual as biological entity is not identical with the behavioral individual, the deposit of the organization and control of human behavior. First, the individual as persona is the selective, deceptive, and coherent semiotic interpretation of the behavioral individual, either by the individual himself or by someone else. It is an interpretation of a randomly assembled package of learned behavioral patterns. The persona construct assumes that the behavioral individual is a conjunctive category (a category in which certain attributes are found in all members of that category), but it is in fact a disjunctive category (a category in which there are no attributes in common to all members, and which is a cultural and social heuristic convenience). Personality is to the individual as culture is to human behavior. Personality organizes and stabilizes the behavioral individual and ascribes value to it. From this it follows that an interest is a strategy that maintains personal stability. This is obvious in noneconomic interests (though an interest can be economically functional, probably a rarity in modern society). An example is collecting. As affluence in this country increased, discretionary income and discretionary time increased. The consequence was an enormous increase in the behavioral phenomenon of collecting. This was a repetition of the collecting behavior which historically has always been a behavioral pattern of members of an affluent class. Interests are the repressive oppressor of the individual upon himself, a way of controlling and stabilizing behavior. Alcoholic or other drug addictions are further examples of interests. Agape and eros are further and almost universal modes of interest. Agape or social love resolves temporarily the tension arising from the struggle to maintain the equilibrium between aggression and control. Eros (whether sexual or mystical) resolves the tension that arises from maintaining the distinction between figure and ground and from maintaining the categorial stability of the figure so distinguished, particularly the persona as disjunctive category. Both arise from the irresolvable tension of maintaining relatively stable explanatory regresses without resorting to or being overcome by the ultimate sanctions. Agape and eros are redemptive modes, safe enough when used as vacations, but immensely destructive, as in revolutionary utopianism, when redemption is hypostatized by language into the ideal of an absolute stability, behavioral, cultural, and institutional, and an absolute freedom from the basic tensions of human behavior, the sources of organic stress. Thus redemptionism is ultimately the attempt to escape from randomness, which is, in fact, the source of human adaptability.

When this randomly assembled package of interests is introduced into an institution, the smooth working of the institution becomes impossible. Directions given from above and feedback from below (corrections of the institutional ideology from beyond the verbal frontier of the institution) necessarily threaten to destabilize the position of the individual of the institution, his "politics." Hence instructions and feedback information are both distorted, one on the way down, the other on the way up. Thus, looking up, the perspective is primarily one of resentment, and looking down, one of contempt. The first regards higher levels as hindrances to aggression, the second regards lower levels as fundamentally incompetent. This increases the randomness within the institution, and paradoxically, can either destroy it or make it more viable, more adaptable.

This fundamentally unsatisfactory condition of the irresolvable conflict between individual and institution yields on the part of a few individuals the behavioral phenomenon known as cultural transcendence. The importance of the Romanticism of the early nineteenth century is that a few innovative Romantics discovered and established within Western culture the basic behavior pattern of cultural transcendence. This arises from the judgment of explanatory collapse (the failure of ideologies), alienation from the culture and the society's institutions, cultural vandalism, social withdrawal, reducing the interaction rate to the minimum, randomizing behavior, selecting a promising emergent innovation, collecting a little group of supporters, and propagandizing the cultural emergent or innovation or "creativity." The Romantic emergent innovation or cultural transcendence was a deconversion from hypostatized redemptionism; that deconversion led to a conversion into a permanent deconversion. But it must always be remembered that no institution works well, whether authoritarian or democratic, for there is always a conflict, an incoherence, between the task or mission of the larger institution and the stability of the individual, for innovation always threatens dissolution of the persona. And it takes the richest possible development of the individual at the highest cultural levels to make such dissolution both tolerable and profitable. It is possible to the degree the individual regards himself as a social dyad; i.e., he knows himself just as he understands another, by observing his own behavior.

Ultimately, then, there is nothing but the individual organism, behaving, and by that device we call semiosis turning behavior into performance. The behavioral individual is the precipitate of semiosis and culture and redundancies and institutions and ultimate sanctions; he is the irreducible surd of existence, the fundamental incoherence of human life, for he cannot but strive with all his might, with all his aggressiveness, for stability; and yet at the same time he is the only source of that randomization from which issue emergent innovations—which if they cannot eliminate can at least modify, not infrequently for the better, our fictive and normative absurdities of explanation.

Explanation is the ineluctable condition, the defining attribute of human behavior, and that proposition is the termination of the explanatory regress of this theory of human behavior.

# I

# THE ROMANTIC TRADITION

# CHAPTER ONE

# Cultural Transcendence

## The Task of the Romantics

I

Will we ever understand the Romantics? Will we ever understand Romanticism? Will we ever understand the people who write about Romanticism? Indeed, will we ever understand those critics who in the past couple of decades have written long and detailed and exhausting explanations about particular Romantic works? The answer to all these questions is, Probably not, at least not very completely or satisfactorily. But this conclusion is by no means pessimistic, although it may sound so. On the contrary, though our understanding of all of these related problems is inadequate, it is surely far more adequate than when I began writing about Romanticism more than thirty years ago, at a time when the question "What is Romanticism?" had almost been abandoned. Happily, René Wellek reopened the problem; since then matters have improved considerably.

Moreover, I do not think we should expect positive answers to the questions I have asked, an answer of a type that to the question "What is Romanticism?" the answer can be "Romanticism is so-and-so," an answer that will be accepted by just about everybody in the academic and literary worlds, except, of course, for the usual number of odd-balls. Here the philosophy of science can be summoned to our aid. I am aware that it is the usual assumption that science and literary study have nothing to do with each other, but I do not believe that to be the case. I think that the student of literature and the scientist not only have much in common but are engaged in the same kind of behavior. But before attempting to say what I mean by this, let me make it clear that I am talking about the literatus engaged in the historical study of literature, not one who uses canonical literature for other ideological purposes.

The virtual identity between scientific research and historical-philosophical research I would establish upon the fact that both emerged at the same time, in the fifteenth and sixteenth centuries, and from the same cultural situation. In spite of the obvious difference between the two in the circumstance that one is engaged in the study of a particular category of verbal phenomena and the other in non-verbal and verbal phenomena of various categories (assuming, obviously, that literature is a category such that we can distinguish between literary verbalization and other verbalizations) both are faced with the same problem: How should one interpret a particular configuration, whether it is a plant or a poem, a crystal or a play? This problem arises because the interpretation of any configuration has no theoretical limits, only pragmatic limits. Now what emerged in the fifteenth and sixteenth centuries was the decision not to interpret a configuration from the point of view of an *a priori* position, primarily theological, but rather from the circumstances or situation in which the configuration emerged and in which it is found. Both historical interpretation of documents surviving from a preceding period and the scientific study of physical phenomena can be subsumed under the more general category of situational interpretation. Since there are only pragmatic limits to interpretation, but no theoretic limits, the problem in any interpretation (and we live in an interpreted world) is to set up controls over an interpretation. Thus when we ask what the "intention" behind a work might have been, we are telling ourselves that the appropriate interpretation is not immediately and unquestionably obvious and that we must seek controlling clues, first, but not exclusively, from other behavior of the individual responsible for the work. As science gradually perfected the experimental method, what it found to be necessary was to limit, experimentally, the factors in the situation from which the configuration to be studied can reasonably be said to emerge. In the same way early fifteenth-century Florentine historians asserted that, contrary to the tradition, Cicero should not be said to be a bad man because he objected to the foundation of the empire, which, as every one knew, was founded by the will of God to provide the secular arm for the church, and its protection, but was to be accounted a good or moral man because he emerged from a situation in which it was impossible to know anything about the church and its future. And just as the scientist found he could best proceed by limiting the situational factors, so the philological-historical study of literature did the same, by beginning with a study of the crucial words of a document or literary text—those words the interpretations of which were most doubtful. A century before Vico there were those who grasped that this limitation was pragmatic, heuristic at best, and that to understand fully the meaning of a document it would be necessary to understand fully the entire culture, as we now use the word in its anthropological sense, from which the work emerged. In the same way there were scientists (Newton seems to have been among them) who knew that to interpret adequately a natural configuration it would be necessary to understand the whole of the natural world, to the farthest limits of space, assuming that there are limits, in itself a puzzling notion.

Nevertheless, for a long time the scientist was, though remotely, under the control of a theological ideology, even though it was vague and had suffered severe attrition as science itself had advanced. Thus it was assumed that the task of the scientist was to discover those basic laws that govern the universe. Presumably such laws would explain literature, though there probably have been few scientists who have been particularly concerned about that problem. At any rate it was not until late in the nineteenth century (although there had been adumbrations) that it was realized that the pursuit of fundamental natural laws is a vanity. On the contrary, it was realized that a scientific law is never more than theory, a verbal and at its best a mathematical construct, a human convenience. And the realization also came that science advances by exploiting the inherent instability of scientific theory—and has advanced by that exploitation, even though scientists themselves thought they were doing something quite different. That is the realization responsible for the overwhelming advance of science in the twentieth century.

In seeking for a final definition of Romanticism, students of the history of literature are engaged in a pre-twentieth-century endeavor. In asking "What was Romanticism, really?" we are asking a question analogous to "What is the natural law that governs this phenomenon?" George Herbert Mead said it as well as anybody ever has. A scientist, he maintained, is happy only when his experimentation reveals that his theory is wrong. Only that kind of feedback enables him to correct and improve his theory. Actually, the historical study of literature has proceeded in the same way. We are so aware of its inadequacies, and so impatient at times with its results, that we forget what has been achieved in the past five hundred years. And that achievement has been as extraordinary as the achievement of science. Nor must we forget that the study of nonliterary documents, what we call history itself, has been even more massive and impressive, even though so many once apparently solid results have turned out to be unsatisfactory. But the dissatisfaction has emerged from the examination of hitherto unexamined documents. History is not about the events of the past but about documents, and literary history is about a pragmatically circumscribed category of documents. What we need to recognize, therefore, is that the theory of Romanticism, like any theory, is inherently unstable. At any stage of its enrichment it has a heuristic function, and the aim of theory is so to direct our exploration of known and hitherto unknown documents that our theory is improved by revealing its inadequacies. We should think in terms of an increasingly enriched and increasingly adequate theory of Romanticism—adequate for the interpretation of Romantic documents, our primary concern—but never in terms of hoping to arrive at an answer to the question "What was Romanticism, really?"

But before engaging directly with Romanticism I should like to make two other observations about what I have called situational interpretation. The first is that situational interpretation is the norm of interpretation in the most ordinary and mundane interaction. Our behavior is overwhelmingly governed by the protocols of a given situation. Our response is automatic, once we have learned it and practiced it a few times. Hence arises the illusion that the response is dictated by the situation, and that the appropriate response is immanent in the situation itself. We actively and knowingly engage in interpretation, however, when what we are responding to is emergent in that category of situation and appears, at least, to violate the behavioral protocols of that category. Under such circumstances we get ourselves going by asking ourselves "What did he mean by that?" Nonsituational interpretation of phenomena, whether or not immediately present, is of quite a different character. It is under the control of an ideology which resists or does not permit or is incapable of correction by feedback. It is the interpretational mode of those who are committed to a final theory of literature, or a final theological or political or psychological or philosophical theory. Such ideologies are verbal cancers, for they are, metaphysically, of the kind of cancer that is neither operable nor treatable. Unfortunately they can survive for centuries, even for millennia.

The second point I would make is that the limitation of factors in situational interpretation, as in scientific experimentation, is always pragmatic and usually more or less arbitrary, and always arbitrary at the beginning of an investigation of a hitherto unexamined phenomenon. Hence both science and historical scholarship are always pressing at their pragmatic limitations. From this arises what has been so striking in this century, the emergence of new scientific disciplines, biochemistry, for example. The same phenomenon is to be found in the historical study of literature. As such scholarship has developed, interdisciplinary scholarship has become an increasing threat to the imagined integrity of literary scholarship. Thus in the theoretical quarrels of literary study, particularly since the First World War, there have been two tendencies, one to limit severely the discipline of literary study, the other to expand literary study into cultural history, particularly the history of the other arts, of the history of philosophy, of the history of scientific theory, specifically the philosophy of science. Here the student of literature faces a peculiar embarrassment. The historical study of art and of music is hardly out of adolescence. Only since 1976 has architectural history even begun to organize information about the monuments of nineteenth-century architectural history; and the history of nineteenth-century painting, aside from those artists who led directly to impressionism and modernism, is hardly a decade old. Likewise the history of music from about 1730 to 1790 is hardly more than in the initial stages of bibliographical organization. In the past twenty years, for example, we have seen a complete revolution in our comprehension of the music of Haydn. As far as that goes, the serious historical study of Victorian poetry is not much older.

Both of these points will have their place in what follows.

II

I shall turn, then, to the problem of Romanticism, more specifically to cultural transcendence as the task of the Romantics. I use the term cultural transcendence in the widest possible sense, to direct attention to the most ordinary forms of it as well as to modes of cultural transcendence at the highest cultural level, a level at which, I believe, the Romantics were operating. As an example of cultural transcendence, consider an automotive engineer who discovers that the redesign of an automobile engine entails the malfunction of any carburetor designed according to the existent principles of design, that is, the current cultural protocols for designing carburetors. The engineer's experimentation with old carburetors on his new engine elicits a feedback which undermines those principles. It is the kind of problem with which the automobile industry has been struggling for a decade, and we all know that the results are not as yet satisfactory. Nevertheless there has been striking improvement in the miles per gallon the fleets of automobile manufacturers have been achieving. I merely wish to emphasize that cultural transcendence in mechanical matters is not different from cultural transcendence in high culture, and to suggest that the Romantics—that infinitesimal portion of the European population at the beginning of the nineteenth century, perhaps at the most a hundred individuals out of a population of perhaps 200,000,000, including Russia, or of about 70,000,000, if we limit the initial Romantic area to England, Germany, and France—proposed to themselves the task of cultural transcendence.

Before, however, I can engage with that problem I find it necessary to deal with a term that many people have long since abandoned, at least in literary studies, and at least in this country, though evidently in England and on the continent and in art history it continues to be used. I mean the term pre-Romanticism or proto-Romanticism. My first objection to this term is that it violates a basic principle of historical scholarship: a document or set of documents or artifacts should be interpreted by deriving controls over the interpretation from the situation in which the documents or artifacts emerged. The notion of pre-Romanticism endeavors to interpret documents which began to emerge forty years before the emergence of those documents and artifacts which it is almost universally agreed are properly called Romantic. Obviously the documents from which interpretational factors are derived are themselves subject to interpretation, and just as obviously such interpretations are themselves unstable. That is one of the reasons for the fundamental instability of historical explanation or theory. Like the situational factors in scientific experimentation, they are relatively stable compared with the documents to be interpreted, or their observable attributes are redundant with observable attributes in the phenomena to be interpreted. In this situation the question is whether or not those works called pre-Romantic can be successfully subsumed by the current stage of Enlightenment theory construction. I believe they can be.

Now let me admit at once that there are few or no themes found in pre-Romanticism that are not also to be found in Romanticism. Why that should be so I shall consider later. At the moment I shall turn instead to what, for my present purposes, I shall call the stylistic character of pre-Romanticism. It frequently happens, especially since around 1600, that music is an excellent clue to the cultural character of a period, simply because the thematic, that is, the propositionally expressible, is eliminated from consideration. In music the most important emergent from the middle of the eighteenth century on was the appearance and development of what is currently being called sonata style. Baroque and Rococo or *style galant* style was under the control of the theory of affects. The point of this is that music was considered to express emotions. I think that this notion is inadequate, though not completely wrong, but for my present purposes it will do. According to Charles Rosen and others, what the sonata style did was to abandon the theory of affects. Insofar as that theory meant that a movement of a work is properly devoted to expressing a single affect, I think Rosen is correct. But he is easily misunderstood. It is clear from other remarks that what he is getting at is that a movement in the sonata style could express a variety of affects, from the most tender to the most violent. The term for such an emotional condition is emotional lability. Webster gives "changeable," "unstable," and "adaptable" as synonyms for labile, and the psychological definition as "tending to discharge rather than retain affect." All of these are very much to my purpose. The years 1766 to 1775 have been called the *Sturm-und-Drang* period in Haydn's style, although the application of this term to Haydn has been objected to as inappropriate because Haydn, off in Eszterhaza, could have known little about the small group of *Sturm-und-Drang* writers. Perhaps so. At any rate, some musicologists have seen an affinity between those writers and Haydn, and I believe that affinity is observable, for certainly emotional lability is a mark of *Sturm-und-Drang* writing. At about this time a term began to be widely used in a very special sense; that term is "the picturesque," which was shortly to be elevated to an equality with the sublime and the beautiful. Two other terms also made their appearance, "romantic" and "sentimental," and something called "feeling" begins to be extolled. In the 1760s Sterne said that the two knobs at the back of his chair were equal in shape and height, just as reason and feeling are equal in importance and value.

These three terms, then, picturesque, sentimental (or sentiment and feeling), and romantic, began to be important about the same time and were to a considerable degree interchangeable. Each brought out a different aspect of the emotionally labile. "Sentimental" focused on the subjective state; "picturesque" on visual variability, or even incoherence, just as the sublime and the beautiful were two modes of visual coherence; "romantic" focused on the notion that the origin of emotional lability was medieval-renaissance European culture, observable in medieval romance and Ariosto, as opposed to the classic, that is, the ancient world as the source of the proper models for the sublime and the beautiful. Among painters the emotionally labile, or visually picturesque, may be found in the later Fragonard, in Gainsborough, in Horace Vernet, and in Hubert Robert. Simultaneously the epistolary novel owed its popularity, I believe, to the opportunity it offered for presenting the emotionally labile, both in the shift from one character to another and, within a letter, in the private emotional instability of the individual imaginary correspondent. It is hardly necessary to mention *Werther* as a supreme example of this sort, along with *La Nouvelle Héloise*. At the same time the emergent character of Rousseau's *Confessions*, written between 1764 and 1770, is to be found in the deliberate emphasis upon Rousseau's emotional instability, or lability, which he presented as the normal or natural condition of emotional behavior. This turn toward emotional lability also accounts for the sudden acceptance of Shakespeare as a natural genius, not subject to the dramatic rules and transcending them. Goethe patterned the *Ur-Faust* on Shakespearean emotional lability, and continued that pattern to the end of Part II.

Two other words increasingly popular at the time were "nature" (and its cognates) and "adaptation." Both are instances of the gradual displacement of religious and metaphysical thinking and the secularization of European culture during the Enlightenment by that mode of thinking emerging in the fifteenth and sixteenth centuries which I have already called situational thinking. An example is Herder's theory of the origin of language. Denying that it was a divine gift or that it was immanent in the rational mind, he asserted that it can be accounted for by considering it as a necessary consequence of interaction among human beings; that is, it was a natural product, emergent from the human situation. At the same time it is easy to see in clothes and domestic architecture a more "natural" style, that is, one adapted to human physiology and comfort. The period saw the invention of upholstered furniture and the emergence of a variety of eating and serving utensils, the latter adapted to the morphology of the particular food being served. One served cabbage soup in a tureen shaped like a cabbage, and fish in a fish-shaped platter.

It is clear that the psychological definition of the labile, tending to discharge rather than retain affect, is entirely serviceable and appropriate to what was going on in a great variety of cultural areas during the period known as pre-Romanticism. The man of feeling became the ideal because he was the more natural man, one who responded to changes in his situation, one who did not retain an affect by controlling it by means of a stable affect. Baroque music retained affect by stabilizing it; sonata style discharged it. To control affect by affective stability is, it was judged, an act of reason, of rational control, of stoicism. Furthermore, it was asked, What is the cultural situation of European man? What indeed are his roots? And the answer was being found by Herder and others. The roots were in the early middle ages, in Christianity, even in the pre-Christian dark ages. Hence the enormous impact of Ossian. Eighteenth-century European man, it appeared, was not a product of the Mediterranean antiquity, of the classic world, but of the culture of tribes untouched, it was thought, by Greece and Rome. Ossian proved that the European situation had a natural origin different from the situation of antiquity. No wonder, since it was written to prove just that.

It may be too succinct, too abstract, but even so, I think it is adequate to say that what was happening ideologically in the second half of the eighteenth century was the pulling apart of nature and reason; but it has been clear for a long time that in later Enlightenment thinking the claims of nature, and above all of emotional lability, were as valid as the claims of reason, and for a good many individuals of the time considerably more valid. The explanation for this divergence, a divergence of central importance for understanding the task of the Romantics, lay in the inherent contradiction, already hinted at, of situational thinking, that mode of interpretation which separates us today from medieval culture, makes us feel something profoundly different about it. On the one hand situational thinking seeks to interpret and explain a phenomenon, natural object, or document in terms of the factors associated with it and, perhaps, responsible for it. On the other hand, since the situation is by definition theoretically unlimited, the selection of those factors must be accomplished by the imposition of a construct not derived from the situation, a construct that must be the product of what we call, too carelessly and too optimistically, the reason.

The perfect example of that inherent contradiction may be found in painting, the invention of perspective in the early fifteenth century. Situational thinking meant that a saint could be presented only once in a painting, and in a single incident of his life, not several times in several incidents, but in the same setting. Perspective gave the painter the control of the situation from a single point of view, the point of view from which an individual perceives all situations. Nevertheless the system of perspective is not derived from perception but is rationally and mathematically imposed upon it, since in fact binocular vision and three-dimensional perception depend upon the fusion of two separate images.

The notion of pre-Romanticism is faulty because it does not depend upon a comprehension of the fact that nature, the natural, the situation, the exaltation of feeling and sentiment, the picturesque, the anti-classic romantic, were just as much part of Enlightenment culture as the rational, the classic, the sublime, the beautiful; that emotional lability was just as much an Enlightenment phenomenon as the rational control of affect by means of a controlling affect. The fact that both strains of Enlightenment culture had a common cultural background is indicated by the fact that in all the arts and in all styles the last few decades of the eighteenth century saw a steady stylistic simplification. Put more precisely, that meant that the output of cognitive energy required to make a perceptual accommodation and adaptation to the work was steadily reduced. This stylistic trend can be seen in, to give a few examples, the work of Boullée and Ledoux, the architects, in David, in the London symphonies of Haydn, in his chamber music, and in his later choral works, in Cowper, in the German painter Hackert, and in Weimarian classicism. The notion of pre-Romanticism emerged, it must be remembered, at a time when the eighteenth century was categorized as The Age of Reason, and it also emerged at a time when the metaphors of evolution and development were widely applied to historical phenomena. Darwin made a bad mistake, I think, when at Spencer's suggestion he adopted the term evolution for the sequence of origins of species from existing species. What years ago I called Darwinisticism immediately took up what was in fact an Enlightenment metaphysical term and imposed an idealistic and metaphysical metaphorical construct upon historical events. Pre-Romanticism tends to drain away from the later Enlightenment everything that was characteristic of it. But to admit, as I have, as I maintain, that the themes of the later Enlightenment were used by the Romantics is not to admit or to maintain that they were used for carrying out the same task. Quite the contrary, and to that problem I shall now turn.

## III

A useful place to begin is with Goethe's old wheeze about the classic being healthy and the Romantic being sick. What he was talking about probably comes clearer when we remember an equally famous and equally fatuous assertion by Freud that to question the value of life is already to be sick. Not to question the value of life, however, is to accept unhesitatingly the platitudes of one's culture, particularly those regnant platitudes we call ideology. It must be recognized that an ideology is always out of phase with the situation in which it is employed, for an ideology has always emerged as a response to a preceding situation, the attributes of which are different from those of the current situation. As an example—one with which, I daresay, many will quarrel—it appears to me that at the present time the ideologies of both the political left and the political right are bankrupt. Both capitalism and socialism are Enlightenment ideologies, and the regnant metaphor of capitalism—the invisible hand—is obviously a secularization of the notion of divine providence, just as socialism is also providential. Original sin having been eliminated by secularization and converted into human error and selfishness, once socialism has eliminated such error and selfishness, man can abrogate his responsibility by trust in the bounteousness of nature and the goodness of human nature. In that sense, nature was merely a secularization of the divine and of the providential. If, then, it is recognized that the ideology of a culture is always failing—and certainly human history seems to support such a notion—then to recognize that failure, to question the ideological platitudes which affirm the value of life, to question the value of life itself, is the first step toward health.

I should like to propose a justification for the Romantics from a very distant position, one with which they were entirely unfamiliar. It has been said over and over again—Stephen Jay Gould is simply the most recent one to have said so, to my knowledge—that the big brain gives flexibility and that man is the most flexible of animals because he has the biggest brain. As Gould has put it, this means that smaller-brained animals are morphologically committed to a set of environmental factors, but that human flexibility means that man is not so committed. I think that this is an error. What he is suggesting is that adaptational mechanisms are likewise maladaptational, in that morphological commitment prevents the emergence of further adaptational mechanisms, the exception being man. But I do not believe that exception to be tenable. Every human being is morphologically committed to language. That language is a wonderful adaptive mechanism is universally recognized; that language is a maladaptation seems to be only rarely acknowledged. Indeed, I cannot remember ever having run across such a recognition. Yet I believe it to be the case. Language operates independently of the physical world; it transcends the physical world; it is not tied down to it by any ligatures. It gives man freedom, which it is wiser to think of as indeterminability. Language does not reflect the world; it is a verbal transformation of the world. To use a word I shall return to, any utterance is always a product of the imagination. Consequently as far back in recorded history as we can go, or guess, it is apparent that language has given men the capacity to construct the most outrageous silliness and to use all the force at his disposal to make that constructed silliness control the behavior of as many human beings as possible.

I do not maintain, obviously, that the Romantics held this notion of language, though a good many of them perceived that language was somehow or other at the heart of the human problem, especially those who had read Herder. Rather I believe it to be the case that to question the regnant ideologies of one's culture is at least a step towards questioning the adaptational validity of the defining attribute of man, language itself, and that health, if health is possible to man, depends upon the recognition that language is a severe human limitation upon species survival. At a time when population growth is conflicting head on with the limits of natural resources, language tells millions of people, in a number of cultures, that the simplest and most convenient and reliable techniques of population control must not be used. I am not aware of any group in any culture that has questioned so severely the regnant ideologies as did the Romantics. They began, I believe, a process of undermining the ideological superstructure of Western culture, and of culture itself, an undermining which, it may be, is the only human hope.

Nevertheless, at the time, in the early decades of the nineteenth century, very few saw the Romantics in that light. Quite the contrary. Let us look at them from the point of view of a contemporary utterly unsympathetic with what they were trying to do and what they managed to do, of such a man as Goethe, for instance, a man who, he said, was in his whole life happy only during the year and a half he spent in Italy and who devoted most of the rest of his life to betraying his genius by being a civil servant in a miserable little German duchy. To such a man the attribute common to all the Romantics was that they were bizarre, bizarre in their lives and bizarre in their works. "What a world, what a set!" Arnold said of Shelley and his circle, and Watts-Dunton was surely responding to a pervasive character of Romantic works when he spoke of their "strangeness." One can but retrospectively congratulate Francis Jeffrey that he was spared *The Prelude,* considering his response to *The Excursion.* If Blake is counted among the Romantics, as I think he should be, but just barely, or minimally, surely "bizarre" is the right word for at least an initial response to the prophetic poems, and possibly one's final and conclusive response. Those proper names! It is difficult to contain one's laughter. Novalis's *Hymns to the Night* and Heinrich von Ofterdingen are hardly less bizarre than Blake. A search for a blue flower, indeed! Or what could be more bizarre, more absurd, to any rational man of common sense than Shelley's claim that poets are the legislators of the world. And so on. Though Goethe's opinion was imperceptive, and even vulgar, it is not difficult at all to assume a position towards the Romantics from which "sickness" is the nicest thing one can say about them.

The valuable thing about looking at the Romantics from such a position is that it recognizes a sudden and powerful cultural emergence, even though it disapproves of it. In the arts it recognizes a stylistic break. At this point it is useful to look at a few painters, for in them one can see readily the striking emergence of new styles. Anton Koch painted landscapes in the spirit of Goethe's *Iphigenia,* an evocation of the classic world, at once sublime and beautiful. As in all landscape painting of the late eighteenth century the human figures are small, so buried in the natural world as to become part of it, and for that reason they are often country folk. Now to turn from Koch to Caspar David Friedrich is to experience an extraordinary stylistic break or emergence. A characteristic of both Friedrich's paintings and those of Philip Otto Runge is that the human figures in both are often large, almost filling the picture space from top to bottom. In Friedrich's, time and again a single large figure stands with his or her back to the observer and faces a vast and highly symmetrical landscape, as opposed to the "natural" irregularity of the landscapes of Koch. The imposition of human interest upon the natural world could hardly be more vividly presented. Or in such pictures as the extraordinary *Monk on the Seashore* and the tragically destroyed *Cloister Graveyard in Snow* the human figures though small are not sunk in the landscape but presented in an alien and even inimical world. Turning to England, we find that in 1808 both Constable and the older Turner started producing sketches of a character quite different from their previous work, Constable in his sketches of spring plowing in Suffolk, Turner in his sketches of the Thames valley. And these sketches were for both men the foundation of new styles; in these sketches they worked out new stylistic principles. In the work of Beethoven we can hear the same stylistic emergence. A pivotal work is the Septet Opus 20, composed in 1799 and 1800. Rosen calls it classicizing, not classic. It was very popular, and Beethoven came to hate it. For myself, I can only admit that I find it the most irritating and exasperating piece of music that I know, at least by a major composer. After it come the striking experiments with the piano sonata, particularly Opus 27 (no. 2 is the "Moonlight") and with the violin sonatas, Opus 23 and Opus 24. In 1803 comes the third symphony, of then astonishing length and power. Even before this the second symphony had been complained of because of its noisiness. And within a few years Beethoven had changed the whole structure of the symphony into its nineteenth-century form. I mean by this that the third and fourth movements are no longer frolicsome rewards for enduring the first and second, as with Haydn and most of Mozart, but rather the heaviest weight and importance of the entire work is to be found in the concluding movements. And this change applies to chamber music and solo instrumental music as well. The violence and aggressiveness of the opening are not brought under control and subdued but rather raised to a higher and more intense level, triumphant, urging the listeners to a more passionate involvement with the forces of life, and to an attack upon them. The Septet is so exasperating, I think, and classicizing because Beethoven could no longer endure the Viennese classic style as perfected by Haydn and Mozart. It was a style he could no longer use. One more step and the work would have been parody.

The stylistic break or emergence, then, can easily be seen, in music and painting and poetry and even in architecture, in Sir John Sloane's house and in the Dulwich gallery, and in some of the almost purely functional designs of Schinkel. And a corresponding change comes over the classic style in the hands of Romantic architects. As I have pointed out, in the last decades of the eighteenth century the arts moved steadily towards simplification, but in the Romantic works there is a striking reversal of that tendency. Art moves towards complexity. In eighteenth-century painting and architecture space is clear and uninterrupted; music and poetry flow smoothly. All are arts of transition. In Romantic works space and flow are interrupted by a saliency of separable configurations. In music the chain of motifs is superseded by the bold melodic and dominating theme. In poetry and painting the reader and the observer cannot avoid the thrusting forward of configurations of intensified realism. But aside from that stylistic break, can anything be determined as common to all Romantic works, any stylistic feature or any theme? I think not.

The assumption all along has been that Romanticism is a conjunctive category, one with certain attributes common to all documents and artifacts subsumed by the word. I think that such an assumption is unjustified, is, indeed, a mistake. Rather, Romanticism is best seen as a disjunctive category, a category justified by something other than common attributes. Certainly anyone familiar with the history of Romantic scholarship has seen the endless proposals to determine conjunctive attributes, and the failure and abandonment of all of them. Over and over we read that Romanticism is indefinable, but that notion is based on the assumption that it is a conjunctive category. Had there been more than a few dozen Romantics at work in all of Europe from 1795 to 1820, had there been even a few hundred of them, the character of the opening decades of Romanticism would be at once apparent. That character is, within the widest limitations of European culture, randomness. I read recently a penetrating remark to the effect that the Romantics let down pails into the past of European culture and pulled up whatever they could find and kept what they could make use of. Otherwise there is no pattern to the Romantic use of the past. Nor is there any pattern to the Romantic use of Enlightenment themes, nor of Christian themes, nor of classic themes and styles. Keats astonishingly used classicisms in *Hyperion* in order to explore the very phenomenon we are concerned with, cultural transcendence. Wordsworth used classicisms quite differently. If, in short, we survey the entire field of Romantic works, what has struck so many students is that randomness which, I have suggested, has been called indefinability. Scholars and critics who have abandoned the effort to define Romanticism have rather abandoned the notion of Romanticism as necessarily a conjunctive category. We believe that there was a cultural emergence which by a kind of accident we call Romanticism because we can observe striking stylistic emergence, but aside from that, Romanticism appears to be random.

At this point I should like to make use of a proposal I made some years ago in writing a book about pornography. In attempting to account for the full range of sexual deviation in every generation, I proposed what I called the delta effect. To the degree a behavioral pattern is badly transmitted, the result is a full spread of deviant behavior. What Gould and others have called the flexibility of the big brain, I would call the human capacity to generate random response, a capacity which emerges when cultural directions for behavior have failed. In such circumstances the individual, to respond at all, is condemned to innovation. When we approve of innovations we use the word "imagination." When we disapprove, we use the words "error" and "perversion."

On the subject of the imagination the Romantics, I submit, are endlessly tiresome. The only people more tiresome are the people who write about the Romantics. And when to "imagination" is added "creative" we have a phrase of inexhaustible flatulence. I find the word "imagination" so exasperating simply because, like Herder, I cannot accept a facultative psychology. Hence I turn my attention to the situations in which the word is likely to be uttered. We use the word, I believe, when we observe that an individual has evaded the cultural protocols of a given situation, when, to use a delightful metaphor, he has gone up the down staircase. Nor must we ever forget that the consequences of such evasion can be as silly and as vicious as the consequences which have been evaded. That evasion occurs when an individual judges, rightly or wrongly, that the protocols of the situation are no longer appropriate for him. From this point of view the Romantics judged that something in European culture, something at the highest ideological level, was no longer appropriate, was no longer usable, had become, indeed, harmful and destructive. Their emphasis upon the imagination, upon creativity, upon the artist and poet as prophet and priest, as unacknowledged legislators, was their way of recognizing that innovation was necessary, their way of defining their task as cultural transcendence. But since they worked as solitary individuals or in very small groups with short lives followed by divergence of the individuals in those groups, their efforts at cultural transcendence were necessarily random.

Moreover we can now understand why almost all of their themes or ideas can also be found in the eighteenth century, in Enlightenment culture, a phenomenon which, combined with the notion of Romanticism as necessarily a conjunctive category, has led to the misleading notion of pre-Romanticism. You can talk about the imagination all you wish, but initially the only materials you can use for innovation are the materials of your cultural situation. All you can do is to engage in a desperate and you hope innovative piecing together of available patterns. It is not merely that the total pattern of Romanticism was random. If one follows carefully all available materials arranged in exact chronological order, one can see that each Romantic engaged in random experimentation and that only after quite some time had elapsed did he either, as some of them did, give up and regress to an Enlightenment or even Christian position, or else arrive at a position which he judged he could stick with and develop profitably. The sketching of Turner and Constable in 1808 is precisely of this randomizing pattern of behavior. In the same way the automotive engineer will try every way of combining available knowledge about carburetors before he hits upon a new one. Indeed, a brilliant physicist I know insists that scientific discovery is a random affair. Thus it took three or four generations of Romantics to develop a Romantic tradition, and Romanticism did not produce a fully innovative cultural evasion for more than a hundred years. It came with the emergence of the modern styles in the first decade of the twentieth century.

But this still leaves the problem of what, in the judgment of the Romantics, had broken down. We can get some insight into the problem if we consider a couple of famous remarks about the imagination. When Wordsworth writes of how the imagination is impaired and how it is restored, it is reasonably clear that he is talking about how the sense of his own value is impaired and restored. If we listen to the talk of individuals suffering from clinical depression, the striking thing about their statements is the ascription to themselves of negative value, or the withdrawal from themselves of the ascription of value. That in the impairment of the imagination Wordsworth was talking about something very like clinical depression is reasonably apparent, just as it is the subject of the first books of *The Excursion*. In those particularly he is clearly concerned with the failure of value institutions and ideologies. In ordinary and stable circumstances, and for most people most of the time, their own value is sustained by value institutions, of which religion and nation and race are the most obvious. The consequences of Enlightenment secularization was, as I have already suggested, that an ideology developed which made nature and behavior based upon emotional lability into value institutions. Value was conferred by response, just as religious value is conferred by response to religious ritual. But Wordsworth found he had to create value from his own resources, that no available institution or ideology could help him. His eventual return to the church was, I believe and he seems to have implied, heuristic and symbolic of his own achievement.

The second illuminating remark is Keats's to the effect that what the imagination seizes as beauty must be truth. Now when an individual affirms that something is the truth he confers value upon himself. Hence the clinging to truths which are no longer tenable. Translated into these terms, what Keats was saying is what the imagination seizes as beauty must be a source or sign of the individual's own value. Upon this kind of decision was founded the whole tradition of nineteenth-century aesthetics and aestheticism and eventually the late nineteenth-century religion of art.

Many years ago George Herbert Mead said that Romanticism was the separation of the self from the role. The self becomes antithetical to the role. Hence success in behaving according to the cultural protocols of a role no longer becomes a source for the Romantic individual of a self-ascription of value. If we assume, as I think to be correct, that there is no such entity as the self, just as there is no such faculty as the imagination, we can understand better what those Romantics were doing—not all of them—who talked about the self, as did Fichte, no matter how bizarre were his metaphysical results. We can see the notion of the self as opposed to the role as a heuristic construct the function of which was to provide a justification for the innovative creation of value, for finding sources of one's own value in configu-

rations not sanctified by existing social institutions and existing ideologies. That is why the Romantics were both so intent upon their
notions of imagination and creativity and selfhood, and at the same
time so exasperatingly vague. Shelley was clearer than most when he
talked about self-respect as the essential of life, and *Alastor* can be
understood as the exploration of the possibilities for value, and their
failure.

The Romantics, then, in talking about the imagination and the self
were talking about the same activity, necessary, they judged, because
something had failed, some cultural pattern could not be transmitted
to them. If we trust Northrop Frye—and I suppose he is as trustworthy
as anybody else on Blake and more trustworthy than most—Blake
responded to what I have already referred to as the increasing late
eighteenth-century divergence between nature and reason, that internal incoherence in situational thinking that was becoming increasingly unavoidable. He rejected both, in favor of the imagination, or
pure selfhood free from the ideologies and institutions of contemporary European culture. To be sure the best he could do with his perception was to regress to an ancient and exhausted redemptionism,
concealing from himself his failure to achieve cultural transcendence
by a clumsy and obsessive mythology. A better example of that divergence between nature and reason can be found in Herder's attack
upon Kant, an attack in which, to my taste, Herder had the better of
it. He made three points: first, Kant was using a faculty psychology
that was long since outmoded. I must confess that when I read Kant
all those mental faculties remind me of nothing so much as the ubiquitous *djinni* in the *Arabian Nights*. When a man does anything, Herder maintained, the whole man does it. Second, he asserted that when
Kant talks about the mind he is only talking about silent verbalization.
It seems a pity that Herder could not make the next step and conclude
that Kant's faculties are nothing but different verbal rhetorics. Third,
he maintained that when Kant, who according to Frank Manuel was
a Utopian, said that the task of the reason was to conquer and eliminate the irrational, he was only smuggling in original sin by the back
door. It is clear that Herder had profited from his studies in the *Ideen*
and had developed a far richer comprehension of human behavior
than Kant ever did. But this is not the point of importance here, which
is rather that Herder thought of the rationality which man imposes
upon that situation in behalf of his transcendentally human interests.
But Herder thought in terms of progress. He too was a man of the
Enlightenment, just as much as Kant was. But the divergence between

reason and nature, between Kant and Herder, revealed the fundamental incoherence of Enlightenment thinking.

Once that incoherence and that divergence had become inescap-
able, at least to a few dozen people, the institutions and ideologies
maintained by Enlightenment thinking lost, for them, their validity,
lost their power to confer value, lost, in Keats's terms, their truth. Only
the individual who by the exercise of the imagination could confer
value upon the world, could sanctify some factor in the world, and
could do so from his own resources, without the aid of current ideologies and institutions, could achieve the cultural transcendence
which was the task of the Romantics.

For many individuals, as with Blake, and Novalis, and Wacken-
roder, and Fichte, and Coleridge, and Wordsworth, this task was assumed in the 1790s, and for a very good reason. The extreme
ideologues of the French Revolution set about to reconcile Nature and
Reason, to create a society in which nature and reason are one, or are
reciprocal factors. The result was the Terror, and the military dictatorship of Napoleon. Yet there was one service the French Revolution
and Napoleon did for the Romantics. Napoleon and the men of the
Revolution provided models for raising the level of aggression, for the
stylistic emergence of Romanticism did not happen in a cultural vacuum. It was an aggressive attack upon the high cultural norms of Europe, and at the time was recognized as exactly that. And that
aggression was necessary, not only to sustain the sense of unique selfhood, but also because the Revolution had bequeathed in virulent
form an epistemological problem which had been gradually emerging
for four centuries and which began to move toward a possible solution
only in the late nineteenth century, a solution which has not yet been
achieved. It may be that if that solution is achieved, philosophy will
come to an end.


IV


Let me conclude by replying to an obvious objection to what I have
said. "You have asserted," someone is bound to say, "that Romantic
theory construction is inherently unstable, and in that instability is
the hope for improving it. Yet you have offered here what you evidently believe to be a stable and even final theory." Let me attempt
to justify myself. I wrote my first piece on Romanticism thirty-two
years ago. Happily I called it "Towards a Theory of Romanticism."

Ten years later I repudiated, publicly, most of it. I do not know how many times I have arrived at what I believed to be a stable theory of Romanticism. I have always turned out to be wrong. And since the middle 1950s, when I undertook the study of the philosophy of science, I have known that I would turn out to be wrong, or at best that my current stage of theory development would prove to be inadequate. I have looked forward to finding the weaknesses of that current theory construction. This evening I have rejected, silently, much that I have said before; I have included much that I have said before; but mostly I have said things that I have never said before. I am reasonably sure that I shall in time reject much I have said today. I certainly hope so. I believe in the inherent instability of theory constructions, and I have endeavored to practice it. Let me address my final remarks to young people and repeat to them what I have so often said to my graduate students. "You must force your ideas to the wall, and if they have nothing in their pockets, you must slit their throats without compunction."

# CHAPTER TWO

# Romanticism, Science, and Gossip

In considering the coherence of science and Romanticism, it is as important to have a clear notion of what we are talking about when we use the word "science" as when we use the word "Romanticism"—as important and as puzzling. In the nineteenth century it is possible to find a number of differing notions of science, but only rarely does one come across a notion that is like the sophisticated current one. It will be useful, I think, to begin by discriminating some of these meanings for the term.

One that is quite easily identified is the sense at work in such a phrase as the "science of theology." Such a phrase, it may be, is still to be found today, but not in circles I am familiar with. It certainly tends to disappear in the English-speaking countries after the publication of Whewell's *The History of the Inductive Sciences* in 1839 and of *The Philosophy of the Inductive Sciences Founded upon their History* in 1840. I believe it to be a reasonably adequate interpretation of "science" in this sense to make it equivalent to "a discourse of logically coherent propositions." Something of this meaning survives in the now rather dreary and so far fruitless philosophical discussions on whether or not historical discourse can be scientific. However, it survives in another area, an area of the highest importance. The claims of Marxism to be scientific are claims founded upon this sense; it claims to be what those following Whewell's line would call a pure deductive science, and hence not a true science at all. It is worth, perhaps, a moment or two to point out that a great many people who believe Marxism-Leninism to be a science are, nevertheless, quite unaware that it is not a science in the sense of the inductive and physical or natural sciences. That is, they are unaware that Marxism uses the term in a pre-Whewellian sense but that they themselves are using it in a post-Whewellian sense. The weakness of claiming that a discourse of logically coherent propositions generated by a deductive process is a science arises from what appears currently to be the fact that only the propositions of symbolic and formal logic can be demonstrated to be logically coherent, and then only if a logically constructed system of logical criteria conventionally established is used to test the coherence. This amounts to saying that even a discourse of such propositions cannot be called finally or immanently coherent, let alone a discourse composed of propositions in a natural language.

The most common notion of scientific activity in the nineteenth century was that it discovers the laws of nature. (This notion subsumes the Whewellian sense, which need not be discussed further.) This seems to us an extremely simple-minded notion, yet the discovery by scientists at the end of the century that it indeed is a simple-minded proposition threw them into consternation. It is to their credit and to the glory of modern science that the best of them rapidly recovered from their consternation and saw in that discovery an immense promise, a promise which has been more than fulfilled, though today, for very interesting reasons, the really sophisticated sciences are undergoing a period of some stagnation, a problem to which I shall return. This notion of the equivalence of science with the laws of nature was still taught in commonplace science when I was in high school and college. One learned that the consequence of experimentation was hypothesis, which was then used as a basis for further experimentation. In a rather mysterious way, when the hypothesis was sufficiently confirmed it was raised to the level of theory, and when the theory was confirmed, in an equally mysterious way, it became a scientific law and a law of nature. The genealogy of this notion of science is also worth a glance. It started out as the will of God, conceived providentially. Regularity justified the transformation, and attrition, of this notion into the laws of God. Further transformation and attrition gave birth to the laws of Nature. This too proved unstable, and the notion of the laws of science was born, a further impoverishment of authority. But suspicion and uncertainty reappeared, and we had the laws of scientists. The next step, very advanced for its time, was Darwin's notion that a scientific law is a mental convenience. I believe he got this notion from the semi-Kantian Dugald Stewart, in whose writings it is already, at the beginning of the century, quite clear. But the end of this procession of the attrition of authority was not yet. Another step and a scientific law becomes a linguistic convenience, or at best a mathematical convenience, the latter being preferred, for mathematics is empty of content. It can meet the criteria of logico-mathematical convention and can with impunity create new criteria because it does not say anything, in the sense that a natural language says something. The result is a heuristic conception of scientific theory, a notion that most scientists can get along perfectly well without, and of those who need it, a good many are uncomfortable with it. If, as has happened to some, it is concluded that the foundations of science are cultural conventions, then science is what scientists do. To such a poverty-stricken notion has the providential will of God been reduced.

Closely related to a midway stage of this procession was not so much a conception of science but a mode of validating scientific activity. The task of science, it was held in what was taken to be the Baconian conception of science, was to establish the mastery of man over nature. This, incidentally, is to be found in Marx as well as Macaulay. It is obviously dependent upon the notion of science as the discovery of the laws of nature. It is in origin and metaphysical character an Enlightenment mode of validating science. At the present moment this mode of validation is undergoing a severe cultural crisis, one party urging that science must be controlled or even stopped, and the other urging that only more science can repair the damage that science has done. The young are understandably more exercised about this than the old, such as myself. Shaw once said something to the effect that one must be very suspicious of old men; they don't really care any more.

My own conception of science, which I feel I must mention if I am to discuss the relation of science to Romanticism, is somewhat different from any of these, though not too far from a heuristic conception of science and even closer to a social conception, that is, science is what scientists do. As I understand cultural history the scientific revolution occurred in the late sixteenth and early seventeenth centuries. It amounted to what, speaking metaphorically, may be called a decision. It was a decision not to ascribe truth-value to a proposition because it was coherent with a body of purportedly true propositions from which it had been derived, by whatever process, but rather to ascribe truth-value to a proposition if and only if it is interpreted as a prediction, and if and only if it is conventionally linked to a nonverbal behavior manipulating the phenomenal world in such a way that the predictive character of the proposition in question is verified. But even to this relatively stringent definition I would add a further qualification. It is not that the proposition is thus verified, but rather that the consequences of the phenomenal manipulation are *interpreted* as verifying the propositions. That this qualification undermines the authority of verification procedures I am aware, and indeed is the point I would make. That point is that the interpretative criteria of the verification procedures are derived, not from the proposition in question, not from the behavior, and not from the consequences of the phenomenal manipulation, but from quite different sources. This qualification is necessary, I think, to account for what Thomas Kuhn calls scientific revolutions, those crises in science in which the foundations of a science or of science in general begin to suffer an attrition of authority. It is at such times that sophisticated scientists begin to become concerned with the philosophy of science. That is what is happening today. Physicists are attending meetings of philosophers of science. The foundations of science are, I would say, not foundations at all but modes of terminating an explanatory regress. To use some of Darwin's notion, a scientific law terminates an explanatory regress and is therefore a convenience. Accumulation of scientific knowledge invariably turns the convenient into the inconvenient. Further, the emphasis I have laid upon interpretation accounts for the common occurrence in science of the reinterpretation of an experiment such that the proposition in question is not verified but falsified. Many humanists, I fear, tend to think of science as something both monolithic and stable. On the contrary, it is far more splintered and unstable even than theology, *because* it is infinitely more intellectually respectable.

Now it would be a very simple matter to demonstrate that a great many writers and even nonverbal artists whom many of us would agree upon calling Romantics, or in the Romantic tradition, had an intense interest in science. Coleridge was but one of the first of many. Even so literary a writer as Swinburne was powerfully affected by at least a popularized notion of Darwinism, inaccurate as it might have been. The explanation for this, however, is only partially that they were Romantics. Those major writers who were interested in science, from one end of the century to the other, were interested because they were men of wide and capacious minds. Like all truly cultivated and intelligent men at any time, they were interested in all culturally emergent, or innovative, notions. But there was also a special reason in their character as Romantics that would make them interested. The inadequacy of the world-picture of traditional European culture had been revealed to them. They were irresistibly interested in anything which justified and contributed to the construction of a new world-picture of greater adequacy. The notion that the task of science was to discover the laws of nature may have been philosophically faulty but it was heuristically of great value, and it had even greater heuristic force for those scientists who continued to believe that the discovery of the laws of nature meant the unveiling of the mind of divinity itself. A nonsensical spur to human activity is no less a spur because it is nonsense. One is tempted to think it is a more powerful spur. Thus the Romantics lived at a time when a scientific revolution was going on, though it was only a curtain-raiser to the scientific revolution of the twentieth century.

It would also be a simple matter to point out that the epistemology of Romanticism is congruent with the epistemology of the more sophisticated philosophies of science. The heart of the Romantic position is, I believe, the acceptance of an irresolvable tension between subject and object, between mind and nature, between theory and empirical data, between language and the world. This is identical with the heuristic conception of scientific explanation, or theory. The revolution that overcame physics at the beginning of this century was, a great many have pointed out, an instance of science catching up with the philosophical idealism of the nineteenth century, for that irresolvable tension can be gathered from the final pages of Hegel's *Phenomenology of Mind* as well as any place I know. I suspect that the revolution in question occurred because the scientists who led that revolution had themselves encountered the nineteenth-century philosophical tradition when they were young men. One of the most instructive books for grasping all this is Vaihinger's *The Philosophy of ''As If,''* which was written in the 1870s and 1880s but not published until 1911, the new material principally being a chapter on Nietzsche demonstrating that the latter's position was virtually identical with Vaihinger's own. It is particularly instructive that Vaihinger apparently did not see his way clear to publication until *after* the revolution of physics.

There is a third way, however, for suggesting the congruence between science and Romanticism which I should like to explore. When a scientist is pushed to the wall in trying to respond to demands for justifying his activities, he behaves just like a humanist. He falls back on the value of knowledge for its own sake. This seems to me a very feeble mode of validation, whether science or humanism is in question. Yet since it is generally felt to be a very powerful mode, and since both scientists and humanists are clearly very proud of pursuing knowledge for its own sake, I am interested in locating its source. I pursue my inquiry on the assumption that no highly sophisticated mode of human behavior is discontinuous from the most unsophisticated and intellectually primitive modes. I do not wish to be misunderstood. I am an intellectual snob; I think highly sophisticated

modes are better, even better for mankind, than intellectually primitive modes, but at the same time I feel that they are grounded on
primitive modes and are refinements of them. When I ask myself the
question, "What is the source in primitive verbal behavior of that sophisticated and refined mode of verbal behavior called 'knowledge for
its own sake'?" I believe that I can discover that source in a rhetorical
mode that is pervasive at all cultural levels. That mode is gossip. The
appeal of science, of philosophy, of history, of the humanistic disciplines, of the content or semantic aspect of the arts, is identical with
the appeal of gossip. Both the nonverbal behavior and the rhetorical
modes of an MLA convention are identical with the behavioral and
rhetorical modes of primitive women gossiping around a well, or
primitive men gossiping around a fire. The difference, of course, is that
*their* well had water in it, and *their* fire gave off warmth.

As a rhetorical mode gossip can be adequately defined, I believe,
as the simplest linguistic mode of cognitively comprehensible hypostatization or reification of empirically inaccessible events. The linguistic condition for gossip is the fact that no verbal analysis can
determine whether a given sentence does or does not have a phenomenally observable referent. Literary critics like to say that a work
of literature creates another world, another reality, and they fancy that
this attribute of literature is unique to literature and adds to its dignity
and importance. But such creation is precisely the attribute of gossip.
Moreover, the behavioral situation or protocol of gossip not only does
not require explanation and testing, it actually discourages and even
forbids both, since both compromise gossip's purity of cognitive comprehension. Gossip is a disengagement from other modes of activity
and other rhetorical modes, the latter encouraging and often requiring
the behavior for which it gives directions, while the only appropriate
response to gossip is to provide further gossip or to keep quiet if one
cannot. Explanation and testing threaten gossip's hypostatization and
the disengagement which is characteristic of gossip behavior. Now this
at first seems incompatible with the explanation and testing in scientific activity, but it is not; for science does its testing in experiments.
Both the experimenter and whatever is being experimented on are
disengaged from ordinary or, if you wish, existential situations, while
the explanation is equally remote, since it only explains the results of
the experiments. Thus the cognitive integrity of comprehension remains uncompromised. So it may be said with some accuracy, I believe, that the hesitation to perform scientific experiments on human
beings in nonexperimental situations does not arise from the ethical
consideration of invading and violating others. After all, invading and

violating others is a condition of all interaction, including interaction with ourselves. Rather, the scientists' reluctance flows from the threat of such experimentation to the disengagement of gossip, and the public's reluctance from the threat from gossip and its disengagement. The guilt that scientists and humanists feel alike is the guilt that accompanies the disengagement of gossip. Gossip is the disinterested and disengaged pursuit of knowledge for its own sake. If it appears to be malevolent it is only because it has no interest in forgiving us our sins. It is interested in our sins only for the sake of knowing about them.

Thus when Wittgenstein said, or at least seemed to say—with him you can never be sure—that the trouble with philosophy is that it is language out of gear and with the engine idling, he was, I think, wrong. It is philosophy's peculiar advantage, as it is the peculiar advantage of the other intellectual disciplines. That is, even in a heuristic theory of science, verbal hypostatization or reification is a necessary precondition to further scientific activity, which depends upon an initial purity of cognitive comprehension. Gossip then may be conceived as the constantly rehearsed behavioral foundation for the intellectual disciplines of high and sophisticated culture, in both its rhetorical and its behavioral aspects. That disengagement and hypostatization make sustained problem exposure and solution postponement possible, and likewise are the necessary preconditions for laboratory experimentation and the refined and intellectually sophisticated construction of explanatory theory. However, just as whenever action is proposed and undertaken on the basis of gossip the gossip is perceived as a source of social disturbance, so whenever it is proposed that the explanatory theories of science be applied to the problem of social management they are at once invalidated as socially destructive and validated as socially redemptive.

But what has Romanticism to do with all this? The cultural indicator of Romanticism is the sense of estrangement accompanied by the judgment that estrangement is of positive value to the estranged individual. One way of seeing the history of Romanticism is to see it as the history of the struggle, through a number of generations to the present, to accept estrangement. It was accomplished by perceiving estrangement as the necessary precondition for transcending the necessarily inadequate cultural modes obtaining in the social world of the Romantic. Both estrangement and gossip are accompanied by guilt, the guilt of disengagement. Gossip itself is a mode of estrangement, for it sees the object of the gossip as an otherness, as socially discontinuous from the gossiper. The feebleness of the validation of science—and similar activities—as knowledge for its own sake is a consequence of science's social disengagement, of its estrangement, its ability to categorize everything as a proper subject for experimentation, and to interpret that categorization as the sole source of the value of anything. Both science and Romanticism are modes of estrangement. Romanticism is not only congruent with science, and coherent with it; it is a cultural support for science. To put it another way, science is a sophistication and refinement of gossip, while Romanticism is the first cultural mode to be firmly founded upon gossip as a pervasive mode of human behavior. The most accomplished gossiper can gossip about himself with the insouciance, disengagement, and estrangement with which he gossips about others. That the Romantics to this day have gossiped about themselves, deafeningly, is a statement that no student of Romanticism will, I think, deny. Such gossip was long since identified as Romantic irony. By validating gossip Romanticism created a cultural situation in which science clambered to its most splendid achievements.

We denigrate gossip, but not because it is trivial. It is not. It is still our most useful source of information about human behavior, and our most common mode of experiencing cognitive comprehension. We denigrate it because it is disengaged and estranging. Romanticism has as its aim cultural transcendence, and it reveals gossip as the fundamental, the most pervasive, and probably still the most valuable source of that transcendence.

# CHAPTER THREE

# Romantic Historicism in Italy

## Opera, Painting, Fiction

On January 22, 1809, Ugo Foscolo, newly appointed professor of eloquence at the university of Pavia, gave his introductory lecture *Dell' origine e dell' ufficio della letterature: Orazione*. But his peroration was startling. "I exhort you to histories, for the arena of orators is narrow; but in histories there is fully displayed nobility of style, the sentiments of the virtues, the charm of poetry, the precepts of wisdom, all the progress and merits of Italian learning."[1] He had just alluded to the documents of Italian history—chronicles, genealogies, and municipal records, and especially to the collections of Muratori,[2] as well as to the forgotten volumes of the history of every Italian city. "But where is a history of Italy?" Even, he complains, Italians have waited for biographies of the great Medici patrons of arts and letters to be done by an Englishman.[3] And so he urges Italians to historical study and writing, for "no people better than Italians can show more sufferings to lament, more errors to avoid, nor more virtues demanding respect, nor more great spirits worthy of being liberated from oblivion." Moreover, Foscolo had prepared for this peroration in two previous works. In the *Ultime Lettere di Jacopo Ortis*[4] the hero, first fleeing from the Austrian occupation of Venice and then from an unhappy love affair in the Euganean Hills, wanders about northern Italy, visiting the tombs and shrines of great Italians. Several years later Foscolo wrote and published his famous *Dei sepolcri*,[5] inspired by a law of the French occupation forbidding tombs with sculpture.[6] Tombs of great men, and of evil men, tombs in which the distinction is observed are, he says, the inspiration for the living, and although most of the illustrative material is classical, he alludes to Machiavelli, Galileo, Dante, and

Alfieri. Within a few months Foscolo published his university lecture in Milan, and though he considered bringing out a second edition, never did so. However, beginning in 1815, that is, shortly after the Austrians took possession of the Po Valley as the Kingdom of Lombardo-Veneto, editions began to multiply, and the essay was frequently reprinted.[7]

Even as Foscolo was giving his prolusion, the first important effect in the composition of a history of Italy was already under way, but by a Swiss, not an Italian. In 1809 J. C. L. Simonde de Sismondi began to publish the work he had undertaken in 1804, *Histoire des republiques Italiennes du moyen age*; the last of the sixteen volumes appeared in 1818. Simonde had spent the years from 1795 to 1800 on his refugee father's farm near Pescia, Tuscany, between Lucca and Pistoia. There, convinced of the noble descent of his family from a powerful medieval family of Pisa, he had added "de Sismondi" to his name. After his return to Geneva he became a friend of Madame de Stael, and through her met Johann von Müller, a fellow Swiss and the historian of Switzerland, who had inspired him to his great undertaking.[8]

In the development of Romantic historicism Simonde's work was of the greatest importance. Not the least of the reasons for its significance was that it was less a history than a chronicle. For the most part it is a year by year account of Italian events, a kind of harmonization of Muratori, Guicciardini, Machiavelli, Villani, and other older Italian historians. Yet this very awkwardness, and Simonde's failure to write a grand sweeping history (perhaps, considering the history of Italy, an impossibility), was of immense service. First, it made Muratori and the others easily available by extracting from the numerous chronicles, some lively and some dry and dull, the interesting and significant events, and especially the good stories. Second, as a result, even though it is beyond human capacity to read Simonde straight through, it is impossible to open any of his volumes and not discover some fascinating event. In spite of the title, Simonde continues his account well into the seventeenth and even eighteenth centuries. To Simonde must be added another work in French, Pierre Daru's *Histoire de Venise*, published in Paris in 1817, in seven volumes. The basic materials, then, for a comprehension of Italian history, at least for writers, artists, librettists, and opera composers, were now readily available. To understand the use to which that comprehension was put requires some consideration of the place of history in Romantic culture and its special place in Italian Romanticism.

The historicization of European culture in the course of the nineteenth century was one of the major consequences of Romanticism.

Indeed, Benedetto Croce has called the nineteenth century "il secolo della storia,"[9] and that Scott, for the general public, was more responsible than anyone else is well known; and Scott was as important in Italy as elsewhere.[10] In Italy, however, Romanticism and Liberalism were fused to a degree and with a completeness not to be found even in France. The explanation lies in the fact that Italy was a unique victim of Napoleonic exploitation, though to be sure it had profited much from the French control; but after 1815 more than any other country Italy was a victim of the reestablishment of absolutism and the ideology and the governmental control of the prerevolutionary regimes. Other countries were at least independent, but Italy was under the domination of the Austrian Hapsburgs, that is, of Metternich; of the various Austrian dependencies, of which Tuscany was the largest; of the Papacy, the existence of which as a secular state was maintained by the restoration engineered by the Congress of Vienna, particularly by Metternich; and of a foreign dynasty, the Spanish Bourbons, in the Kingdom of the Two Sicilies (southern Italy and Sicily). Only in northern Italy, principally in Milan, was there much cultural and intellectual life, and that, in 1815, was hardly more than feeble. In fact, its most vital figure, Foscolo himself, fled to Switzerland in March 1815 and shortly after to England, establishing the pattern of exile for the Italian liberal patriot, a fact widely recognized in the course of the next decade or two. Consequently historicism had a dual function. Its purely Romantic aspect was its employment as a strategy for establishing and maintaining Romantic alienation and what that alienation made possible, cultural transcendence.[11] Its second aspect or function was the establishment of a national consciousness by an exploration and exploitation of the Italian past, as Foscolo had urged. To call either of these two aspects "sentimental nostalgia," as has Croce, among many others, is to be guilty of a serious lack of understanding of what was going on.[12]

This second aspect was ancestor worship rather than nostalgia, and this phenomenon of behavior is common in both primitive and advanced societies, though in a less obvious form in the latter. The cultural position of the Italians was not too different from that of the now famous tribe of the Ik, who, forced to move from their traditional hunting grounds and to develop a new economic mode, suffered an extreme social collapse as a result of economic collapse. And this collapse was accompanied by a mythological collapse. The shock of Colin Turnbull's book about the Ik was the revelation that if bees and ants are social animals, then man is not.[13] The mythological collapse meant that the Ik no longer had an explanation of their existence as a tribe which demanded and justified the ascription of value to others and of each individual to himself, an ascription which as a verbal mode of behavior may be called an *agape* system of a culture. Hence individuals became indifferent to the starvation and suffering and death of members not only of their own tribe but even of their own families, and even to their own. The situation was a double bind. For each individual all of his energy was necessary to maintain life; hence none was left over to maintain the mythology which maintained the *agape* systems. On the other hand the removal from their traditional home destroyed and undermined that mythology. As one witch doctor made quite clear, the problem was to renew communication with the ancestors. The problem of the Italian intellectuals and artists was identical, even though the economic substructure had not been destroyed.

What, then, is ancestor worship? Clearly it is a form of mythology, but what mythology is, it is only too obvious, is a matter on which there is very little agreement. To my mind, mythology is a level of explanation which lies between words which categorize perceptual configurations by subsumption and words which categorize those words by more inclusive subsumptions, by, that is, what we call abstract terms. Mythology explains the lowest level of subsumptional categorization (concrete words, in traditional terminology) by using such words and ascribing to them the attribute of divinity, a recognition that these words are more regressive from the nonverbal than concrete words. To take a specific example, Plato observed that the attributes of an "idea" when used to subsume a configuration did not correspond completely with the attributes of that configuration. Consequently he called the configuration an "imitation" of an "idea," since the "idea" is more "real" than the configuration in the sense that the categorization, not the configuration, controls our behavior. But he also observed that the ideas, since they are shared by human beings, do not emerge from the interaction of individual mind, or organism, with the phenomenal world. He explained their existence by ascribing to them a divine, transcendental, nonhuman origin. That explanation was mythological. Hegel, in the *Phenomenology*, took the important step of maintaining Plato's observations and at the same time of demythologizing Plato's explanation for the existence of the ideas. For *geist* we have now substituted "culture," in the anthropological rather than the humanistic sense. "Culture" subsumes learned behavior, and can further be defined as directions for performance. Ancestor worship, then, is an explanation at the mythological level for the readily observed behavioral phenomenon that so much of human behavior as is culturally transmitted (almost all of it) is directions for performance. The Ik witch doctor wanted to communicate with the ancestors in order to get directions for how the Ik should act in a crisis situation. The Italian liberals of the early nineteenth century were in exactly the same position. Before the Spaniards had locked Italy in a prison and thrown away the key—to use that famous metaphor—Italy had been independent, wealthy, powerful, and almost inconceivably creative. That disaster had happened in the early sixteenth century. It was the theme of Guicciardini's great history of Italy. Since then nothing had happened except the illusive Napoleonic interlude and the substitution of the Austrians as jailers for the Spaniards. "Sentimental nostalgic historicism" was the effort to get in touch with the ancestors, to derive cultural instructions from Italian medieval and Renaissance history.

To renew Italian life meant to create Italy anew and, as more and more liberals and even conservatives came to realize, to create *Italy* for the first time. The cultural renewal involved also a cultural transcendence. What made Italy, then, was not its political entities, but its cultural unity and continuity. But that cultural unity could not be brought into existence until there was brought into existence a corresponding political unity which would be independent of control not so much by another country as by the still feudal control of the Hapsburgs. In this endeavor several ingredients need to be distinguished. One was the revival of Giambattista Vico's *Scienze nuovo.* That was begun by Foscolo and continued by Giuseppe Mazzini, among others. To me it seems more than likely that Herder also played a very important part in this development. Vico had a number of ideas of the first importance, but the one most important to Italian historicism was precisely the notion of culture, of a cultural continuity that transcends the momentary judgments of rationalism. Another ingredient was nationalism, an Enlightenment idea, the consequence of the Enlightenment secularization of culture. The myth that had maintained what I have called the *agape* system was Christianity. The attempt to substitute for it the myth of man has been only partially successful, and only to a few intellectuals; for that myth is too vague—too regressive from the phenomena—to maintain the sense of membership as a source of *agape.* Membership in the feudal tradition was still powerful for the majority of the population; it involved subsumption by a suzerain. It was, however, but an easy step from feudal membership to membership in a nation, the possibility that Herder offered. Thus was created the myth of the nation, and made effective. Nevertheless in Italy this secularization created a difficulty; for the peasants, illiterate and untouched by the Enlightenment, had been neither secularized nor defeudalized. Throughout the struggles of the Risorgimento the failure of the peasants to support the movement (almost entirely an urban phenomenon) and frequently their hostility to it were the results. Manzoni aimed *I Promessi Sposi* at subverting confidence in the aristocracy, but Mazzini thought that quite unnecessary and even undesirable.[14] Hence propaganda for nationalism as well as the renewal of Italian culture was constant in the political and artistic agitation built on Romantic historicism. The immediate problem was what to select from the great past which might be useful in the present for these two purposes, cultural renewal and forging a nation. The misadventures of the Carbonari and the ease with which they were suppressed first by the monarchy of Naples and then by the Austrians in northern Italy made it apparent that a much wider popular support for independence and a more massive involvement of the population in the movement for independence were equally necessary. As best as I can make out there were two schools of thought: one was moral, its aim the moral regeneration of the population, a moral aim which meant the control of the population by the Church. Its leader was Manzoni, at least if Mazzini's analysis can be trusted. To that school what was useful in the past was by no means the continual internecine warfare, the murders, the cruelties of which so much information could be had from the Italian historians, now codified by Simonde. But the other school was quite different. It was precisely those cruelties, that strife, which was to be the aspect of Italian culture to be recaptured. In his essay on the current state of Italian literature in which he briefly attacks Manzoni, Mazzini quotes extensively from the preface to Francesco Guerrazzi's *L'Assedio di Firenze*, published in Paris in 1836 under a pseudonym. Why French publication was necessary is clear from the preface.

So long as your hands when raised to heaven feel the weight of hostile fetters, pray not. God holds with the strong! The measure of your abasement is full: to sink lower is impossible; life consists in motion, therefore you shall rise. Meanwhile bear rage in your heart, menace on your lips, death in your hand. Break to pieces all your divinities; adore no other God than him of *Sabaoth*, the spirit of battles. Ye shall rise . . . once more shall we trail through the dust to the Capitol the crowns of the tyrants of the nations—And shall we be happy? What matters it? Come, oh come ye days so dear to Italian pride! Bitter is the pleasure of oppressing, but it is a pleasure, and vengeance for atrocious crimes is grateful even to the spirit of God.[15]

This passage provides the key to much of what happened in fiction, in painting, and in opera from the mid-1820s to the first significant outbreak, initiated by the Sicilians in January 1848, and to 1860, the proclamation of the Kingdom of Italy, and even beyond to the final unification in 1870. If the Austrian domination was to be overthrown, the level of aggression in enough Italians to make that possible must be significantly raised. But the very publication of this passage in France reveals the problem. The censorship, even in relatively liberal Tuscany, was so severe that verbal exhortation was difficult, except in the mode of exemplification. For the purposes of raising the level of aggression it made no moral difference if historical romances, paintings, and operas show Italians as brutal, bloody, and revengeful. They were Italians being highly aggressive. An Italian fictional or operatic villain was ambivalent and had a dual function—to raise awareness of oppression and to show an Italian as highly aggressive and capable of seizing and wielding power. That was all that was needed.

Nor need it be imagined that to put the arts to such uses in any way violates their true character, though Mazzini, in the essay quoted above and in his essay on the philosophy of music, recognized that what he calls *l'art pour l'art* was an ideology very much in the way. These Risorgimento artists were merely putting to a specific use the most common attribute of art, its redundancy. The tradition of criticism which selects for consideration only a tiny fraction of art marked by a certain amount of originality, though always far less than most critics imagine, is incapable of perceiving that when one considers the entire field of art, from the joke to the *Iliad,* from graffiti to the Sistine ceiling, its most obvious attribute is redundancy, the continuous repetition of the same cultural elements, and in such redundancy art is merely part of all human behavior; for culture, directions for performance, can be kept stable only by redundancy of those directions. Most art exemplifies ideologies; only a small amount modifies regnant ideologies; only an infinitesimal proportion of it undermines ideologies. Intellectuals and artists, therefore, turned for their means for a redundant raising of the level of aggression in a critical mass of the population to the two artistic traditions which had never lost their vitality in Italy, painting and the opera, and in addition, modeling themselves on Scott, though not morally or politically, created a tradition of the historical romance.

Before continuing, it is necessary to understand the place of opera in nineteenth-century culture and also the significance of music, both operatic and "abstract." The simplest analogy for nineteenth-century opera is the cinema from its large-scale establishment in the second decade of this century to the time television undermined its immense popularity. As late as the 1920s opera singers were still stars rivaling movie stars, although opera would have succumbed far sooner had it not been for the invention of acoustical recordings. In the nineteenth century there were opera houses everywhere, and opera performances everywhere, not only in Italy. In all the newly emerging nations, eager to establish their own cultural traditions—Poland, Russia, Bohemia, the Scandinavian countries—the establishment of a national opera was considered to be absolutely essential, and if possible the establishment of a national school of opera composers. Yet in musical historiography one of the most significant aspects of opera is neglected, the libretto. It is extraordinarily difficult to find what any opera is about if it is no longer in the active repertoire. Musicologists are concerned with music. That is understandable, I suppose, though there does seem to be an excessive preoccupation with key changes, presumably because that is very nearly the only aspect of music, given their impoverished vocabulary, they can talk about. But opera was the most popular form of music in the nineteenth century, and it was through opera libretti more than through any other medium, even the theater, that Romantic ideologies were disseminated to a large public. It was, in fact, not until late in the nineteenth century that in Italy the title page of libretti and scores gave the name of the composer first. The author of the libretto was given the more important position and frequently was printed in larger type.

Moreover, the character of opera must be understood. I do not believe that I am attacking a straw man when I say that it is a common opinion that opera is artificial. In any theatrical performance in which the actors pretend that the audience is not present there is already an artificiality which no singing to an orchestra can alter very much. Indeed it can be reasonably argued that opera is the most complete form of theater. Certainly at the present time great operas are more frequently performed than great plays, and to larger audiences. Furthermore, since it is widely believed that opera libretti are silly, the usual operagoer assumes that it is so. In many an opera-lover is a love of singing, not of theater, and he is familiar with the plot only through a summary. All fictional plots seem silly when reduced to a couple of paragraphs of summary, and I cannot see that opera plots are any sillier than those of any other kind of narrative fiction, that is, less silly and certainly less strange than life itself. Now, that artificiality of opera is alleged to lie especially in the fact that in real life people do not stand around singing to each other. But in fact they do. All aspects of music are derived from the human voice, from that nonverbal aspect of linguistic behavior known as intonation. The whole theory of *bel canto* is that singing is no more than sustained speech. If you blot out from awareness the words of any utterance, you will hear a melody, and indeed some children practice the melodies of sentences *before* they start using words.

Moreover, though melodic intonation is usually categorized as expressive it is as culturally controlled as words or any other mode of culture, that is, of learned behavior. Furthermore, since culture exists only in the behavior of individuals, every individual in his behavior is engaged in giving directions for performance of others or of himself, of controlling his and their behavior. Music abstracts the intonational mode of behavioral direction and control and intensifies its attributes. We respond to that intensification, even though we may never hitherto have heard anyone sing or play an instrument, because we have been listening to and uttering that intonation all of our lives. It is one of the most redundant of the behavioral redundancies which maintain behavior. But what in the behavior of the individual to whom the utterance is made is the object of this endeavor to instruct and to control? I believe it is the level of the recipient's aggression. This proposition assumes that all behavior can be understood as aggressive, passivity being merely covert aggression or seduction. This may seem startling and probably absurd until it is remembered that this formulation is a behavioral explanation of a very ancient tradition in philosophy, the theory of the will. The medieval philosophers, for example, were always arguing about which was the more important, which really ruled the mind, the will or the reason. It is no accident that Schopenhauer, a Romantic philosopher, insisted that a man is but the individuation of the ground of being, the will. Intonation, then, endeavors to control redundantly the level of aggression, and hence music is a semiotic system which, as a cultural redundancy, regulates the level of aggression. Robert Craft has recently called music "innocent"; nothing could be further from the truth.

Little could be more useful to the Risorgimento movement than music, for since it was thought to be innocent and meaningless, it was scarcely an important object of censorship. With music, censorship could be circumvented, though to be effective music had to be presented in a context of aggression. The historical opera on medieval and Renaissance violence, even when there was no analogy to the current political situation—and often enough there was—was obviously the perfect medium for raising the aggressive level of a critical mass of the population, since opera was by far the most popular art form. Moreover the fundamentally Enlightenment nationalism of the drive towards liberation in Italy was perfectly matched with the character of Romanticism. For almost all Romantic philosophy, art, and literature is marked by a much higher level of aggression than that

which preceded it, particularly the neoclassic. This raising of the level
of aggression was essential to maintain Romantic cultural vandalism,
the attack upon the regnant cultures, which, for the Romantic, had
collapsed, even though for the overwhelming majority of the European population the traditional culture was still unquestioned. That
very stubbornness, that dead monolithicity of European culture, as
the Romantic saw it, required a cultural vandalism of great intensity.[16]
When we are talking about the Romantic "self" or, in old-fashioned
terms, Romantic individualism, what we are talking about is precisely
a high level of aggression not under the control of existent sociocultural institutions. It is an aggression devoted either to cultural vandalism or to sociocultural withdrawal, a contemptuous denigration of
the regnant culture which requires nearly as high a level of aggression
as engagement.

It is not surprising, therefore, that Rossini was identified by his contemporaries as a Romantic composer. He was the Beethoven of Italy,
for Beethoven had raised music to hitherto unknown levels of aggression, particularly in the Fifth Symphony, in which the last movement
was the most aggressive of all, and thus was profoundly different from
the symphonies of Haydn and Mozart. In almost all of those works
even a rather low level of aggression was restricted to the first movement. Mazzini, among others, recognized the Romanticism of Rossini,
for, as he put it, through his melody Rossini raised what Mazzini calls
"individuality" to new levels.[17] "Rossini was a Titan in power and
daring: the Napoleon of a musical epoch. A careful study of Rossini
will convince us that the mission he fulfilled, with regard to Music,
was identical with that fulfilled by *Romanticism* with regard to literature. . . . *I advance.*" But Rossini did more than intensify melody; he
also increased volume and tempo, and made particularly striking use
of sustained crescendi. And his storms were famous. To his detractors
he was noisy. And that was the point. He recommended a great increase in the level of aggression. Yet for a long time his libretti remained untouched by Romanticism. That of *Elisabetta Regina d'Inglhel-
terra* (1815), his first opera for Naples, then recently restored to the
Bourbons, contains such typically Restoration remarks as "And mer-
ciful heaven regards with wonder the defender of princes," and Elizabeth's concluding utterance, "No other passions do I wish than glory
and mercy."[18] The resemblance to the historical Elizabeth is almost
nonexistent. Like eighteenth-century operas on other than classical
subjects it could perfectly well have been on a classical subject. Historical realism, the endeavor to set imaginary characters in an accu-

rately and carefully realized historical situation, was still in the future, and to that development it is now useful to turn.

In the winter of 1973–1974 an extraordinarily interesting exhibition was held in Florence. The occasion for the exhibition was the public opening of the restored Meridiana suite of rooms in the Pitti palace. It had been many years since the rooms had been open to the public. The suite was begun by the last Grand Duke of Tuscany and remained unfinished when the palace was occupied by the King of Savoy in 1860 and Florence became the capital of an almost united Italy. The Grand Duke Leopold II had been responsible for commissioning the original frescoes, scenes from Manzoni's *I Promessi Sposi,* done between 1834 and 1837. King Vittorio Emanuele II ordered the decoration completed with frescoes from the history of Florence (the conspiracy of the Pazzi and the Siege of Florence, among others) and scenes from the life of Tasso. The reopening of the Meridiana was celebrated with an exhibition of Italian historical painting from 1820 to 1870, and with a conference on Francesco Guerrazzi, a native of Leghorn, one of the principal Italian historical novelists of the nineteenth century, a powerful publicist for the liberation movement, and, briefly and unsuccessfully, the dictator of Florence when it was temporarily free from Hapsburg control in 1848.[19]

The catalogue, however, is much more than a mere catalogue of the exhibition. It represents a tremendous amount of work and breaks much new ground not only in the history of nineteenth-century Italian painting but also in cultural history. It is unfortunate but true that nineteenth-century Italian painting is still vastly underestimated outside of Italy. The Italians never lost their feeling for design and color, and nineteenth-century Italy had dozens of excellent painters, and not a few of the first quality. Now that the history of nineteenth-century art is moving away from what for so long has been its sole preoccupation, the tradition that led to the French Impressionists, now that Rudolf Zeitler has revealed that the nineteenth century in terms of art history is generally "Das unbekannte Jahrhundert,"[20] the remarkable achievements of the nineteenth-century Italian painters may become better known, and the Italian museums of such paintings may be less deserted, or not visited only by the Italians. Perhaps those now closed will eventually be reopened. At any rate the catalogue has certainly paved the way, for the first part establishes the principal themes of historical painting during the period selected, and lists 1,649 paintings (including a few pieces of sculpture, but not including 105 paintings on Mary Stuart and Faust). Even so Sandro Pinto, the compiler of this

section, "Il soggetto storico dalla Restaurazione all' Unità," has excluded pictures on Romeo and Juliet and other Shakespearean figures, common at the time; Byronic subjects, except for Lara, Marino
Faliero, and the two Foscari; Beatrice di Tenda; subjects taken from
Scott, Victor Hugo, Chateaubriand, etc.; a number of Dantesque subjects; and stories from Boccaccio. The list is thus almost completely
confined to true historical scenes. The second part of the catalogue,
by Paola Barocchi, is "Il Camp Storiograffico," an anthology of passages from essays of the time devoted to the examination of and
justification for historical painting, and to criticisms of particular
paintings. The third part, "Il Melodramma," by Fiamma Nicolodi, is
a list of 131 operas on subjects (not including Faust and Mary Stuart)
identical with those of the painting. To these I have been able to add
a couple of dozen on similar themes from Italian history. A good many
of the operas are described, with plots and quotations from contemporary reviews. The fourth part is a full catalogue of the 100 paintings
in the exhibition, particularly valuable for the identification of sources
and for datings of the paintings.[21]

When the operas and paintings in Parts III and IV are arranged in
chronological order and when those lists are compared with a similar
list of historical poems and fiction, a significant fact emerges. The great
majority of both operas and paintings was created after their subjects
had appeared in literature, and the particular literary work or works
were definitely the source of the opera or painting. The literary work
was itself based upon an historical account, or a narration in Dante.
The bulk of the work in all three fields, however, finds its source in a
recent history or in an old chronicle, just as Byron founded *Marino
Faliero* on old chronicles but *The Two Foscari* on Simonde and Daru.[22]
Donizetti wrote *Marino Faliero* for Paris in 1835, the libretto based
both on Casimir Delavigne's play (1829) and Byron.[23] Verdi's *I Due
Foscari* (1844), the finest to my mind of his early works, was derived
directly from Byron.[24] Francesco Hayez, the greatest of the Italian historical painters, created his excellent "Il Doge Francesco Foscari des-
tituito con decreto del Senato Veneto" in 1844 (Milano, Brera), and
one of his masterpieces, "Gli ultimi momenti del Doge Marino Faliero" in 1867 (Milano, Brera).[25] There were other paintings on both
subjects.

The categories used in the catalogue are I: The crusades; II: Foreign
invasions into Italy during the middle ages; III: The heretics and the
great persecuted; IV: The principal personages of romantic poetry; V:
*I Promessi Sposi* and *Ettore Fieramosca*; VI: Lombard history; VII: Venetian history; VIII: Florentine history; IX: The hegemony of Piemonte;

X: Famous men (Dante, Petrarch, etc.). There are operas in each of these categories except III and IX. For III the lives of Arnold of Brescia and Fra' Paolo Sarpi do not lend themselves very well to operatic treatment, but it does seem rather surprising that there are no operas on Savonarola, possibly because of religious-state censorship. As for IX, the rest of Italy regarded Piemonte with great suspicion until 1848. For one thing the government was more repressive than that in any Italian area, except for the Papal dominions, and far more priest-ridden. For another, republicans suspected that if the House of Savoy became involved in the movement of independence and unification, the result would be less a unification of Italy than a conquest of the rest of Italy by Piemonte, a suspicion that was pretty well verified in the course of events. Moreover, none of the major composers (Rossini, Verdi, Bellini, Donizetti, Pacini, Mercadante) and only two of the seventy-seven minor composers came from Piemonte. Other subjects not used in operas will be discussed below, but here a few other notes may be of some interest. The omission of the conspiracy of the Pazzi from operatic subjects is surprising, since there is a play by Alfieri. Goethe's precedent would justify the use of Tasso, and the Raphael operas were built on his love for La Fornarina. Since the one opera on Dante was less an opera than a visionary pageant, possibly Petrarch, Boccaccio, Giotto, Leonardo, and Michelangelo were considered as too noble or sacred for the stage.

The best place to begin in comprehending the character of these works, in particular their contribution to raising the level of Italian aggression, is to examine the literary materials. Before this can be undertaken, however, two problems need to be disposed of. The first is that of introducing imaginary characters into an historical situation. This is always a problem of criticism of historical fiction, and Italian criticism after the 1820s, when the problem was first considered, was no exception. But the emergence of the problem is considerably more interesting than the problem itself, which is scarcely a problem at all. The difference between imaginary characters and historical characters was, until the emergence of Romanticism, hardly existent. Until then an historical character, even in history, even in such a writer as Gibbon, was highly simplified and abstract, since he was presented, for the most part, as exemplifying a moral ideology not of his time but of that of the writer, whether a writer of fiction or of history. Romanticism, however, with its drive toward reality, steadily increases its demand for historical accuracy, a demand that eventually resulted in the realistic novel, an historical novel about the present.[26] Thus in all the arts the demand for historical accuracy by authors, critics, and the public was constantly intensified. But as that happened the resemblance of imaginary characters and historical characters disappeared. A consideration of the historical figure in "scientific" or modern historical writing shows on the one hand an increasing disagreement about how to interpret that character and on the other a dissolution of the character into the discontinuity and incoherence of individuals in life. The more details of the life and behavior of a historical individual which research uncovers, the less amenable he is to any ideological control and subsumption, while characters in fiction are always under ideological control. Even when the personality shows a high degree of discontinuity in the course of a work, the decisions about what discontinuities to present are ideologically controlled. Thus the critical problem in itself is an exemplification of an ideology the tendency of which was to undermine existent notions of the past and of its individuals. The aim of Romantic and modern historiography has been to dissolve not merely the regnant constructs of the past but, far more important, the ideologies which those constructs exemplified. Manzoni's conclusion that in fact this problem of the historical novel—to unite the historically real and the imaginary in the same work—was insoluble is properly understood as a symptom of the effect of historiography as an analytic critique of regnant ideologies.[27] It seems probable that the emergence of this problem led to its resolution in the realistic novel, which began to appear in Italy in the 1850s. Ippolito Nievo's superb *Confessioni d'un Italiano* (1861) marks the transition.

The other problem is the place of the love story in fiction, opera, and painting. The best clue to its place is that, in Italian historical fiction, unlike Scott's, the lovers do not have a happy ending. One or both die, or one dies and the other commits suicide, or dies of despair over the dead body of the other. It is generally believed that these tragic conclusions to love affairs were merely tacked on to the primary plot for the sake of providing "love interest" to please the sentimental public. That there is truth to this is unquestionable, but it is by no means perceptive of what is really going on. Those plots which are primarily love stories, such as Romeo and Juliet, Paolo and Francesca, Parisina, or Bonifazio and Imelda (the Bolognese equivalent of Romeo and Juliet) show exactly the same pattern as that to be found in plots in which lovers are not the central figures, in which the central figure is an old historical character. The love stories either have to do with the consequences of internecine struggle, particularly that between Guelf and Ghibelline, or they have to do with social oppression, usually that of a father or a husband or a seducer who is a social or feudal superior. Love is presented as a refuge and a withdrawal from an unbearable social-cultural situation. It is an instance of what I have called covert aggression, a denigration of the situation in which the lovers find themselves. The disastrous consequences of the love are, as it were, proof that the social situation is in itself destructive of human value, or generally the love is presented more as a matter of *agape* than of *eros*, more, that is, as a mutual confirmation of the individual's value than as a dissolution of the distinction between subject and object, such as that found in *Tristan und Isolde* or in any form of fetishism, the object of which may be a man, a woman, or an old shoe. That is, the love in these works is more social than mystical. Since the destruction of the lovers is a critique of the existent social order, the effect was to raise the level of aggression against the social order of the audience.

The first work to achieve fame was Silvio Pellico's tragedy, *Francesca da Rimini*, its source in Dante. Published in 1815, it was constantly performed throughout the century, and by 1860 had been the subject of fifteen operas and by 1870 of sixty-seven paintings and sculptures. The most famous was that of Ingres (1819). Although Ingres had considered the subject before 1815, it seems highly probable that he knew Pellico's drama. At any rate, the picture was painted before Ingres left Italy. It is not surprising that the first of the Romantic historical operas was based on Pellico by the librettist Felici Romani. The composer was F. Strepponi, and the opera was presented in Vicenza in 1823. Pellico's play has considerable power, and the lovers are destroyed not by the jealousy of Lanciotto but by his feudal power to kill them with impunity. Since Paolo and Francesca have made every effort to escape from each other, that is, to obey the social rules, the play reveals a profound incoherence within the social structure. This is subtly emphasized by Paolo's patriotic speech, one which became a necessary ingredient in subsequent historical literature and opera, and was often present by implication in painting. Paolo is destroyed, then, by the country which he loves. The power of the tragedy, as well as its popularity, was enhanced by the fact that Pellico himself was arrested in 1820 by the Austrians and sent to the infamous Spielberg. After his release he wrote an account of his experience, the famous *Le Mie Prigioni*, a work which probably did more to make the rest of Europe sympathetic with the Italian struggle than did any other work or even any political action.

In 1819 a minor work created considerable stir because of its historically realistic presentation of the brutality of the middle ages. Diodata Saluzzo-Roero's *Il Castello di Binasco* tells the story of how

Filippo Maria Visconti married Beatrice di Tenda in order to acquire the wealth of her dead husband, the famous *condottiere* Facino Cane, and thus gain possession of Milan. Falsely accusing her of adultery, Filippo had her executed. Thus the theme of high Italian aggression is introduced, and the story was used several times in a little more than a decade. Bellini's opera appeared in 1833.[28]

The most important works for the future of both drama and fiction were the two plays by Manzoni, *Il Conte di Carmagnola* (1820), the story of a just man destroyed by a ruthless political force, Venice, and *Adelchi* (1822), the theme of which is the destruction of the noble Langobard royalty by the invading Charlemagne. In preparation for the writing of the play Manzoni did a great deal of historical research, as indeed he had for the previous tragedy, and wrote an account of the Langobards in Italy. Pellico's play was fundamentally in the manner of Alfieri, with very little historical setting, but Manzoni abandoned the dominant Alfierian model and turned instead to Shakespeare, as did so many Romantic dramatists. Manzoni, however, observed the unity of treatment; there are no comic elements. Two important themes were thus introduced into the emerging tradition, together with the introduction of the demand for historical accuracy, barely adumbrated by Pellico.[29] By 1860 there had been three operas based on *Adelchi* though none on *Il Conte di Carmagnola*, probably because it was a complete failure when presented on the stage in 1838.[30] During the next few years a number of new subjects were treated, the invasion of the Hungarians and Pia de 'Tolomei, a woman unjustly destroyed by her husband, then thought to be Dante's Pia.[31] Pia was a popular subject for paintings (fifty-seven by 1870) and in the 1830s was used in two operas, all based on Sestini's novel in verse (1822). Buondelmonte introduced a new theme, internecine or fratricidal strife within a community, a subject which on the one hand warned Italy of the consequences of its political disunity, and on the other showed Italians capable of violent action in revenge, the theme so powerfully presented in Guerrazzi in the passage quoted above. A work of 1826, however, shows the reverse of this, Rommasco Grossi's once famous *I Lombardi alla prima Crociata*, a poem then thought to be a rival or equal of Tasso. Here the theme of the healing of such strife is presented, with the implication of the virtues of cooperation, and also the capacity of Italians for vigorous action. Verdi's opera based on Grossi appeared in 1843, and the subject was repeated in several paintings, including four by Hayez.

The most important work of this period, however, and the greatest Italian novel of the nineteenth century, was Manzoni's *I Promessi*

*Sposi*, published in three volumes from 1825 to 1827.[32] Manzoni was of course profoundly influenced by Scott, from whom he learned a great deal; nevertheless, Manzoni's novel is far greater than anything Scott ever accomplished. Probably the most important thing Manzoni learned from Scott was the very device that makes Scott great—the introduction of ordinary people onto the stage of history and into the novel. Yet *I Promessi Sposi* is an anomaly in the fiction, painting, and opera of the Risorgimento. The events take place from 1628 to 1631, when Italy had already long been under the heel of the Spanish, and only in the story of the Nun of Monza is there any suggestion of rebellion against the demands of society. But she was Spanish and is morally condemned. Political and social power is to be circumvented, or submitted to. Morality is the cultivation of acceptance of the human situation, of the fundamental tragedy or failure of humanity, not the tragedy of Italy. Even though the aristocracy is presented harshly and their brutality and immorality projected forcefully, nevertheless a great aristocrat, cooperative with the Spanish, Cardinal Federigo Borromeo, intervenes and saves Lucia. It is not surprising that people of a mind with Mazzini objected strongly to Manzoni's morality of acceptance. The lovers end happily, and that alone is enough to separate the novel from most of the rest of the historical fiction and opera of the Risorgimento. Yet the very quality for which Mazzini praises Rossini is to be found here, the almost hallucinatory individuality of even minor characters.

Although there were seven operas on *I Promessi Sposi*, none has survived. It was not until the later nineteenth century that opera began to be able to deal successfully with the people whom Scott had introduced into fiction. On the other hand, for painters, subjects from Manzoni's work were among the most popular, Part I of the Florence catalogue listing 150, including series of works, such as those in the Meridiana. Most of these paintings, however, show Renzo and Lucia in situations in which they are at the mercy of the powerful. They fall within the general category of a critique of the social order, and thus form part of the tradition of raising the level of aggression. Cianfanelli's frescoes in the Meridiana, commissioned by the Grand Duke of Tuscany, are not surprisingly an exception.

Other novels of the same years are very different and far more typical. G. B. Bazzoni's *Il Castello de Trezzo* (1826) has as its theme the imprisonment and murder of Bernabo Visconti by his nephew Gian Galeazzo, one of the most powerful and unscrupulous of the Visconti, and that is saying a good deal. In 1829 G. Rosini told the full story of the Nun of Monza, picking up the subject from Manzoni and emphasizing what is always emphasized in that terrible story, the forcing of a beautiful and vital young woman to take the veil against her will. Her rebellion was dramatic and powerful, and according to the most recent study, based on documents now fully available, even after years of incarceration she subtly renewed her rebellion and quite deceived her spiritual advisor.[33] The most important novel of these years was *La Battaglia di Benevento*, by Guerrazzi, the story of the destruction of Manfredi, the son of Frederick II Hohenstaufen, by the French, called into Italy by the Pope, the beginning of the disastrous intervention by the French into Italian affairs, an intervention that eventually destroyed Italian freedom. That destruction was the theme of Guicciardini. And the novel was an equally powerful attack upon the secular power of the Papacy, which, with Spanish support, was ultimately to destroy the cultural and political vitality of city after city, culminating in the Massacre of Perugia by Papal troops in 1859. It is not surprising that the novel became the theme of dozens of paintings and four operas, including two on Corradino, or Conradin, the last of the Hohenstaufen, pursued with equal success by the Pope.

In 1830 D. Sacchi introduced a new subject in his *I Lambertazzi e i Germei*, telling a Romeo and Juliet story set in Bologna, and concerned with the consequences of internecine strife within a city. Within a year Donizetti had set the story to music in *Imelda de' Lambertazzi*.[34] Even today only Italians, I suspect, can respond significantly to these savage partisan struggles within the same city. In a milder form such a quarrel continues to this day in the division of the old aristocracy into two noninteracting groups of families in Lecce, a beautiful city in the heel of Italy, and probably in a good many other cities. To non-Italians the enmity between Montagues and Capulets in Shakespeare seems at best a convention and on the whole quite incomprehensible. To Italians, particularly to Italians at the time, these violent and murderous quarrels between families, quarrels in which the original distinction between Guelf and Ghibelline had within a century or so virtually lost its original meaning, created a powerful and immediately comprehensible situation. The theme could easily be transferred to the enmity between those who wished to make peace with the Austrians and those who wished to rebel against them. There were even neo-Guelf and neo-Ghibelline schools of historiography. Hence it is not surprising that the censor deleted "Guelf" and "Ghibelline" from Tottola's libretto.[35] All such novels, operas, and paintings were covert references to the cost of this internal division within Italian opinion. By 1850 there were three operas on this Bolognese subject and sixteen paintings, one by Hayez.

In the last years of the 1820s two operatic subjects appeared which are not represented in the Florence catalogue. The first is the story of Masaniello, who in 1647 led a revolt against the Spanish masters of Naples. In 1827 Carafa wrote an opera on Masaniello, and in 1828 appeared Auber's much more famous Parisian opera, *Le Muette de Portici*, or *Masaniello*, a work which established the French pattern of the heroic grand opera. In 1829 came Rossini's last and greatest work, *Guillaume Tell*. Both of these operas have to do with the rebellion of natives against foreign masters, the Italian rebellion eventually a failure, the Swiss a success. The final patriotic hymn in Rossini's work would make it immensely popular in Italy.

A somewhat similar theme, the defeat of foreign invaders by Italians, was that of Massimo d'Azeglio's *Ettore Fieramosca; ossia, La disfida di Barletta* (1833). D'Azeglio was even more talented than Guerrazzi, for he was a notable painter, a novelist, and a political publicist of considerable power, and eventually an important political figure as prime minister for Vittorio Emanuele and governor of Milan. The challenge at Barletta comes from an obscure passage in Guicciardini.[36] In 1503 during the war between the French and the Aragonese certain Italian soldiers of fortune were serving with the Aragonese. A French prisoner accused the Italians of cowardice, and the Spanish commander arranged a tournament between French and Italians, announced by a challenge or *sfida*. Thirteen fought on each side, and the Italians won. In 1831 d'Azeglio painted a famous picture on this subject (now in a private collection in Milan) and was inspired to write a novel, combining with the story of the *sfida* a tragic love story. At the end Fieramosca leaps into the sea from a cliff on the peninsula of Gargano, horse and all. This leap was the subject of a picture by d'Azeglio and also of a particularly fine painting by Filippo Palizzi, one of the best nineteenth-century Italian artists (1855, Rome, National Gallery of Modern Art). D'Azeglio, who was of a noble Piemontese family, was already involved in political activities, and the subject he chose was highly suitable for the principal Risorgimento task, the restoration of aggressive confidence among the oppressed. Like the two previous subjects, this one was a struggle against invaders, one in which the Italians were victorious. Moreover, a tournament emphasized individual courage and military prowess, and the period in which it took place, when Italy was losing her independence, made it even more attractive, a quality intensified by the fact that it was a great foreigner, an Aragonese, who insisted on the courage of the Italians and arranged for the fight. It is not surprising, then, that Ettore Fieramosca and his beloved, Ginevra di Monreale, were the subjects of ten operas by 1870 and three more by 1883, nor that the subject was exceeded in popularity among painters only by *I Promessi Sposi* and the siege of Florence.

In the same year as *Ettore Fieramosca*, appeared Rosini's novel *Luisa Strozzi*. Luisa was the intended victim of the vicious Alessandro de'Medici, who, it must be remembered, had been placed in power by the cooperation of the Pope and the Spanish and who was murdered by Lorenzino de'Medici, his distant cousin. These two subjects, then, combined foreign oppression with oppression by those in positions of power, irresponsible and degenerate members of the aristocracy, thus supplementing, in a sense, Manzoni. By 1862 there had been five operas on the subjects of Luisa, Alesandro, and Lorenzino, the best probably being Pacini's *Lorenzino de'Medici* (Venice, 1845). A dozen or so paintings were devoted to these subjects, most of them to Lorenzino, for here was a character almost as debased as his victim, yet one who performed a heroic act in defense of his compatriots. One is reminded of Guerrazzi's point that Italy was so debased it had nowhere to go except upwards, through violence and revenge.

In 1834 appeared one of the most successful and popular of the Italian historical romances, Tommaso Grossi's *Marco Visconti*. This Visconti was the son of Matteo I Visconti, *il Magno*, the founder of the Visconti power. Marco was a remarkable military leader, murdered in 1327 by order of his nephew, Azzone, who feared him as rival for the lordship of Milan, granted by the emperor but not yet by the people of Milan. The novel is given length and body by a love story in which the heroine, captured by a misinterpretation of Marco's wishes, is hidden in a castle vault and discovered too late to save her life. The indirect, as well as the direct, consequence of the abuse of power is the theme. An important incident has Marco achieve the lordship of Lucca with the aid of German mercenaries, whom he is then unable to control. He enters on discussions with Florence to sell Lucca to that rival city, a plan aborted by the people of Lucca. The theme of the horrors of occupation by foreigners is thus brought into the picture, as well as the power of the people and their love for liberty. Except for the character of the heroine's father, amusing enough, though more of a nineteenth-century gentleman than a medieval noble, the medievalism is reasonably convincing, though not up to the level of either Scott or Manzoni. Five operas and nearly three dozen paintings were derived from this work.

Two powerful works were based on a single subject, the siege of Florence, historically preceding the theme of Alessandro de'Medici. The subject is the end of Florentine independence in 1530, the reestablishment of the Medici, and the end of Italian independence, for Florence was almost the last state left free from the control of foreign power, either directly or indirectly. Venice, Genoa, Lucca, and Siena were still free, but Siena was to be captured in a few years by Cosimo I of Florence. The capture of Florence by the troops of the Emperor Charles V is the climax of Simonde and very nearly the conclusion. Everything thereafter is an anticlimax. The first of these novels was Guerrazzi's *L'Assedio di Firenze* (1836). Part of its inflammatory preface has already been quoted. The other novel was d'Azeglio's *Niccolo da Lapi* (1841). By 1865 seven operas had been based on one or the other of these two novels, and five more were to follow, one of them by Pacini (1873). As with *Ettore Fieramosca* d'Azeglio had already painted several pictures on themes of the siege of Florence and was probably led to the novel by these paintings, as well as by the discussion of the siege in Guiccardini, no doubt his original inspiration. The capture of Florence was the climax and virtual conclusion of Guiccardini's great history. Eventually d'Azeglio was to paint fourteen pictures related to his novel. It became a subject enormously popular with other painters. The Florence catalogue lists a total of 116 paintings derived from the fiction of Guerrazzi and d'Azeglio. The subject of the siege of Florence intertwines several themes—the heroic defense of the destruction of Italian liberty, the presence of two of Italy's greatest men, Machiavelli and Michelangelo, in charge of the fortifications, and, particularly in Guerrazzi's work, what he had learned from Scott and Manzoni, the struggle of a great people. There are also love stories which show the destruction of private happiness by public struggle and disaster. More than anyone Guerrazzi established the character of the Italian historical novel.

After Guerrazzi's *L'Assedio di Firenze* few more novels of great significance were written. Even those by Guerrazzi, though popular, added little to the themes already established. The most striking phenomenon is the wide range of subjects now employed in opera and paintings. Part of this effort was, of course, the result of the need for writers, composers, painters, and librettists to find new subjects that would be useful for exemplifying the well-established themes. I shall examine what followed more briefly than in the previous discussion, and in several groups. The chronological limit for fiction and operas is 1860; for paintings, 1870.

First are works of fiction. In 1838 Cesare Cantu published *Margharita Prusteria*. The setting is Milan in the mid-fourteenth century. The villain is the then duke of Milan, Luchino Visconti, the brother of Marco Visconti and the successor of Azzone, and the theme is the

abuse of power as well as the high energy of the powerful. Three operas were based on this novel, the first in 1844, and twenty-six paintings. One play needs to be mentioned, for it introduced an extremely
popular theme. Giuseppe Rovani's *Bianca Cappello* tells the famous
story of the Venetian girl who fled her home with a lover of lower
class, went with him to Florence, and became the mistress and eventually the wife of Duke Francesco I, the events taking place in the
1570s and the 1580s. According to the legend, now generally discredited, both the duke and the duchess were poisoned by the Med-
icis. The theme appears to be the degeneracy of the Medici and the
Italian aristocracy after Italy had lost its independence. At any rate
there were two operas on the subject and twenty-seven paintings.
Giovanni Rosini's novel *Il Conte Ugolino della Gherardesca e i Ghibellini
di Pisa* (1843) presents again the theme of the tragic consequences of
internecine struggle. The subject comes from Dante, and though there
are no operas on Ugolino, there are twenty-three paintings, some of
them certainly not dependent upon Rosini. In 1844 Guerrazzi published another historical novel, *Isabella Orsini*, the story of the murder
of Isabella de'Medici by her husband, the Duke of Bracciano, convinced of her adultery, either rightly or wrongly. In either case it is the
conflict between love and brutal feudal power and authority. Two operas were based on it, the first as early as the year of publication of
Guerrazzi's work, and there are nineteen paintings on the subject. All
of them appear to be later than Guerrazzi. The final work is on a subject not included in the Florence catalogue, nor have I been able to
discover an opera on this subject, at least before the twentieth century.
It is Guerrazzi's wild, absurd, and frequently powerful novel *Beatrice
Cenci*, its theme the oppression of innocence by vicious power, both
of Beatrice's father and the powers of Rome, including the Pope.

The next group consists of subjects on which there were both operas and paintings. The story of Parisina, based on Byron's poem,
taken from an incident in Gibbon's "Antiquities of the House of
Brunswick,"[37] became very popular. In the early fifteenth century
Nicolas III of Este had his wife and bastard son executed for incest and
adultery, yet he was responsible for bringing them together and encouraging their friendship. The theme is very much that of *Isabella
Orsini*. Besides Donizetti's opera (1833) there are twenty-one paintings. In 1834 Buondelmonte Buondelmonti[38] appeared on the operatic stage, the beginning in 1215 of one of the most terrible struggles
of all, that between the Guelfs and Ghibellines in Florence when
Buondelmonte was murdered by the relatives of a girl he had been
betrothed to but left for another. No other opera was written on this

subject, but there are twenty-five paintings. In 1835 the tragic story of the Venetian Doge Marino Faliero was set by Donizetti. Again the theme is unscrupulous power and revenge. In 1840 an opera was written on Cosimo I de'Medici, and there were six paintings on the death by torture or outright murder of Filippo Strozzi, one of the last of his opponents. In 1844 appeared Verdi's *I due Foscari*, again the theme of oppression, injustice, and revenge, a subject for twenty-five paintings. In 1855 there was an opera on Bernabo Visconti, presumably based on Bazzoni's novel. There have been eleven paintings. Other operas and paintings (the number of paintings is indicated in parentheses) were based on Conradin, the last of the Hohenstaufens (13); on Aldechi, based on Manzoni's play (9); on Piccarda Donati, a subject taken from Dante about a nun forced to leave the convent by her brother for a political marriage (11); and on Dante (133), Petrarch (41), and Galileo (53). Though the story of Columbus is not Italian, he was counted among the great Italian figures. Before 1860 there were four operas and by 1870 sixty-nine paintings.[39]

Subjects not in the Florence catalogue on which I have located at least titles of operas, and occasionally more, and the subjects which I have been able to identify are Verdi's first opera, *Oberto, Conte de San Bonifacio* (1839), in which the heroine loses both lover and father, but the story is given historical depth by being set in the court of the terrible Ezzelini. Others are Alberigo da Romano, the last of the Ezzelini; Giovanna I, queen of Naples, supposed to have been implicated in the murder of her husband; Caterina Cornaro, deprived by the Venetians of her rule of Cyprus; and Salvator Rosa, the painter, famous for his wild life, the most modern of the subjects.[40]

The final groups consist of subjects found in paintings but in neither operas nor, so far as I have been able to discover, in novels or poetic romances: the preaching of the first Crusade (5), preparations for the second Crusade (3), Frederick Barbarossa, i.e., subjects other than the Lombard League and the attacks on Milan (12), Arnold of Brescia, the great early medieval populist (14), Savonarola (33), Fra Paolo Sarpi, historian of the Council of Trent and Venetian patriot (8), Caterina Visconti (1), Muzio Attendolo Sforza, who succeeded to the Visconti rulership in Milan (3), the Conspiracy of the Lampugnani, resulting in the death of Galeazzo Maria Sforza in 1476, based on a 1779 play by Pietro Verri, Lodovico Sforza il Moro, whose court was magnificent but who opened Italy to the French invader (8), Il Conte di Carmagnola, Manzoni's hero (14), Valenza Gradenigo and Antonio Foscarini, another story of brutal Venetian power (11), the expulsion of Walter of Brienne, Duke of Athens, from Florence, where he had abused the power granted him, and from which he was chased by the people (7), the exile of Giano della Bella, the leader of the people's party of Florence (1), the conspiracy of the Pazzi against the Medici, in which the great Lorenzo almost lost his life (17), the expulsion of Alessandro and Ippolito Medici from Florence in 1527 (5), and four great men: Boccaccio (15), Giotto (30), Leonardo (28), and Michelangelo (41).

As one thinks over these subjects or examines the paintings reproduced in the Florence catalogue, the dominating impression is one of violence, oppression, and the struggle against it, of love destroyed by power, and above all the presentation either of a high level of aggression or of its consequences, when that oppression is the result of injustice and brutality, particularly that of foreigners or of Italian powers dependent upon foreign rulers. Even so quiet a picture as that of Puricelli, representing the Venetian senators visiting Paolo Sarpi, reminds the knowledgeable observer of the attack upon Sarpi by assassins hired by the Papal Curia and possibly by the Pope himself (1863; Milan, Civic Gallery of Modern Art). In 1836 A. Bianchi Giovini had circulated the story once again, for modern readers, in his biography of Sarpi, published in Zurich, and the picture was painted at the very time that the Papacy was almost the last impediment to Italian unification.

These themes can be summed up by some examination of three operas by Verdi. The first of these is *La Battaglia di Legnano*.[41] In 1162 the Milanese resisted the power of Frederick Barbarossa, who desired to deprive them of autonomy. Aided by other cities jealous of Milan's power and wealth, Barbarossa besieged, sacked, and completely destroyed it. And then he turned upon the cities which had aided him and subjected them to brutal oppression. In 1167 in Pontida the Lombard League was consecrated, and on May 19, 1176, the League defeated the Emperor. In 1183, by the peace of Constance, Barbarossa was forced to recognize the principle of the autonomy of the communes. No subject could be better chosen to show the cost of internal division, the brutality of foreign oppression, and the validity of high aggression. On April 20, 1848, a month after the "Five Days of Milano," which drove the Austrians from Milan and precipitated the first war for independence, Salvatore Cammarno wrote to Verdi and suggested as a subject the Battle of Legnano. "A story like that should stir every man with an Italian soul in his breast."[42] But the opera was not ready for performance until the following January 27, 1849. In the meantime, in July, at the battle of Custozza, the Piemontese had been defeated and were shortly driven from Lombardy. On the other hand, Pope Pius had already fled the city, and the declaration of the Roman Republic, to be dominated by Mazzini, was only two weeks away. It was a time when it seemed as if the first rebellion for independence still might be successful. Such hopes ended soon. The disaster of the battle of Novara on March 23 virtually brought the struggle to an end, though it lingered on for several months. On June 30, 1849, the French entered Rome. The subject of the Lombard League had already been used for an opera once, Buzzi's *La Lega Lombarda*, but it had been presented in Paris in 1846. For the Paris performance Meucci, the librettist, had written an inflammatory preface to the libretto. For the performance of the opera in Rome, two years before Verdi's opera, it had been necessary to give it a Spanish setting and title, *Gusamo di Medina*. Such transformations were common, and Buzzi's opera was occasionally presented as *The Siege of Harlem*. Presumably when such transformations were necessary, the public would be quite aware of what had happened and what the original subject had been. Even were they not, although the setting was no longer Italian, the theme remained a victorious struggle against foreign oppression, achieved by a league which resolved a country's internal divisions. All this also lies behind the forty-five paintings of the burning of Milan, the founding of the Lombard League, and the defeat of Barbarossa.

In the 1850s Verdi wrote for Paris an opera on a similar subject, *I Vespri Siciliani*. After the defeat of Manfred at Benevento (1266) the French of Charles of Anjou took over Sicily, but in 1282 the War of the Sicilian Vespers broke out, lasting until 1302, when the French gave up; for in 1282, their leader, Giovanni di Procida, had called in Peter of Aragon, the husband of Constance, daughter of Manfred. The heart of the matter was a spontaneous uprising of the people of Palermo, set off by a minor incident. The subject had already been used in painting, and by 1870 there was a total of twenty-two paintings with the Sicilian Vespers as subject. *I Vespri Siciliani* was written for the Paris Opera and presented there on June 13, 1855. The recent revival at the Metropolitan in New York was not too well received and Francis Toye's strictures are typical.[43] He calls the libretto, by Scribe and Duveyrier, "transparently insincere," and the Sicilians "a treacherous crew." This, it seems to me, is completely to misunderstand the story. First, the theme, the rebellion of Italians against an occupying foreign army, could not possibly have been presented anywhere in Italy, except perhaps Piemonte. To be sure, the censors were remarkably stupid. *Rigoletto* (1851), originally involving Francis I of France in Hugo's play *Le roi s'amuse*, had to be reset in Mantua, for it involved the disgraceful conduct of a king. But to Italian interests, whether a French king or an Italian duke was presented as vicious made no difference. In either case the subject was the abuse of power, one guaranteed to arouse aggressive indignation against such creatures and the society which supported them. The surprising thing about *I Vespri Siciliani* is that it presents the French in such a bad light. First of all, no knowledgeable Italian would be unaware of the fact that the Sicilian Vespers was a direct consequence of the papal introduction of the French to destroy the Hohenstaufens. That Manfredi and Corradino were Italian heroes has already been pointed out. Second, historically one Frenchman was seen to make an improper gesture to a Sicilian girl, but in the opera a chorus of Frenchmen makes off with a bevy of Sicilian brides, thus emphasizing the repeated offenses of the French, and the luxurious life of the French is contrasted with the simple and defenseless life of the Sicilian people in a striking scene. The Sicilians who have lost their girls are left dejected and helpless, until aroused by Giovanni di Procida. Of course they are "a treacherous crew." Italians had been plotting against foreign domination for half a century. Monforte, to be sure, wishes to reconcile Sicilians and French, but only for the sake of recovering his long-lost son and that son's affections. His act of doing so precipitates the finale, in which the Sicilians hurl themselves on the French, as the opera ends. Monforte, in short, is interested in reconciliation, and therefore a betrayal of the Sicilians, only for private reasons.

But how could it be that a Frenchman prepared for Paris a libretto at best ambiguous and one easily interpretable as denigrating to the French? At the time the French were in fact occupying Rome and supporting the Pope, his only real support, in maintaining the secular power of the Papacy. This was the policy of Napoleon III. Yet a great many Frenchmen were highly sympathetic with the Italian desire for freedom and independence, and a great many were opposed to Napoleon III, both for his troops in Rome and for other reasons. On the other hand Napoleon had already indicated his sympathy for the Italian cause, and in the spring of 1855 at the Congress of Paris Cavour had been given the opportunity to express before the representatives of the European powers the grievances of Italy. The substitution of Italians for Sicilians and Austrians for French by members of the audience would have been remarkably easy, something in which the audiences of Italian operas were already well trained, especially now that the plight of Italy had become a European concern, as it had ever since the publication of *Le Mie Prigioni* in 1832. In Verdi's *Nabucco* (1842) the substitution of Jews for Italians and Assyrians for Austrians was absolutely transparent, and accounted for the success of an opera far below what Verdi was to accomplish. In short, when examined in the light of the Italian situation in 1855, six years after the defeat of Italians by a foreign invader, *I Vespri Siciliani*, which takes place fourteen years after the defeat of Italian interests by a foreign invader, looks very different. Irving Kolodin in his introduction to the libretto for the recent recording is as imperceptive as Toye. It all "ends in confusion—bloody confusion." To Italians there was nothing the least degree confusing about Italians hurling themselves on brutal and exploitative foreigners in possession of Italy. To respond to the end of this opera it is wise to remember Guerazzi's introduction to *L'Assedio di Firenze*, quoted by Mazzini in an article written for an English journal read and respected in France. Verdi had read the book and had considered it as the subject for an opera and was to do so again. It is obvious that both Toye and Kolodin are controlled by an historiographical ideology which was only beginning to emerge forcefully in European culture in the 1850s and which had not affected opera, nor was to until the twentieth century. The characters are indeed pasteboard, *if* one brings to them no significant knowledge of either medieval or nineteenth-century Italian history. In addition, in opera the third dimension of personality is provided by the music.

Moreover, Toye says, "There is, then, little of musical interest in *I Vespri Siciliani*."[44] At this point I must become personal in a way which I hope may be useful to others. In the course of writing this essay I have taken the occasion to listen to four Verdi operas with which I was not very familiar, having heard three of them but once. These were *I Due Foscari*, *La Battaglia di Legnano*, *I Vespri Siciliani*, and *Simon Boccanegra*. From the perspective I have gained from doing the research for this essay and from writing it, I have perceived in Verdi's music a quality to which I have hitherto responded, I admit, inadequately. For the first time the grandeur and strength of his music have seized me, and above all its aggressiveness. I hear what Mazzini heard in Rossini, the introduction to a higher level of aggression in Italian operatic music, but raised by Verdi to a far greater power than one finds in Rossini. I hear now in Verdi's music the voice of Guerrazzi, "Ye shall rise." The ideology which controls Verdi's music is an ideology that demanded that the level of Italian aggression be raised to the level common in the middle ages.

The third Verdi opera of the period that I wish to discuss is *Simon Boccanegra* (1857), the next work after *I Vespri Siciliani*. It was not successful at its first presentation in Venice on March 12, 1857, at least with the public, though the critics praised it.[45] It was based on a play by the Spaniard Guiterriez, who had been consul in Genoa and had become fascinated with its history. In 1881 Boito revised the libretto, improving it greatly. Verdi added long sections to the score and revised the whole quite thoroughly. As in the immediately preceding opera, the people play an important part, and the struggle is between the Guelfs and Ghibellines in Genoa, reconciled at the end by Simon, a man of the people, originally a sailor, raised to the position of Doge because of the strife between the leading families. By 1857 it was a standard theme, except for the striking figure of Simon himself, who as hero, sacrificed to internecine struggle, represents the people of Italy with a new power and energy. It is not fanciful, I think, to discern behind the character of Simon Garibaldi, himself born near Genoa in Nice, not yet sacrificed to Napoleon III by Cavour. The politicians always regarded Garibaldi with suspicion, but no one had done so much to arouse the Italian people from their submissiveness. Had they not been so aroused, Vittorio Emanuele could never have unified Italy. The plot, to be sure, hinges upon the usual long-lost child, as does *I Vespri Siciliani* and many other operas. But this device requires careful consideration, and it would be unwise to dismiss it merely as plot machinery. The child is almost always lost as the consequence of the oppression of one or more of its parents, and its rediscovery has the power of the theme of the emergence of truth from suppression, concealment, and oblivion. It is a redundancy of considerable potential in raising the level of confidence in revitalizing a lost cause.

It is now apparent that the primary tasks of the Risorgimento, the raising of the level of aggression and the establishment of the myth of the nation, so that Italians could take pride in their past achievements and be convinced of their ability to dominate their situation, were central to the writing of fiction, the composition of operas, and the painting of pictures. It is also clear that this theme was side by side with and often coupled with the task of the analytic critique of society, and that the effort of these artists during the period from the 1820s was principally devoted to historical themes. But what is even more striking is the enormous effort, the great output of energy and devotion, that went into this cultural activity, for one must include the work not merely of artists, but of publishers, of critics, of the arts, of the organizers of painting exhibitions, of which there were dozens, and of all the personnel involved in opera production. That the audience was responsive and increasingly so is evident; not only were paintings popular, judging from the Florence catalogue, along with many operas, but also the more successful historical novels went through numerous editions. Nor must it be imagined that this activity

was confined to only a few major centers in northern Italy. First performances of operas took place all over the country.[46] It is true, of
course, that Italian opera production, especially in the 1820s, 1830s,
and 1840s, was generally not of a high standard. That is why all European opera composers wanted to be commissioned to write for
Paris, for only in the state-supported Grand Opera could adequate
productions be accomplished. The situation was almost as bad in Germany. Italian poverty, of course, is the obvious explanation. The opera
managers did the best they could, and most of the impressarios had
to make a profit, and usually did, so great was the demand. Certainly
standards improved in the course of the century; but one of the reasons that we are now discovering forgotten operas by Bellini, Donizetti, and Verdi is that only in the last thirty years have they ever
received adequate productions and performances.

On the other hand the reports of travelers to Italy give almost uni-
formly a picture of a completely decadent and lethargic society. Tour-
ists, and even serious travelers, however, rarely know what is really
going on in the cities they visit. This study of the relations of fiction,
opera, and painting has made it clear, I hope, that the traditional picture is quite in error, that, in fact, the cultural situation in the first half
of the nineteenth century was extraordinarily lively. Oddly, this vigor
was aided by the Austrians, for Austria received one third of its annual
income from the Kingdom of Lombardo-Veneto; it is not surprising
that they were reluctant to give it up. Hence they encouraged economic development, and in doing so dug their own grave. One has
only to consider the many popular editions of the novels of d'Azeglio,
Guerrazzi, and Grossi, as well as Manzoni, inexpensive and richly illustrated with woodcuts, works which were increasingly in demand
as the level of literacy rose, to realize the enormous importance of
these works in creating, through redundancy, the sociocultural at-
mosphere which made the unification of Italy possible. Opera, as the
most popular of the arts, available even to illiterates, was as important
as fiction. But such considerations lead to another irony, one which
destroyed the Italian regimes of the early nineteenth century. Since
the censorship of the Austrians, the Papacy, the Neopolitans, even the
rulers of Piemonte denied political discussion and political action, the
energies of the Italians turned to the arts in which their tradition was
so great. De Sanctis on this subject is worth quoting.

The sciences, the arts, literature, music and song, all of them flourished exceedingly. The place that politics left vacant was occupied by discussions of
Taglioni and Malibran, of Rachel and Ristori, of Rossini and Bellini, of literature and science, of the French and Italian novels. . . . Italian aspirations

were vibrating in this literature [and painting and opera, he might well have added], and every son of Italy was conscious of it: the smallest allusions, the most distinct analogies, were caught on the wing by a public that was one with its writers.[47]

It must be admitted that Italian rhetoric never dies, and certainly has not departed from de Sanctis, for all of his talk about criticisms. But it is to be remembered that this passage was written in 1870 or 1871, with Italy at last unified, when the great cultural effort of which this paper is some account had at last achieved what certainly seemed to be fulfillment.

Ugo Foscolo told the Italians to write histories. They took his advice. I know of no other time or country in which historicism in the arts made possible a political revolution. However, the nineteenth century is still the unknown century, and the interrelation of the arts in maintaining and transforming a culture is still a subject scarcely studied.

## NOTES

1. "Io esorto alle storie, perché angusta è l'arena deglie oratori: . . . Ma nelle storie tutta si spiega la nobiltà dello stile, tutti gli affetti delle virtù, tutto l'incanto della poesia, tutti i precetti della sapienza, tutti i progressi e i benemeriti dell'italiano sapere." (Ugo Foscolo, Opere, ed. Mario Puppo [Milan, 1964], p. 673).

2. The reference is to the great work of Lodovico Antonio Muratori (1672–1750) of Modena, 25 folios of medieval chronicles and documents, Rerum italicarum scriptores (1723–1738).

3. William Roscoe, The Life of Lorenzo de' Medici (1795, Italian trans., 1799), and The Life and Pontificate of Leo the Tenth (1805, Italian trans., 1816–1817). It should be noted, since cultivated Milanese tended to speak French better than Italian, not yet standardized, that French translations appeared in 1799 and 1808, respectively.

4. First published in Bologna in 1799 in an incomplete edition, finished by Angelo Sassoli. In 1801 Foscolo published a protest against this edition and completed the novel; he published it in its authentic form at Milan in 1802. In the same year two more editions were published, more or less under his control, and these were followed by numerous pirated editions. In 1816 in Geneva he published a revised edition (falsely dated London, 1814), and in 1817 brought out a definitive edition in London, published by John Murray. Foscolo, Opere, p. 1,152.

5. Brescia, 1807.

6. Foscolo, Opere, p. 1,133.

7. Foscolo, Opere, p. 1,197.

8. J. Christopher Herold, Mistress to an Age: A Life of Madame de Staël (Indianapolis and New York, 1958), pp. 293–296. A new edition of the history appeared in 1826. In 1832 Simonde published an abbreviated version in En-

glish, *A History of the Italian Republics: Being a View of the Rise, Progress, and Fall of Italian Freedom*, written for the "Cabinet Cyclopaedia." My 1951 statement that it was not is an error ("Dr. Lardner's *Cabinet Cyclopaedia*," *Papers of the Bibliographical Society of America*, vol. 45 [1951], pp. 37–58).

9. The title of the first chapter in *Storia della storiografia italiana nel sec, XIX*.

10. For the publication of translations of Scott see Sergio Romagnoli, "Narratori e prosatori del Romanticism," *Storia della Letteratura Italiana*, ed. Emilio Cecchi e Natalino Sapegna (Milan, 1968), vol. 7, pp. 7–88. The *CBEL* is inaccurate.

11. For an extended discussion of Romantic historicism see my essays, "Romanticism and Behavior," "The Function of History in Nineteenth-Century European Culture," "Reflections on Historical Modes in the Nineteenth Century," and "Rebellion and Deviance," in *Romanticism and Behavior: Collected Essays II* (Columbia, S.C., 1976), pp. 3–89.

12. Croce made this charge in various essays, but see particularly his "La storiografia del romanticism" in *Teoria e storia della storiografia*. A translation is available in *History: Its Theory and Practice*, a selection of essays translated by Douglas Ainslie (New York, 1923), pp. 264–288.

13. Colin M. Turnbull, *The Mountain People* (New York, 1972). See particularly chapter 8, "Retreat of the Icien God."

14. See his "On Italian Literature since 1830," *Westminster Review* (October 1837), reprinted in *Life and Writings, II*, "A New Edition" (London, 1891). The passage referred to is on p. 178.

15. Mazzini, "On Italian Literature . . . ," pp. 189–190.

16. For a more extended discussion of this point see my essay "Romanticism and Behavior," referred to in note 11.

17. In "The Philosophy of Music," *Life and Writings, IV*, pp. 24ff.

18. "E ciel pietosa ammira de' regi defensor." "Altri affetti non vogl'io che la gloria e la pietà."

19. The catalogue of the exhibition *Romanticismo Storico* was prepared by Paolo Barochi, Fiamma Nicolodi, and Sandra Pinto. The exhibition was the responsibility of Sandra Pinto, and the restoration of the Meridiana of Marisa Conti Forlani. The catalogue was published by Center Di. Unspecified identifications of sources are taken from this catalogue.

20. The title of the introductory essay in *Die Kunst des 19. Jahrhunderts, Propylaen Kunstegeschichte*, vol. 11 (Berlin, 1966).

21. Whether the catalogue is still available I do not know. I purchased mine from St. George's Gallery Books Ltd., 8 Duke Street, St. James, London. It may be that this admirable firm still has some available. Part I of the catalogue does not date the works listed, only the date of the source of the information about the existence of the painting; nor does it indicate the location of the pictures. Very possibly many of them no longer exist. Certainly many must be in private collections.

22. *The Works of Lord Byron*, ed. E. H. Coleridge, *Poetry*, vol. 4, pp. 324–329, and vol. 5, pp. 115–119.

23. William Ashbrook, *Donizetti*, London, 1965, p. 484.

24. Julian Budden, *The Operas of Verdi: From Oberto to Rigoletto* (New York and Washington, 1973), p. 475.

25. Both of Byron's plays were translated into Italian in 1845 by P. G. B. Cereseto and published at Savona. However, a translation of Byron's dramas

by P. de Virgilii was brought out in Brussels in 1841. Whether this volume included these plays I do not know. French translations were later. (*CBEL*).

26. For further discussion of this point see my essay "Reflections on Historical Modes . . . ," referred to in note 11. "It appears to be the case that the central drive of nineteenth-century fiction throughout Europe was the drive to construct a critique of society; that this drive first found satisfaction in nineteenth-century historicism, as was sociology, and that the self-conscious exploitation of the techniques of research made it possible to solve the problem of the intuitive sociological novel by fusing it with the historical novel" (p. 54).

27. "Del Romanzo Storico," published in *Opere Varie*, 1845–1855.

28. It was based on Carlo Fores's play *Beatrice di Tenda* (1825). Herbert Weinstock, *Vincenzo Bellini* (New York, 1971), p. 514. Another opera using the same libretto appeared in 1837, the composer R. Ticci.

29. I have not considered other plays unless they were sources for operas or paintings because I have been unable to find the kind of widespread information available for operas in the Florence catalogue. Subjects of historical plays were Eufemio da Messina, Buondelmonte, Beatrice di Tenda, Antonio Foscarini, the Fieschi and Doria, Corso Donati, Ezzelino III, Lodovica il Moro (2), Pia di Tolomei, Bianca Cappello, Arnold de Brescia (2), Beatrice Cenci, Tasso. With few exceptions these subjects had already been treated in historical poems and novels and in paintings.

30. Manzoni, *Opere*, p. 1,004.

31. *Purgatorio*, V, 133–136. See the commentary of Charles S. Singleton (Princeton, 1973), pp. 107–109.

32. I cannot forbear offering a public tribute to Archibald Colquhoun for his splendid translation, published in 1951 and now available in Everyman's Library.

33. Mario Muzzuchelli, *La Monaca da Monza* (Milan, 1961), translated by Evelyn Gendel as *The Nun of Monza* (New York, 1963).

34. Ashbrook in *Donizetti* says that the source is unidentified, but Sacchi was a very minor figure, easily overlooked. Though Tottola, the librettist, changed the ending of the story, his references to the original ending seem to refer to Sacchi (Ashbrook, p. 474). This is also Nicolodi's opinion in the Florence catalogue.

35. Ashbrook, p. 474.

36. *Storia d'Italia*, vol. 5, p. 13. *Opere*, ed. Vittorio de Capraiis (Milan and Naples), pp. 592–595.

37. *Works, Poetry*, vol. 3, p. 502.

38. This was Donizetti's opera *Maria Stuarda*, which had to be refashioned because the Queen of Naples almost fainted during the dress rehearsal at the sufferings of another Queen (Ashbrook, p. 152).

39. Wagner's *Rienzi* (written 1838–1840, first presented in 1842) deserves to be mentioned as an indication of the extension of the fashion for Italian historical opera beyond Paris. Mary Russell Mitford's play appeared in 1828 and Bulwer-Lytton's novel in 1836. Verdi considered the subject as early as 1844 and again in 1848 for the Rome opera which became *La Battaglia di Legnano* (Budden, p. 390).

40. Subjects tentatively identified or not identified: the siege of Brescia (probably that by Gaston de Foix, 1512), the siege of Messina (probably that

by Charles of Anjou, 1282), Giulio d'Este (probably the Ferrarese prince blinded by his ducal brother), Carlo Gonzago (Mantova), the Council of Ten, Mastin I della Scala (Verona), Morosino (Venice), the Saracens in Sicily (possibly the Saracen invasion of Sicily, since several plays are about Eufemio di Messina, supposedly responsible), the duke, and the knights of Valenza (possibly a rebellion against a Milanese overlord), the count of Lavagna, Marie di Ricci. Other titles suggest an historical setting.

41. A recent recording is available.

42. Budden, p. 390.

43. In his *Giuseppe Verdi: His Life and Works*, first published in 1946; references are to the paperback edition of 1959, pp. 328–329.

44. Toye, p. 329.

45. Toye, pp. 97–98.

46. Trieste, Verona, Cremona, Napoli, Genova, Torino, Chieti, Sira, Milano, Roma, San Severo, Vicenza, Lucca, Venezia, Livrno, Rimini, Ferrara, Casalmaggiore, Bologna, Piacenza, Malta, Firenze, Palermo, Parma, Arezzo, Lecco, Messina, Pesaro, Aquila, Padova, Urbino, Pistoia, Terni, Lugo di Romagna.

47. Francesco de Sanctis, *History of Italian Literature*, trans. Joan Redfern (New York, 1959), vol. 2, pp. 938–939.

# CHAPTER FOUR

# Frederick the Great

It is difficult to write about Carlyle's *History of Friedrich II of Prussia Called Frederick the Great,* for it seems a pointless and useless undertaking. Almost no one has read it, and it seems unlikely that anyone will read it because of a mere essay. Those who find this essay valuable will probably conclude that they are saved the trouble of reading the work; while those who dislike the essay will decide that it has not offered convincing reasons for undertaking the book itself. During the fifteen years since I first read it, constant inquiry among other Victorian scholars has not uncovered anyone else who has done so. In fact, one scholar who has written in some detail about it and with an air of considerable authority turned out only to have skimmed through it. Another, one who likewise found the work to be a failure, does not give me the impression that he has done more than a rapid skimming. When I recommend reading *Frederick* to other Victorian scholars, my enthusiasm is received with skepticism and more often than not a politely but barely concealed implication that my judgment is grotesque. To be sure, one friend to whom I recommended it did read it and, though he detested Carlyle, thought it to be a marvelous book. But then, he was not a Victorian scholar but a music critic, and besides he died not long thereafter.

I shall make no attempt, therefore, to argue that *Frederick* is a success or a failure, a great book or a poor one. When I first read it I felt that I was having one of the greatest and most thoroughly satisfying reading experiences of my life. My second reading was less agreeable, but it was done not at leisure but under deadlines pressure. I look forward to reading it again, but at my ease and after I have retired. I think it is a fascinating and wonderful work. If one wants to understand Carlyle and the culture of the nineteenth century one should read it; if one wishes professional success and status, to read *Frederick* is clearly unnecessary, since so many Victorian scholars who enjoy both have not troubled to do so. Rather, I shall be concerned with certain rhetorical peculiarities in *Frederick* and in proposing explanations for them, since they raise interesting questions not only about Carlyle but also about the very nature of writing history.[1]

I

Approaching *Frederick* initially as a piece of historical discourse, one first notes the oddness of its proportions. Almost a third of the work is over before Friedrich succeeds to the throne. The last half of his reign takes up a little less than a tenth of the whole. Thus almost 60 percent of the work is concerned with the years from 1740 to 1763. This is the period of the Silesian Wars; Friedrich invaded Silesia in December 1740, less than seven months after his accession. Moreover, Books I to III, almost 10 percent, are principally taken up with the history of Brandenburg and of the Hohenzollerns before the accession of Friedrich's father, Friedrich Wilhelm. Books IV to X, about 23 percent, ostensibly taken up with Friedrich's youth, are as much concerned with Friedrich Wilhelm as with his son. Thus anyone who wishes to read a balanced account of the career of Friedrich will be both disappointed and puzzled.

A clue to this way of laying out the work is to be found in the great space and immense detail devoted to Friedrich's campaigns and above all to his battles. Carlyle himself visited most of the battle-sites, and it is obvious that no one who had not done so could have written about the battles as he did. If he could not go to the field itself, he procured the most accurate and informative maps and descriptions he could lay his hands on. Two themes of the book emerge here, that of struggle and that of reality.

The theme of struggle emerges in the long accounts of the history of Brandenburg and of the Hohenzollerns, though it is not explicitly set forth until Book XXI. Carlyle is discussing the rapid recovery of Prussia from the devastations of the Third Silesian War:

Prussia has been a meritorious Nation; and, however cut and ruined, is and was in a healthy state, capable of recovering soon. Prussia has defended itself against overwhelming odds,—brave Prussia; but the real soul of its merit was that of having merited such a King to command it. Without this King, all its valours, disciplines, resources of war, would have availed Prussia little. No wonder Prussia has still a loyalty to its great Friedrich, to its Hohenzollern Sovereigns generally. Without these Hohenzollerns, Prussia had been, what we long ago saw it, the unluckiest of German Provinces; and could never have had the pretension to exist as a Nation at all. Without this particular Hohenzollern, it had been trampled out again, after apparently succeeding. To have achieved a Friedrich the Second for King over it, was Prussia's grand merit. (XXI, i, 8)

The interactions of Hohenzollerns and Brandenburg, the long history that lay behind the achievement of "Prussia's grand merit," is the theme of the first three books.[2] It is the struggle on the one hand of the Hohenzollerns to establish themselves, and on the other of the people of Brandenburg to establish themselves as an independent nation. The central theme is the struggle of Brandenburg and the Hohenzollerns to adapt themselves to each other, a struggle almost completed by Friedrich Wilhelm, who left to Friedrich an army and a disciplined population. In the Silesian wars Friedrich consummated the century-old struggle and created a modern nation.

Carlyle conceived of his task as the creation of an epic, the first true historical epic, although he was convinced that his cultural situation did not allow him to create that epic.

Alas, the Ideal of History, as my friend Sauerteig knows, is very high; and it is not one serious man, but many successions of such, and whole serious generations of such, that can ever again build up History towards its old dignity. . . . "All History is an imprisoned Epic, nay an imprisoned Psalm and Prophecy," said Sauerteig there. . . . But I think all real *Poets*, to this hour, are Psalmists and Illiadists after their sort; and have in them a divine impatience of lies, a divine incapacity of living among lies. Likewise, which is a corollary, that the highest Shakspeare producible is properly the fittest Historian producible. (I, i, 17–18)

Arms-and-the-man is the theme of epic, and to Friedrich the Electorate of Brandenburg and the Kingdom of Prussia were his arms, forged by his Hohenzollern ancestors.

But the joint struggle of electorate and family to realize themselves and each other was not enough to account for Friedrich. Not only must the arms be forged but also the man. Hence the long and lovingly detailed discourse on the reign of Friedrich Wilhelm and on what, for Carlyle's purposes, was the real point of that reign, the fearful conflict between father and son, the result of which was the creation of a man and a king out of a sensitive, dilettantish, Francophile prince. It is therefore of great significance to the design of the work that Carlyle makes much of the reconciliation of father and son, of Friedrich's grief at his father's death, of his love for his father, and particularly of his continuation of his father's internal policies and administrative personnel. Thus by the end of the original first two volumes (Books I–VIII) both country and man are forged and ready for each other.

The next twelve books (IX–XX) are taken up almost entirely with the three Silesian wars, except for seven months of peace after the accession and two intervals of two and ten years (Books XI, XIV, and XVI). From these wars Friedrich and Prussia emerge, the one as finally a true King, the other as finally a true Nation. Book XXI, which Carlyle calls a "loose Appendix of Papers," is not a "finished Narrative" simply because to his theme such a finished narrative would be inappropriate. All that was needed was a demonstration that, in the last twenty-three years of his reign, Friedrich truly ruled a consummated nation. The whole metaphysical point is to be found here.

In the chaos of the eighteenth century—that it was a chaos the French Revolution, to Carlyle, sufficiently proved—Friedrich had created an island of social order. Not that he was alone. Carlyle saw in that chaotic century of lies two other focal points of truth. One was Voltaire; the other was Pitt. Carlyle judged Voltaire to be no more perfect than Friedrich, yet he saw him as a counterpart. Voltaire had an intellectual grasp of his cultural situation; Friedrich, whom Carlyle saw as intellectually superficial, nevertheless had a practical nonintellectual grasp of a similar sort. Pitt stands on the sidelines; he helps Friedrich, but his help is validated by his intelligence in grasping that America must be English, not French, France, of course, being at once the most brilliant and the most corrupt of eighteenth-century nations. America is presented as the hope of the future; Pitt was great because he saw that hope as something that could be destroyed if France controlled America.

Further, Carlyle saw the nineteenth century as the inheritor and the continuator of the collapse of eighteenth-century culture in the French Revolution. The first chapter of Book I begins with that theme and the first chapter of the final book reiterates it, "New Act,—of, we may call it New *Part*; Drama of World History. Part Third" (XXI, i, 2). This is not a casual remark here but a proper introduction to that Book. The work cannot be allowed to end triumphantly, heroically, in a blaze of Friedrich's glory. Friedrich, it is true, created an island of order, but it was bound to be temporary, since it came toward the close of Part II of World-History. The world in which Carlyle was living was the opening chaos of Part III. That is why the true Historical Epic lay far in the future, why Carlyle could not write it. To do so it would be necessary to understand the meaning of Part III, and though Carlyle guesses at it—("unappeasable Revolt against Sham-Governors and

Sham-Teachers,—which I do charitably define to be a Search, most unconscious, yet in deadly earnest, for true Governors and Teachers")—the result of that search cannot be envisioned. Friedrich, he implies in the next sentence, is not particularly significant for what he did, but that he existed may be of the highest relevance. At the beginning of Book I Carlyle writes, "To many it appears certain there are to be no Kings of any sort, no Government more; less and less need of them henceforth, New Era having come" (I, i, 16). At the beginning of Book XXI he defines Part III of World-History as "the breaking-out of universal mankind into Anarchy, into the faith and practice of No-Government" (p. 2). That is why he says in Book I, "My hopes of presenting, in this Last of the Kings, an exemplar to my contemporaries, I confess, are not high" (I, i, 17). In short, if Carlyle has understood World-History, true Governors and true Teachers— political and moral agents of social control and management—will arise; if he has not, mankind will find a way of living satisfactorily without social control and management. Since Carlyle cannot be sure of how the problem is to be resolved, if at all, he cannot write a true Historical Epic, since such an epic would require an understanding of the meaning of World-History. He can only show the struggle, he can only demonstrate how one man became a true King, but he cannot be sure that such struggle and becoming can really be useful. (I cannot forbear interpolating that, disagreeable as the notion may be, I cannot imagine mankind without techniques of social control and management. My reason is that notions of society without social control and management are founded upon love, but love, in all its forms, appears to me to be the most stringent and oppressive of the various modes of social control and management. Possibly Carlyle was hinting at this when he proposed that Part II of World History began with Christ and ended with the French Revolution.) The future, then, may not need such exemplars as Friedrich, or, on the contrary, it may need them but be unable to use them. From this point of view the real hero of *Frederick* is Carlyle himself, for he engaged in and persisted in the immense struggle to complete the work without any confidence that it was worth completing. This is the difference between the redemptionist Carlyle (and Marx) of the 1830s and 1840s and the Carlyle of *Frederick*.

The theme of *Frederick*, then, is the theme of all Carlyle's work from before 1830: the struggle to create order out of chaos, and the struggle to penetrate through shams and lies to reality. However, the notion that that penetration is redemptive is now gone or at best has suffered a severe attrition. What had sustained Carlyle so long, up to *Latter-Day Pamphlets*, was the conviction that the penetration through lies and shams revealed the reality of the world as a symbol of the divine, or that the hero was a symbol and instrument of the divine. All this has disappeared from *Frederick*. We hear often enough about the Laws of Nature and the Laws of God, but we are not informed precisely what those laws are, except that they tend on the whole to be disagreeable, and except that the heroic man can face their disagreeableness and act in spite of it. Indeed, Carlyle's conception of God becomes remarkably like that of Kierkegaard's at much the same time: from the belief in God no moral or metaphysical propositions can be deduced. The only reality the not very intelligent or perceptive Friedrich was capable of was the reality of creating an island of order in the chaos of the eighteenth century, the reality of knowing what he wanted; yet his island was to be washed away by the French Revolution. The best Carlyle can suggest is that Friedrich's achievement enabled Prussia to survive several inferior kings, the French Revolution, and Napoleon. Thus the marked difference between *Frederick* and the works of the 1830s and 1840s is not sufficiently explained (and to my mind not at all explained) by postulating failing powers or loss of "creativity" (whatever that is). One must recognize a radical difference of vision. Recent writers on *Frederick* have been young (and platitudinously liberal). Their rejection of the work may, possibly, be a function of their youth (and their ideology), not of their critical insight nor of their social comprehension.

2

A second oddity of *Frederick* is typographical. A very large portion is in small print. It was the result of a very idiosyncratic decision, and I have never seen it discussed, though it seems impossible that it has never been commented on. Why did Carlyle set up this additional barrier to the reader?[3]

Many of these small-print passages are, to be sure, quotations from letters and other documents, but most of them are not. Some of them are summaries of documents; others are elaborations of minor points; for only a few of them is there any suggestion that they can be profitably skipped by all but persevering and determined readers. A sampling of how they are introduced will be of some interest. "Says one whose Note-books I have got" (I, i, 58); "says one of my old Papers" (I, i, 75); "the following Excerpt" (I, i, 77); "perhaps I had better subjoin a List (V, i, 15); "the following stray Note" (V, iii, 31); "accept this Note, or Summary" (V, iii, 39); "a most small Anecdote, but then an indisputably certain one" (V, v, 48); "One glance I may perhaps commend to the reader, out of these multifarious Notebooks in my possession" (IX, vi, 78); "excerpted from multifarious old Notebooks" (IX, viii, 91); "the following chronological phenomena of the Polish Election" (IX, viii, 95); "As to the History of Schlesien . . . I notice . . . Three Epochs" (XII, i, 4); "Read this Note" (XII, ii, 17); "says an Excerpt I have made" (XII, ii, 20); "and this Smelfungus" (XVI, iii, 233); "I have something to quote, as abridged and distilled from various sources" [it is not a quotation] (XVI, vi, 273); "says a certain Author" [unidentified] (XVI, viii, 306); "take this brief Note" (XVIII, vii, 228); two paragraphs without introduction, but placed in quotes (XVIII, viii, 264); "Smelfungus takes him up, with a twitch" (XVIII, ix, 304); "Four our poor objects, here is a Summary, which may suffice" (XX, v, 299); "some glances into the Turk War, I grieve to say, are become inevitable to us!" (XXI, iv, 100); "a rough brief Note" (XXI, v, 132); "Here, saved from my poor friend Smelfungus (nobody knows how much of him I suppress), is a brief jotting, in the form of rough memoranda, if it be permissible" (XXI, v, 181).

A thorough study of all the small-print passages, the categories into which they fall, and their various introductions, when present, as they usually are, might be of considerable interest, but probably would not change drastically the impression one gets from a thorough reading of the entire work. One group, as suggested, consists of direct quotations from letters and other documents. Here the small print is clearly a typographical convention. The effect of the other group, however, is quite different. For these passages Carlyle has innovated not merely a typographical convention but one that may properly be called a rhetorical one. The effect is by no means one that indicates that the material is skippable or unessential in any way. Often enough the effect is quite the contrary; it is an effect of emphasis. There seem to be two quite different functions, subordination and superordination.

In the first category are materials which only remotely impinge upon Friedrich, events which affect his activities and his purposes, but only indirectly, through some other agency. Although it is not in small print, the following passage gives some clue to this function. It is about the Italian War from 1742 to 1748: "War of which we propose to say almost nothing; but must request the reader to imagine it, all along, as influential on our specific affairs" (XIV, ii, 381). And every now and then there is a reminder that it is indeed going on, and occasionally more than a reminder, sometimes in small-print passages. Excellent examples of this kind of subordination are to be found in the accounts of Wolfe in Canada (Books XVIII and XIX). What Carlyle was attempting to do is clear enough. To carry out his theme of Friedrich creating an island of order in the European chaos of the eighteenth century, he had to present that chaos both vividly and in considerable detail. To feel Friedrich's struggle, the reader has to feel as intimately what he was struggling against. The effect is certainly precisely that. As the reader continues to burrow his way through the book, gradually he gains, as several readers at the time noticed, an extraordinarily comprehensive and detailed imaginative grasp of the political life of Europe during the twenty-three years of Friedrich's role as Friedrich Agonistes, not Carlyle's own epithet but justified by the identification of Friedrich with Samson Agonistes in Book I (p. 5). From this tremendous detail emerges a pattern of forces marshaled against him, at various times and in various combinations, England, France, Austria (above all), Russia, and Sweden. I know of no sustained historical discourse, even of much lesser length, in which the general contours of political and military events emerge with such grandeur and clarity. The convention of subordination by small print certainly, I think, contributes greatly to this. Such a passage is to the large print as a subordinate clause is to an independent clause. The equivalent of a logical articulation is achieved in large-scale historical articulation.

The second category, superordination, is equally important. The effect is cinematic, a close-up, together with a slowing down of the tempo of narration. A more appropriate nineteenth-century term would be "vignette." One of Carlyle's constant minor themes is the difficulty of getting a clear picture of Friedrich, or of his contemporaries, such as Voltaire or Czar Peter III. Just as Friedrich's effort was to penetrate through the shams and lies and illusions of the eighteenth century, so Carlyle presents himself as engaged in an equivalent struggle to penetrate through the mass of documents and formal histories—subsumed under the imaginary Prussian historian Dryasdust—to get at the living reality of a human being. The large-print discourse, then, carries forward the events in a more or less normal historical rhetoric, but it is apparent that Carlyle recognizes such narrative rhetoric as an abstraction, a simplification, a reduction to a spurious order of the infinitely complex interactions of human beings. The small-print superordination not only serves, then, to penetrate through that abstraction and to offer relief from it, but also—and this is the most important effect—to reveal its abstract character.

Moreover, the conventions of rhetorical articulation of subordination and superordination effected by small print are themselves part of a larger and even more interesting rhetorical strategy, the dissolution of the narrator into a group of narrators. First, of course, is "I." This is the modest struggling historian, attempting to set forth clearly the history of Friedrich, to disentangle immense complications, such as the Schleswig-Holstein question, or the case of the Miller Arnold, to present clearly what cannot be presented clearly, a battle, to explain the movements in Friedrich's campaigns. Above all—and this is of the highest importance—the "I" is struggling with an immense accumulation of documents. This "I" often calls himself "Editor." This not only emphasizes the physical presence of the documents but also links *Frederick* with Carlyle's truly editorial role in *Cromwell* and with the fictitious editor of *Sartor Resartus*, also struggling with a confused mass of miscellaneous documents from which he has to construct some kind of meaning. Closely related to this primary "I," and almost identifiable with him, is the "I" of some previous stage in the construction of the book. This former "I" has left behind him notebooks, scraps of paper, annotated maps, and so forth, which the current "I" uses. Part of the humour of the current "I" is the pleasure he takes in burning up materials he no longer needs. More remote is an unnamed "predecessor," transparently Carlyle himself. Dramatized in this figure is the experience every researcher has of feeling that his earlier notes must have been made by someone else, a justified feeling, since as one studies and writes one does become a different figure. Still more remote is the unnamed tourist, transparently again Carlyle himself. Here also is dramatized the feeling that the historian in his study, consulting his notes and his documents, is not the same man as the historian in the field, actively engaged in examining the battleground, or the palace, or the gardens, or the portrait. All these figures are anonymous, and each indicates a different and psychologically accurate relation of the historian to his materials.

Over against these are two named figures, each with quite a different function. "Sauerteig" is the author of the discussion of Ideal History, of the identification of history with imprisoned epic, quoted above. "Sauerteig" means yeast, or leaven. He is the ultimate interpreter not of history itself but of the historian's activity. He is the metahistorian. At the opposite pole is "Smelfungus," presumably meaning "smelling of the mould of ancient documents." He is the polar opposite of Sauerteig. He is the researcher; he occasionally seems to be Joseph Neuberg, Carlyle's immensely valuable assistant. He is spoken of with contempt and affection, and with sorrow for his endless and often profitless efforts, for he often produces the useless or the barely usable. He is, therefore, a useful means of subordination, a way of bringing in material of very peripheral interest, which is, however, at least above the level of the negligible, though often enough he turns up with that as well. These two figures likewise indicate psychologically accurate relations of the historian to his materials.

Against these named and nameless figures is the enemy of all of them, Dryasdust. He is not only the unimaginative, noninterpretative historian, usually Prussian; he is not even competent and reliable in presenting his materials. He is particularly incompetent—and he often gets cursed for this—in providing indices; either they are nonexistent or they are bad. Thus he is as unimaginative in comprehending the relation of the historian to his documents as he is uncomprehending of the extreme pole of the competent construction of historical discourse—meta-history, the role of Sauerteig. Dryasdust cannot give a rational account of a sequence of events of any complexity; he cannot even construct a simple chronological table of such a sequence. He is entirely overwhelmed by the maelstrom of historical documentation; he himself is only caught up in the perpetual whirlwind in the dustbin of historical documents. He is therefore a constant threat to the other narrators; without knowing it, he continuously undermines and subverts the activity of constructing a historical discourse. And he too is an aspect of Carlyle, of the narrator of the narrators, as he is of any historian.

This dissolution of the narrator into a variety of roles is of the highest interest. It is a device which, without compromising *Frederick* as historical discourse, nevertheless pulls it into the general field of art. The narrator, the "I," as increasingly in the novels of the time— *Vanity Fair*, for example—is not a category with a fixed and stable set of attributes.[4] He becomes something like the central figure of a major work of fiction, a proper-name category with a constantly changing set of attributes for which there is no attribute that subsumes the remaining attributes into a coherence. Thus the narrator resembles not only the narrator of sophisticated fiction but also the narrator of many lyric poems and of the informal essay. This dissolved narrator, in fact, tends to become more interesting, because of attributional discontinuity, than Friedrich himself, who shows greater attributional stability and coherence than Friedrich Wilhelm, his father, a character recognized by some of Carlyle's contemporaries as one of the great creations of English literature.

This attributional dissolution of the narrator into various named roles is on the central line of Romanticism, the separation between self and role, as George Herbert Mead pointed out many years ago. The usual procedure in Romantic fictions of one sort or another, including poetry, is the creation of an antirole, the Bohemian, the Artist, the Dandy, the Virtuoso, and the Historians.[5] The antirole establishes and defines the self, which, of course, is a pure concept and has no empirical existence, or at best is a feeling-state, a sense of continuity as one shifts from one social role to another. In dissolving and sub-dividing the antirole of the Historian, Carlyle has gone one step further in this, anticipating Nietzsche, who insisted that the effort to create a coherent interpretation of his thousands of aphorisms and paragraphs would be a profound miscomprehension of what he was trying to do. Carlyle has shown the similarity of the construction of antiroles to the construction of socially validated roles. The self, as it were, can man-ifest itself only in roles, and from this point of view, even the creation of an antirole itself belongs to the socialization process. The person-ality is thus revealed not as a manifestation or embodiment of the self but as part of the social world from which the self is alienated. This is again an instance of the radical difference between the redemp-tionist Carlyle of the years before *Latter-Day Pamphlets* and the Carlyle of *Frederick*.

Nevertheless, the continuity of the self behind the roles is symbol-ized. The prose style is that symbolization; for whatever role is being played, even a minor role not yet mentioned, the Translator, there is a stylistic continuity. However, that continuity is by no means iden-tical with the style of Carlyle's previous writings. It is different from the style of *Latter-Day Pamphlets,* in which appears an unusually high percentage of complex sentences. On the other hand, *Frederick* shared with the *French Revolution* and *Latter-Day Pamphlets* a most unusually high percentage of sentence fragments. Again, only *Past and Present* and *Latter-Day Pamphlets* show a higher average of expressive punc-tuation marks than *Frederick,* to which the average in *Heroes and Hero-Worship* is equal. The latter, of course, was designed for public pre-sentation in lectures, and *Past and Present* was written after several years of public lecturing. *Latter-Day Pamphlets,* on the other hand, was specifically polemic, designed to bring about changes in attitudes and action. Sentence fragments and expressive punctuation are the marks of a style aimed at oral delivery. The self underlying the various roles in *Frederick* can be usefully categorized as a man speaking to other men, but a man separated from other men by an alienation more thorough-going than at any previous stage in Carlyle's life. Thus the style of *Frederick* is often more like Carlyle's journal style than is the style of any of his other published works. This is perfectly consonant with the implications drawn above from the passages on No-Govern-ment, and with the conviction that the true Historical Epic cannot be written at the present time by anyone.[6]

But this is not all, for that alienation is further dramatized by the narrator's alienation from the task he is engaged on, the construction of a history of Friedrich. That this alienation was perfectly sincere is indicated by Carlyle's journal entries at the time. That sincerity, however, is of no importance; the evidence for it serves little more than to support a rhetorical analysis developed from other evidence. It is more interesting that the alienation from the task itself is consonant with Carlyle's lack of conviction than that the whole enormous effort was worth the trouble it was taking to do it. All of the devices so far discussed are employed to dramatize that alienation from the effort. *Frederick* is unique in the way it forces on the reader an awareness of the narrator's struggle with documents and with previous histories on this and related subjects. Everyone who attempts to construct a discourse from primary and secondary materials and from his own notes experiences that struggle; but the normal and socially validated attributes of the scholarly narrator's role are the suppression of that awareness, the presentation of an air of quiet confidence, and a dramatization of perfect competence, even though in fact the author is constantly trembling with professional anxiety. The competence of the scholar and the historian is one of those shams and illusions and lies, one of those "univeracities," which Carlyle is attacking. This is often dramatized amusingly, as when the narrator admits he has lost a note, or has inadvertently destroyed it, or can no longer locate the source of a quotation or a reference. The highly unsatisfactory and fundamentally incompetent behavioral processes of the scholar and historian are thus brought out into the open. Perhaps this is why younger scholar-critics have rejected *Frederick*. Their professional ambitions and longings for validated professional status do not permit them to become aware of and examine the illusory and unveracious attributes of the social role they are playing. That incompetence and wasted effort are fundamental attributes of humanity is neither an attractive nor a sustaining notion. Nevertheless, it sustained Carlyle through the immense struggle of writing *Frederick*. It is worth speculating on how this could have been the case.

3

In the first place Carlyle saw the ultimate task of the historian as the interpretation of historical events:

That the man of rhythmic nature will feel more and more his vocation towards the Interpretation of Fact; since only in the vital centre of that, could we once get thither, lies all real melody; and that he will become, he, once again, the

Historian of events,—bewildered Dryasdust having at last the happiness to be his servant, and to have some guidance from him. Which will be blessed indeed. For the present, Dryasdust strikes me like a hapless Nigger gone masterless: Nigger totally unfit for self-guidance; yet without master good or bad; and whose feats in that capacity no god or man can rejoice in.

History, with faithful Genius at the top and faithful Industry at the bottom, will then be capable of being written. History will then actually *be* written,— the inspired gift of God employing itself to illuminate the dark ways of God. (I, i, 19)

This is spoken by Sauerteig, the yeast of historical discourse, the metaphysical historian. In this passage two things are to be noted: interpretation as the ultimate task of history, and the insistence that though history may be the gift of God which illuminates the dark ways of God, the time for the exercise of that gift has not yet come. This is Sauerteig's hope. The fact that it resides in the realm of hope, however, suggests something about how Carlyle was able to sustain himself. The central epistemological thesis of Romanticism, not often uttered but constantly exemplified, is the irresolvable tension between subject and object. In this passage the hope for the future historian appears to be, for history at least, that the interpretation of fact, the illumination of the dark ways of God, will ultimately involve a resolution of subject and object. But it is to be remembered that this is Sauerteig speaking, and that Sauerteig is a role. Thus what he says is displaced from Carlyle's own position. A hope is offered, to be sure, but the ultimate Romantic position of nonresolution of subject and object is not ultimately compromised. It is as if Carlyle were stating that Sauerteig's hope has its primary attractiveness in its emotional satisfaction, that such satisfaction cannot be rejected simply because it is satisfying, but also that it cannot be accepted on the same grounds either. This is one of the more subtle Romantic epistemological strategies, one at which Browning was particularly adept. "The tension between subject and object is irresolvable, but insofar as that proposition is itself object, it is necessary to maintain an irresolvable tension between the subject and that proposition as object." It was a very Hegelian way of considering the problem.

*Frederick*, then, rests upon a historian's alienation from his task of constructing an historical discourse, but the task could be, in spite of that, continued since it was sustained by the Romantic epistemology of subject-object tension. That alienation, moreover, particularly as it is manifest through the reader's intense awareness of the historian's unsatisfactory struggle with the documents and already existing instances of historical discourse, raises a further question about historical discourse which cannot be answered in terms of the Romantic epistemology, at least as it had developed for Carlyle and his contemporaries. That question is, "What is historical discourse, really?" Now there is a fallacy in Sauerteig's remarks, a fallacy revealed by the actual discourse of *Frederick*. The historian does not in fact interpret fact, that is, historical events. He interprets documents and historical discourses. Carlyle seems to have some self-conscious inkling of this. He urged the student of history to seek for portraits, just as he himself collected all the portraits of Friedrich he could acquire. The portrait, he said, was "a small lighted *candle*, by which the Biographies could for the first time be read with some human interpretation."[7] Though I do not know of any passage in which he spelled it out or even hinted at it, other than this one, here, at any rate, Carlyle seems to have had some notion that there is a profound difference between interpreting fact and interpreting documents. The latter, the historian's task, is the interpretation of language before him, not of events in the past. The past is inaccessible; only language is accessible. The historian constructs a linguistic discourse which is related, somehow or other, to a selected assemblage of discourses, a package of discourses held together by the wrappings of the package, not by internal affiliation. Their affinities are elected, but the historian does the electing.

History, then, is language about language, language that refers to language. A notion of history thus is properly subsumed by a notion into the question, "What is language?" One can find a way into this maze by focusing upon the term "refer." Now it seems to be reasonably clear that language does not refer. "Refer" when applied to language is a metaphor. Human beings refer; *language* does not do anything. It consists of signs to which human beings respond. Furthermore, responses to particular signs are not stable over time nor at any given moment, since to any single sign an indefinably wide range of responses is always possible. Further, human beings *learn* how to respond to signs and learn, with considerable imprecision, what responses to a given sign or set of signs are appropriate in a given situation or set of situations. Like Fritz Mauthner, and others before him, I think the most adequate resolution of this problem is to define language as instructions or directions for performance, effective only for those who have been previously instructed how to respond to those directions, even when the proper response is to produce further linguistic utterances. Such a position avoids completely any notion of immanent meaning and accepts fully both conventionality of meaning and the imprecision (that is, the constant flow of innovation) which is characteristic of responses to language. Much else remains to be said about historical discourse, but a conclusion about history from this notion of language can serve to explain the extraordinary and unique character of *Frederick*. A historical discourse is a set of instructions for reading primary and secondary documents originating in the past. The drama of *Frederick* is the drama of a historian struggling to learn how to read his documents.

The charm of historical discourse is its capacity to elude our human demands for the probable, a demand to which fiction is disgracefully obedient. If one likes to read history merely for the sake of reading history, Carlyle's *History of Friedrich II of Prussia* offers a hugely enjoyable experience. Beyond that it derives a further interest because it raises questions of great interest both about historical writing in Carlyle's own cultural situation and about the philosophy of history, or more precisely, the philosophy of historical discourse.

### NOTES

1. A few bibliographical details may be of some interest, particularly since the first edition is less frequently encountered, in my experience, than the Centenary Edition.

*First edition*: Vol. I, Books I–V, pp. 634, 1858; Vol. II, Books VI–X, pp. 694 (with index to p. 712), 1858; Vol. III, Books XI–XIV, pp. 759 (index to p. 770), 1862; Vol. IV, Books XV–XVII, pp. 615 (index to p. 632), 1864; Vol. V, Books XVIII–XIX, pp. 639, 1865; Vol. VI, Books XX–XXI, pp. 698 (index to. p. 781), 1865. The total pages (excluding indices) amount to 4,039. The first installment (Books I–X, 1858) ends with the death of Friedrich's father Friedrich Wilhelm; the second installment (Books XI–XIV, 1862) recounts the events through the First Silesian War and Friedrich's subsequent two years of peace; the third installment (Books XV–XVII, 1864) carries the account through the Second Silesian War, Friedrich's ten years of peace, and the first year (to March 1757) of the Third Silesian or Seven Years' War; the fourth installment (Books XVIII–XXI) concludes that war (1762) and in Book XXI gives a summary of Friedrich's last years (1764–1786).

*Centenary Edition*: Vol. I, Books I–IV, pp. 435, 1897; Vol. II, Books V–VII, pp. 406, 1897; Vol. III, Books IX–XI, pp. 413, 1897; Vol. IV, Books XII–XIV, pp. 501, 1898; Vol. V, Books XV–XVI, pp. 410, 1898; Vol. VI, Books XVII–XVIII, pp. 435, 1898; Vol. VII, Books XIX–XX, pp. 494, 1898; Vol. VIII, Book XXI, pp. 321 (index to p. 390), 1898. Total pages (excluding index): 3,415.

The work is about the same length as Gibbon's masterpiece. Comparison is difficult because so many passages in *Frederick* are in smaller type. References in the text are (by Book, chapter, and page) to the *Works*, XII–XIX.

2. Here "Prussia" means what it meant when Carlyle was writing, all the territory of the former Electorate of Brandenburg. As King of Prussia Friedrich was in fact *King* only of East Prussia, separated from Brandenburg by West Prussia, acquired in 1772 by the first Polish partition (except for Danzig).

3. The large print yields about 2,160 characters to the page; the small print about 2,910. If 900 pages in the Centenary edition are in small print, and if those pages were printed in the larger type, there would be about 300 pages

more than the present 3,415, an additional bulk of less than 9 percent. Since 900 is probably too high a figure, though not extremely far off, a reasonable guess would be that if the entire book were presented in the large-type font, not including the index, it would grow by about 7 percent or perhaps 240 pages. In the original edition there might have been about 300 additional pages, or 50 pages per volume. The cost of paper might have been responsible for the decision to print much of the book in small type, but the book was so splendid and even luxurious a piece of publishing that this explanation is most unlikely. The immediate model was probably Macaulay's *History of England.* The decision to use smaller type may have been the publisher's, but, in view of Carlyle's fame and prestige, it seems most likely to have been Carlyle's.

4. See my "Discontinuity in Fiction," *The Triumph of Romanticism, Collected Essays* (Columbia, S.C., 1970), pp. 318–340.

5. See my "The Dilemma of a Century," *id.,* pp. 36–57.

6. I owe the above information to the kindness of Professor Robert Lee Oakman III of the University of South Carolina, who has allowed me to use his unpublished dissertation, *Syntax in the Prose Style of TC, A Quantitative, Linguistic Analysis* (Indiana University, 1971). Professor Oakman is not responsible for my statement about Carlyle's journal style.

7. "Project of a National Exhibition of Scottish Portraits," *Works,* XXIX, p. 405.

CHAPTER FIVE

# Browning and Romanticism

The interpretation of the term "Romanticism" governing my general orientation in this chapter is that it is a name for the attempt to resolve the crisis of European high culture of the late eighteenth century, that it was to be found, eventually, in all fields of high culture—philosophy, literature, painting, music, ballet, opera, religion, scholarship, science, and political theory—and that it took nearly a hundred years for what I call the Romantic tradition to recognize the only possible solution—at least so far—to the problem the crisis of the Enlightenment exposed. The recognition of that solution, which was the achievement of Nietzsche more than of anyone else, led to the extraordinary cultural redirection that took place in virtually all fields of high culture between 1905 and 1915. The names of Picasso, Schönberg, and Wittgenstein are enough to indicate what is meant here. Such a striking redirection has been experienced by no other culture.

To understand the place of Browning in this tradition would obviously entail a much more extensive study of his work than is possible or even desirable here.[1] Rather I shall also use the term "Romanticism" in a more restricted and traditional sense—the emergent culture of the first decades of the nineteenth century. Browning grew up in the second and third of those decades, and early in the fourth, when he was in his twenty-first year, he wrote the poem with which I shall be concerned, *Pauline: A Fragment of a Confession* (written in 1832 and published in March 1833). By 1832 the accomplishment of the Romantic tradition, or of Romanticism (if one wishes to think of it as dying away at about this time and yielding to something not properly called Romanticism) was already massive enough. The hypothesis of this chapter is that *Pauline* is the consequence of Browning's encounter with this accumulation. Apart from the famous passages on the "Sun-treader," identified by Browning himself as Shelley, there are in the poem traces and echoes of Wordsworth and Byron, almost certainly of Coleridge, possibly of Keats and Hazlitt, and also possibly, if the setting of 950–985, the description of the homeland of Pauline, is to be identified as Switzerland, of Senancour's *Obermann* (1804). However, I shall not be concerned with specific influences, echoes, and traces, but rather with the indications *Pauline* may be with some justice said to yield about Browning's comprehension of that tradition, particularly with the problems it had raised and with the solutions so far available. None of them, to be sure, turned out to be viable for the advanced thinkers in the rest of the century, or for Browning himself, though they have by no means disappeared from the present cultural scene.

The first step is to construct a hypothesis of how the poem should be read. The usual hypothesis has been succinctly stated in a recent essay on John Stuart Mill's famous marginalia to *Pauline*.[2] The authors refer to Mill's "distaste for Browning's self-indulgent confessionalism in *Pauline*." This is Mill's own judgment, and there is no doubt that it has been pretty generally accepted. Its dissemination and the confirmation of Mill's hypothesis are probably owing to DeVane's discussion in his *A Browning Handbook*.[3] His interpretation depends upon a hypothesis that the poem is "Browning's autobiography to his twentieth year."[4] But if, as he says, Pauline is "a mere lay figure," the phrase "thoroughly autobiographical" seems somewhat exaggerated; if there was no Pauline in Browning's life, he can hardly be said to be writing autobiography. Furthermore, when Browning republished the poem for the first time in the 1868 *Poetical Works,* he asserted that it was his

earliest attempt at poetry always dramatic in principle, and so many utterances of so many imaginary persons, not mine, which I have since written according to a scheme less extravagant and scale less impracticable than were ventured upon in this crude preliminary sketch—a sketch that, on reviewal, appears not altogether wide of some hint of the characteristic features of that particular *dramatis persona* it would fain have reproduced.

The inadequacy of the Mill-DeVane hypothesis has been convincingly discussed by Roma A. King,[5] but something remains to be said, since Professor King does not exhaust the theoretical possibilities of his position that the speaker of the poem is situated between the objective persona of Browning's claim in 1868 and the purely subjective autobiographical speaker of Mill and DeVane.

The first step in constructing a hypothesis for interpreting the poem appropriately is to recognize it as an exercise in self-definition. Like most adolescents and young men, however, Browning had as yet very little in the way of a unique self to define. At this stage of life the young imagine they are defining a unique self when they are but defining themselves in terms of a culturally available and validated social role. That this is what Browning was doing is suggested very strongly by the line in which the speaker identifies himself as properly both "priest and prophet" (l. 1019), a mode of self-definition that was already very nearly a Romantic commonplace, at least within the Romantic tradition. Thus insofar as the poem is autobiographical, Browning was identifying himself as an exemplification of the primary Romantic figure or role. But we may go a little further than this. Culture in the full anthropological sense is a set of directions for behaving in interaction with the nonhuman world, with other humans, and with oneself, which amounts to the same thing, since the individual is most usefully considered as a social dyad. Just as culture institutionalizes behavior in persistent patterns of behavior known as social institutions, so the individual in issuing himself directions for his own behavior institutionalizes himself and becomes a dyadic social institution. Thus in *Pauline* Browning was institutionalizing himself as a Romantic Poet, and in the standard Romantic way was presenting the development or historical emergence of that role as a means of organizing and directing his behavior. In his personal history only those tendencies and events which contributed to the emergence of that role or which hindered it and frustrated it are considered important and related to his "true self." The process, of course, is no different for someone who defines himself in terms of the role of automobile mechanic or literary scholar. The peculiar twist of the situation, responsible for the almost irresistible autobiographical impression the poem makes, an impression which must however be resisted, arises from the fact that a central ingredient or factor in the role of Romantic Poet (or any kind of Romantic figure) is the notion of self as opposed to role. (This is responsible for the various judgments that the poem is sincere or insincere, or partly one or the other, or, as Professor King suggests, that its insincerity demonstrates its sincerity. But since "sincerity" is transparently a normative term, to raise the question of Browning's sincerity in *Pauline* and to resolve it is merely to terminate investigation.)

The problem of the first Romantics, such as Wordsworth and Coleridge, was to create a new social role, but since the problem emerged from the rejection of available social roles, the solution was to create an antirole, that is, a "self." Now it is true, to be sure, that each individual is a self, but only in the sense that in performing a role his performance is necessarily a greater or lesser deviation from the current conception of how that role should be played, a circumstance made more apparent by the fact that each individual differs in his judgment of what the essential factors of the role performance actually ought to be. The two standard ways of justifying role deviation are, first, to point out the unique factors in the situation eliciting the role which required that the role be adapted to a situation with novel factors; and, second, to point out the formative or historical factors in the individual life which are responsible, it is asserted, for the role deviation. Both these justifications are to be found in *Pauline*; the speaker presents what he conceives to be the unique and distorting factors in his personality and life and uses the Sun-treader as a surrogate for his cultural situation.

Both of these strategies are to be found in the first Romantics, and were responsible for what can, I believe, be identified as subjective and objective historicization, the historicization of the personality as a strategy for identifying and justifying the resources for deviance into an antirole, and the historicization of the situation as a strategy for identifying and justifying the necessity for that deviance. The two great exemplars in English literature are Wordsworth's *The Prelude* and Carlyle's *Sartor Resartus*, but neither of these works, though written before *Pauline*, was as yet published. In thinking about the problem Browning was undertaking in *Pauline* it is essential to keep in mind that these two works were as yet unknown, and that the other models, *Childe Harold*, *Alastor*, *Endymion*, and the figure of The Solitary in *The Excursion*, were incomplete and in part as yet incomprehensible. (Indeed, *Endymion* is still inadequately comprehended, and very likely always will be.) The Romantic antirole, then, was something by no means clearly outlined in the tradition of English Romanticism, insofar as it was available to Browning, nor, unlike Carlyle, had he found additional and more firmly outlined exemplars in German Romanticism, particularly in German Romantic philosophy. What Browning was attempting to do in *Pauline*—this is the hypothesis proposed here—was late adolescent self-definition in terms of a recently emerged and incompletely and inadequately defined social role, the Romantic antirole of poet-prophet-priest. We must turn, then, to the problem of why the Romantic antirole was conceived in these terms, or why, more precisely, certain attributes of each of these metaphors were combined in the Romantic antirole, and to a clearer understanding of why that antirole was identified as a "self."

In any culture the priest is the regular, customary human instrument by which the divine is made accessible. The prophet, who also operates under the aegis of the established religion, is the divine instrument at times of crisis. Insofar as both are not merely witnesses to the divine and channels of the entrance of the divine into the human but are also individuals who utter specific directions for behavior in specific situations, that is, moral propositions, the difference is that the priest utters validated morality while the prophet innovates morality by extending the validated morality to meet what he perceives to be the novel demands of a novel situation. The position of the poet, as conceived in one tradition of European culture from the time of Plato, and perhaps before, is unstable, moving along a continuum from a validated notion of divinity to an innovative notion, and from a validated morality to an innovative morality. Lacking the authority of both prophet and priest, his position often permits the negation of dominant notions of divinity and dominant moral notions. Milton, for example, self-defined as a poet, permitted himself innovation in both areas of conceptualization. The priest asserts that redemption is always available for those who behave properly; the prophet asserts that redemption is available if the demands of an emergent situation are met as he recommends; the poet asserts that redemption is available through channels other than the normal or validated channels of the culture, and in this he may be anything between boldly innovative and utterly platitudinous. In using the metaphors of poet, prophet, and priest to define his antirole the early Romantic combined the attributes of permissive innovation of the poet (which Plato justified by asserting that the poet himself does not understand his own utterances and therefore is not truly responsible for them), of crisis innovation of the prophet, and the priest's normality of being a channel for the divine. Thus Coleridge, for example, asserted the truth of Christianity, but on wholly novel grounds, by reinterpreting, for one thing, the theological meaning of the Trinity. This amounted to a claim that the socially validated grounds for accepting Christianity were false, or at least inadequate. He claimed to be not merely an alternative, secular channel for divine knowledge, but a channel that superseded the cognitive aspect of established religion. That was in the 1820s, but as early as 1798 in *The Ancient Mariner* he developed at least the beginning of a new mythology of redemption, the innovative character of which was brought out by the failure of the Mariner to be successful in demanding validation by a recognized instrument of grace of the established Church, and by the fact that he is condemned to repeat his story indefinitely. Perhaps we are to assume that the occasion of repetition is always to be an interruption of the religious validation of a social ritual, as it is in the narrative poem we have.

In defining himself as at once poet, prophet, and priest, the early Romantic was making the most extraordinary claims. He was doing something different from what Thomas of Münster, for example, had done. Innovative prophets, often claiming for themselves the status of priesthood, had appeared with considerable frequency in the history of European Christendom. Luther himself was one of such. His unique achievement was not religious but political. He was able to create for himself so powerful a secular support that he and subsequently his religion, although branded as a heresy by the Church, were able to resist the best efforts of the Church's secular arm, and to survive. Thomas of Münster's secular support was minuscule by comparison and easily overwhelmed and destroyed. The early Romantic, however, was in a different position and made a different claim. First, the rationalism of the seventeenth century, its notable scientific achievements, and the secularization of culture by the Enlightenment had already created a situation in which it was relatively safe to propose an alternative mode of redemption. Next, the French Revolution and subsequently the Napoleonic sweeping away of feudalism and the secular power of the clergy made it even safer. Ever since the Revolution and the Napoleonic cultural reorganization, Europe has experienced a permanent measle-like rash of strange religions. Nor are they always independent of the Romantic tradition. Yeats was interested in such phenomena because of fundamentally Romantic reasons. Next, the fact that philosophy had already become independent of religion gave to the early Romantic analytic instruments which he could and did use to dissolve the cognitive claims of established theology; he could also turn them against previous philosophy. The fact that most of the Romantic writers were not technically good philosophers is of no importance. But the most important factor was that at the level of high culture there was a vacuum. For the most acute spirits of the time the traditional explanation of the world had dissolved from its own internal incoherence and from the failure to make its claims good.

The Enlightenment, it has long been recognized, was a secularization of the Christian scheme of redemption. Redemption was to be accomplished by the philosophical, rational, and sentimental fusion of man and nature, a fusion that became the channel for the entry of the divine into the world. Since philosophy, reason, and sentiment comprehended the character of that divine, it was possible to generate a set of moral propositions of such a character that, if they were used to direct and control behavior, an adequate, or even a perfect, social order would be the result, the equivalent of Heaven. To be sure, a good many Enlightenment figures, especially towards the end of the century, had their doubts about all this, but generally speaking they were committed either to trying or to asserting, like Burke, that given the natural circumstances and human limitations, an adequate society already existed, or at least one existed that could be redeemed by rational reforms. The great moral force of the Enlightenment lay in the ease with which it could demonstrate that the traditional, Christian explanation of the world was responsible for social situations which could not possibly be reconciled with the attributes of deity. But that moral force was lost when the French Revolution and Napoleonic imperialism attempted to put Enlightenment redemptionism into effect.

To put it in different terms, according to the traditional Christian explanation of the world, the subject (the divinely illuminated reason of man) absorbs the object; that is, the categories of the subject exhaust the attributes of the object. That which cannot be absorbed or exhausted is defined as evil, in turn defined as the absence of divinity; it need not be absorbed or exhausted. The Enlightenment version was that the object (divinely created Nature) properly absorbs the subject, Man, or the natural reason; that is, the categories of the object exhaust the attributes of the subject. That which cannot be absorbed or exhausted is defined as error and ignorance, which the enlightened reason can eliminate. Through the analysis of Hume and Kant, arriving at results which others, such as Wordsworth, arrived at independently, and through the violent, chaotic, and dictatorial imperialism of the French Revolution and the Napoleonic enterprise, it became apparent, even before Napoleon for some English and German figures, that the Enlightenment version of the subject-object relationship was not a true negation of the Christian version but a mere inversion of it. If the subject claims that the object absorbs it and exhausts its attributes, it is nevertheless making a subjective claim. The boasted objectivity of the Enlightenment was thus transformed into a willful self-delusion. This is the explanation for the ease with which certain adherents to the Enlightenment, such as Manzoni, returned to Christianity. From this point of view the Enlightenment was identical with Christianity; the only thing new was terminology. But for others, the failure of the Enlightenment in theory and practice, philosophically and politically, meant the failure of Christianity. To them there was no turning back.

Browning was perfectly aware of this development and describes it in *Pauline* with great accuracy. The relation of the speaker to the

Sun-treader changes in the course of the narrative. At first he accepts the ideology of the Sun-treader (one who walks on the sun, often presented as the location of heaven in early nineteenth-century England); although he says that his "choice fell / Not so much on a system as a man—" (ll. 403–404), this is not to disclaim that he accepted the system, as indeed he did. However, that system turns out to be a dream:

> First went my hopes of perfecting mankind,
> And faith in them—then freedom in itself,
> And virtue in itself—and then my motives' end,
> And powers and loves; and human love went last[6]
>
> (458–461)

The next paragraph spells out the result:

> My powers were greater, as some temple seemed
> My soul, where nought is changed, and incense rolls
> Around the altar—only God is gone,
> And some dark spirit sitteth in his seat
>
> (469–572)

At the end of the poem the reason for emphasizing the man rather than the system becomes clear. In the last paragraph the Sun-treader is appealed to without any reference to his system. He is not even a role model; he is reduced to a mere supportive function. It is fairly evident that in Browning's development Shelley presented primarily Enlightenment values which Browning had already rejected by the time he wrote *Pauline*. This is suggested even in the first and most famous Sun-treader passage:

> And I, perchance, half feel a strange regret,
> That I am not what I have been to thee
>
> (191–192)

At this point, since I am discussing in behavioral terms the Romantic problem of defining an antirole, it is necessary to attempt to clarify in such terms the notion of the divine and of redemption. In the Christian explanation, strongly influenced by Platonism, and Neoplatonism, meaning emanated from the subject to the object, that is, from language to the world. In the Enlightenment view meaning emanated from the object to the subject, from the world to language. If both the Christian and the Enlightenment view of the subject-object relation are abandoned, any immanent, necessary, and inherent link between language and the world is broken. And this is what Kant, stimulated by Hume, accomplished when he asserted that we cannot know the *Ding-an-sich*. And in the other direction he asserted that though we can know God exists, we cannot know anything else about him. This is tantamount to saying that "God" merely terminates an explanation. The history of Romanticism in the fuller sense is the history of the gradual recognition of the consequences of sundering any necessary relation between subject and object, of the consequences of tearing language loose from the world.

We may now return to "divine" and "redemption." A redeemed individual is one who returns from a deviant mode of behavior to a validated mode. "Deviant" is here used in two senses: one, behavior that follows a well-established pattern, such as adultery, but is invalidated by instructions maintained by a social hierarchy supported ultimately by arbitrary power; and two, innovative behavior that is not yet validated and perhaps never will be. Redemption, then, involves conforming to a validated mode of response to a particular category of situation, such as marriage, and to a particular set of either verbal or nonverbal instructions, or both, as when the individual is told to respond to his rosary by uttering certain prayers for a given period of time or a given number of repetitions. To be truly redeemed involves a change of heart. This means that the response to a given stimulus, it may be successfully predicted, will in the future not be deviant, in either sense. It is a change of heart because the individual imposes upon himself a limitation of response to the stimulus in question and sanctions it with a self-imposed application of the ultimate sanction, power. Hence in a wide variety of cultures redemption is maintained by self-inflicted flagellation.

In Heaven, however, the application of power is not required. Heaven is a place where there is no possibility of deviant behavior; it is a place in which one always "knows" how to respond. It is instructive that most visions of heaven are marked by a singular limitation of the range of behavior. A place of eternal redemption is a place in which all behavior is marked by the attribute of the individual who has been redeemed from one particular kind of deviant behavior. To put it somewhat differently, if the bulk of human energy goes into the strategies for limiting the range of behavior, in heaven the range of behavior is limited without any expenditure of energy. Or, any expenditure of energy is immediately returned by emanation from the Deity who rules the heaven in question, as in Milton's vision of Heaven before the revolt of Satan.

God and the ultimate social role in a social hierarchy have a number of attributes in common, a not surprising fact if one is aware that the explanatory regress is identical in structure with and is carried out by the power of regress of social hierarchies. The Divine Right of Kings is but one of innumerable instances of the interdependency of explanation and social power. Those conservatives of the seventeenth century who asserted that to deny the Divine Right of Kings was to head society towards a severe crisis were quite right. The first of these attributes, of course, is power itself. To be redeemed, whether on earth or in heaven, is to have immediate, intimate, and unquestioning contact with the ultimate source of power. An intimately related pair of attributes is made up of love (i.e., valuing) and chastisement. Absolute monarchs always chastise their people in the name of love: Gods and Kings are called fathers and sometimes mothers. The inseparability of love and chastisement, and the necessity for self-imposed chastisement for redemption gives the figure of Christ its immense charismatic power. A final attribute common both to God and ultimate social roles is creativity, which is the innovative adjustment of sociocultural systems to emergent situations, sanctioned and validated by power. By establishing new modes of response and limiting and channeling those modes creativity becomes redemptive.

There are, then, two modes of redemption, in symbiotic relationship, verbal and political. By "political" I mean redemption carried out by social institutions: thus even self-flagellation is political behavior. Pre-Enlightenment societies found their ultimate verbal sanction in "God," post-Enlightenment societies in "Nature." The United States of America used both, since it was founded during a transitional period; it was both Christian and Enlightenment, a source of endless confusion to this day, when representative assemblies, in spite of the separation of Church and State, employ chaplains and begin their deliberations with prayer. This is why when the social institutions charged with exercise of verbal redemption are discredited and are judged to be deleterious, destructive, and decadent (Voltaire's *l'infâme*) the institutions charged with political redemption, unless they dissociate themselves from the verbal institutions, are threatened; thus the Enlightened monarchs of late eighteenth-century Europe frequently downgraded the church and separated themselves from it. The Jesuits, on the whole a relatively harmless group and socially more valuable than many of the Catholic orders, were destroyed. But of course, as Voltaire's case shows, the discrediting of a mode of explanation exercised by verbally redemptive institutions necessarily involves the innovation of an alternative mode of verbal redemption. And this alternative mode, to maintain itself, necessarily must gain control of the ultimate roles in politically redemptive institutions. Hence the French Revolution and its Napoleonic aftermath. In Italy, for example, the unification of Italy, in reality the conquest of the rest of Italy by Piedmont, was made possible by the memory of the innovative verbal and political redemption introduced by the French conquest of Northern Italy, and of Murat's brief rule of the kingdom of Naples.

The Revolutionary-Napoleonic enterprise and liberation of Europe from feudalism and the Church also saw the ultimate source of political redemption, social power based on force, exposed in all of its nakedness and arbitrariness. To those who accepted the verbal redemption of the Enlightenment, the Revolutionary-Napoleonic enterprise was acceptable. To those who rejected the Enlightenment mode of redemption and still accepted the Christian mode, that enterprise was not acceptable. It was these who restored the Christian verbal and political modes of redemption after 1815 but who also incorporated in their political institutions a large share of the modes of Enlightenment political redemption, and in their verbal institutions even bits and pieces of Enlightenment verbal redemption. To that tiny group of Europeans, however, for whom the Christian and the Enlightenment modes of political and verbal redemption were seen as mere inversions of each other and not true negations (as, for example, the naked exercise of the Revolutionary-Napoleonic power made perfectly clear), both were unacceptable. Hence arose the Romantic alienation from both social institutions and explanatory modes available in the European tradition. The problem of the Romantics, then, was to draw the consequences of the true negation of the Christian-Enlightenment explanation of the world, the breaking of the link between subject and object, the sundering of any necessary tie between stimulus and response.

Now the history of Europe, and especially the history of the Enlightenment, demonstrated that any large-scale innovation must begin with verbal redemption, the reason being that political institutions find their sanctions in the extremes of explanatory regress when the directions issued down from hierarchically ultimate power are no longer effective in relating institutions to the extralinguistic world, a fact that Hegel was the first to realize fully. It is why he asserted that history is the history of *Geist*. (Marx, in the 1840s, emphasized the relation of language to the world, but in failing to realize fully what Hegel was saying fell back on a Christian-Enlightenment pattern of redemption. He thought he was negating Hegel when he was merely filling out what Hegel had sketched.) Thus Hegel quite correctly placed philosophy higher than religion, since for him and a few of his European fellows religion as an institution of verbal redemption had clearly failed; it must, therefore, be subsumed by philosophy. Consequently Romanticism first emerged in literature and metaphysics. Furthermore, since these alienated individuals had no access and wished no access to political institutions (except for small groups of the like-minded), of the various attributes in common to deity and the ultimate power levels of political institutions, they chose creativity. The poet-prophet-priest figure emerged as the Romantic figure with access to the divine (ultimate explanation) and to the redemptive (an ultimate mode of limiting and channeling response), but unlike their predecessors the Romantics claimed the attribute of radical creativity. Since the innovative task was not to adjust political and verbal redemptive institutions, but to discover the foundation for new modes of redemption, the old modes having failed, creativity was located within the individual as the precondition for the innovation of verbal redemption and, it was hoped by some at any rate, eventually the innovation of political redemption. This is to be seen, for example, at the end of Hegel's *Phenomenology* (1808), when the fully self-conscious spirit, having transcended all modes of explanation and redemption, turns once again to the phenomenal world, the material on which to exercise its creativity.

The early decades of the nineteenth century were the early decades of Romanticism, or, if one wishes, were the period of Romanticism. Its history can be summed up very briefly. The implication of the breaking of the link between subject and object was not yet recognized, the implication being that final redemption, political or verbal, is impossible and that the explanatory and political institutions of man cannot solve the fundamental human problems. The significance of the irresolvable tension between subject and object, that is, the impossibility of redemption, was not yet recognized, even though the fact of that tension was accepted. The explanation for this failure is that overwhelmingly the European cultural tradition was founded upon the possibility of and necessity for redemption, verbal and political and final, as for the most part it still is. It was difficult and virtually impossible to imagine anything but an alternative yet innovative mode of redemption. (Senancour and Hegel were two of the very rare exceptions, perhaps the only exceptions. Neither was understood.) Consequently Romanticism, or the first stages of Romanticism, depending on how the term is used, was marked by an extraordinarily wide-ranging effort to create an alternative and viable final mode of redemption. That is, though the Christian and Enlightenment modes were seen as mirror-like inversions of each other, not true negations, it was still believed that a negation of that mode was to be another redemptive mode; it was not yet perceived that the possibility for final redemption had been culturally exhausted. But since it had been exhausted, the only possibility was to begin by locating the source of redemption in the self, as distinguished from the role, since the existent roles were necessarily part of the existent verbal and political redemptive modes and institutions. Further, only the existing redemptive fields of verbal and nonverbal high culture were available as institutions in which creative innovation was possible. Hegel identified them as philosophy, religion, and art. The early decades of the century, then, were marked by redemptive innovation in each of these fields. Browning was born into and grew up in a cultural situation in which were to be found available Christian, Enlightenment, and a wide variety of Romantic redemptive modes. It was to define himself in this situation that he wrote *Pauline*. Moreover, since he was a very young man, hardly more than an adolescent, we cannot assume that he had mastered the full range of any of these in anything like the great variety and confusing interrelationships and interactions of all three possibilities. Given his extraordinary intelligence and the rich culture of his upbringing, he could still do no more than his best in an extraordinarily confusing cultural situation. It is my own opinion that he did very well indeed, and that *Pauline* is by no means the confusing failure it is usually judged to be. It is not merely, as he was to claim in 1868, that it was the first of his dramatic monologues; it is also the case that *Pauline* established the pattern of his use of the genre, for the great monologues to follow were to be more than anything else exercises in self-definition by their speakers.

The subtitle of *Pauline* is *A Fragment of a Confession*. The poem, then, is not to be read as a complete statement of an experience, but the word "confession" is not ordinarily used unless there is something to confess, a reason for feeling guilt, or, the word used in the poem, shame. Deviance in either sense has been at work in the life of the speaker, but it is not, it develops, a Byronic deviance, some violation of the validated norms of behavior, but rather verbal deviance, deviance, to use the terms of the poem, of mind and thought. It is moreover, it appears, innovative deviance. The speaker condemns himself throughout for that reason. In the second paragraph, for example, he speaks of a

> wandering aim
> Sent back to bind on Fancy's wings and seek
> Some strange fair world, where it might be a law
> (32–35)[7]

Confession is the second step in the path to redemption, the first step, of course, being the admission that there is something to confess, that deviance has taken place. The subtitle establishes the redemptive theme.

The epigraph from Marot is equally important, for it asserts that an irreversible change has taken place. This again reappears in the poem several times, that the speaker cannot return to his former condition. This theme is of prime importance, for it explains why the confession is made to a representative of neither a political nor a verbal institution. Pauline, to whom we shortly learn the poem is addressed, is a redemptive figure but a completely secularized one, a woman who loves the speaker but who in return is "to receive not love, but faith" (l. 43), thus emphasizing Pauline's redemptive function, a task facilitated by her beauty. Love, beauty, a beloved woman as instruments of redemption were already Romantic commonplaces and—through fiction, the drama, and the opera, as well as poetry with its more restricted circulation—were in the 1830s and 1840s presented as redemptive instruments to a more general non-Romantic public, which, however, had been sufficiently unsettled by the events of the preceding hundred years to welcome alternative redemptive modes, at least so long as they were not regarded as necessarily excluding the traditional modes. To the Romantic, of course, they were innovated because the traditional modes were unusable, culturally inaccessible. The possibilities of this triad for redemption arise from the fact that awareness of deviance is a source of tension, of a sense of internal incoherence. Whatever else redemptive behavior might accomplish— and recidivism indicates that it does not necessarily accomplish much—at least it reduces tension. For the Romantic there were two sources of severe tension, one his cultural deviance, and the other the fact that that deviance when properly apprehended involved an irresolvable tension between subject and object. Since the whole tradition of redemption emphasizes tension reduction as the highest human value, this was yet another reason for the desperate effort in the early decades of the nineteenth century to create alternative redemptive modes. It took nearly a hundred years of the Romantic tradition for a few individuals to arrive at the notion that tension is not of negative value but of positive. Erotic love, therefore, and eroticized beauty, both of which had long been used by religion as weapons in its arsenal of redemptive strategies, since both have as their goal total tension reduction, could easily be separated from religion in such a way that their redemptive attribute, gained from religion, could function independently of it. Although Goethe's *Faust II* and its *ewige weib-*

*liche* appeared in the autumn of 1832, perhaps while Browning was writing *Pauline,* it is unlikely that he knew of it. Nevertheless, the cultural convergence is striking because Pauline is given the same function as Goethe's "eternal feminine": "It draws us on." Pauline's redemptive function, it turns out at the end of the poem, is to re-introduce the speaker to his tension-raising innovative deviance. Browning had already gone beyond Wagner, whose Senta can only redeem his alienated Wandering Dutchman from a life of alienation into what certainly seems to be a Christian paradise. The poem for *Der Fliegende Holländer* was written in its first form in May 1841.

From this point of view the second epigraph, from Cornelius Agrippa's *De occulta philosophia,* is comprehensible.

They will say that I teach forbidden things, lay the seeds of heresies, offend pious ears, and corrupt pure minds. . . . My book . . . is harmful and very poisonous. In this book is the gateway to hell; it speaks hard words.

In a note to this quotation published in 1888 Browning was to call it "absurdly pretentious," but it should be taken seriously. It shows his clear comprehension that he was undertaking a deviant self-definition. In relation to the culture as a whole and even to high culture, Romanticism was in 1832 still a deviant mode; hence the fact that Romantic spokesmen are so often presented as wanderers, outcasts, Cains, poets with a curse on them, and so on, and that so often Romantic individuals acted out this self-definition in their personal lives. The only significant deviance in Browning's life at this point—at least that we know of—was his refusal to continue his studies in London University after a very brief trial. At the time the older Carlyle was still acting out the outcast role in Craigenputtock. Tennyson had acted it out at Cambridge and was to continue his Bohemian experiments for several decades to come. And even then he withdrew to the Isle of Wight. Browning, however, seemed to have as early as this that cultural objectivity towards his own self-definition which made such acting-out unnecessary. Instead, he developed his peculiar version of the dramatic monologue, disclaiming personal responsibility for his characters, and in life in the course of time, and perhaps—there is some evidence for this—even in the 1830s adopted that sociocultural *doppelgänger* strategy in which in later years he was adept.

The opening paragraph of the poem establishes Pauline's initial function, to provide the traditional protection of the confessional. But what is to be confessed is not sins, but rather a

sleepless brood
Of fancies from my soul, their lurking-place.
(6–7)

These thoughts are clearly presented as dangerous, but it would be even more dangerous not to unlock them. Unlocking them is the precondition of song, that is, creative utterance. Sad confession of their presence in the soul must precede—what? "Ere I can be—as I shall be no more" (l. 27). This reveals the purpose of the confession to create an unknown subjective condition. The second paragraph speaks of shame, but it is not the shame of harboring such thoughts, but rather, it would seem, the shame of confessing that the thoughts, the "wild dreams of beauty and of good," have not been allowed issue. What is to be confessed, it transpires in the next paragraph, is not guilt for deviance but weakness in not being deviant. It is Pauline's wish, he says, that he "essay / The task which was to me what now thou art" (ll. 53–54), clearly a redemptive task. The fourth paragraph continues the theme of shame and weakness, and presents the initial confession to Pauline, which took place in the natural world in the spring.

This introduces a theme which recurs several times in the rest of the poem, and towards the end is crucial, the redemptive power of nature. But to put it this way is to offer the possibility of a confusion of the Romantic attitude towards nature with the Enlightenment attitude. For the latter, nature was exemplary; it provided nonverbal exemplifications of verbal propositions; the attitude towards nature was still allegorical, as the order of nature was an allegorical exemplum of the ordering power of God. For the Romantic the first important thing about nature was not so much the presence of nature as the absence of man. This in turn facilitated the "aesthetic" response to nature, a tension-reducing feeling state elicited by the natural world and ultimately inexplicable. Not the explicability of nature, but the inexplicability of the response to the natural world indicated its redemptive power and made it not into an allegory of divine attributes but a symbol of the sense of divinity. Wordsworth was probably right when he traced it back to what we could call today the preconscious awareness of the infant in relation to its mother, the felt fusion of subject and object, a fusion from which, however, no further propositions could be deduced other than that of the divine character of that fusion; divine because it was a creative act of perception on the part of the subject. It is best understood as an eroticization of nature, or at least can be so understood if eroticism is seen as having its origin not in sex but in the preconscious fusion of subject and object which for most individuals is most successfully repeated and recalled—or regressed to—in sexual behavior. From this point of view it is not surprising that Pauline's erotic function should first appear in a natural setting. Eroticized nature was, of course, a redemptive mode which by 1832 had been richly explored and well established. Browning had only to make use of it.

The paragraph concludes with an interesting passage beginning

> thou art not more dear
> Than song was once to me; and I ne'er sung
> But as one entering bright halls, where all
> Will rise and shout for him. Sure I must own
> That I am fallen—having chosen gifts
> Distinct from theirs.
>
> (76–81)

This equivalence in value of Pauline and song indicates the redemptive function of song, and the next lines suggest the redeemer who is recognized as such. Yet the supportive group is only potential, and that potentiality has been sacrificed to other interests. In the concluding lines of the paragraph, however, that potential group is spoken of as having once actually existed. This is something of a puzzle, but it can be resolved—if at all resolvable—by the explanation that the self-created isolation of the Romantic alien or deviant was responsible for an inextinguishable longing for that support which any radical and innovating deviant always seeks. The personal history of the great Romantic figures shows a continuous record of gathering about themselves such supportive groups. Among lesser Romantic figures the same conditions were responsible for the emergence of the Bohemian subculture. Here again Browning turned out to be something of an exception. Insofar as he had a little group it consisted, it would appear, solely of Elizabeth Barrett, and that for less than two decades. Indeed it may be worth noting that the more one studies *Pauline* the more one is tempted to see Browning using Elizabeth in much the same way that the speaker uses Pauline. At any rate, in this passage the imagined group is spoken of as having existed. And of course it had. It was the audience for the traditionally redemptive poet, the audience in which the speaker refused to find his support, though he feels that he had the power to have done so.

The next paragraph, beginning with line 89 (not a paragraph in 1833), identifies the "chosen gifts." They were the dangerous gifts of total self-involvement:

> my soul had floated from its sphere
> Of wide dominion into the dim orb
> Of self.
>
> (90–92)[8]

"Soul" seems, then, to mean here the capacity to establish successful relations to the objective world. The isolated imagination, turned in upon itself, can only destroy the traditional values of beauty and divinity. The effect in the next paragraph is the sense of aging and of loss of value. The next section of the poem is concerned with how the Sun-treader rescued the speaker from this condition. Yet, as indicated above, the redemptive power of the Sun-treader fails; even though the speaker feels himself once again cast down into an abasement, he refuses to imitate him, to use him as a role model for self-definition. The Sun-treader was only a temporary interruption of the value-destroying self-isolation already defined. The result has been the probing of "life's vanity" (l. 237), a condition from which Pauline rescues him, "won by a word again / Into my own life" (ll. 237–238). But still this gives him no sense of having "part in God, or his bright world" (l. 251). All he can do is to sing, thoughtlessly, without confidence—of himself.

At this point the autobiographical narrative of *the speaker* begins. Five things, he says, formed his native endowment. First is

> a consciousness
> Of self—distinct from all its qualities,
> From all affections, passions, feelings, powers; . . . linked
>     . . . to self-supremacy,
> Existing as a centre to all things,
> Most potent to create, and rule, and call
> Upon all things to minister to it.
>
> (269–276)

It is hardly necessary to point out this attribute as the defining attribute of Romantic self-definition. The second of his native gifts is

> A principle of restlessness
> Which would be all, have, see, know, taste, feel, all.
>
> (277–278)

This is obviously the central theme of Goethe's *Faust*, but it is also to be found in Fichte, and among English works in *Childe Harold, Don Juan, Endymion,* and *Prometheus Unbound,* and it was to be the theme of *Paracelsus.* Like the presentation of self-consciousness as a native gift of the speaker, Browning apparently believed that it was already so well-established as an ingredient of Romantic self-definition that it required no further explanation. Still, the use of the word "rest-lessness" indicates Browning's rather remarkable insight that to want to know everything, to be forever restless, is to deny the redemptive power of tradition. Even the Enlightenment looked forward to a human condition in which such restlessness would be stilled. It is antiredemptive because such behavior exposes one, as Goethe makes quite clear, to a condition in which one does not know how to behave. It violates the basic principle of redemption, the limitation of the range of behavior. It presents, therefore, a violently alternative redemptive mode, one which necessarily raises tension, rather than reduces it. In the next paragraph the destructiveness of such a desire is clearly understood: that which saves it from destructiveness is of his powers "the only one / Which marks me"—imagination (ll. 283–284), defined by the metaphor of an angel, thus ascribing to it the attribute of divinity. The Romantic change of meaning for the term "imagination" invariably, to quote from a passage above, indicates that divine "creativity was located within the individual as the precondition for the innovation of verbal redemption." The whole passage shows an interesting cultural convergence with Hegel, with whom it is unlikely that the young Browning was familiar. In short, the Romantic self-definition as poet, prophet, and priest could not be clearer.

In what follows the speaker asserts that he has always yearned after God, even though neglecting his laws, and even though he came to doubt his existence, always felt his presence. It must not be imagined, as it often is, that the mere approving mention of God, even when it is clearly the Christian God, means that the Romantic writer accepts Christianity. An acquaintance with the cultural history of the period, especially the more obscure areas of religion and philosophy, not only among the Germans, indicates that one of the more common modes of innovative verbal redemption was a reinterpretation of Christian propositions, both theological and moral. God was retained, and it was claimed that it was a Christian God, yet the word terminated a quite different explanatory regress. Yet it is also perfectly true that a great many Romantic figures, in the interest of social safety and of being let alone, quite deliberately deceived a non-Romantic public by referring to God, or, as Carlyle did, seduced them into a Romantic redemptive mode. Hegel realized that God was dead (that philosophy subsumes religion), but he was almost alone. The persistence of the term is like the persistence of redemption. European culture overwhelmingly demanded both. On the other hand, the creation of alternative redemptive modes the explanatory regressions of which were terminated by "God" was in the development of Romanticism one of the more important means by which the function of that term as a mere means of terminating such a regress was revealed. Kierkegaard, for example, within the next two decades after *Pauline* was to make that function almost painfully clear. His final refusal to accept the identity of Christianity and an established Church in symbiotic relationship with the state indicates his awareness of having created a deviant innovative mode of verbal redemption. Less clearly, this recognition also emerges in *Pauline*.

The final native attribute comes as a surprise: "I can love nothing." Yet "sense supplies a love / Encircling me and mingling with my life" (ll. 310–312). This seems best interpreted as on the one hand a rejection of traditional modes for eroticizing experience and on the other the acceptance of the aesthetic mode, initially, in Romanticism, applied to nature, and subsequently applied to art. The passage appears to assert the autonomy of the self and by dissociating the self from sensory experience sunders the subject from the object, the self from the world. To ascribe love, the fusion of subject and object, to mere sensation is to assert more precisely what was asserted earlier, that affections, passions, feelings, and powers belong to the object and that any sensation of fusion of subject and object is an illusion. The importance of this denial of the capacity for love to Browning's future development can scarcely be overestimated. It was a factor in Romantic self-definition that did not emerge in the development of Romanticism until several decades after *Pauline*. Once again it shows Browning's remarkable grasp of the Romantic problem.

The next section of the poem presents the speaker's encounter with ancient literature and then, with a sense that his powers were bursting out, his encounter with the Sun-treader. His vowing himself to liberty and subsequent disenchantment, already discussed, was the central experience of those who originated Romanticism. The effect here is not despair but light-heartedness, wit, and mockery, shortly followed by the disappearance of God and the appearance in his place of a dark spirit. But the further effect was the effort to chain his own spirit down. Browning, then, is different from the early Romantics, who had to discover the true "self." The Romantic self-definition had been by his time at least well enough formulated and established so that he could postulate its five attributes as a native endowment. Thus shame at self-betrayal takes the place of the earlier guilt over violating established social modes. This stage is in turn succeeded by an elaborate rationalization for avoiding the vanity and suffering of genius, for such the speaker thinks himself. To abase himself before the remembered figure of the Sun-treader and "feed his fame" (l. 588) is now his only ambition. The result was a defiance of all hopes for glory, but a corresponding reward in the return of music, "my life" (l. 565), and other "old delights" such as classical literature. The importance of music in the Romantic tradition and its emergence in the nineteenth century as a major art lay in its simultaneous inexplicability and its somehow convincing meaningfulness. It was therefore interpreted as the most intimate and truest expression of the "self," and consequently as the best, perhaps sole, mode of redemption. This tradition contributed powerfully to the survival of art as the sole means of redemption, a position arrived at in the late nineteenth century and powerfully continued into the twentieth. Nevertheless, the speaker discovers, all faith had left him, and what he took for a returning spring was but a fading autumn, a sunset glow. It was in this condition that he encountered Pauline, as previously narrated (ll. 55–88).

The argument of the poem has proceeded in the classical way of justifying deviation, a unique personal history and a novel situation, represented by the Sun-treader. However, the shameful deviation is not from a socially validated but from a Romantically defined self. As Paracelsus later was to say, the crucial matter is to let out that which is within. But these inner attributes, as a result of personal history, have been frustrated and suppressed. The rest of the poem is the exploration of possible strategies for undoing these bonds. Nevertheless, a striking sentence indicates Browning's penetration into the Romantic problem.

> I will tell
> My state as though 'twere none of mine.
> (585–586)

This desubjectification of the personality is one of the most interesting notions of Romanticism, one, of course, immensely difficult to accomplish; furthermore, it is exactly what Browning was doing in *Pauline* and clearly indicates the origins of his peculiar use of the dramatic monologue. It is similar to Carlyle's distinction between the I and the me, between the noumenal and the phenomenal selves. The same impulse is behind Flaubert's objectification of himself in *Madame Bovary*, and it accounts for the peculiar impression that Browning's poems make that they are at once autobiographical and nonautobiographical. It was a notion that was to flower in the 1870s in Nietzsche and in Vaihinger, though the latter did not publish his philosophy of "as if" until 1911. The term "construct," now so widely used, is a development of this factor of Romanticism, and amounts to an objectification of cognitive processes.

The speaker proceeds by asserting that it is impossible for him to maintain the frustration and suppression of his powers. Thus he defines the character of the redemption he seeks:

> So my baffled hopes
> See out abstractions; I would have but one joy,
> Delight on earth, so it were wholly mine;
> One rapture all my soul could fill.
>
> (607–610)

This is the clearest possible indication that his undertaking is redemptive, his aim a single mode of limiting the range of behavior, dominating and subsuming all others. One certainly suspects that the delight is necessarily linked to the singleness. Of his initial endowment, the factor now singled out is the restless craving after knowledge, which he has suppressed, for reasons already suggested. He calls it a "sleepless harpy" (l. 624), a striking metaphor for the awareness that such an endowment must necessarily violate traditional redemptive modes, that it necessarily leads to innovative deviance. Admitting that he "cannot but be proud of my bright slave" (l. 634), he goes on in the next paragraph first to assert that this gift must be freed, and then to indicate the source of his self-hate, the fear that to attempt satisfaction of this instinct, which involves soaring beyond the earth (the validated social modes of verbal and nonverbal behavior) would be a vain effort and would entail the loss of normal earthly satisfaction. We now see the real source of his shame. He wants to eat his cake and have it too. He will not take the risks his gifts require. This is the spell that needs to be broken (l. 698).

Whatever else one may say about the works and the lives of the first two generations of Romantics (and there are still many who can have no sympathy with them) no one can deny that they took major risks. The recognition of their cultural situation, as I have outlined it, demanded either that they take great risks or suffer total collapse. Halfway measures were difficult and, to the degree each recognized the demands of the situation, impossible. In his struggle to achieve self-definition, Browning has clearly seen this attribute of his great predecessors. To abandon normal modes of limiting behavior is to expose oneself to a degree of disorientation that can threaten sanity and undermine that steady continuity of behavior that makes risk-taking possible. Browning is very accurate, then, in linking the craving after knowledge with the fear of risk-taking, but the example of his predecessors makes it clear that risk-taking is his only possible mode of redemption. The problem of risk-taking—and it was the central psychological or decisional problem of Romanticism—is that the direction that limits behavior is one that directs expansion of behavior. This is the true Romantic paradox, and it explains why so many Romantic lives were filled with disturbance.

That the speaker is capable of it, he asserts, his past behavior shows, but defenses against the disorientation of risk-taking are, he realizes, necessary, and this is perfectly true. One is the power of empathy, to cease temporarily being a self and to become a plant, a bee, a sunbeam, a bird, a fish, a flower, or a tree. The other is the standard method of social withdrawal. Just as Browning's task was made more difficult by his lack of access to *The Prelude,* so his investigation of the strategy of withdrawal was made more difficult by the nonpublication of *The Recluse,* which did not appear until 1888. Nevertheless his imaginary construction of "A home for us, out of the world; in thought—" (l. 730) is as much Wordsworth as it is Shelley. Even so, the imaginative construction of withdrawal proves unsuccessful: "But my soul saddens when it looks beyond; / I cannot be immortal, nor taste all" (ll. 809–810). For this there are good reasons. Exposure to problems and postponement of solutions, that is, verbal (intellectual, cultural, spiritual) risk-taking, requires both psychic insulation and social protection, in actuality, not in imagination. Imaginative withdrawal, which is what he attempts here at some length, leads directly to the awareness of death. Indeed, the opening request to Pauline, to "bend o'er me," introduces in the first line of the poem the principle of protection. But at this point, the awareness of death, Browning uses a strange device, a long footnote, in French, signed by Pauline herself!

Several things about this note are worth comment, apart from the suggestion that the genre of the poem is the literary epistle and that Pope's "Eloisa to Abelard" may have been a primary model. The note clearly indicates the structure of the speaker's life, a succession of increasingly lofty plateaux, each with a more extended view of the circumstances of human existence. It is an interesting anticipation of what subsequent study of learning has shown, that we do indeed learn by sudden leaps to new plateaux. To this ascent forgetfulness and slumber, Pauline suggests, will put an end. This transparent denial of immortality is cautiously suggested by Pauline to be as incomprehensible to the speaker as to herself, yet rest of the poem makes it fairly clear that the notion of immortality is in fact abandoned.

This denial of immortality leads to the next point, the desire of the speaker's soul to

rest beneath
Some better essence than itself—in weakness;
This is "myself"—not what I think should be,
And what is that I hunger for but God?
(818–821)

Two things are of note here, the desire for submissive dependency, and as the next paragraph shows, a nonmediated access to a clearly eroticized deity, as eroticization is defined above. Obviously it is verbal redemption that is at work here, a redemptive mode which dismisses all culturally available modes of a redemptive relation to the term "God." This submissive dependency, for all the talk about Romantic pride, well founded, to be sure, is nevertheless an important ingredient in Romanticism, particularly in its early decades, since all redemptive modes involve a submissive dependency upon some stimulus which is responded to by limiting the range of behavior. When in the course of the century the most important source of redemption came to be art, the relation of the "aesthetes" of the nineteenth century to art was a submissive dependency upon it. Further, the submissive dependency which is inherent in all modes of redemption, whether verbal or political, was given a double strength by the psychologically regressive effort to eroticize the source of redemption, of which the eroticization of nature, as described above, was but one form. This accounts for the diffused sexual eroticism to be found throughout the Romantic tradition, but particularly in the period generally known as Aestheticism. As I have suggested, many religions, particularly Christianity, have used eroticized sexuality as an instrument of redemptive control. Romanticism frequently reversed the process and eroticized religion, as in this passage and in the ensuing discussion of Christ.

This is followed by a rapid transition from an assertion that the speaker can envision spending the rest of his life in teaching the faith to an assertion that he is Pauline's forever and that he does love her, a passage which is concluded with the reversal of their relative positions. Pauline is now beneath, looking up. Pauline now assumes the role of submissive dependence, willing to die for the beloved. What has happened here is that the immediate apprehension of God and the empathetic experience of Christ and the crucifixion has successfully accomplished an innovative redemption, utterly deviant from the traditional Christian modes. Consequently the speaker, who was self-defined as incapable of love, is now capable of it, but it is a love in which he is the dominant figure, thus indicating at last a sense of being in command of his own gifts and able to put them to use. This dominating dependence upon Pauline suggests that the best interpretation of "love" in this passage is "value—in the object's own right," to value another's subjectivity. It is the love of a ruler for his people, as suggested above. Thus Pauline henceforward ceases to be a redemptive figure, or even a protective one, but becomes rather a supportive figure, the need for which was so great to the Romantic. The relationship, after this sudden reversal, changes to a relation of equality, rather like that of Wordsworth and his sister Dorothy, or more precisely of the first among equals.

The speaker is thus able to turn his back upon the past and project a genuine withdrawal to Pauline's native country, evidently Switzerland. Nevertheless, he anticipates a return from his self-imposed exile to his native England, a return to be marked by strength and calm, since the retreat to Switzerland will involve a reinvestigation of the cultural tradition and a new examination of the mental treasures of the speaker. But even, he goes on to say, should none of this happen, he has achieved a moment of "perfect joy," a claim he repeats. The redemptive pattern, then, is a sequence of the discovery of his fear of risk, the taking of that risk in an immediate, deviant, and innovative relation to "God," the traditional termination of an explanatory regress, and the assumption of a dominant relation to an object valued in its own right, and to his own powers. He can therefore claim that he will be calmer and purer, that "beauteous shapes will come for me to seize" and that "unknown secrets will be trusted me," that in short he will be "priest and prophet as of old" (ll. 1015–1019).

The final paragraph is once again addressed to the Sun-treader, to whom the statement is made that "I believe in God and truth / And love" (ll. 1020–1021). The Sun-treader, like Pauline, is now reduced to a supportive role, as is to be expected, since the speaker is now prophet and priest in his own right. This subordination of the Sun-treader is made possible because the speaker has arrived at an innovative conception of deity, a conception of truth which entails the unknown and thus innovation and deviancy, and a conception of love in which is the source of valuing. Thus he is able to extend the range of his awareness and of a potential supportive group beyond the Sun-treader and Pauline, concluding the poem in an epistolary manner. He is therefore free of doubt and fear. The purpose of the poem is achieved, self-definition as Romantic poet-prophet-priest, a role with a genuine social function, even though the role and its function should be recognized and validated by but a small group of people. Even so, the possibility of creating a nucleus for an alternative mode of redemption suggests an alternative society. But most important, as the phrase "moment's pride" suggests (l. 993), finality is grasped as the *sense* of finality, a psychological condition, a feeling state, not an absolute truth, not a goal. He asks his friends to "wish me well" (l. 1031). The future is open; the goal is unknown. There is at least the faint implication of a goal-less existence, of the abandonment of finality and redemption as anything more significant than cognitive vacations. *Pauline* either marks the end of Romanticism, or, if one accepts the larger and more inclusive definition, the beginning of a new stage in its century-long emergence.

NOTES

1. I have made a tentative sketch of this in my essay "Personality and the Mask of Knowledge," *Victorian Revolutionaries* (New York, 1970).

2. William S. Peterson and Fred L. Standley, "The J. S. Mill Marginalia in Robert Browning's *Pauline*: A History and Transcription," *PBSA*, 66 (1972): 138.

3. First published in 1935; 2nd ed. 1955. As Browning scholarship develops, it becomes distressingly evident that DeVane's *Handbook* must be used with extreme caution and scepticism.

4. DeVane, *Handbook*, p. 42.

5. *The Focusing Artifice* (Athens, Ohio, 1968), pp. 4–10.

6. 1833 text. The 1889 text is a little clearer: "First went my hopes of perfecting mankind, / Next—faith in them, and then in freedom's self / And virtue's self, then my own motives, end / And aims and loves, and human love went last."

7. Unless otherwise indicated the text is that of the 1833 edition for all subsequent quotations, as derived from the variants in *The Complete Works of Robert Browning* (Athens, Ohio, 1969), vol. 1, as I have corrected them.

8. "Wide" is so preferable to the 1868–1889 reading "wild" that it is possible that the passage should be emended to its original reading. Work on the Ohio Browning Edition has revealed that Browning, though an earnest proofreader, was no more successful at achieving perfection than anyone else is, and less successful than some.

CHAPTER SIX

# An Explanation of "Realism"

"Thinking" about "thought," that is, the semiotic transformation of
semiotic transformation itself, engaged in for the purpose of controlling semiotic transformation, throughout human history has been almost infinitely complex and various, and is ordinarily subsumed by
the term "philosophy," in itself a term of markedly high polysemy.
Nevertheless, it appears to me that all of this complex process can be
reduced to, or at least subsumed by, three factors.

The first is the preservation of perceptual attributes. A trivial but
illuminating example is the following interchange: "Let's go to the
movies." "Right on! Let's go to the movies!" Here the verbal perceptual attributes of the original utterance have been perfectly preserved,
though not the intonation, as the "!" indicates. And in "Right on!"
there has been an addition, a fact which I must momentarily post-
pone. On the other hand, in *Modern Painters* Ruskin preserves by verbal categorial subsumption the perceptual attributes of trees, clouds,
and waves with a completeness no one had hitherto achieved, at least
in English, pointing out, for example, that clouds have no curved lines
but only straight ones. The effectiveness of Ruskin's control of the
reader's behavior is that after reading such Ruskinian semiotic transformations one feels that one has never really *seen* a cloud, a tree, or
a wave. In the following interchange, just the opposite has occurred.
"Let's go to the movies." "Let's not; I hate popcorn." Here there is
almost no preservation of perceptual attributes, and the semiotic
transformation is not only a negation of those attributes but is also
ironic, in that it proposes the inappropriate judgment that one goes
to the movies to eat popcorn, with the implied judgment that popcorn

is the only justification for going to the movies, a judgment not ironic but a negation of the value of moviegoing and of movies.

The second factor is the inherent limitation of the semiotic modality into which the transformation takes place. A drawing of a piece of sculpture cannot preserve all of the perceptual attributes of the sculpture, or indeed very many of them, since it is a transformation of a three-dimensional semiotic mode into a two-dimensional mode. The factor at work here can be further indicated by the probability that if Debussy's *La Mer* had neither title nor subtitles but were merely presented as a three-movement symphony, no one would guess that it is a semiotic transformation of the sea, or even of Debussy's "feelings" (whatever that means) about the sea. Further, for all of Ruskin's brilliant preservation of attributes in his semiotic transformations of clouds, waves, and trees, the inherent limitations of verbalization as a semiotic modality do not permit him to equal in such preservation what Frederick Leighton could do in his nearly contemporaneous drawing of an almond tree. The explanation, of course, is that words preserve no perceptual attributes, though in combination they can preserve some attributes of sounds, as in the highly sophisticated rhetorical figure of onomatopoeia. But that is the only exception. It is precisely the independence of verbalization from attributional preservation in semiotic transformation that makes possible the indeterminability of human behavior, or, sentimentally, "human freedom." An amusing example of semiotic preservation can be found in the recent, quite dreadful film *Close Encounters of the Third Kind*. The hero is inspired by beings from another planet to create a scale model of the distinctive terrain where the UFO people planned to land. But this example is instructive, for it brings out the third factor, the factor which controls the selection of perceptual attributes and manipulation of the semiotic modality.

That third factor has been called all kinds of names: mind, spirit, soul, ideas, the divine, feelings, ideologies, the subjective, the inner world, the *a priori*, preconceptions, expectations, and so on. But I think the most useful term is "style," a term, to be sure, almost excessively polysemous. But that very polysemy makes the term useful here. For "style" is various in its application simply because it is a contrastive term. That is, it contrasts the unique attributes of an instance with the attributes common to other instances in the same category. Furthermore, because thinking or explanatory behavior proceeds by subsumption away from the phenomenal, "style" is also used to contrast the attributes of a category from other categories subsumed by a more regressive category. Thus we can distinguish the "realistic style" of Balzac from that of Zola, Thackeray, Fielding, or any other writers of "realistic fiction" that we can manage to think of or judge to be justifiably subsumed by the literary category "realism." The sources of style, or the factors in style, are simply the factors of culture, that is, learned behavior, or, more precisely, interactionally transmitted instructions for performance. In the individual human organism, as it develops, cultural factors are uniquely combined, partly from postulated but as yet unknown genetic influences, but principally by the brain's random response to controlled learning and combination of cultural factors. Within a given culture these factors tend to be controlled and organized by explanations at a level distantly regressive from the phenomenal. One mode of organized explanation is mythology, which in modern times becomes UFOism, Freudianism, Jungianism, Marxism, the mythologies of an insufficiently secularized culture. But a better term, one that recognizes a level of explanation more regressive than mythology, is "ideology." The ideologies of a culture—and the more modern the culture the greater the number of ideologies at work within it—are the ultimate controlling explanations of a culture, and its justifications; they are invariably maintained by the ultimate sanctions for the control of force, the instrument of governmental and economic power from the family to the state.

With this notion of semiotic transformation it is now possible to approach directly the problem of "realism." First, it must be recognized that realism is an attribute of style, an ideologically controlled principle for selecting perceptual attributes and manipulating the semiotic modality into which the semiotic transformation is made. As such it is not a factor that can be analyzed in itself but only contrastively. A given work is either more or less realistic than some other work or category of works. Second, in that contrastive use, what "realism" directs our attention to is the preservation of perceptual attributes of whatever segment of the phenomenal the individual writer is responding to. A literary work tends to be called "realistic" if it is marked by a preservation of perceptual attributes greater than that of a work with which it is judged to be appropriately subsumed by the same category. It is, moreover, obvious that the phenomenal field to be transformed in the literary work is under the control of an ideology, as well as the selection of the perceptual attributes to be preserved. And this is also true of the semiotic modality, that is, the degree to which the current rhetoric of literature is to be employed with or without significant modification and extension or narrowing. In the realism of "naturalism," for example, the semiotic modality of the rhetoric of fiction is at once narrowed by the exclusion of the traditional literary vocabulary and widened by the use of terms not hitherto used in that rhetoric.

Although we can refer perfectly successfully and appropriately to the realism of Chaucer and Shakespeare and, at least in certain passages, even of Milton, in the fiction of the last several hundred years two waves of realism can be discerned, that of the Enlightenment and that of Romanticism. But to understand the significance of either it is necessary to turn again to nonliterary semiotic transformation and consider the development of realistic semiotic transformation in ordinary semiotic behavior, both verbal and nonverbal. It is, I think, usually assumed that "thinking" moves, as the individual grows and matures, from the concrete to the abstract. And this assumption is valid up to a certain point, in that the vocabulary of the individual, as his education, in its largest sense, proceeds, becomes more abstract, that is, more regressive from the phenomenal by means of categorial subsumption in an increasing depth of levels. Yet in actuality the reverse is the case; that is, "thinking" proceeds primarily from the abstract to the concrete. Hegel, in a brilliant essay of unknown date, insists that it is not the philosopher but the man in the street who thinks abstractly.[1] If we examine the drawings of children it is obvious that the semiotic transformation is highly abstract; that is, initially, an enclosed shape, roughly circular, subsumes all configurations. That is, whatever details of the phenomenal world children may see, their semiotic transformation into nonverbal signs is at a very regressive level of abstraction, or categorial subsumption.[2] It is only gradually that children learn and are sometimes demandingly taught the semiotic conventions for the preservation of perceptual attributes. And this is just as true of verbal semiosis. Consequently, "realism," whether in philosophy, in science, or literature, is always a highly sophisticated attribute of semiotic transformation, a characteristic of high culture.

If, in objection to this, the cave paintings of paleolithic man are appealed to, it is only necessary to remember that such paintings were necessarily preceded by eons of semiotic transformation onto organic materials, materials which have long since returned to dust. Indeed, the surviving sculpture and paintings of paleolithic man, as is increasingly recognized, have many of the characteristics of sophisticated high culture, a culture which has recognized "thought," or semiotic transformation, as a mode of behavior, and which has engaged in manipulating that mode, a recognition which is the necessary consequence of recording semiotic transformation and of preserving it beyond the moment of transformation. If semiotic transformation is the attribute of human behavior, then we must recognize that the recording or preservation of a semiotic transformation is a further transformation, and that the conventions of the one are different from the conventions of the other. Hence, the preservation of perceptual attributes in the conventions of recording can and do vary independently from immediate semiotic transformation. And this variability is of the highest importance in understanding the various literary realisms of the past three hundred years.

An excellent example of Enlightenment realism is to be found in Thomson's *The Seasons* as well as in the fiction of Fielding. Such realism was governed by the ideology of "Nature," of man as a creation of natural forces to which it was appropriate that he adjust his behavior. It is hardly necessary to point out that the Enlightenment notion of "Nature" was itself a highly abstract ideology. What it accomplished was the displacement of God into a realm which removed God from Providential interference with human behavior. God and Natural Law were identified. Under the impact of seventeenth-century science the Enlightenment proposed that man discover those laws (established, to be sure, by a *deus absconditus*) and correct his mythologically controlled behavior accordingly. Now the important aspect of realism in this enterprise was this: an ideology is undermined by a literature (or a science or a philosophy or a sociology or a psychology) which investigates the perceptual attributes of a phenomenal field other than those dictated by the regnant ideology, and by preserving attributes ignored, or not selected, by that regnant ideology. The ideological objective of Enlightenment realism was to undermine the ideology of Providence, and it did so by preserving perceptual attributes which that ideology could not successfully subsume. Enlightenment realism was thus culturally convergent with the contemporaneous argument about miracles, which in its anti-Providential and occasionally atheistic endeavors simply presented evidence which the ideology of miracles could not successfully subsume.

From this cultural situation there began to emerge the notion, not fully arrived at until the twentieth century, but nevertheless at the heart of Romanticism, that ideologies are human creations, are human semiotic transformations of semiotic transformations. The keynote of the new cultural epoch, revolutionary in its aims and its consequences, an epoch which I have called Romanticism, was struck by Hegel, who asked in his *Phenomenology* why men created ideologies; his notion of *Geist* proposed the first theory of human culture.[3] In the preceding cultural epochs of European and other civilizations the aim of "thought" was a true and stable ideology capable of subsuming all phenomena under a single explanation. The aim was synthesis, and analysis was in the service of synthesis. The modern (or, to my mind, Romantic) ideology is the reversal or negation of that traditional aim. Analysis became the primary and dominating ideology of that tiny portion of high culture, gradually growing in size and strength, but still immensely in the minority, which is best understood as an anti-ideological ideology, or, in the American version of Hegelianism, pragmatic ideology. What had been discovered in the Enlightenment, the capacity of "realism" to undermine a regnant ideology, now became an instrument of that analytic undermining of the European cultural superstructure, that is, of all European ideologies. The past 180 years have been the age of analysis. Marx was an incomplete analyst, still controlled by synthetic-redemptionist ambitions. Popular Marxism is synthetic, and therefore tyrannical and authoritarian. Sophisticated Marxism is increasingly analytic.

It takes only the most cursory examination of the history of the various realisms of the nineteenth and twentieth centuries to recognize how the tradition of literary realism has progressively undermined the ideologies of western culture. Initially, as was to be expected, that undermining was controlled by culturally emergent ideologies, such as sociology, or Darwinism, or science. Zola has been ridiculed for his notion of the experimental novel, for, after all, an experiment cannot be carried out in words. Yet in the structure of semiotic transformation, Zola can be seen as justified in his claim. Science proceeds by experiment, that is, by testing and necessarily modifying, correcting, and on occasion completely undermining a current scientific ideology. By the twentieth century it began to be perceived that the proper object of the analytic culture was to exploit that inherent instability of ideologies. That is, any ideology is the product of a preceding situation, and therefore to a greater or lesser degree inappropriate for application to a current situation. Man's continued existence depends upon that exploitation.

It is this analytic aim that was responsible for the fact that in the course of the nineteenth century the novel displaced poetry as the primary literary form. Because the novel's rhetorical conventions were undefined, it was the literary genre most capable of preserving perceptual attributes hitherto ignored or exploring phenomenal fields hitherto ignored and often enough forbidden. The limits of realism in poetry were reached in the first third of the century by Byron and Pushkin. And it was Stendhal who first fully grasped the analytic possibilities of fiction. The widespread effort to distinguish the novel from the romance was the result of the recognition that the romance had its origin in poetry and still was confined by the rhetorical conventions of its origins. In the twentieth century the novel has been able to extend the conventions of its semiotic modality by incorporating literary devices and conventions hitherto limited to poetry. The most brilliant recent effort of this sort is Carlos Fuentes's *Terra Nostra*, a work which uses the techniques of surrealism and of realism to undermine the current ideologies of synthetic redemptionism and Utopianism. For these reasons the novel has become the primary literary genre for exploiting the inherent instability of all ideologies, the primary representative in literature of the analytical tradition of anti-ideological ideology.

## NOTES

1. The essay has been translated by Walter Kaufmann as "Who Thinks Abstractly" in *Hegel: Texts and Commentary* (Garden City, New York: Doubleday & Co., Inc., 1966), pp. 460–465.

2. See Rudolf Arnheim, *Art and Visual Perception*, 1st ed. (Berkeley: University of California Press, 1954), a book far less about art than it is about nonverbal semiosis.

3. It can be argued that Vico preceded Hegel. It is beginning to be recognized that Hegel was not an idealist but a materialist and an empiricist, though of a new kind. From him Marx learned the notion of economics as the basis of all human behavior and of the cultural superstructure built upon that basis but capable of operating independently of it.

# CHAPTER SEVEN

# Victorian Counterculture

As I consider the topics of this conference, the exhibits, the performances, I suspect that just about everything we still consider valuable and interesting from the Victorian decades will turn out to have belonged to the Victorian counterculture. Even Queen Victoria herself can no longer be seen as the perfect exemplar of what we usually mean by "Victorian." As one biographical study after another penetrates behind the veil of royal public relations and governmentally inspired iconography, she is seen to have been far more of a belated hangover from the Regency, of whom it was typical to complain to Palmerston of the closing of parks and museums on Sundays. Helen Lynd once said that we, meaning the Americans of the 1950s, are the true Victorians in our sexual mores, for we live—or lived a couple of decades ago—by the morality that the Victorians themselves merely uttered. If today the *Playboy* morality is a counterculture, then what we mean by the Victorian morality of sexual prudery may very well have been a counterculture of the Evangelical middle classes, a counterculture that became in time the dominant culture. In the 1850s and 1860s pornography was almost as easily available in London as it is today, and the law that put Oscar Wilde in jail was but a few years old when it was enforced upon him. To be sure, in the 1820s a bishop lost his benefices for having been discovered in unnatural relations with a guardsman, but the accounts of the affair suggest that his crime lay in having been discovered. Indiscretion is always the only crime that really counts. At least I suspect that was the attitude of the British upper classes, to which this eventually unfortunate Bishop belonged. What, after all, is the point of wealth and social position if you cannot enjoy yourself, particularly in ways forbidden to lesser and poorer mortals?

Yet if the publicly uttered sexual morality was one of sexual constraint and if the actual sexual behavior was marked by sexual freedom, or even license—the word is hardly too strong—then which was the counterculture? Writers from one end of Europe to the other, writers and publicists of every kind, emphasized the supreme value of sexual virtue. Was this because such virtue was so rare? Freud denounced nineteenth-century culture for having induced widespread neurosis through sexual repression, but the memoirs of Arthur Schnitzler, only six years younger than Freud, suggest that Vienna could have used a little sexual repression. Jung has made fun of Freud because the latter, as a nice middle-class Jewish boy, did not know about the realities of sexual behavior, whereas Jung, a country boy, knew all about all the sexual aberrancies and normalcies by the time he was ten.

It is evident that there were two sexual cultures in nineteenth-century Europe, a public culture of constraint and a private one of license. Nor must we imagine that the private one was individual, in the sense that it was natural or free from cultural control. Quite the contrary, if we can judge by what we know about the sexual culture of the twentieth century until a decade or so ago, or in the thirties, when the *New York Times* refused to accept advertising for *Studs Lonigan*. The culture of license was also culturally transmitted, but for the most part it was a nonliterate or oral culture. It was what Philip Rieff has called a remissive culture, one that took place in situations in which the sinfulness of sinful talk and behavior was remitted. To be sure, there was some circulation of pornography, but nothing, of course, to be compared with what we have today. Pornographic bookstores today belong to such a remissive culture. The importance of oral transmission of culture is brought out if we contemplate the fact that such stores have come to be called adult bookstores. They are permitted if they are not available to the young, on the grounds that we do not wish to corrupt the young. However, as every one who has ever been young knows very well, pornography is not necessary to corrupt the young. They corrupt each other very well without such cultural aids. Sexually, the culture of adolescence is a culture of license, and, so far as we can tell, always has been. Likewise it has always been, at least under the Christian dispensation, a remissive culture, one in which the constraints of the public culture are acknowledged in their violation.

From this point of view it seems reasonable that the effort to stamp out the remissive culture of sexual license, the effort, as I have suggested, of what was initially a rather small group of mostly middle-class evangelicals, was the true sexual counterculture of the Victorian world. This counterculture gradually became dominant, as in the removal of street solicitation by prostitutes in post-World War II London, or during that same war, the suppression of the red-light district in Charleston, South Carolina, which in happier days had the largest number of brothels per capita in the United States, just as it had the largest number of churches. In saying that neurosis was a result of the sexual repression of the nineteenth century, Freud apparently was quite wrong. To be sure, his neurotics were sexually repressed, but their sexual timidity was a symptom of their neurosis, which had other roots. Yet in putting his finger on sexual repression as a significant factor in contemporary culture, Freud possibly was treating some members of a small counterculture of sexual repression which by the end of the century was becoming dominant and beginning to be able to enforce its cultural values upon much of the rest of society and all of its public culture.

Nevertheless, if we step back a bit and look at the problem from a wider point of view, one at first wonders if the emerging culture of sexual repression is correctly to be called a counterculture. In deciding whether a behavior is indicative of the presence of a counterculture or is itself countercultural, caution is necessary. Consider a contemporary phenomenon, the pot culture, so intensely identified with the emergence of the very term counterculture. For two reasons it is doubtful if the use of marijuana can be called countercultural. In the first place, I do not know of any culture more complex than that of simple food-gathering that does not depend upon the introduction of a chemical substance, a drug, into the body, the effect of which is to reduce the activity and the range of activity of the individual and thus contribute to the maintenance of cultural stability. The consequence of this in the high days of the counterculture in the 1960s was a great deal of rhetoric but not much action. It was mostly confined to college campuses, not very important places, and had little or no lasting effect there. To be sure, a minority of faculty members began to spend a little time thinking seriously about what they were doing, but the days of that particular cultural aberrancy are long since over. In the second place, the youth of that counterculture did not learn the use of drugs as a tension-reducing mechanism—tension being the precondition of cultural innovation—from an innovative counterculture but from their parents, and their parents learned it from the medical establishment, physicians and pharmaceutical manufacturers. This country became an alternative drug culture, alternative to alcohol, that is, in the early 1950s when the medical establishment introduced tranquillizers into the culture. The use of pot was only the most superficial indication of a generation gap. The young had been taught by both precept and example that when one is upset one introduces a chemical substance into the physiological system. The young use pot because they have been trained by their parents and the dominant public culture in the use of drugs as a behavior-limiting strategy.

Thus if we look at Victorian culture we see a public culture of sexual constraint, a remissive culture of sexual license, and an emerging culture, eventually to be reasonably successful, though not until the twentieth century, of sexual repression. What all of these have in common is a tremendous emphasis upon the importance, the supreme significance of sexual behavior, a significance constantly validated by the culture's most sacred text and by what for the immense bulk of the population was the highest cultural level which they encountered, the pulpit. However, to be sure, it is only from the very rare pulpit and to a small and highly select congregation that then or now or at any time issue exemplifications of truly high culture. And that tremendous emphasis is still true today. But let us remember that we are told by our culture, and told in continuous redundancy, that sexual activity is of the highest importance. I doubt if there is anyone here who has not been instructed to the point of belief that sexual fulfillment—whatever that is—is an essential condition for mental, emotional, and physical health. This belief is dependent, of course, on Freud and even more on popularized Freudianism, which is not precisely identical with Freud's writings themselves. It is dependent, then, on Freud's misapprehension of actual behavior, but only in part, for the reason that Freud has been so widely accepted is that in placing a tremendous importance on sexual behavior he was merely saying what practically everybody else in the society was saying, whether overtly or covertly, publicly, remissively, or repressively. A true countercultural judgment of sexual activity would be that it is actually very unimportant, aside from the economic consequences of the production of offspring. However, in the Victorian era the economic consequences were less than at first glance they might seem, for the rate of infant and childhood mortality was high and the incidence of infanticide of considerable significance. It is well known, for example, that at times of unemployment it was quite common for the unemployed to allow the younger children to die so that the burial insurance could be used to keep the rest of the family alive. Today, if there is a sexual revolution (and if there is, it may be only a return to the pre-regressive culture, an overturning of the countercultural sexual repressiveness that emerged in the nineteenth century, plus a public though still minority culture of sexual license) that sexual revolution is as much as anything else, as all the world knows, a consequence of the increasing ease in circumventing those economic consequences. Moreover there are, happily, a number of ways of sexual activity with no economic consequences whatever, though of course one could wish for more. To assume that sexual activity is one of the trivialities of life gives one at least a fresh perspective on the matter.

There is, I submit, some reason for thinking so; for one thing, consider the enormous redundancy of cultural instructions that sex is of the greatest possible importance. There is no question that such redundancy raises the frequency of sexual arousal and activity. The objection to the repression of pornography is not that it does not arouse people sexually. Of course it does. That is what it is for, and that is why it is both popular and enjoyable. The objection to repressing it lies rather in the statistical triviality of pornography, even when it is freely circulated, compared with the multitudinous other cultural instructions that sex is of central importance. The objection to repressing pornography, certainly now that it has entered our society so richly, is rather that such repression would make no difference, and that the economic costs, both in policing expenses and in loss of business activity, would be monumental compared with the infinitesimal reduction of frequency of sexual arousal and activity that would be accomplished. I myself doubt if there would be any reduction. My point is that the sexual drive is not at all powerful, and that it is to the interest of society to make it as powerful as possible.

Now it is hard to imagine anything so immediately available to human beings for the purpose of limiting the range of behavior as sexual activity, for it is exciting, pleasurable, and sooner or later tension-reducing, all three of which are desirable though not of course necessary for focusing interest and channeling behavior. All the individual really needs for survival is food and water; sex may be necessary for the survival of the race, but the number of individuals at any time genuinely interested in the survival of the race, as distinguished from being interested in talking about it, is very small. Perhaps there are none. For survival, individual sex is unimportant, but there is little that human beings do that is more capable of being made important by means of cultural manipulation. It is so beautifully suited in its very triviality for limiting the range of response, for controlling the sociocultural innovation that is the consequence of the brain's capacity for randomness, that one is tempted to revive the argument from design.

As for the second reason for judging sexual activity to be one of the trivialities of life, that is easily seen. What is important? Well, I would say that what is important is what people start revolutions about; I mean real revolutions, serious revolutions in which the shedding of blood and even wholesale slaughter are considered matters of relative unimportance. I do not mean metaphorical revolutions, such as what our overheated imaginations call today's sexual revolution. As for what is responsible for the outbreak of a revolution, it is a little too easy to say that economic interests are at the root of the matter. Certainly revolutions seem generally to involve a judgment about the unacceptability of the current distribution of goods and services, but that judgment is itself controlled or directed by an explanation of the world, an ideology, or, if you prefer, a metaphysic. Neither an ideology nor economic conditions by themselves seem to be able to spark sufficient revolutionary fervor for something interesting to happen; they appear to require each other. The relationship is perhaps best thought of as dialectical. In any case, it is not sex that starts revolutions. However, sex often and in recent centuries almost invariably plays a part in a true political revolution, for the revolutionary forces encourage an ideology or public culture of sexual license, or strengthen the remissive culture of license. The explanation is that it is useful to transfer the energy locked into sexual activity by the diversionary strategy of sexual overestimation from sexual activity to revolutionary activity. Sex is made guilt-free, easily accessible, "natural." However, the ideology of sexual license is at once suppressed as soon as the revolutionaries either take power or are unquestionably defeated. What has followed the failed counterculture of the 1960s is the wide dissemination of an ideology of sexual license. During revolutionary periods sex is something you can engage in if you feel like it. A sexual ideology of license makes sex into something you *ought* to engage in. Guilt arises if you do not, and social condemnation. That is, to procure the desirable effects of sexual overestimation, sexual constraint, sexual license, and sexual repression are equally effective. *Playboy* and *Playgirl* are among the most conservative magazines now being circulated, and the free circulation of pornography is likewise deeply conservative. The revolutionary use of sexual ideology, then, is a strategy of trivializing sexuality, of making it unimportant. The effect is to release tremendous energy for the service of other interests. In revolutionary situations sex is reduced to the simple role of tension reduction. Tension is, of course, the condition of aggressive action, but in situations in which both ideology and power centers are under violent attack, the tension can easily rise to the point at which it interferes with action. In such situations, the social protocol of sexual conduct is dispensed with, and sexual activity serves the purpose of both reducing tension to a manageable point and at the same time of enhancing the sense of aggressive adequacy, for such enhancement is one of the primary values of sexual conduct.

As the author of a book on pornography I have been asked to speak on the subject by a number of colleges and churches, though only Episcopalians and Unitarians among the latter. Nothing I say seems to cause any particular perturbation, except for one thing—the suggestion that sex is a trivialty. I remember with amusement that when I first made this suggestion in public, at the University of Illinois, there were in the discussion that followed my remarks expressions by a number of members of the audience of barely controlled fury. Whenever I speak on the subject, it is certainly this point that rouses the most intense interest and not infrequently anger. Though my intentions are innocent enough, it is clear that in making this suggestion I am attacking a central factor in the culture's belief system. One young man, when he finally understood the theory of the diversionary overemphasis of sexual activity, said that it was the most cynical thing he had ever heard. Actually, in my innocence, such a response was a surprise to me. It is clear that in uttering the notion that sex is a triviality, I am committing an act of cultural vandalism.

It seemed to me appropriate to begin a discussion of counterculture by way of sexual behavior because there seems to be an unavoidable connection between a counterculture and sexual conduct, and I have attempted to offer something in the way of explanation as to why this should be so. Sexuality is not necessarily central to a culture—the Aztec culture is an obvious instance of a culture in which, at least in its art, it was not—but it is certainly central to ours. That is, it is one of the primary strategies, probably the most important strategy, whereby the range of behavior is limited and channeled. It is a central interest of the culture, and a true counterculture is marked by its attack on the central interest of the dominant culture. But an attack on the validity of such an interest is, to those members of the dominant culture who maintain that interest, an act of vandalism. To those initiating and carrying out the program of a counterculture, of course, the attack is anything but vandalism; on the contrary, it is an attack on falsehood and hypocrisy for the sake of making way for the emergence of truth and honesty.

The behavioral forces involved here deserve a little attention, and we may take as our model the adolescent who vandalizes an empty house. In doing so, of course, he is attacking one of the central and most sacred values of our culture, private property. Yet it is doubtful if his attack is in any way ideological. Rather, this apparently pointless act has a great deal of point. In a situation in which destructive acts are safe, in which they can be done with impunity, the act of vandalism gives the individual the sense of aggressive adequacy. That is obviously precisely the sense which the well-brought-up middle-class vandal is most in need of. Caught in a transitional stage between a family life in which aggressiveness is discouraged and under heavy control and the first steps into the extra-familial society in which aggressiveness is necessary, above everything else he needs a sense of aggressive adequacy. Vandalizing an empty house, especially if it belongs to a family higher than his own in economic status, is a rehearsal of aggressiveness, a rehearsal which convinces the adolescent that he is capable of aggressive adequacy in situations in which there is no impunity, in the ordinary situations, that is, of adult life. In vandalism he learns the feeling which is the necessary accompaniment of aggressive adequacy; he learns what it feels like to stand up for himself. The feeling can be practiced successfully because the feeling is separated from the conditions in which aggressive action is required.

This tells us much about the mounting and above all the maintaining of a counterculture. A counterculture is not done in situations of impunity. It is risk-taking and can be dangerous for the individual. Furthermore, the countercultural individual in vandalizing the beliefs of his culture is vandalizing his own beliefs. Moreover, the initial stages of a counterculture are invariably met with defeat, and often enough after great efforts met with final defeat. The countercultural vandal is in the position of the adolescent vandal. He needs to sustain the sense of aggressive adequacy. Hence much countercultural activity seems as pointless as vandalizing empty houses, as, for example, the famous Berkeley dirty-speech movement. Likewise in the nineteenth and twentieth centuries, countercultural efforts very frequently have a sexual character. In insisting upon making a remissive culture a public culture, or in attacking a repressive culture and insisting on the validity of a licentious culture, the countercultural vandal is eating his cake and having it too, for though his insistence is vandalistic, the implication of that insistence, that sexual activity is of supreme importance, is deeply conservative.

Wilde's *Salome* is itself an excellent example. What does Salome do that is so terrible? First, she fuses the sexual and the sacred. The religious as a metaphor for the sexual and vice-versa is certainly nothing novel in European literature. They are among the oldest and the most common of our literary metaphors. And Pope had already done an excellent job of literalizing that metaphor in "Eloisa to Abelard," not to speak of St. Teresa and Bernini. Wilde's fusion of the two is scarcely novel, but is always good for a *frisson* of horror. The feeling state of religious apprehension is identical with that of erotic apprehension of sexuality. This is the basis for the metaphor. However, the two are kept separate by the use of different public rhetorics. In presenting that identity publicly Wilde was vandalizing that separation, but at the same time was most conservatively making a culturally redundant assertion of the identity of the two. Second, Salome is determined to get what she wants and succeeds in getting at least some of it. Wilde, using a theme that had been commonplace in high culture for some decades, transfers aggression to a sex that is by definition submissive. Nevertheless, female aggressiveness is also a very ancient theme. In violating or vandalizing the public morality, he was nevertheless affirming the morality of aggressiveness. Third, the Princess Salome in insisting on getting at least something of what she wants is exhibiting the fundamental pattern of any aristocracy. Wilde presents us with a corrupt aristocracy and thus offers a countercultural attack upon aristocratic institutions. A defense of an aristocracy by one who is not a member of that class and has none of its privileges is always far more shocking than an attack upon it, far more countercultural. The reason is that in any hierarchical institution, and all institutions are hierarchical, resentment directed up and contempt directed down are the normal strategies for problem avoidance, that is, for tension reduction and social stabilization. All academics, for example, express resentment towards administrations, but genuine acts of academic rebellion are remarkably uncommon. Wilde thus at once attacks aristocracy but at the same time redundantly confirms social structure. Fourth, Salome kisses the severed head of Jochanaan. Terrible, of course, and marvelously effective in the theater, particularly when set to music by Strauss. Nevertheless, kissing the corpse of a loved one is a widespread practice. Not to do so, in fact, is often considered a serious breach of manners when the corpse is publicly displayed, and certainly Salome makes a public display of her affection for the so recently deceased Jochanaan. Wilde shocks, of course, by fusing death and eroticism, but after all "to die" is a very old metaphor for sexual intercourse, and in the remissive culture the rhetoric of sexuality often makes use of the rhetoric of death to indicate the extremity of sexual delights. Thus in this apparently countercultural attack upon public standards of sexual acceptability, Wilde confirms the overwhelming power of sexuality, its diversionary overemphasis. And that conservatism is confirmed by the fact that poor Salome, for whom I confess I am beginning to feel a certain sympathy, is crushed to death for her wickedness. It would be interesting, I think, and perhaps refreshing, to see a revised version of *Salome,* a second act in which, Salome's mother having conveniently died, Salome has married Herod and has taken up childbearing and good works. That might be genuinely countercultural, for it would imply that the fusion of religion and eroticism, the natural aggressiveness of women as well as of men, the self-indulgence of an aristocracy, and the fusion of sex and death are matters of very little importance compared with the serious problems of the human species, such as its controlling itself with drugs and locking its innovative powers into trivialities, both of these being strong hints that humanity is maladapted not so much to the natural world but to itself.

Any movement, then, that offers itself as countercultural needs to be looked at with some care, first, because much of its activity is pointless, that is, not aimed at achieving the countercultural ideology but only aimed at maintaining the sense of aggressive adequacy; and second, because it is always possible that a counterculture is only superficially so. It is always necessary, then, to ask just exactly how counter any counterculture is. Let us consider a current countercultural movement, women's liberation. So far as I can tell, it appears to have two incoherent aims, that women ought to be able to be as aggressive as men are, and that nobody ought to be aggressive. As for the first of these, I doubt if there is a man here who has not been a victim of a woman's aggressiveness and has not submitted to it. But I also doubt if there is a man who has not submitted to another man's aggressiveness, nor a woman who has not submitted to a woman's. A remark by a woman colleague of mine is instructive. She was not interested in women's liberation, she said to me once, because she always feels at an advantage dealing with a man. In short, all behavior is aggressive, that is, an effort to control the environment, including the environment of other human beings and indeed of oneself. The alternative is submission, which is seduction, a mode of reducing the aggressiveness of the agressor and limiting his behavior, or hers, as the case may be. As we all know, the public culture has assigned aggressiveness to men and submission, or seduction, to women. In the remissive culture, however, arrangements are different. Aggressiveness and submissiveness are permitted and are assigned to both men and women. Now women's liberation is hardly a novelty. There was a countercultural outbreak of women's liberation in the years before World War I; there was a widespread outbreak of it in the middle of the nineteenth century, another at the end of the eighteenth, another at the end of the seventeenth, another in the sixteenth, and another, in the form of Mariolatry, in the Middle Ages. In European culture, at any rate, it has been a recurrent phenomenon, and in the remissive culture it has been a constant.

What is going on here can, I think, be understood if we consider the phenomenon of violence in movies and in television, not to speak of the violence that was common in nineteenth-century popular literature, a violence which became more widespread as literacy became almost universal, nor of the violence in folklore and other literatures. Social interaction depends, of course, on the control of aggression, and among very primitive food-gatherers, the noneconomic cultural life is almost entirely devoted to such control. Among the Eskimos, an outbreak of aggressive violence is treated in a therapeutic group of the entire community and is judged to be symptomatic of a psychic illness. However, as the cultural boundaries within a society and between societies become penetrable, and as the density of population increases, aggressiveness must be increased to gain control of economic goods and at the same time must be lowered to permit economic exchange of goods. Modern societies, made up as they are of innumerable and mutually incoherent cultural strains, of a great variety of incompatible modes of limiting the range of behavior, that is, of interests, are filled with occasions for occurrences of aggressive violence. Consequently the threshold of aggressiveness must be raised, or God is a god of Love. On the other hand to maintain itself as an ongoing enterprise, a modern society, that is, the individuals in that society, must also maintain a certain level of aggressiveness, or God is a god of Wrath. The threshold of aggressiveness must be lowered. Now it is not true that women are less aggressive than men, either by nature or in practice, but it is true that the culture in distinguishing between aggressiveness and submission, or seduction, has assigned to men aggressiveness and to women submissiveness. That is, masculinity and femininity are the two factors in a dichotomous semiotic system. But of course a culture consists of sets of directions for performance, people follow those directions, and women tend thus to adopt a semiotic system as a social rule. Thus, just as the violence in imaginative fiction, both verbal and visual, serves to maintain a necessary level of aggressiveness, so outbreaks of women's liberation serve to maintain the aggressiveness of women. The female colleague I have mentioned is more aggressive than most men, certainly more aggressive than most male academics; she has little need for women's liberation. In short, women's liberation as counterculture is neither very innovative nor very counter, since it does little more than confirm a state of affairs which already exists, but which is not publicly recognized. From a sufficiently remote position, the apparent incoherence of the aims of women's liberation, raising women's aggressiveness and reducing everybody's, is a special case of the general problem of culture, controlling aggressiveness and maintaining it at an effective level.

The question then raises itself as to whether a genuine counterculture is even possible. After all, what I have called the nineteenth-century counterculture of sexual repressiveness was scarcely novel, though its widespread, albeit temporary, success was. Sexual repression in the form of culturally induced celibacy is not only as old as Christianity but far older. Physiologically arranged celibacy in the form of a castrated priesthood was not the only form. On the other hand, Norman O. Brown's countercultural claim for the validity of polymorphous perversity is little more than an attempt to validate publicly what has been going on all along in the remissive culture. In making the world go round, incest is probably more important than love. I do not mean to imply, however, that the introduction into the public culture and thus the attempted validation of the remissive culture is unimportant. If the problem of any individual, and therefore the problem of a society, the sum of individual behavior, is the irresolvable problem of continuously being engaged in raising the level of aggressiveness and seductiveness and also of lowering it, then a countercultural attempt to change the conventionalized and culturally validated strategies for handling the problem is obviously of great importance. It is an attempt to restructure the standardized mode of limiting the range of behavior, and therefore of decision making. This can be understood better if we consider what is meant by the term "culture."

Culture is not some vague entity that floats around in our heads; it is not a collection of what we call ideas. It is, on the contrary, something quite specific and easily observable. I have suggested that culture emerges as the brain becomes increasingly capable of producing randomness of response. Culture, then, consists of limitations upon that randomness. But it can be put more precisely than that. Culture is directions for performance, and such directions are easily observable. They consist of verbal and nonverbal signs, and not only humanly produced signs but signs in the nonhuman world to which response has been conventionalized. A cultural object, then, is anything to which response has been conventionalized, and from this point of view words and sentences are objects. But in addition, performances in response to cultural directions are themselves instructions for performance. For example, as soon as there was one airplane hijacking, there followed immediately a number of them. Likewise, recent studies of suicide have shown that when a conspicuous and well-publicized person commits suicide, there is at once a wave of suicides. Evidently, there are always some people in such a state of indecision about what to do next that any resolution of that indecision is attractive. But such cases are only special and conspicuous instances, that is, newsworthy instances, of the ordinary condition of everybody. What to do next is a continuous problem. That is, controlling randomness and raising and lowering aggression are ever-present problems. When we put this together with the attractiveness of vandalism in providing the sense of aggressive adequacy, it is easy to see why a well-publicized countercultural effort immediately attracts a following. A counterculture effort is, after all, something to do. We can be sure that the really quite imaginative undertaking of the Symbionese Liberation Army will be widely imitated.

A counterculture, then, may be defined as an effort to change by negation and inversion the conventionalized instruction for performance as redundantly uttered in the public culture. Moreover, a counterculture is also ideological, or, if you wish, metaphysical. A counterculture, in its effort to change performance, must negate the explanation, justification, and validation of that performance. This is the explanation for the ideological vandalism which is a necessary factor in any countercultural effort. Whenever there is a countercultural effort, it is always attacked because it is accused of undermining the very foundations of society. What this means is that the counterculture is attacking the explanatory validations of the public culture, and such accusations are entirely justified. That being the case, the question also arises as to why the counterculture should wish to do so, and that raises the more general question of why countercultures do indeed emerge.

One reason may be briefly disposed of. The nineteenth century experienced a greater frequency of the incidence of countercultures than had ever previously occurred in so short a period. By the end of the century there had emerged the paradoxical situation that the mounting of countercultures had become a factor, even though a minor factor, in the public culture itself. If, as seems to be the case, the incidence of the appearance of countercultures increases as the century goes on, then we have the same phenomenon that is to be observed in the incidence of airplane hijacking or suicides after the suicide of a well-publicized individual. To mount a counterculture had become something to do, and the techniques for doing so had become well established.

Nevertheless countercultures are mounted in response to something in the sociocultural situation, something that is seen by a few individuals as a failure or breakdown in the culture and in social management. I believe two varieties can be discriminated, one an incoherence in the ideology of the public culture, and the other a gross antithesis between the public culture and the remissive culture. Of the first the nineteenth-century American abolitionist movement is an instance. On the one hand the public culture maintained that all men are and ought to be free, but on the other hand it also maintained that some men, specifically blacks, are and ought to be slaves. This counterculture was eventually successful, at least legally. But in terms of performances, of course, it was not. That is, freedom for the slaves meant the emergence of a remissive culture which was in gross contradiction to the public cultural ideology of social, cultural, and economic freedom. Thus some fifteen years ago the black liberation counterculture was mounted. The explanation for the timing of that effort can probably be found in the fact that as the country became strikingly wealthier, the blacks were not sharing that prosperity. Thus for a few blacks, and even fewer whites, the gross contradiction between the public culture and the remissive culture for the social management of blacks became intolerable. But only for a few, of course. For the overwhelming bulk of Americans, black and white, the contradiction continues to be quite tolerable, although, to be sure, the incidence of such toleration is probably higher among whites than blacks. By tolerable, of course, I do not mean that it is approved of; merely that it is not seized as an occasion for the mounting of or participation in the counterculture of black liberation. It will be interesting to observe, as the country becomes progressively less prosperous, as I suspect it will for the rest of this century and probably indefinitely into the future, whether or not the black liberation counterculture recedes. I rather suspect it will, and I think it is possible already to see signs of that recession. That is, the grossness of the contradiction will become more tolerable as it becomes less gross, not through the economic improvement of blacks, but through the economic deterioration of whites.

An example of a counter-counterculture will make this principle a little clearer.

I have suggested that what we think of as Victorian sexual repressiveness was actually a counterculture that emerged in the course of the nineteenth century. It was successful as a public culture because, given the gross contradiction between the public and the remissive cultures, it was able to govern much remissive behavior—though probably a statistical minority of it—by the public culture, and thereby bring some of the remissive into the public. The publication of the first Kinsey report, however, revealed that the culture of sexual repression had not been nearly so successful as had been thought. In that publication began the counter-counterculture that led in time to what is now called the sexual revolution. It is not, consequently, a simple return to the prerepressive system, for the difference is that sexual license has now assumed a place within the public culture. The contradiction is no longer between the public and the remissive, but rather in the incoherence of two aspects of the public culture. The struggle is now ideological. What will happen remains to be seen. The public culture of sexual license may quite possibly overwhelm the public culture of sexual repression and exterminate it, or more likely it will force it into the remissive culture, so that people will pay lip service to sexual license but secretly live lives of sexual repression. Self-castration may become the remissive style, as it has in the past. Possibly the countercultural and sexually repressive Jesus movement is already a symptom of what is to come. On the other hand it is equally possible that the repressive may defeat the licentious. Since the wealthy have always lived lives of license, the increasing impoverishment of the country may bring about a return to the domination of the public culture by sexual repression.

But all of these examples are superficial in the sense that they are not aimed at the foundations of society; they do not challenge but confirm the necessity for conventionalized patterns and roles of aggression and submission and the centrality of the sexual strategy for limiting the range of behavior. I describe this kind of counterculture as polarized. By this I mean that a contradiction or incoherence is observed and that the counterculture responds to that observation by assigning negative and positive poles and assuming the role of urging the unique value of the positive pole. Either pole can be made positive or negative, of course, as in the two countercultures of sexual repression and sexual license. Furthermore, in the nineteenth century—and today—the situation is further complicated by the fact that, in the level of high culture or the regressive ideological level, there was not a single culture but in fact three, which we may compare with three geological strata. The oldest and the least important at the highest cultural levels was that of Christianity, or, preferably, the Platonistic-Christian tradition. The great shock to European culture was, of course, the French Revolution. Its effect on those whose Christianity was not disturbed was to intensify Christian behavioral repressiveness, and not least in the centrally important sphere of sexual conduct. Since to this tradition the French Revolution so clearly demonstrated the sinfulness of man, the Christian countercultural effort was the invasion of the remissive, the social space where sinfulness was in effect remitted, and more, encouraged. The intensification of evangelicalism after the French Revolution is well known. Thus, this kind of countercultural effort was of the polarization type.

The second stratum was the Rationalist-Enlightenment tradition. The failure of the French Revolution and its transformation into a military dictatorship did not by any means discourage this cultural tradition. There was, by the end of the eighteenth century, a sufficient injection of pessimism into Enlightenment optimism to make failure tolerable. Many of the countercultural efforts of the nineteenth century emerged from this tradition and were efforts to extend into the public culture, and particularly into politics, the principles of the French Revolution. An example is the women's liberation movement of the mid-nineteenth century, which extended from America to Russia and of which *A Doll's House* was by no means an early manifestation. Similar were many of the countercultural efforts called positivistic, which only apparently stemmed from Comte, who was generally misunderstood, as indeed, judging by references to him in the literature of the behavioral sciences, he still is. In England, of course, the tradition of utilitarianism was more obviously Enlightenment in origin, while in Russia the name given by Turgenev, "nihilism," concealed the Enlightenment tradition. This also was a counterculture of polarization. A recent Enlightenment counterculture, that of the 1960s, the ideology of which can be found in Schiller's late Enlightenment *Kabale und Liebe,* shows the vitality and even the dominance of this tradition in the public culture. The third stratum laid down—and I think there has been no stratum laid down since—was that of Romanticism. This was the innovative counterculture of the nineteenth century, because it was a response to what was perceived as the consequence of the French Revolution, the collapse of European explanations of the world, and it judged the Enlightenment itself to have been little more than a secularized version of Christianity. The countercultures in this tradition were like those of the first at least in this: the century saw a series of countercultural efforts, independent of one another but showing the same pattern.

Three romantic countercultural traditions may, I think, be discerned. The first two were based on the perception of, as I have suggested, the collapse of European explanations of the world, metaphysics if you wish. The first, which dominated the first forty or fifty years, consisted of a series of attempts to create new explanations of the world, and, like the explanations of Christianity and the Enlightenment, they were redemptive explanations, in the form of new interpretations of Christian rhetoric, or in the form of reasonably innovative religious and metaphysical schemes and systems, or in the form of social redemption, such as that of Marx and of so many others in the 1830s and 1840s. After the events of 1848 and 1849 it was extremely difficult to mount this kind of counterculture. These were polarized countercultures, in that the possibility of redemptive explanation was selected from the traditional public culture, but the rest of that public culture was pretty generally rejected.

A second kind was more subtle, lasted longer, and still continues, as indeed does the first. The effect of the French Revolution was the collapse not of explanations of the world but of explanation itself. Explanation and redemption were shifted from the verbal to the subjective experiential, to the redemptive experience of the fusion of subject and object, to, in short, a feeling state. In this tradition are to be found principally the countercultures of aestheticism and eroticism, which are frequently found together. The *Playboy* philosophy is probably best understood as a vulgarization or, to be a little nicer about it, a penetration of romantic erotic redemption into a lower cultural level. I believe the deliberate destruction of the arts by the *avant-garde* artists of the last fifteen years is in fact a countercultural rejection of the once counterculture but subsequently public culture of aesthetic redemptionism. This tradition too is a polarized counterculture, since it selects from the traditional culture religious or mystic experience, although it rejects the theological or verbal explanation, justification, and validation of that experience.

Finally, the third tradition of Romantic countercultures is, for the first time, a nonpolarized or genuinely alienated counterculture. So far it has had little effect, except at the highest cultural levels. The second Romantic tradition rejected explanation but accepted existential or experiential redemption. The third Romantic tradition rejected both. A late manifestation may be found in the penetrating Freud, Freud the moralist, not in the superficial Freud, the scientist and psychologizing metaphysician. When Freud asserted in his grim optimism that civilization, what I have been calling culture, presents irresolvable problems and that the only hope lies in facing that fact, and when he implied that neurosis cannot be cured but only lived with and used, he was in the tradition of alienated counterculture. To use old-fashioned terms, the Christian tradition asserted that the object could be absorbed and redeemed by the subject, and the Enlightenment that the subject could be absorbed and redeemed by the object. This is the most ancient tradition of human culture, for it is the redemptive-explanatory-apocalyptic tradition. It asserts that the highest aim of man is the resolution of tension, the final and permanent limitation of the range of behavior, the freedom from decision making, the absorption into God or into Nature, according to whichever explanatory stratum you belonged to or happened to prefer. It is this redemptive tradition, traceable from the early Paleolithic, and in all culture, which is the overwhelmingly predominant and redundantly maintained ultimate of human culture, the tradition which makes it possible for the public culture and the remissive culture to live side by side, in spite of the occasional outbreaks of the kind of countercultural efforts I have discussed. And it is this most ancient cultural tradition with which the third type of Romantic counterculture drastically broke, which that counterculture so utterly vandalized. It can be found as early as Senancour's *Obermann,* the last book of *The Prelude,* and Hegel's *Phenomenology,* and as recently as the last period of Wittgenstein. It can be found in Boltzmann, Vaihinger, and Nietzsche, and in Dostoevsky, when he was able to maintain it and did not collapse into sentimentality. It asserts that the relation between subject and object is one of irresolvable tensions, or, to use my own repulsive jargon, that the gap between sensory input and semiotic process cannot be crossed either explanatorily or experientially. Its implications are frightening, for it asserts that the human species must develop a genetically transmitted ability to tolerate tension which it does not have, and it takes about a million years to establish a new genetic attribute.

The student of nineteenth-century countercultures, then, will find them in great numbers and in four polarized traditions, countercultures which are superficial and fundamentally, in spite of appearances, confirmatory of the culture which they are apparently countering. But he will find only one countercultural tradition which is genuinely an alienated counterculture, for it is counter to the central tendency of human culture itself, as it has so far existed. It may be that this last mode of nineteenth- and twentieth-century countercultures is the only valuable one, the only one which is not, in the last analysis, comic.

# CHAPTER EIGHT

# Edgar Saltus and the Heroic Decadence

From questioning academic colleagues at my own institution and elsewhere I have gathered that Edgar Saltus is now scarcely known and even less read. To be sure, there have been dissertations about him and an occasional article or two, and a book in the Twayne series. Yet on the whole Saltus seems to have been pretty well forgotten. I have been surprised at this disappearance, for fifty years ago and still in the early 1930s his was an important name. About him there was a certain mystery and advisability of caution, as of a man somewhat dangerous and certainly very daring. It was the opinion that he had led directly to the modern world, or at least to the modernism of the 1920s, by way of James Huneker and H. L. Mencken, his heirs and descendants. In 1925 and 1926, for example, Brentano's republished most of his work.

The socioeconomic crisis of the 1930s and the social consciousness of writers and critics wiped him out. A "decadent" was considered to be just that, and the decadence, thoroughly misunderstood, was judged to be a totally extinct movement. In recent years, however, the late nineteenth century has begun to be taken a little more seriously, at least in the visual arts. Decadence, Symbolism, Aestheticism, and particularly their culmination in Art Nouveau are not only fashionable again but are coming to be seriously studied. It is beginning to be grasped that what these names together subsume was not an aberration, or a mistake, or a minor episode, but on the contrary had emerged necessarily from what had preceded and was the necessary precursor to what follows. In art history it is a serious question as to whether Art Nouveau should be thought of as the last of the nineteenth-century styles or the first modern style. The important matter is not how this question is resolved but that Art Nouveau be understood. Its importance was placing style itself as central to art. Once that had been done, the stylistic freedom and radical innovation of modernism became possible. And this very centrality of style marks the work of Saltus and shows that his contemporaneity with the emergence and temporary domination of Art Nouveau made Saltus and Art Nouveau culturally convergent. Saltus, insofar as he is remembered at all, is remembered as a brilliant stylist, and when I was young it was for his style that he was judged to be of the first importance in the development of modern American literature. To understand the place of style, then, in the complex of Aestheticism, Decadence, Symbolism, and Art Nouveau is to understand the historical position of Saltus in the history of nineteenth-century culture, best comprehended if Europe and the Americas are conceived of as a single culture area.

In *Beyond the Tragic Vision* (1962) I proposed that the term "Stylism" be used in the place of "Aestheticism" as a more satisfactory term for the cultural character of the late nineteenth century. If "aestheticism" is appropriately interpreted as meaning the centrality of art in the work of art rather than the centrality of morality or ideology or political commitment, and so on, then aestheticism is by no means a defining attribute of late nineteenth-century cultural history. It is to be found in Gautier quite explicitly in the 1830s, and implicitly from the beginning of the century, most obviously in the form of the radical creativity of the artist—the notion that artistic creativity in itself is the primary and even the exclusive value of the work of art, rather than any propositional meaning the work of art is interpreted as implying. The "Religion of Art," art as the source of value and even redemption, has indeed been a central issue of Romanticism from its earliest days. On the other hand, when one examines the critical writings of Aestheticism, it is obvious that the central concern at this period was not art but style. The centrality of the issue of style is to be found in such widely diverse phenomena as the writings of Nietzsche and the revival and validation of Dandyism.

The first clue to this placing of style as the central issue is to be found in the fact that style is a universal attribute of all behavior. That is, all behavior is styled. To be sure, ordinarily we do not respond to the style of an individual or his products unless it is significantly different in its attributes from the attributes of other individuals in the same context, or significantly, unless we wish to distinguish an individual from other individuals, to indicate how he can be told apart from the others, or separated from them. That is why we can discuss the style of a category of any size, from an individual to an entire culture, why we can talk about the difference in philosophical style of Eastern and Western culture, or of Schopenhauer and Hegel, near contemporaries within the same culture.

If, however, we wish to understand how style emerges in the behavior of an individual, without reference to other individuals belonging to the same category, we must understand that in this sense also style is a behavioral universal. Every individual is marked by a unique style, and furthermore that style tends to be more marked as the individual ages. To understand this it is appropriate to consider the behavioral (not biological) individuals as precipitate of culture, and moreover a randomly assembled package of behavioral patterns, learned from others. But in both the precipitation and the learning the behavioral consequences are unique for each individual. First, the precipitation, since it is randomly assembled, necessarily results in behavioral uniqueness for each biological individual. That is, no two individuals will be assemblages of precisely identical package contents. Second, each behavioral pattern learned is distorted, or modified, randomly in the learning process. No individual can learn any behavioral pattern perfectly or precisely, and the learning can be marked by anything from a fairly close replication of the learned pattern to a widely divergent one. Third, the individual is not a passive recipient of the cultural package or any of the contents of behavioral patterns, but rather interprets the patterns and above all innovates the combination or interactions of the learned patterns as he learns them, in addition to the fact that the various patterns interact and affect each other in ways unique for each behavioral individual. Fourth, as he grows, the behavioral individual develops a "mental construct" (as I shall call it for the moment) of himself, a persona, a coherent interpretation of his behavioral patterns, an interpretation which is both selective and deceptive, modeled as it must be on personal patterns in his cultural environment.

However, "mental construct" is an inadequate and deceiving term. Rather, what we are responding to when we use the term is a transformation in the individual's behavior of the materials of his culture. That transformation is, of course, observable, as certainly a "mental construct" is not. That latter term merely is our attempt to explain and subsume the uniqueness of the behavioral attributes resulting from the transformation. As the individual grows he tends to maintain his persona, the result of that transformation, and the persona itself now governs his behavior, with the result that it becomes less deceptive. The transformation, which involves all of the factors considered above, is the style of the individual.

Moreover, it is easily observable that as an individual distinguishes himself from individuals of the same category he intensifies his style, just as whenever we wish to single out a member of any category, we select its distinguishing attributes. The way we distinguish the style of one A&P from the style of another is identical with the way the individual separates himself from others by stylistic intensification. In the same way the neurotic or the psychotic will either intensify his persona or abandon the attempt to maintain it. The former strategy brings out the defensive possibility of stylistic intensification, of style itself. But such defensiveness can also be interpreted as an aggressive strategy. The difference between the style of the individual and that of his individual situation provides him with a platform of distinctiveness to which he can ascribe value and which he can use as a position for denigrating others. The history of Romanticism is the history of style as a strategy for maintaining alienation and for aggressive attacks on the surrounding culture, an action made desirable because the ideological justifications for the persona styles and their supporting culture had, for the Romantic, collapsed into invalidity. For this reason there is no Romantic style, as there are Baroque, Gothic, Rococo, or Renaissance styles, and so on. On the other hand, style itself became in the late nineteenth century the central issue of the Romantic tradition, for the central importance of style as a strategy for maintaining alienation and cultural vandalism was consciously realized.

This development, occurring in individual artists and writers with increasing frequency in the course of the 1860s and 1870s, was precipitated by the culturally advanced tone of the 1850s. The failure of the revolutions of 1848 and 1849 terminated a period marked by a transcendental redemptionism, the conviction that the Romantic tradition—peculiarly fused with Enlightenment thinking, from which Romanticism had not yet fully separated itself—was capable of redeeming society by reforming it, revolutionizing it, and reconstructing it, according to new principles of a transcendent origin, even if, like Marxist historicism, it was disguised as a nontranscendent materialism. The almost accidental revival of Schopenhauer in the early 1850s, facilitated by the publication of his essays, *Parerga and Paralipomena* (1851), was symptomatic of the new pessimism, the abandonment of the notion of redeeming the social order, and of the hope for the possibility of a society responsive to the needs of all individuals yet marked by an absence of conflict among individuals, that is, marked by community. This pessimism about society and the dominant culture required for justification and for self-protection an ideology which was free of ideological commitment. Not a metaphysical explanation and justification of the human enterprise was the necessity but, as Henry James later put it, a figure in the carpet. Thus style, implicit in the Romantic tradition, emerged as offensive and defensive armor against the economic conditions of society and the cultural superstructure of those economic conditions.

The transition from what I have called "objectism," the pessimistic mood of the 1850s and the early 1860s, to Stylism can be seen in the shift in the history of what is inaccurately called Impressionist painting. About 1880 the program of these painters shifted from an interest in presenting the world of appearance as pure object to an interest in creating a surface of color, one in which the object subjected to semiotic transformation in the painting was less important than the imaginative style, increasingly expressionistic, governing that transformation. The next logical consequence was the kind of painting, and poetry, known as Symbolism, the creation of a work which so juxtaposed recognizable configurations that the impulse to explanation was both aroused and frustrated. The result was that an inexplicable feeling was both the source of the work and what the work elicited. From this it was but a step, in the visual arts, to the creation of Art Nouveau, an entirely self-conscious effort to create a unique style evocative of feeling but not of meaning. In the United States, the equivalent of Art Nouveau is the work of Frank Lloyd Wright, who, in fact, never moved out of it, even in his latest works.

This, then, was the cultural situation of Edgar Saltus, for like most American writers of the nineteenth and early twentieth centuries, he is far more easily understood in terms of what was happening in European culture than in what was happening culturally in this country. Born in 1855, he was twelve years younger than Henry James, and like James traveled extensively in Europe and came to know European writers and artists. James's grand tour as an adult was in 1869 and 1870, Saltus's from 1873 to 1878. The intense "aestheticism" of both emerges with great power from James's letters of that tour. But among other people that Saltus called upon during those years was Edouard von Hartmann, the successor of Schopenhauer in the philosophy of pessimism, and even more pessimistic than his master. Hartmann published *Die Philosophie des Unbewussten* in Berlin in 1869; it was translated by W. C. Coupland as *The Philosophy of the Unconscious* and was published in London in 1884. In 1885 Saltus published his first study of pessimism, *The Philosophy of Disenchantment*, a work in which in Chapter 5, "The Great Quietus," he described his visit to Hartmann, who was living in Berlin. This presumably occurred during the period in the 1870s when Saltus was studying in both Heidelberg and Munich. It seems probable that the current enthusiasm for Schopenhauer, by no means then novel, led him to the study of Hartmann.

Saltus's first book was a brief essay on Balzac. This first effort was not inappropriate to his interest in pessimism, for Balzac was a naive sociological novelist, while the Goncourts and Zola, who in the 1880s was publishing the first part of the Rougon-Macquart series, were examples of the ideologically self-conscious stage of sociological fiction, marked by an extreme social pessimism. Saltus's next two books, then, are fruitfully understood as the effort to get at the strain in the Romantic tradition which underlay Balzac and was obvious in the most important fiction of the 1880s. These two interests, the philosophical and the sociological, emerge in Saltus's third book. *The Philosophy of Disenchantment* was not a work of formal philosophy but rather a popularization—and a very good one—of a philosophical tradition of the nineteenth century, as found in the magnificent poetry of Leopardi, in Schopenhauer, and in Hartmann. *The Anatomy of Negation* is particularly interesting because it is an effort to study the pessimistic negation of the value of existence from ancient times, beginning with the Buddha, to the 1880s, and to study that tradition in terms of the religious and social human conditions from which it emerged. The climax is a passage on Leconte de Lisle, "perhaps the most perfect poet of France" and certainly the most austerely pessimistic.

The other step forward in this second study of pessimism was the appearance of Saltus's style, not yet perhaps in its full maturity, but certainly remarkable for its crispness and its vividness. In her book on Saltus (New York: Twayne, 1968) Claire Sprague has analyzed that style too well for further discussion to be necessary here. At this point it is enough to recognize the emergence of that style from an intense study of pessimism and negation. What lay in the future for Saltus at his best is the use of that style to relate historical circumstances which in their horror justified that pessimism. His novels, together with his extremely voluminous journalistic essays, are, with the exception of the first novel, *Mr. Incoul's Misadventure*, a commercialization of both his style and his philosophy, a condition that necessarily softened the latter. (A collection of some of these popular essays, *The Pomps of Satan* [1904], is an excellent demonstration of how his position could be made amusingly fit for popular consumption.) That first novel, however, is at least a fairly successful effort to present that inherent human viciousness which justifies pessimism and negation. For it is a story of how a proud American aristocrat revenges himself upon his wife and her lover, and is both undetected and unpunished.

A full justification for pessimism, however, is to be found in history; and in *Imperial Purple* Saltus used the history of the Julian and Claudian emperors to exemplify the human capacity for viciousness. Mr. Incoul is a worthy companion of these emperors, for he too is thoroughly protected from the consequences of his two murders by his wealth and his social position. The Caesars had unlimited power and wealth. There was no ideology capable of imposing a morality, nor any social power capable of controlling the pleasure to be found in exerting the most brutal and revolting subjection, exploitation, humiliation, torture, and murder on less powerful human beings. Saltus's point certainly seems to be that when human beings can do exactly as they wish, this is the way they are likely to behave. *Imperial Purple* was published in 1892. Nearly thirty years later the Russian Revolution gave him the opportunity to repeat his message. *Imperial Orgy*, an account of the horrors of Russian Czars beginning with Ivan the Terrible, is even more powerful than the first analysis of imperial pleasure seeking, though not so well written; for it countered the point that the Caesars were pre-Christian. Russia was a Christian country, and the Russian czars were Orthodox Christians. Nevertheless, their autocratic viciousness was if anything even more spectacular than that of the Roman Caesars. Saltus had the prescience to perceive that, given the tradition of Russian rulers, the new intellectual and proletarian rulers would be little different, and they have not been, though certainly less imaginative, except in their steady continuance of the Czarist tradition of imperialistic expansionism.

The shudder of human history became Saltus's most serious interest, one which extends to the analysis of religion and its consequences in *The Lords of the Ghostland* and of the relation of sexuality to power in *Historia Amoris*. A passage from the latter illustrates his position.

The boredom came from precocious pleasure that had left [Louis XV], without energy or conviction, a cold, dreary brute, Asiatic and animal, who, while figuratively a spoke in the wheel of monarchy then rolling down to '89, personally was a minotaur in a feminine labyrinth which he filled, emptied, renewed, indifferent to the inmates as he was to his wife, wringing for the various Petticoats prodigal sums from a desolate land, supplying incidentally to fermiers generaux and grand seigneurs an example of Tiberianism which, assured of immunity, they greedily followed, and, generally, making himself so loathed that when he died, delight was national. (*Historia Amoris*, 1925?, p. 247)

Saltus was willing to face the horror of history, of religion, of sex—of human behavior—and for this reason I have used the word "heroic." For that willingness he shared with the other decadents. The term "decadence" was used by the decadents themselves. But does it mean they were living in a time of decadence, or that they were decadents in a time of social health? Certainly it has been the second meaning that has been used against them, and has justified both their denigration and the failure to comprehend the cultural significance of their movement. It was, I think, a moment within the larger movement which I have called Stylism, and exhibits the offensive and vandalistic potentialities of Stylism. I have called the decadents heroic, for at a time of sentimentality and bourgeois optimism, they had the courage to see the horror of humanity, evinced when it is not under social control, and the shudder of history.

Yet, much as we may regret it, Saltus himself was not able entirely to sustain his position. Like so many of the decadents he turned to an innovative transcendentalism, specifically theosophy, at the end of the *Lords of the Ghostland* and in several of his novels. "It would certainly be a species of snobbery to accept theosophy in Yeats and to reject it in Saltus," Clair Sprague writes (p. 42). I am not a snob; I reject it in Yeats. It is particularly depressing that Saltus was capable of conceiving of Russian bolshevism as a force directed from transcendental realms and designed to cleanse the world for a redemptive rebirth. This failure of nerve on the part of Yeats and Saltus and other decadents, though by no means most of them, is indeed depressing. But it is not difficult to account for it. Religious belief, together with various forms of philosophical transcendentalism and idealism, was the enormous redundancy of the culture surrounding Saltus, and there is more excuse for him than for Yeats, who lived in a more intellectually sophisticated and realistic cultural environment. Saltus's failure, though not complete, nor so complete as Yeats's, nor so intellectually damaging, reveals the necessity for stylism and the "decadence," and shows the extreme importance of style as a strategy both for maintaining protection against culturally redundant absurdities and for mounting heroically vandalistic attacks upon that culture and its untenable beliefs. But that failure also shows that style is not in itself enough, nor are art and beauty as instances of style. None of these turned out to be powerful enough to sustain a self-ascription of value. To find a more powerful strategy remained the problem of the next stage of Romantic tradition of European culture.

# CHAPTER NINE

# Romanticism, Surrealism, *Terra Nostra*

That *Terra Nostra* is a surrealistic work is at least the most obvious way to categorize it. Yet it may be surrealism with a difference, a work which uses the devices of surrealism but in which Carlos Fuentes has transcended the ideology of surrealism. The simplest definition of surrealism is that it is an artistic strategy which expresses the unconscious. At least that is the sort of definition which I have encountered, and it certainly was the claim for surrealism when the first large-scale American exhibition of surrealism was presented at the Museum of Modern Art in the 1930s. Yet I do not believe for a moment that this notion of surrealism is at all satisfactory, or in any way is descriptive of what is going on in surrealist strategies.

My principal objection is the very notion of "the unconscious." It never fails to surprise me that people talk about the contents of the unconscious with all the confidence of a Southern Baptist informing us, frequently in the daily press, all about the will and intention of God; or of an orthodox Marxist telling us all about the meaning of history and the consummation towards which it necessarily moves. I am reminded of Matthew Arnold's remark about the evangelicals of his day, who talked, he said, about the Trinity as if it (they?) lived just around the corner. I am perfectly willing to accept the notion of an unconscious mind, though I have very strong doubts about the usefulness of the notion of a conscious mind. And as for the content of the unconscious, the unconscious is precisely that, unconscious, and it is going to remain so. All that we can know about unconscious thinking is that its processes are analogical, but since analogy is ultimately the only strategy that any kind of thinking has or can have, it is neither surprising nor very instructive that analogy is also the process of unconscious thought. Moreover, the word "thought" is so vague and so regressive from the phenomenally observable that it is hardly more than a card we play in order to win a trick or two, a kind of joker in the pack.

What then are these alleged accounts of the content of the unconscious? I think it is most useful to judge them to be the mythologies of a secularized culture. Sometimes, indeed, such mythology is barely secularized, a secularization, as in Jung, that is hardly more than a scanty fig leaf scarcely hiding an embarrassing religiosity. That the surrealists in their heyday may very well have believed that their art really was a projection of the unconscious we need not doubt, but we need not take their claims seriously. It is instructive, for example, that the popularity of psychoanalysis and the subsequent effort of surrealism were immediately preceded in European culture by a widespread revival of the occult, of spiritualism, of theosophy, a popularity that extended from San Francisco to Moscow. Skryabin and Yeats are but two of the many superb artists of the time whose justifying ideologies make one blush for them. At a lower cultural level and at the present time we have the same phenomenon in the widespread belief in close encounters of the third kind, not to speak of the first and second.

Still, it is hardly fair to call psychoanalytic interpretation and surrealism constructive mythologies without committing oneself to some notion about what mythology might be. Plato caught Western thinking in a trap from which it has barely been able to escape when he attempted to build a concept of mind from the perceptual experiences of the individual organism. He observed that an idea does not correspond to a phenomenal configuration subsumed by that idea. Or— to avoid the use of that vexing term "idea"—he observed that the attributes of a categorial expectancy do not correspond with the attributes of a configuration which otherwise satisfies the demands of that expectancy. Where, then, did that categorial expectancy come from? It came, Plato said, from a divine or transcendent source. That explanation of his is a mythological explanation. We can say today with considerable confidence that perception is not under divine control, but is under cultural control; like the nature of the brain, however, cultural control varies in its effects from individual to individual, that variability being subsumed by the word "mind." Or else, in the individual mind, perception is a more or less distorted precipitate of culture. Surely that has been evident ever since Hegel, whose "Geist" is virtually identical with "culture" in the anthropological sense.

Continuing to see Plato's observation for the moment, mind is the negation of the phenomenal, or the other way around. It makes no difference. But substituting for Plato's unfortunate "idea" the term culture, we find that culture is the negation of nature. This gets us a little closer to understanding mythology. To understand it better we must imagine the remote period when a group of higher hominids, already adept in semiosis, like all higher animals—that is, already governing their behavior by culture rather than by genetic programming—when a group of higher hominids, then, freed semiosis from its former dependence upon the perception of phenomenal configurations. That is, on a foundation of nonverbal semiosis they invented verbal semiosis, or language. Semiosis became free from immediate stimulation of perceptual configurations, except for a limited category of sounds. That extraordinary act of analogical generalization gave man his freedom. But we need not indulge ourselves in the metaphysical pathos of the word "freedom." It is sufficient to say that the invention of language made man's behavior indeterminable, no longer tied down to or locked into the phenomenal world. And that indeterminability made man a liar, that is, a mythologist. Man's capacity to lie is the only interesting thing I know about him. The indeterminability of human behavior requires, for the sake of economic interaction, human control over that indeterminability. And that control is human culture, a very different matter from animal culture, for human cultural control is both required and made possible by language. For this reason human culture is the negation of nature. Culture, then, consists of instructions for human behavior, instructions made necessary by the indeterminability of behavior that language has given to man. Mythology is an explanatory exemplification, a justification, and a validation of those instructions. Mythology is the ancient form of precisely that activity which today we call cultural anthropology.

The economic expansion of European civilization into other cultures brought about the analogical coordination of the mythologies from a wide variety of differing cultures, an investigation that continues today. That coordination was made possible because European civilization had already developed an abstract language which subsumed and explained its own mythologies, a development made necessary by the analogical similarities and dissimilarities of the various mythologies of the Mediterranean region, principally Greco-Roman and Judeo-Christian. The pre-Socratics were, so far as we know or ever can know, the first who generalized from mythologies into explanations more regressive from the phenomenal than are mythologies proper. As I have suggested, it is not difficult to see the persistence of mythology in Plato. That is, when he gets stuck in his abstract explanatory constructions, he falls back on mythology. In short, culture contact leads to syncretism, and syncretism gives birth to metaphysical abstraction.

The work of the surrealists, then, consisted of the mythologies of an insufficiently secularized culture, and I say "insufficiently" because it appears to be the case that the surrealists really believed that they were revealing the contents of the unconscious. But if they were not doing that—as I do not believe they were, partly because their work is so obviously under the control of their own high European culture—what were they doing? The technique of surrealism is very simple. It exploits the indeterminability of human behavior, and it does so by juxtaposing and combining categories which the controls of culture had hitherto kept separate and unrelated. That is, the surrealists exposed and exploited the cultural conventionality of categorization. The mythology of psychoanalysis provided the ideology and the cultural control which enabled them to do so. And it also provided the justification and direction for the inclusion in their work of a high degree of sexual content, a content which made it possible to vandalize the regnant cultural controls of their time and place, a vandalization which continued the vandalization initiated by psychoanalysis itself.

Let me make my position clear. I think cultural vandalism is an admirable activity, for it is the first and necessary step in exposing the inadequacy of those ideologies which are the ultimate verbal controls, the ultimate cultural controls, except for force itself, over our behavior. And ideologies are always inadequate to the situation to which they are applied, for they always have emerged from a preceding and necessarily different situation.

Now if this vandalization of the conventionality of European categorical modes, made all the more forceful by the inclusion of the forbidden, or at least forbidden for public display, was what the surrealists were up to, why were they doing it? To find answer to this we must go back nearly 180 years to the origins of Romanticism. Briefly, my notion of Romanticism is this. The Enlightenment was a mere secularization of Christian ideology. It was synthetic and redemptive. That is, like Christianity, it endeavored to construct an explanation of the world which would subsume all phenomena and which had as its aim the overcoming of the negation of nature and culture, of phenomenon and idea, of spirit and matter. To a handful of Europeans the failure of the French Revolution, its transformation into a bloody tyranny and then into an imperialistic dictatorship, a repetition of the history of Christianity itself, meant that the synthetic effort of human culture was a failure. Hitherto analysis had been in the service of synthesis. The aim of analysis—and this is still true to a great extent of Kant himself, with his impossible notion of duty—had been to clarify synthesis and increase its coherence. The twentieth century has been called the age of analysis, but I believe the age of analysis began with Romanticism, and in that sense the implications of Romanticism are still being realized and still have affected only a tiny fraction of the world population. The bulk of human explanation continues to be synthetic and redemptive; that is, the aim continues to be the final solution to the instability of human value by transcending the negation of nature and culture. But the Romantics accepted the irresolvable tension between subject and object, between nature and culture, between world and spirit. Romanticism struggled from the beginning to rid itself of synthetic redemptionism. It struggled throughout the nineteenth century to become an antimetaphysical metaphysic, an anti-ideological ideology.

A great step in the emergence of that position was the consequence of the failure of the revolutions of 1848 and 1849, a failure which Alexander Herzen, one of the most penetrating observers of his day, called the end of liberalism. In the 1850s Wagner rewrote the conclusion of the *Ring* so that it no longer ended with a synthetic redemptionism but rather with an analytic recognition of the insolubility of the dilemma of the human enterprise. *The history of Romanticism to this very moment is the history of the dismantlement of the ideological superstructure of Western culture.* It was the indeterminability of behavior that language has given man that was responsible for the fact that, under the control of culture, Wordsworth's Michael never lifted up another stone. But the most important question was asked by Hegel. He was not, I conclude from my study of Hegel, an idealist. He was a materialist, and I am not alone in thinking so. After all, Hegel said, What is mind but what human beings do? Nor, much more significantly, was he a great system builder, let alone a worshiper of the state. On the contrary, he asked a wholly novel question. The old metaphysical systems having failed, he asked, Why do men construct metaphysical systems? With this question, which the *Phenomenology* is engaged in posing, the analytic enterprise of Romanticism was out in the open, though to be sure not very many people were capable of recognizing it, so overwhelmingly powerful were the redundancies of synthetic redemptionism, as for the most part they still are.

Hegelianism, misunderstood, foundered, and the Romantic enterprise continued under the rubric of the words "self" and "identity."

I started using these words thirty years ago as a clue to Romanticism, and by now I am more than a little tired of hearing them. As I see it now these words have been the central terms of an ideological rhetoric which maintained the alienation of the Romantic from his culture, and in so doing maintained the high aggressive level of the Romantic's necessary and to me admirable vandalizing dismantlement of the superstructure of Western—and now, with the knowledge of cultural anthropology, of human—culture. I call it necessary and admirable, for there is not much hope for us unless we recognize the limitations of the human enterprise, those limitations being the indeterminability of human behavior, brought about by language, and the consequent necessity for ideological control of behavior, together with the recognition that all ideologies are and must be failures, not merely sooner or later, but as soon as they are applied without correction from that failure, as they almost invariably are.

Hence to the Romantic only the self remains sacred, that is, only the mythology of the self is capable of conferring value upon the individual, but because it is a mythology of the Protean self, the persona—a selective, deceptive, and coherent construct of our own behavior—Romanticism avoids the stabilizing effects, necessarily bloody, of the sacred in its religious modes and of the secular ideologies in their equivalent modes. But even a mythology of the self requires a social institution, and the Romantics found the appropriate institution in art. Hence the aestheticism of the late nineteenth century, the misnamed religion of art. For art, being the exemplification of ideologies, can exclude ideological discourse or, in the nonverbal arts, ideological symbolization, and thus can covertly undermine and vandalize the regnant ideologies of the culture, sustained by oppressive governments. Fuentes himself has pointed out this task of the arts to have been the traditional task of Latin American literature. In this enterprise the techniques of realism and naturalism are wonderfully effective, and are central to Romanticism, not a departure from it. It was art, then, that became the ideal vehicle for the vandalizing and culturally subversive ideologies of the various forms of psychoanalysis, even when, as was usually the case, psychoanalysis was synthetically redemptive. In the long run Freud was not redemptive—and here I agree with Philip Rieff—though Jung was. It needs to be noticed, however, that Freud has been misunderstood as thoroughly as Hegel, and psychoanalysis has been perverted from Freud's vision into an Enlightenment redemption. This need not surprise us, for psychiatrists are the moral policemen of a secularized society. At any rate, aestheticism as a strategy of institutionalizing value, the sacred, in the teeth of a culture overwhelmingly synthetically redemptive, was infused by the surrealists with the mythology of the unconscious. Historically, surrealism was of the greatest importance and essential to the Romantic enterprise of dismantling the superstructure of Western culture. For, as I have suggested, surrealism exposed the conventionality of human categorization, using the forbidden, sexuality, as its explosive force, a strategy inherited from those heroic individuals called the decadents.

For this reason surrealism was the most appropriate literary strategy for a writer deeply concerned with the Mexican experience, the current juxtaposition of the categories of Meso-American culture and European culture, an incoherence possibly more striking in Mexico and Peru than elsewhere in Latin America, for the pre-Conquest cultures in those areas were more developed than elsewhere in the Americas. The surrealistic tradition made it possible for Fuentes to avoid syncretism, to avoid the syntheses of Virgins of Guadaloupe and of bloody Christs renewing the fertility of the earth. Surrealism was the appropriate vehicle if one wished to expose the failure and the bloody destructiveness in the history of our earth of all Utopias, all synthetic efforts to resolve the indeterminability of human behavior into the determinability of nature. *Terra Nostra*, I believe, is in the high Romantic tradition. It is analytic. It uses surrealism to dismantle the pernicious pretensions of synthetic redemptionism, whether of Christianity, of popular millennialism, or of Aztec religion. It says, I think, that the only way man can resolve himself into nature is by dying, and that all attempts to do so are death bound.

And I would say that this way of looking at the book perhaps provides a way of understanding the last page. It has puzzled me greatly, for it appears at first glance to deny the marvelous analytic negative force of the rest of *Terra Nostra*. Paris, you will remember, is empty. Only "you" and Celestina remain. They don the masks. And are these not the masks of man the liar, the illusionist, the redemptionist? And in their sexual union they become one, and that one chatters, hysterically, I think, of future generations. But then comes the final sentence.

Twelve o'clock did not toll in the church towers of Paris; but the snow ceased, and the following day a cold sun shone.

Here I think Fuentes shows how far he had gone beyond surrealism. The surrealists believed in the mythologies of the unconscious. Fuentes does not. He merely uses them. He penetrates the mythologies language had created, and above all the mythology that is what we call history. But he has gone further. He has exploded the very explosive device of surrealism itself—sex. What is the redemptive synthetic mythology of modern Western man? It is sex.

If redemptive illusions, including the redemptive illusion of sex, are not hopeful, nothing about *Terra Nostra* is hopeful. But from the perspective of the reality-driven enterprise of Romanticism, the existence of *Terra Nostra* is hopeful, but only its existence.

# II

## THE USES OF IDEOLOGIES

# CHAPTER TEN

# Philosophy and Art
# as Related and Unrelated
# Modes of Behavior

Let me make it clear at once that the word "behavior" in the title of this paper has nothing to do with academic professional behaviorism, or neobehaviorism. A reading of the forty-five papers in the *Handbook of General Psychology,* edited by Benjamin B. Wolman, published last summer, has led me to the conclusion that traditional behaviorist psychology, though capable of low-level generalizations, many of which can be used advantageously by the observer of philosophy and art, is not capable of constructing a general theory of human behavior above the level of such generalizations. This does not mean, however, that I find humanistic psychology more promising, since a great deal of it is made up of instructions and recipes on how to live. I daresay the reasons for the development of this alternative psychology are the departure of most professional academic philosophers from such areas of human concern, and the secularization of culture, a process which has made religiously validated instructions and recipes of this sort unacceptable or unavailable to most highly educated people.

My own use of the word "behavior" is governed by a desire to observe what human beings do and to discover as well as I can the patterns and modes of their behavior, the term "mode" subsuming "patterns." Further, since for me "human" is properly subsumed under the category "animal," I am also interested in attributes of behavior common to both human and nonhuman animals. If the human is explained as emerging from the nonhuman, a commonality of attributes prevents ascribing uniquely human status to attributes also observable among animals. Thus observation of animal behavior circumscribes more precisely unique human attributes. My purpose in the present paper is to find a way of looking at philosophy and art which does not look at either from the point of view of the other. To look at art from the position of the philosopher, or at philosophy from the position of the artist, tends to result in apologias for the one or the other, nor does the point of view by any means determine which of the two is the subject of the apologias. Such an apologia is little different from the attempt to explain one in terms of the other.

I shall, then, attempt to explain philosophy and art from the point of view of a general theory of behavior, though I can present that theory here in only a highly abstract and schematic way. Controlled by this theory, I shall undertake to indicate the differences between the two, considered as modes of behavior, as well as their similarities.

I shall enter the problem by way of art. First, I believe art to be a uniquely human mode of behavior. I am aware that various animals are said to engage in aesthetic behavior. The evidence is that such creatures gather materials which do not appear to be useful but are bright and colorful and variegated. Because a biological function has not been imagined for such behavior, it is concluded that the bird acts as it does simply for the sake of sensory pleasure. This, it is somewhat hastily concluded, is the prehuman origin of art. Well, bears are said to eat honey, presumably for the sake of sensory pleasure. It is not unlikely that sensory pleasure is to be found at the prehuman level, though that is something we can scarcely be certain of until the animals tell us so. But granted the existence of sensory pleasure, such as a monkey's having its lice removed by another, or any animal grooming, we nevertheless have here a splendid example of semantic drift. "Aesthetic" began, so far as we know, simply by meaning sensory; then proceeded to sensory pleasure; and then jumped to the sensory pleasure of nature and of art; and then to art alone; and then, the attribute of pleasure having been dropped, became hardly more than the equivalent of "artistic" or having to do with the theory or philosophy of art. To claim that sensory pleasure at the prehuman level is the origin of art is simply to glide along this sequence of meanings without observing the semantic discontinuities in that sequence. This argument, then, cannot be taken seriously, and art remains a uniquely human attribute. That makes it much easier to explore the relatedness and nonrelatedness of philosophy and art, since both are now at the same explanatory level. At least, so far as I know, it has not yet been claimed that philosophy exists at the prehuman level.

Having disposed of that minor but not insignificant strategy for defining art, my next problem is to define art, or at least define it for my purposes. And I go about this by asking a question which, in such defining, is rarely asked. How do we know that a particular artifact was a work of art in the culture of its origin if that culture did not have the general category art, or even such lesser categories as painting, sculpture, dance, poetry, and so on? After all, it is little more than a couple of centuries ago that our culture had such a term, and it was only in the course of the nineteenth and twentieth centuries that the notion developed that all the arts are the expression of a single impulse, that impulse being ordinarily defined as the impulse to create works of art, and shorthandedly as the creative impulse, perhaps a slightly circular definition. The answer I propose is based on a fairly elaborate theory published some years ago which I can scarcely summarize here, except for certain pertinent parts (*Man's Rage for Chaos*, 1965). My answer to the above question is that an artifact was a work of art in the culture of its origin if, once the artifact has been placed in a chronological sequence of such artifacts, that sequence shows nonfunctional stylistic discontinuity. By "function" here I mean its tool use or its meaning, two words here interchangeable. Thus an archeologist digging in a Neolithic cave comes across an object with a serrated edge. That edge, he says, means that it is a saw. The meaning of a tool is what it is used for, and this is also the meaning of a verbal utterance or a nonverbal man-made configuration.

Let me give a couple of examples of what I am talking about. Scientific instruments until late in the eighteenth century were designed successively in Renaissance, Baroque, Rococo, and Neoclassic styles. The tool use did not change but the appearance did. After that, however, the artistic character disappeared and changes were made only to improve the efficiency of the instrument. Thus scientific instruments moved out of the field of art. Before the late eighteenth century such instruments show nonfunctional stylistic discontinuity. After that the stylistic character, a bare utilitarianism, was unchanged; the only change was in the design of the working parts of the instrument. Another example is the typewriter. Until a few decades ago all makes of typewriters looked more or less alike. Then in the 1930s in response to competition the appearance was varied from one maker's model to another. Successive changes in nonfunctional style, as in the automobile, became the rule. Typewriters entered the field of art, and about the same time most kitchen appliances and kitchens themselves underwent the same kind of change. Another example, from verbal texts, must suffice. Philosophy at one time had something in the way of literary charm; writers of philosophy were to a certain extent under the control of the protocol of literary rhetorics. I know of little philosophical writing today that has any literary charm at all, and it has even been a reproach to Bertrand Russell that his philosophical work is not entirely free of it. But if we look back, it is apparent that Plato's dialogues fall within the realm of literature, though Aristotle has little of the appeal of literary rhetoric. Few, I think, would praise Aquinas for his literary charm, but Berkeley and even Hume are a different matter. Philosophy is functional always, but occasionally its rhetoric is nonfunctional, having a literary character. Had Nietzsche not written so well and had he not used clearly nonphilosophical devices, he would probably be taken today more seriously than he is. Thus philosophy moves in and out of the field of art.

This nonfunctional stylistic discontinuity or dynamism of art arises, my theory goes, from the fact that works of art are differentiated from nonartistic artifacts by the presentation of perceptual disorder or discontinuity. As one boy said, on being told which one of a sequence of stylistically matched pairs of work was the better one, "Oh, I get it. The best one is always the crummy one." Since the decision on which was the better had been made by art historians, artists, and art students, the anecdote also exemplifies another principle: the higher the cultural level the greater the disorder or discontinuity and the more problematic the task of grasping it perceptually. This is the internal character of works of art; the external character is the historical dimension, or stylistic discontinuity.

But this is only one aspect of art. The other is the tool-use, or meaning, or function, or semantic aspect. Most definitions of art I have seen have been attempts to find in the semantic aspect of art its defining attribute. Such efforts must fail. There is no semantic function in art which cannot be found outside of art. This does not mean that it cannot be said that a culture or subculture "assigns" to art certain semantic responsibilities, but these can be anything at all. Analysis invariably shows that efforts to derive a definition of art from its semantic aspect can be traced successfully to the semantic character of art validated at the cultural level at which the attempt is being made. When I was young, Victorian poetry was highly regarded; then came a period when it was denied that it was poetry at all; now once again it is highly regarded, but for different reasons, usually because of a hermeneutic effort which ascribes to it hitherto unsuspected meanings. Swinburne (it appears at least from my writings) is not intellectually superficial but profound. This assertion will be made more frequently for some decades to come, not because of what I have said, but simply because my work was part of a cultural convergence. When enough critics have said so, it will be so, and no doubt a new definition of poetry will be the result.

In the semantic aspect of art may be found, moreover, another kind of disorder or discontinuity, semantic discontinuity. But this is not a defining attribute of art. To a considerable extent it is a phenomenon of the late nineteenth and the twentieth centuries, though it may be found as a minor device in early periods. A work of art may cause little or no semantic disorientation, or as in *Ulysses* it may cause a great deal, to a point close to incomprehensibility, at least when it first appears and perhaps forever, as may be the case with Pound's *Cantos* and much surrealistic painting. Semantic disorientation in art is a historically local phenomenon.

Thus far we may locate certain relations and nonrelations between art and philosophy. Philosophy may, at any time, manifest certain artistic attributes, but this is likely to happen at some times rather than at others. It is a culturally linked phenomenon. On the other hand, philosophy never offers semantic disorientation. This statement no doubt will seem a surprising and indeed quite unjustified remark to philosophers and especially to nonphilosophers. I mean that the semantic disorientation philosophy offers is not a function of philosophy; the philosopher always tries to present semantic orientation. The failure to grasp a philosophical work is a consequence of unfamiliarity with philosophical discourse or with that particular philosophical style of discourse, or of the emergence of innovative meanings. When one is so familiar with a work of art that it offers no disorientation one tends to be bored with it; when he is so familiar with a work of philosophy that it offers no disorientation, then interest truly begins, and the reader has a sound foundation for pleasure or distaste. Furthermore, stylistic discontinuity in philosophy is invariably external, that is, only by contrast with previous philosophical works. If philosophy employs literary rhetoric and charm and thus falls within the field of art, that rhetoric almost invariably will be continuous throughout the entire text.

We may now make a few preliminary statements about the relatedness and nonrelatedness of philosophy and art. Philosophy may or may not show nonfunctional stylistic discontinuity, but art, in its formal aspect, always does, though at times, when, for example, a purely functional object is displayed in an art gallery, the discontinuity may be only external. But such cases are exceptional and almost invariably displayed to make some theoretical point about art, that is, that it is culturally linked. Philosophy always, however, tries to present internal semantic continuity, but art may or may not. It is a matter of indifference to its perceptual function of disorientation, the defining attribute of art. Furthermore, art, as in *The Testament of Beauty*, can fall within the field of philosophy, though so long as it presents perceptual disorder or discontinuity it remains also within the field of art. In short, the fields or categories of art and philosophy can overlap, though such overlapping tends on the whole to be atypical as well as culturally linked.

The last point, however, raises the question of the semantic relation of art and philosophy, and the conclusions so far arrived at suggest that the relatedness and nonrelatedness of art and philosophy are to be found in the semantic aspect of both as well as in the formal or perceptual aspect. Now I do not propose for a moment that the semantic aspect of art is unimportant, though I believe the formal aspect is the defining attribute. The importance of the semantic aspect is indicated by the fact that most efforts to define art have been semantic, and also by the fact that a culture tends to assign, as it were, particular semantic responsibilities to artists. Nevertheless, the defining attribute of philosophy is that it tends to be orienting; it tends to control and limit response, not merely to itself, but to other kinds of discourse, to other modes of behavior, and ultimately (at least philosophers always hope this, though sometimes quite secretly) to all stimulus fields. Art, however, offers the opportunity to experience disorientation; it tends to offer the opportunity to lose the sense that one's response is controlled; it offers the experience of not knowing how to respond. To explain why this should be so will, by a circuitous route, bring us back to the semantic relatedness and nonrelatedness of art and philosophy.

Any theory of human behavior must explain two attributes of behavioral continuity, both within the individual's life and within the historical existence of culture and society. The first is continuity itself, or channeling, as I shall call it. I mean the fact that an individual tends to repeat the same behavior in similar situations, and that within the culture such behavior is common to the individuals of that culture, frequently over very long periods of time, even, so far as we can guess from the meager evidence, from the Paleolithic or earlier to the present. The other factor is the reverse; it is innovative deviance from that channeling. When a behavior pattern is inadequately channeled, the result is a widening of the range or limits of the pattern into a delta-like spread. Deviance, however, is an unsatisfactory term, since it ordinarily means behavior judged invalid from the stance of socially validated behavior. It may be, however (and indeed usually is among criminals) itself channeled behavior. But deviance may also mean innovative or unchanneled behavior. To avoid this confusion, therefore, I shall permit myself a neologism and use "deltified behavior," derived from the noun deltification as an equivalent to innovatively deviant behavior.

Art is a counteradaptation to channeling. This can best be understood by glancing at science, which has often been thought to have affinities with art, and rightly so. From the point of view presented here science may be regarded as the explanatory exploitation of negative feedback encountered at the empirical frontier. This is nothing new, of course. It has always happened in human life, so far as we can guess. But until the institutionalization of science in the sixteenth and seventeenth centuries, it affected only low-level generalizations. The heart of science lies in the frustration of expectancies aroused by the verbal directions emanating from a hierarchical institution at the empirical frontier. The effect of such frustration is disorientation, which may be behaviorally defined as inability to respond, followed by random response. If a random response is judged to be successful, we explain its success by appealing to the highly regressive explanatory word "intuition." In the many-leveled regress of scientific explanation such a response can have a deep effect, sometimes modifying the explanatory termination itself. In the early days of institutionalized science, for example, the termination was the word "God," but so powerful was the novel exploitation of negative feedback that the word became a hypothesis, as Laplace put it, that was not necessary. It is a curious phenomenon of cultural convergence that as modern science was emerging, so was the modern business institution. The extraordinary success and power of the modern corporation, which, it certainly seems, is on the way to transcending the nation-state, arises, as with science, from its exploitation of negative feedback. Historically, it is the first large-scale social institution to do so.

It is often said that the affinity between science and art is that both are creative. Since we do not even know how we get from one sentence to the next, unless the movement is controlled and channeled by an explanatory regress the directions of which we follow, what form of verbal behavior is not creative? And since the same ignorance holds true of the movement from one nonverbal sign to the next, what nonverbal behavior of this sort is not creative? No, the affinity between science and art is not in their creativity, for creative behavior is merely a bit of deltified behavior that has been socioculturally validated. Rather, the affinity between science and art lies in the disorientation that art almost always offers and that science can offer at the empirical frontier. Not knowing how to respond is, in a mode of channeled behavior, the condition for fruitful negative feedback. Since science merely developed a mode of behavior already in existence for virtually the entire length of human history, art can be understood as a rehearsal or tempering in exposure to disorientation and also as a way of training individuals to seek disorienting experiences outside of the art situation. The success of channeling behavior has been and is an adaptation and a maladaptation. Art is a counteradaptation to channeling. Art is training in not knowing how to respond. It counters the limiting effect of channeling by increasing the probabilities of deltification and fruitful innovation. Since, however, the social situation of the art perceiver does not require overt response and indeed by protocol excludes it, it accomplishes nothing in itself. Nelson Goodman has suggested that art has an effect upon what he calls cognition, and this, I think, is the effect it has. That is, it does not necessarily accomplish negative feedback, though in any individual it might, but it prepares the individual to tolerate and look for the disorientation which precedes negative feedback. But these statements have only to do with what I have called the perceptual or formal aspect of art, not with the semantic aspect.

Philosophy is quite obviously very different from this formal aspect of art, for its effect is quite obviously to control and to channel verbal behavior at levels of explanatory regress lower than itself. This becomes easier to understand if we remember that it is not enough to say that philosophy emerged from theology. Rather, philosophy is secularized theology. This indicates at once the relation between philosophy and the terminating levels of socially institutionalized power. Like all high culture, philosophy is economically parasitic upon the centers of wealth and power, but it has a symbiotic relation with them. It has always been and still is subservient to the interests of those centers, and independent from them. And the peculiar thing is that when it declares its independence it continues to receive their economic support. To resolve this puzzle, once again it is useful to turn back to animal behavior, in which seduction is the complement to force and enabled hierarchical social organization to develop. Seduction is a means of postponing and circumventing the use of force. The verbal equivalent of force is threat; the verbal equivalent of seduction is enticement, or flattery. Civilization is the multiplication and complication of strategies for postponing the use of force, always uncertain in its outcome. The verbal strategies (or adaptive verbal mechanisms) are threat and enticement. The power centers keep threat to themselves; the province of high culture is the control and direction of enticement. The power centers are the regressive termination of hierarchical institutions; high culture has as its business the regressive terminations of explanatory systems. The verbal technology of high culture is enticement, of which the three modes are explanation, justification, and validation. Philosophy (continuing the mission of its predecessor, theology) is the most regressive mode of high culture; it is the most civilized mode of behavior in which it is possible to engage, because it manipulates the purest modes of verbal enticement. Less pure modes are found in the other humanities, and if the teacher of the humanities in educational institutions is not engaged in enticement I do not know what he is doing. To be sure, in the marking system he has access to power, but that does not make him unique in high culture. Criticisms of philosophy and of the arts are merely more sophisticated modes of the marking system. No philosophy can effectively channel behavior unless it is backed up by power, as the history of Christianity, Communism, Confucianism, and the American mode of the Enlightenment all show equally well; the last is the ultimate explanatory mode for the vast bulk of social institutions in this country. In short, what philosophy attempts to do is to control the movement from one sentence to the next in high-level explanation and ultimately in low-level explanation and at the empirical frontier. This is why the heart of philosophy is logic, the control of sentential interaction. As the ultimate mode of enticement, as the ultimate mode of direction-giving culture, all branches of philosophy, whether epistemology, or ontology, or aesthetics, are normative, and most normative of all, supremely normative, is logic.

This can be put another way. Language is not isomorphic with the world. Thus it has often been said, and usually with an air of smugness, that language enables human animals to lie, to themselves as well as to each other. But there is no reason to be smug about this. Language makes it impossible to do anything else. Verbal interaction is a complex system of mutual deception. Its instability arises from the internal conditions of a society and its institutions, of its external situations, and the continuously disturbing consequences of deltification. Thus philosophy's search for the true statement, or a set of rules to determine whether or not a statement is true, is its response to that instability. It is engaged in constant repair work to the constantly disintegrating system of high-level explanatory deception. This is another way of saying that the most civilized mode of behavior it is possible for man to engage in is philosophy.

It is now possible to turn to the final question I have raised, the relation between philosophy and the semantic aspect of art. Except for an important qualification which I shall discuss later, that relation can be briefly stated: art in its semantic aspect exemplifies explanations. A dirty joke told in a bar (or the same joke in the most refined drawing room) exemplifies the verbal and nonverbal channeling controls over sexual behavior. This does not mean, let me add, merely the socially approved controls. Noninnovative deviant behavior, as in criminal behavior, is also explained, justified, validated, and channeled in the same way that nondeviant behavior is. Like the dirty joke, the Peking Opera under the Communist regime and the frescoes of the Sistine Chapel also exemplify verbal explanations, or channeling strategies. So do *The Faerie Queene, The Divine Comedy,* and Pound's *Cantos.* The difference between these and the dirty joke, however, is that the former exemplify philosophical utterances. That is, the higher the cultural level at which the work of art aims and to which the artist belongs the more likely it is to exemplify not merely philosophical statements but rather philosophical systems. One source of the richness of a complex work of art is that it can exemplify all of the levels of an explanatory regress. No explanatory or abstract utterance can be said to be understood unless examples can be generated. In teaching, the constant provision of examples is a necessity, and the level of teaching can be determined by the frequency of the examples. The lower the level the more frequent the exemplification. It is an instance of controlling behavior by redundancy. Thus art is the handmaiden of philosophy in its task of channeling behavior by means of the rhetoric of enticement, a rhetoric multiplied in its force by redundancy. Philosophical discourse, with its tiny and highly trained audience, minimizes redundancy, but art, directed to a far larger audience, even at the level of high culture, is exceedingly redundant. The lower the cultural level, of course, the more redundant is art, both within individual works and in the number of works maintaining the same redundancy. Man does not live by bread alone, but principally by platitudes, and art is even more platitudinous than philosophy.

The question inescapably arises as to what music signs are signs of, or what semiotic categories music signs categorize—and channel. The answer is obvious from the verbalizations of music, a sample of which I have suggested. Music signs categorize states inside the surface of the skin. What happens is more easily understood by using the notion of the individual organism as a social dyad. The brain transforms a semiotic stimulus into a physiological response which immediately is interpreted as a semiotic stimulus. Whether these internal physiologic stimuli are feelings or emotions is a question that can be safely and even wisely ignored. The usage of those terms is so unstable, so inadequately conventionalized, that academic psychology itself has been unable to bring about stabilization. At this point it is clear that some novel terminology is needed to differentiate between signs of internal conditions and internal conditions as signs. The latter I shall call internal signs; the former I shall call internality signs, signs of internal conditions. That both internal signs and internality signs are channeled can be readily indicated. A composer can produce internality signs without himself experiencing inside his own skin the appropriate internal signs, and a listener can verbalize the semiotic character of internality signs in the same fashion. Such verbalizations are probably less well conventionalized than the internality signs themselves, a point that can explain Mendelsohn's famous remark that music is more precise than language.

Two other points need making. The first is that all of the arts, including poetry, as in alliteration and other modes of phonic over-determination, present internality signs. Examples are color, line, verticality, horizontality, space and spatial relationships, energy release and conservation, orientation and disorientation, and so on. The second is that art is by no means the only kind of semiotic field in which such signs may be found. They are ubiquitous. Indeed, art did not create them or invent them. It simply appropriated them from ordinary behavior and exploited them. "I will lift up mine eyes unto the hills, from whence cometh my help." The social mechanisms for correcting deltification of internal signs are such devices as the confessionals of priest and psychiatrist, and what is currently in our culture even more important, the newspaper columns of Abigail van Buren and Ann Landers. It is instructive to observe how often the letters they receive ask questions about how the writer ought to feel about various problematic situations, and equally instructive to observe how the instructions offered attempt to correct a kind of behavior by recommending a different kind of feeling; in both letter and response the request for channeling and the channeling have to do with internal signs. When we consider, moreover, the ubiquity of art (as I once said to a young Danish critic, "The damned stuff is all over the place") it is obvious that art itself is one of the most important sources for channeling response to both internality signs and internal signs, and that it does so by the collation of situational signs and internality signs. Two paintings of the same landscape may present a high degree of visual, perceptually analogous signs, except for color; color differentiation can change the whole internality sign character, a point made by Monet in his haystack and cathedral series. The development of nineteenth-century landscape without human figures into twentieth-century abstract painting was both controlled by and itself carried or exemplified an ideology or exemplificatory system, a central aspect of which was that selfhood may be experienced by concentration upon internal signs. Thus Pater's famous remark that all art tends to approach the condition of music was confirmed by the redundant assertion that abstract art is visual music.

This brings me to my final point, the important qualification mentioned earlier. Art can be antiexplanatory as well as exemplificatory. The general characteristic of literature is that the overwhelming bulk of its rhetoric consists of low-level exemplification, as close to the nonverbal, to speak very loosely, as the verbal can get. It is thus closely allied to that kind of semiotic behavior known as subjective imagery, of which a special case is dreaming. Subjective imagery can be used for a variety of purposes, including channeling by self-generated redundancy. This seems to be an important function of fantasizing. But imagery can also be employed in problem solving. We have probably all had the experience of solving a verbally stated problem by the sudden generation of the solution in the form of subjective images or a series of such images. Only a couple of months ago I thus arrived at the solution of a difficult problem of textual criticism. I *saw* the solution. It was an innovative deviance of an extremely radical sort, quite counter to the received notions of editing and the presentation of edited texts. My point is this. Highly exemplificatory language and subjective and objective nonverbal semiotic behavior are a long way from the high-level explanatory regress at which philosophy manipulates its rhetoric of enticement. Friedrich Hebbel once remarked that poetry is as unpredictable as dreams. Well, dreams are not really all that unpredictable, nor is poetry. Nevertheless the point was well made. Every teacher knows the difficulty of choosing the right examples for his explanations, examples that do not introduce categorial attributes which confuse the explanation or even subvert it. The movement from one sentence to the next is hard enough to control, and the movement from one nonverbal sign to the next, as in music or the dance or abstract painting, is even harder. The language of literature shares this difficulty of controlling sentential movement, simply because it is so highly exemplificatory. Since the time of Plato, at least, the arts have been regarded with suspicion by the centers of power. Thus there is this peculiarity in the semantic aspect of art: its very mission of channeling behavior by exemplifying explanation is made more difficult by its technology of exemplification. The maximization of exemplification of the nonverbal increases the probability of deltification, of introducing into well-defined social situations innovative deviancy. To indulge once more in a bit of cultural history, Romantic artists of all sorts, since their ideology was in itself antiexplanatory, learned to exploit this subversive capacity of art. The eventual result was such works as *Ulysses*, works which are wonderfully resistant to explanation. It is no wonder that one of the first things revolutionary dictators do is to subject the arts to rigid explanatory control, especially since the Romantics discovered the subversive potential of art.

To sum up, philosophy and the formal aspect of art are related modes of behavior only in their opposition to or negation of each other, the first having as its function the channeling of behavior, the second as its function the increase of the probability of generating unchanneled or random behavior. Philosophy and the semantic aspect of art, on the other hand, are related modes of behavior in that the primary task of art is to exemplify philosophy, whether it be the philosophy of the street or that of our most abstract philosophers. Yet even so, because of the highly exemplificatory character of the semantic rhetoric of art, it can be and historically has been subversive not only of philosophical explanations but of explanation itself. It can generate unchanneled or random behavior and occasionally does so.

# CHAPTER ELEVEN

# Man's Use of Nature

The latest news about man's use of nature is that if we continue to use aerosol cans we will damage the atmospheric shield that protects us from solar radiation. The probable result will be an increase in the cancer rate. Or perhaps this is not the latest news. Very probably since this was written something even more devastating has been discovered. But this will do. That man is using nature very badly, and that nature is, in a sense, fighting back, summoning its resources (to be anthropomorphic about it) to destroy the creature that is destroying it, is in itself hardly news anymore. It is presumably why this symposium is being held.

To consider that question we have to examine a little more carefully how man uses nature badly, that is, in such a way that he damages his own chances of survival on this planet. The probable consequence of the use of aerosol cans makes that "how" easy enough to understand. The damage to nature comes from manipulating nature, in this case the chemical aspect of nature, for a particular human end, but that manipulation does not take into consideration the unanticipated, undesirable, and damaging effect of that manipulation. But this is not merely a matter of carelessness, nor of the simple-minded desire of great corporations to make a profit. Nevertheless, one thing is quite clear. Most of the damage to nature is indeed a consequence of the desire to make a profit. But we need to be cautious here. Profit in business is not an end in itself. It is rather the proof and the measure of success in the business enterprise, which is to produce goods and services which people can be persuaded to find desirable or necessary, and often enough are really both. We cannot always say that such goods and services are desired in themselves. Nobody desired aerosol cans until they were invented and placed on the market. Once marketed, however, they became desirable, partly through advertising and partly through simple availability. Since they offered certain conveniences they did indeed become desirable. Aerosol cans are now what people want, and it follows, to the business mind, that they must therefore be provided. It is the argument of commercial television: give the people what they want. But of course they do not want it until it is made available.

The peculiar situation of a business establishment in these matters can be brought out by comparing legal or establishment business with organized crime. For several years I have amused myself by calling organized crime the counterbusiness. To my mind it is quite evident that organized crime does far less social damage than legitimate business. One reason is simple. Organized crime is much smaller. But there is another and more significant reason. Organized crime has traditionally made its profit from providing goods and services which people are not supposed to want. As we all know, prohibition was responsible for the organization of crime on a national scale, and it was the genius of Al Capone to realize that the way to proceed was to organize crime on the model of national business organizations, or corporations. However, as once again we all know, in recent years organized crime has been investing its illegally gained profits in legal businesses. The corporate leadership of the counterbusiness is behaving more and more like the corporate leadership of establishment business. Since the counterbusiness has modeled itself on establishment business, this imitation is not surprising. Nevertheless, the financial resources which have enabled this development were derived and are still derived from providing people with goods and services they are not supposed to find desirable, or if they find them desirable, are supposed to refuse to try to get them. Thus organized crime (or the counterbusiness) has a power only over people, and a minority of people at that, and even so for a fairly minor portion of their daily lives, principally their leisure hours. The counterbusiness, I think, spends little on research and development. But the establishment business spends enormously. Hence aerosol cans and all the other newly invented goods the proliferation of which is so alarming.

The result is a cultural crisis which is the unrealized motivation for this symposium. It has been central to the American belief system (let us call it the American ideology) that if a business enterprise produces a profit it is socially beneficial, even though there might be undesirable side effects, which it is, so to speak, the task of government to mop

up. But in recent years—it was one source of the despair of the rebellious 1960s—it has become obvious that the production of profit
is *not* the proof of social benefit. This, I think, is the source of the deep-
seated malaise in this country. But we must not think it is purely a
problem of this country. The Russian government is doing everything
it can to increase the proliferation of automobiles. Yet the American
experience with the automobile has been such that one would think
that an intelligent government with the almost total power of the Russian government over its society and its economy would do everything
it possibly could to discourage the use of automobiles, and to use its
tremendous propaganda machinery to persuade the Russian people
that the last thing they ought to want was a lot of automobiles—a
chicken in every pot, perhaps, but certainly not a car in every garage.
When one considers what has happened to the quality of *our* food and
to the quality of *our* automobiles, what we seem to have gotten is a
chicken in every garage and a car in every pot. The Russians surely
could learn something from the example of Western Europe. There
the automobile did not proliferate on anything like the American scale
until the 1960s. The result has been the destruction of old European
cities as centers of civilized living and great damage to the countryside,
not to speak of an air pollution considerably worse than ours. Europe
has learned nothing from the American experience, just as the Russians have learned nothing. We long, for example, for mass transportation, but our economy is so involved with the production of
automobiles that we are able to do nothing more than make rather
pitiful gestures. Part of the economic effect and involvement of the
automobile has been the spread of the population into the suburbs
and the use of the suburbs to absorb the growing population. Now
not only are the suburbs deserts in which the only cultural resources
besides television are alcohol and adultery; they have also completely
changed the pattern of urban movement. A metropolitan area is no
longer a hub along the spokes of which people move back and forth
from homes to jobs. Rather, it is a vast network in which people move
daily long distances in all possible directions and in such complicated
patterns that the result is in effect a random movement. No one has
yet come up with a system of mass transportation which can meet the
demands of this entirely novel metropolitan movement pattern. And
to this we must add that enormous areas of valuable agricultural land
have been removed from production by the spread of the suburbs.
Really good land is, in fact, limited. South of San Francisco, immense
nut groves have been destroyed to make room for suburbs, but in the

United States land of a quality suitable for growing nut-bearing trees is very uncommon.

But if the Russian government cannot act intelligently, and if Western Europe has failed to act intelligently, in spite of our appalling example, and if we have permitted the destruction of the civilization of urban centers, if we also have failed to act intelligently, then, as in all failure of intelligence, the explanation must be sought in the beliefs of culture, in its ideology, an ideology which is increasingly riven with incoherence. An ideology explains the world, and justifies our behavior in it and towards it, and validates that behavior. An ideology tells us what to do and tells us that we are right in doing so. What we need to do, then, in order to understand our present plight is to understand the historical sources and character of our ideology, to understand why our ideology is failing, and ultimately to understand why any ideology must fail.

We must not imagine that the destructiveness of the establishment business enterprises is the cause of our failure to deal intelligently with nature. The difference between business and counterbusiness is not that the former does greater social damage than the latter, but rather that the former does a damage to nature which the latter does not do at all. Modern business not only employs the physical and natural sciences; it is founded on them; it is made possible by them. Historically, it is the consequence of science. It is the economic arm of the society, or more specifically of the society's ideology. The counterbusiness has a mere negative and minor relation to that ideology. And both, after all, are united in the belief that life is something to be enjoyed. It is, therefore, idle to blame business and the great corporations, national and international, for our troubles—for the fact that for a long time we have been using nature badly. Business has merely done what the ideology has told it to do. And whether we like it or not, the same ideology controls the decisions of the Soviet government. That government tries to control its economic arm, but its decisions are, if anything, even more stupid than the decisions of ours. Marx, the cultural instrument by which Western European ideology in one of its more important manifestations was carried to Russia, said that man must master nature, that the mastery of nature was the goal and indeed the historical purpose of humanity. And our ideology says exactly the same thing.

One of the most interesting facts about Eur-American culture is that it alone has developed modern science. Other cultures have adopted European science, and it is European science which is homogenizing the world, which, if not destroying other cultures, is modifying them and making them into extensions of European culture. But no other culture has developed modern science. We must attempt, therefore, to understand something about the nature of science, and why (for this is really our problem) it is such an enormous success and, as is becoming increasingly evident, such an enormous failure, a failure which, so far at any rate, we seem to be able to do almost nothing about.

In its more primitive forms ideology appears as mythology, and as cultures become more modern and intellectually sophisticated, mythologies are transformed into abstract or metaphysical language. A transition period can be seen in the works of Plato, in which both kinds of language may be found. Indeed, *if* we have the correct notion of his intellectual development, at the end of his life he turned once again to myth, as if abstract or metaphysical language were inadequate for what he wanted to say. The basic myth of European society, and this includes Russia as well, is obviously the story of the Fall of Man and his expulsion from the Garden of Eden. The following passage comes from the New English Bible, but neither the King James version nor the Vulgate is very different.

So God created man in his own image; in the image of God he created him;— male and female he created them. God blessed them and said to them, "Be fruitful and increase, fill the earth and subdue it ["subdue" is also the word in the King James version], rule over the fish in the sea, the birds of heaven, and every living thing that moves upon the earth." God also said, "I give you all plants that bear seed everywhere on earth, and every tree bearing fruit which yields seed: they shall be yours for food." God then created a garden in Eden, and he placed Adam and Eve in the garden. [Unfortunately, Adam and Eve disobeyed the Lord. They sinned. They were cast forth from the garden and informed], "Accursed shall be the ground on your account. With labour you shall win your food from it all the days of your life. It will grow thorns and thistles for you, none but wild plants for you to eat. You shall gain your bread by the sweat of your brow until you return to the ground; for from it you were taken. Dust you are, to dust you shall return."

Initially, then, man was perfectly adapted to the natural world. That was his Edenic existence. To expiate his sin, to return to that Edenic existence became the goal of Judaeo-Christian culture. It took two principal mythological forms. One was that the sin was expiated by the appearance of God in human form. As a result of His suffering and death man, or at least a fairly small number of men, would go to heaven and return to an Edenic existence. Another form was that the earth would be destroyed and then recreated, but all of it would be

Edenic and all men would live in terms of Adam's original Edenic existence of perfect adaptation to nature and dominion over it. The earth would be completely subservient to the interests of man. This millennial vision particularly emphasized, then, the mastery of the natural world which was Adam's original gift.

But we must not imagine that European culture and its myths had exclusively Judaeo-Christian roots or were governed solely by the Adamic mythology. Important cultural forces were pre-Christian and survived into and alongside of Christianity and in contradiction to it. One was pre-Christian scientific thought, that is, scientific theory. As we will see, it was not yet what we mean today by science, which has quite a different character, but after it was reintroduced into Western thinking from the Arabians, it presented alongside of Christianity and in uneasy relationship to it the idea of the intellectual comprehension of nature, an intellectual mastery of a dominion over the natural world. Even more important was a cultural phenomenon that is to be found in almost all cultures, magic. There have been a great many scholarly arguments over whether or not science grew from magic, or whether or not science is the antithesis of magic. Both positions are, in fact, justifiable, but for the present purposes the important thing about magic is that it presents an ideology of mastery over natural forces. It makes no difference from our point of view that magic indeed gives precious little of that mastery. The important thing is that it gives the feeling of mastery and embodies the possibility of dominion. It is not surprising that orthodox Christianity condemned magic. To it, the magician was in league with the manifold devils to be found in the world, devils who are fallen angels and who, after the Fall, were loosed upon the earth. For this position any dealings with nature not devoted to the recognition that God created nature, that is, any dealing with nature for its own sake (even for its beauty) or for the sake of that dealing, were sinful, were in league with the devil. The reason, I think, was that since magic contained the ideology of mastery over nature, it circumvented the will of God, for the will of God clearly was that, upon the expulsion of Adam from the Garden in Eden, Adam and all his descendants should lose that dominion and mastery.

Nevertheless, as civilization slowly, very slowly, developed, it became increasingly apparent that with the aid of reason and the aid of trial-and-error man could gain control over certain natural forces. How else, for example, could the vast medieval cathedrals have been built? Popular mythology was constantly ascribing these extraordinary edifices, this suspension of vast masses of stone over immense empty spaces, this building of walls of fragile glass, to the interference in man's activities by angels. But the builders, and the architects, and the intellectuals knew better.

At this point we must call to mind that medieval Europe created nothing more remarkable than what Arabian or Indian or Chinese civilizations created. Indeed the science of astronomy was more advanced in those cultures, and even more advanced in the Mayan culture when Europeans discovered it in the sixteenth century. But from the point of view of the development of modern science, astronomy is not particularly important, for astronomical knowledge does not make it possible to change the stars in their courses. You until very recently could not do anything with it. You could just know it. It embodied the ideology of the intellectual mastery of nature, thus being like Greek science, but it did not embody the idea of the manipulative control of nature, except for the uncertain aid it gave to navigation. Why, then, did this slowly gained manipulative control of nature, not only in building, but also in mining, in shipbuilding, in painting's exact reproduction of nature, in metallurgy, have such an explosive effect upon Western culture but have no such effect on cultures that had accomplished even more remarkable masteries?

I think the explanation lies in the fact that this steadily increasing control over natural forces, even in agriculture, created in Europe an ideological incoherence. This slowly emerging manipulative control was not reconcilable with God's denial of such control to Adam after the Fall. The incoherence was made all the more powerful by the fact that the most extraordinary dominion over nature which medieval culture achieved was in the construction of temples to God, in the great medieval cathedrals and innumerable great churches which were not the seat of a bishop. Though they were built to the glory of God, they nevertheless circumvented and denied the power of the will of God. And at the time there were people who said so. Splendid monuments as they were to the majesty of God, they were nevertheless also emblems of man's pride, above all his pride in his increasing economic success, his achievement of economic surplus, something he was not supposed to be able to do. The great cathedrals and the great investment that built them were an attempt to atone for that success. They were emblems of man's pride, the chief of the seven deadly sins, because pride asserts man's independence, his self-sufficiency, his defiance of the will of God, his creation of economic surplus. And that self-sufficiency, that pride, was supported by a revived tradition of classic science, after its Arabian transformation and after an eventual return to the original classical sources. And that pride was also supported by the anti-Christian but widely practiced tradition of magic.

The word "science" did not gain its present meaning until the 1840s, when for this first time it was restricted to the physical or natural sciences, to the manipulative sciences, with the exception of astronomy, which was vaguely seen to occupy a very special position in the field of science. Thus when Marxists assert that Marxism is a science, they are using the word in a pre-1840 sense, even though they do not know it (hence their intellectual confusion); they are using it in the sense that a science is an internally coherent explanation of anything at all, including theology. The importance of magic in the developing ideology of modern science can be grasped by realizing that in the sixteenth and seventeenth centuries science was called "natural magic." That term indicates the profound importance of the manipulation of the natural world to the modern ideology of science.

The incoherence between the belief that man had been justly denied his original dominion over nature and the fact that man was steadily gaining a control over nature, even in the service of God, created great cultural strains. Clearly, that incoherence needed to be resolved, just as we need to resolve the incoherence between the belief that profit is proof of social benefit and the fact that it is not. An important step was made in the middle of the sixteenth century when Copernicus placed the sun in the center of the solar system. It has often been said that this decision was a blow to man's pride, displacing his home and himself from the center. Not at all. On the contrary, the earth after the Fall had been conceived as a fallen earth, physically as well as morally an aging earth, doomed to destruction, with the worst of existence, Hell, in the very center of it. By placing the sun in the center of the solar system Copernicus removed man from that bad condition—the cesspool of creation. He was placed in a position in which he was constantly warmed and fed by the sun, which was, moreover, conceived as the emblem or almost embodiment of Deity itself. It became increasingly difficult to think of this as a fallen world. That is why Milton kept the old Ptolemaic geocentric system in *Paradise Lost*. The new system, which he mentions as an interesting theory, was incoherent with the story he had to tell, the story of the Fall. Moreover, Copernicus placed the sun in the center of the solar system not merely because that decision resolved certain mathematical and observational problems. The idea occurred to him because of his familiarity with the tradition of classical science. He placed the sun in the center precisely because it was the emblem and instrument of the source of physical and spiritual life. It is not surprising that by the end of the seventeenth century Lord Shaftesbury was literally worshipping the sun.

However, this revision of the human conception of the visible universe was only astronomy. It was not manipulative. It merely prepared the way for the resolution of the incoherence. That resolution was accomplished by, among others, Francis Bacon, who was simply the best propagandist of the new point of view. And the point of his resolution was the inclusion of manipulative science in his creation of ideological coherence. His claim was that the laws by which nature operates are few, are simple, and are discoverable; and more importantly his claim was that discoverability is made possible by experiment, that is, by manipulation. He set out to write a vast treatise on these matters, but completed and published only a part, though other parts were written and eventually published which he had intended to incorporate in his great book. The title of the book was *Instauratio Magna*, the great renewal, and by that he simply meant the Great Path to the Restoration of Man's Dominion and Mastery over the Natural World, the Restoration of what Adam had lost. And this was to be done not by revelation from God but by the powers of God-given but not God-controlled human mind, aided by experiment and observation. Bacon resolved the incoherence between belief and fact by simply asserting that if we freed ourselves from various mythologies we could restore the Edenic existence with the powers God had granted us; and since God had granted us these powers, it was clearly his intention and will that we should do so. By the sweat of our brows we could regain that lost mastery and dominion over the natural world.

These ideas of Bacon had an astonishing effect. The philosopher Whitehead has called the seventeenth century the century of genius, and in a sense all modern science is a development of the ideas of that century, which culminated in the great work of Isaac Newton. It has also been called the century of rationalism, and certainly mathematics was popular to a degree hardly understandable today. One of the great ideas of the century was that of the sufficient reason; the reason is sufficient to the comprehension of the universe. Descartes set out to think the world afresh, as it had never been thought before. But these are but a couple of almost haphazard incidents from that century. The fact that the new vision had penetrated deeply into high culture, at least, and had virtually taken it over is to be seen in what happened to gardening.

Until well into the eighteenth century, gardens continued the medieval tradition. They were surrounded by a wall, and they were laid out formally, and in the seventeenth century mathematically. In the sixteenth century they often had an artificial mound in the center, an emblem of the mountain on which it was conceived the Garden in Eden had been placed. The traditional garden was modeled on paradise, and often was called precisely that. The ideology exemplified by such gardens was exactly the ideology exemplified in the great cathedrals, in the Abbot Suger's invention of the Gothic style, which above all was characterized by immense walls of colored glass. If paradise could not be regained, it could be symbolized. To be inside a Gothic cathedral was to be inside the spirit of the divine. It was to be entirely separated from and protected from the fallen world without. In the same way a garden was a place in which nature could be safely viewed in its aspect of the attributes of deity, for it was separated from and protected from the natural world as it is, a world in which one could be tempted to contemplate the beauties of nature for their own sake and so be exposed to the temptation of those devils that lurked everywhere, devils who used the natural world to tempt the mind to stray away from the contemplation of deity. Hence the wall. All one could see beyond the wall was what lay above it, heaven itself, the abode of deity. The axis of observation was vertical, from God to man, not horizontal, not from man out into the fallen world.

In the early eighteenth century, however, an extraordinary gardener, a man named William Kent, created an entirely new style of gardening. In the words of Horace Walpole, Kent leapt over the wall and saw that all nature is a garden. As a result of this vision Kent laid out the garden itself not in the geometrically controlled patterns which were an emblem of the once unfallen perfection of the world, but in a way that concentrated the landscape around the garden. He removed the wall. Paths were wandering, no longer straight, and for straight canals were substituted naturally flowing brooks and streams. The importance of all this can be seen in Walpole's words. In the Western Christian tradition the word "garden" always evoked the Garden in Eden, and even today the devotion to gardens still does, though more subtly. To many people even now the planting and care of a garden is a religious act. But to see all nature as a garden is to affirm the proposition that the world has not in fact participated in the Fall of Adam, that there has been physical decay to the world. Not long before, the Alps were seen for the first time not as horrible evidences of the sin of Adam, but quite otherwise, as sublime emblems of the attributes of deity, of the grandeur of God. The garden, instead of being a symbol of the Fall of man and a nostalgic reminder of what he had lost, became a symbol of the Baconian way of thinking that man can recover his lost relation to nature. Standing in the eighteenth-century garden and looking out upon the landscape (a landscape often made more beautiful by Kent's great successor, Capability Brown, who restored what he judged to be its true character) one could experience a harmony with nature, a feeling of the possibilities of man's relation to nature, possibilities which science was bringing true. It is instructive that in this very century of the Enlightenment, when these new gardens were being brought into existence by Baconian enthusiasts, Adam Smith laid the ideological foundations for our conception of business profit, a concept now coming apart at its seams. If, he said (or was interpreted to have said and possibly meant), the individual followed his own economic interests, an invisible hand would so manage affairs that all men's economic interests would be beneficially served. There is then a natural force governing economic affairs which can be relied upon to be beneficial; if natural economic laws are but understood, it will be possible to master them and create economic harmony and plenitude.

After two centuries of running the economic affairs of the world according to this idea, we are today not nearly so optimistic. Indeed, there are sophisticated economists who doubt very much if there are economic laws, let alone the possibility of understanding them. Many economists have abandoned the effort to understand economic arrangements as they actually operate. The statements important economists make to journalists for public consumption are to be understood as an effort at the management of public opinion, not as a reflection of a profound understanding of economics, an understanding which in fact they do not have. We must always remember that in the public management of opinion the governmental spokesmen and the university professors of economics are depending upon our basic myth that we can be redeemed from our economic troubles, which are, indeed, troubles in exploiting the natural world, and that we can be restored to an economic Eden. But like all of us, these men are not merely depending upon the myth; they are victims of it. Those among us who believe that redemption is to be found in eating natural organic foods and in wearing earth shoes are manifesting the same mythology.

Thus one result of the Baconian resolution of the late medieval cultural incoherence was the belief that human reason can restore us to Edenic mastery over nature, and that belief was supported by innumerable works of art, which like the eighteenth-century garden gave us the feeling appropriate to such mastery, the feeling of being in harmony with nature. But that belief and that feeling were not the only result of Bacon's writings. They were aspects of the nonmanipulative ideology. Far more important for what was to ensue was the manipulative aspect of his thinking, his emphasis upon the importance of experiment, an importance so dramatically, and independently, emphasized by Galileo.

In Florence, the home of Galileo, is one of the most fascinating of museums, *Il Museo Nazionale di Storia della Scienza,* actually a museum of scientific instruments. Inaugurated in 1930, its nucleus and still the most important segment was the great collection of scientific instruments made by the Medici and by their successors, the Lorraine-Hapsburgs. In the seventeenth century Florence was one of the great centers of scientific instrument making, stimulated by the work of Galileo and also by his successors, the Galilean Academy. Not in Florence alone, however, were groups of private individuals gathered into academies for the sake of Baconian experimentation. In England there was the Royal Society, originally the Philosophical Society, founded in 1645 for the study of natural philosophy, the name given science after "natural magic" was abandoned. All over Europe there existed such societies of people we would today call amateurs, academies of all kinds. Although cultural history, including the history of science, has paid little attention to it, the academic movement was for several centuries the principal instrument by which not only science but all branches of learning and scholarship were developed. Indeed, as late as the 1850s John Henry Newman asserted that the academic function of research was not a proper function of universities and should be kept institutionally separate from the universities, the function of which was the teaching of what was known, not the discovery of the unknown.

A study of what the scientific academies were doing reveals that they were not engaged in Descartean speculation about the universe, were not engaged in rethinking it from scratch. On the contrary, they were engaged in physical experiments, in the manipulation of nature. And to engage in such research they had to have instruments. Hence the fascination of the Florentine museum. The seventeenth century saw an immense proliferation of scientific instruments, and the making of such instruments became an established craft and trade. Whitehead called the seventeenth century the century of genius, but he was thinking of ideas, of the intellectual foundations of modern science, for he was a philosopher. His attention naturally fell upon the rational or theoretical development of science. I think that was a distortion.

Oddly enough, for all the importance of science to the modern world, there are not many histories of science. Only since World

War II have professorships and courses in the history of science been established in universities. In all of the histories of science that I have read, and in virtually all philosophical discussions of scientific theory I am familiar with, there is a serious underestimation and sometimes a complete neglect of the importance of scientific instruments. The philosophy of scientific theory is currently engaged in a passionate discussion of whether scientific theories can be proved, or whether they can only be disproved. I think both positions are mistaken. Scientific theories are neither proved nor disproved. They are abandoned. And they are abandoned because of scientific instruments.

How does a scientist proceed? On the basis of the data available to him he develops a theory. He then designs an experiment to prove or disprove his theory. To carry out his experiment he must have instruments, for Baconian that he is, he does not believe that any theory can be proved or disproved without manipulation of the physical world. Let us be careful about this, for it is important for what will follow. The scientist does not really create a theory. When we state that he does that, we are trying to *explain* what he does, but we are not stating *what* he does. He generates certain verbal utterances. He puts words together into sentences which for the time being satisfy him. His next step is to respond to his own statements by generating new sentences which predict what will happen when he carries out his experiment. He then develops his instruments, or uses an existing instrument for his own novel purposes. After the experiment he judges (observe that word, "judges") that his predictive sentences have or have not been confirmed. If they have, he then judges that his original, or theoretical statements, are true statements—true until further experiment, he judges, falsifies them. For the intelligent scientist scientific truth is always truth only for the time being.

Now it is very interesting to examine all of his behavior and all of the consequences of his experiment. Thomas J. Kuhn in his brilliant book, *The Structure of Scientific Revolutions,* makes the point that if data is uncovered which does not provide, in the judgment of the scientist, information pertinent to his experiment, he tends to neglect it. But Kuhn I think fails to draw the important moral of this, the significance of scientific instruments. For what scientific instruments do is to provide more data than the scientist's theory can handle and also irrelevant data. Scientific instruments invariably are responsible for a certain randomization of data. When that randomization becomes so obvious that some scientist or other can no longer manage to ignore it, a scientific revolution occurs. That is, the theory is abandoned and a new one is created to take its place. Let me put the point differently.

What scientific instruments do is to undermine the theories responsible for their invention, and they have this destructive effect upon scientific theory by providing more data than the theory can handle and by providing data irrelevant to the theory, that is, by randomizing it. And this randomization forces the creation of new and more powerful theories. The history of science is the history of scientific instruments, which are responsible for creating cultural incoherence; for scientific theories themselves are under the control of a culture's ideology, its way of explaining the world. We have already seen an example of this. Medieval man's increasing control over natural forces undermined the theological theory that the descendants of Adam are forbidden by God to have such control. Or, to give another example, Copernicus placed the sun in the center of the solar system because he was faced with more data than the current theory could account for and with a kind of data it could not account for at all.

But this is by no means the only impact scientific instruments have. When you go into any factory or oil refinery or machine shop or chemical plant, what you see are scientific instruments enormously magnified. To be sure, they have been modified as well, but that modification is hardly more than the result of the scale on which they are built. From this point of view the oldest scientific instrument is the potter's wheel, from which was developed the lathe, perhaps the prime instrument for making scientific instruments. Moreover, if you study what went on in the Royal Society, as described in the diary of Samuel Pepys, what is observable is the intense interest of these early academicians in the commercial possibilities of their discoveries, and therefore in the commercial possibilities of the instruments that made those discoveries possible. In the eighteenth century, when the insufficient supply of flax made crucial the endemic shortage of paper, academies offered prizes to anyone who could discover a new raw material. We must not forget that the architects and masons and sculptors and stained-glass makers and all the other artists and workmen involved in building the great medieval cathedrals were engaged in commercial enterprises. Those cathedrals cost money, lots of it, and the officers of the cathedral were as busy as can be in persuading the public to donate the money to build them. That is why practically all of them remained unfinished. It is not that the economic resources of the middle ages were insufficient to complete them; it is rather that the techniques of social management were too crude to raise the money. We do better today at that sort of thing. As I suggested before, business is merely the economic arm of the culture's ideology—and ideologies.

I have been proposing that an ideological revolution of the early seventeenth century, by resolving a late medieval incoherence, precipitated that manipulative science which is responsible for the extraordinary dynamic of European culture in the last three and a half centuries, a culture so powerful in its mastery of nature that no other culture can withstand it. In spite of China's immense and traditional devotion to social stability, which it has fairly well regained, it is being changed and its culture is being undermined by the introduction of Western technology. And technology is the consequence of the development of scientific instruments, and those instruments are the result of an ideological revolution. That revolution, however, was incomplete because it retained the ideology of redemption. Just as the naive scientist (most of them) believes that he can develop a final explanation of what he is studying, and just as he believes that that explanation will fit into a final explanation of the entire universe, an explanation that will redeem us from our ignorance, so the economic arm of our ideology believes that we will finally create for everybody in the world a life so perfect that everybody will live just the way suburban Americans live—a horrifying prospect. Perhaps I may appear to be exaggerating, but only five years ago I heard with my own ears some of the most famous and prominent scientists in this country and in the world state quite seriously that the quantitative, or economic, aspects of human life were on the verge of final solution, and that it was only a matter of time before the only question remaining was the quality of life people proposed to live. Quality of life, they affirmed, can be a billion-dollar business. Well, now we know that India is worse off than before the green revolution, because the green revolution depended upon irrigation, and that depended upon oil, and oil is now too expensive for India to afford in the quantities it needs. But an oil refinery is only an enormous magnification of scientific instruments developed *before* the revolution in the scientific instrumentation of the seventeenth century. Those instruments were developed by alchemists, and alchemy was a form of magic, the attempt to manipulate and control natural forces.

This blindness of enormously competent scientists is the same blindness that has for so long led historians of science and philosophers of science to ignore the revolutionary and all-important role of the seventeenth-century scientific instrument inventor and craftsman. When people are incapable of seeing what is right in front of their eyes, you may be sure that their ideologies are responsible, for a culture's ideologies are the ultimate controls over what we see and the ultimate sources of instructions for interpreting what we see. Because

of the neglect of the history of science and its failure to penetrate beyond a very small circle of interested scholars, and above all because
of the neglect of the importance of scientific instruments, because of
the failure to realize that the history of science is indeed the history
of scientific instruments, the commercial arm of our culture has neglected and indeed been ignorant of what the history of scientific instruments reveals, that scientific instruments invariably produce more
data than the scientist can handle, and data irrelevant to his purpose—
that, from the point of view of the theoretical statements that control
his behavior, scientific instruments produce a randomization of data.
And we are back to our aerosol cans.

Nobody imagined, nobody dreamed, that the use of aerosol cans
might damage the atmospheric layer that protects us from solar radiation and makes human life possible. For an instructive analogy we
need only turn to the exceedingly primitive and barely developed science of medicine, in which over and over again new drugs turn out
to produce unanticipated side effects, many of which are undesirable
and some of which are murderous. We must never forget that the
medical establishment (doctors and drug companies and hospitals)
gave this country a drug culture alternative to alcohol when they introduced tranquilizers. Nor, of course, do we yet have any knowledge
whatever of other equally undesirable side effects the enormous use
of aerosol cans might have, though I seem to remember a newspaper
account that suggested such consequences. An aerosol can is a scientific instrument because by manipulating natural products, or products derived from natural products, such as hairspray, it changes the
world. Scientific instruments of all kinds are now in the hands of millions upon millions of people, but we think that because these instruments give us control over nature they are and must be beneficial
to us, that they will bring us that much closer to the Edenic world
which we have lost and which it is our sole purpose to return to.

Let me give an example of the kind of thinking responsible for this.
It is a poem by Matthew Arnold, "In Harmony with Nature," and it
is addressed to a preacher, a detail in itself historically amusing, because any preacher who asserts that we should be in harmony with
nature is no longer Christian but is under the control of the gardening
ideology of the eighteenth-century Enlightenment.

> "In harmony with Nature?" Restless fool,
> Who with such heat does preach what were to thee,
> When true, the last impossibility—
> To be like Nature strong, like Nature cool!
> Know, man hath all which Nature hath, but more,

And in that *more* lie all his hopes of good.
Nature is cruel, man is sick of blood;
Nature is stubborn, man would fain adore;
Nature is fickle, man hath need of rest;
Nature forgives no debt, and fears no grave;
Man would be mild, with safe conscience blest.
Man must begin, know this, where Nature ends;
Nature and man can never be fast friends.
Fool, if thou canst not pass her, rest her slave!

It is doubtful that man is sick of blood, but it is probably true that he would like to be blest with safe conscience, though not necessarily at the price of being mild. But the important word is *"more."* Man has more than nature has; indeed man begins where nature ends. Man thus transcends and is of greater value than nature. Arnold not only knows all about man, he knows all about nature. Nature is strong, he says, and I think of endangered species; nature is cool, he says, and I think of an atomic pile. But Arnold of course is talking about spiritual values, that in man which is not natural, that which differentiates man from nature. And if nature ends where man begins, then everything man does is nonnatural, is spiritual. And that is indeed the case. But if we abandon this Arnoldian self-congratulation for our difference from nature, if we resist the sin of pride, we will recognize that Arnold is really saying (though he did not know it) that our ideologies, another name for our spiritual values, do not correspond with nature, that our beliefs and our explanations of the world are not isomorphic with the world, not of the same shape, or form, or structure, or with the same attributes or properties. For our ideologies, our spiritual values, when we come right down to looking at them, are words and sentences. They are verbal behavior. And language is the creation of man.

In our examination of the behavior of a scientist we have already seen how language works. His ideology tells him what kind of theoretical statements to generate. Those in turn tell him what experimental statements to generate. And those in turn tell him what instruments he will need. And those instruments provide him the information he is looking for, or fail to provide it. But because he is ultimately under the control of his ideology, he will if he possibly can, ignore the data he cannot use, ignore the randomization for which instruments are responsible. Or he will create a better theory, one which will give greater power over nature. To the question, What is language? we can answer, Language is directions for verbal and nonverbal performance. And I use the word "performance" quite carefully and consciously, for language is directions for performance only for one who has been trained to respond to those directions with that particular performance. Moreover this notion of language as directions for performance can be successfully extended to the broad anthropological term "culture." Some years ago the anthropologist Karl Kroeber brought together all the anthropological definitions of culture. They were many and remarkably various but all of them can be subsumed or covered or taken care of, I believe, by defining culture as directions for performance. Now what an ideology does is to explain those directions, to justify them, and to validate them—to affirm that they are socially valid and that they ought to be obeyed. On the whole, people obey them. On the whole, people do exactly what you tell them to do. If you examine anyone's life for a day, minute by minute, you will observe how rarely people negate an instruction, though the capacity to negate is the indication that a child is a human being and not a Mongolian idiot. Furthermore, what is true of language is true of all culture. It does not and cannot tell us what the world really is; it can only tell us how to find our way around in it. But since it cannot tell us what the world really is, the manipulative relation to the world is bound to have unpredicted and to us random consequences. And thus all ideologies must eventually be undermined and fail.

Therefore if our ideology tells us, as it does, that the aim of human culture is to understand the natural world completely, and to master it and dominate it, and if in doing so it gives us our basic myth, if it tells us to redeem our culture into a perfect isomorphism with the natural world, it is telling us something we cannot do. On the one hand the incomplete ideological revolution of the seventeenth century confirmed the Western European belief that the mind of man (human culture) is capable of dominating and mastering the natural world, that man's reason is sufficient for that purpose, that, as Arnold so blindly said, the mind transcends the world, that man transcends nature. But on the other hand the revolution in scientific instrumentation made it equally clear that the manipulation of the world necessarily brings unanticipated and, with great and unpredictable frequency, undesirable and even deadly consequences. Thus we can see that what we call the Baconian resolution of a late medieval ideological incoherence itself was internally rent by an ideological incoherence. And that is the incoherence with which we are now faced. We set out to master Nature, and when you do that, it turns out, Nature masters you right back. Arnold was wrong. We *are* the slaves of nature, and the scientific revolution has made us more abject slaves than ever.

# CHAPTER TWELVE

# Two Ways of Using
# "Creativity"

I confess I find the word "creativity" as useless as the term "imagination" and almost as repellent as "self-fulfillment." The word has been so extended that it is applied to kindergarten finger painting and rearranging the living room furniture. Like "imagination" it cannot be restricted. Our efforts to restrict it result in terms such as "creative imagination," a phrase doubly useless. Nor does the term "innovation" seem to be an acceptable synonym or substitute. "Innovation" is milder; we seem compelled to couple it with "significant," "important," "powerful," or the like, even "creative." A decade ago I proposed that creativity is socially validated error, and that error is invalidated creativity, both being modes of innovation. This distinction at least suggests that an innovation has to be validated for it to be crowned with the glorious term "creative." Hence we can distinguish between two uses of "creativity," the process of producing something that might be designated as creative, and the designation of something as creative. Thus there are two problems in accounting for the impossibility of restricting the term's application—distinguishing creative behaviors from other behaviors, and exploring the social behavior of designating some human product as creative. Let me say here, to prevent misunderstanding, that the fact that I use the term "behavior" does not mean that I am a behaviorist in the usual sense. I see no reason a group of academic scientists should have the exclusive control over and use of a very valuable word.

To deal with the first problem, it is useful to pull back a very great distance and to begin with the problem of what is "real." Plato proposed—or at least most commentators think that he proposed—that only ideas are real, and that the material, or perceived, or sensorily apprehended world is a mere mimesis—a word puzzling enough—of the ideas. His further notion—though I am sure that someone will say that this wasn't Plato's notion at all—that the ideas had a divine or at least supernatural origin can mean anything or nothing, but at least it means that the idea and its attributes did not originate from the sensory response to the material world. Other philosophers—a breed that I find it increasingly difficult to take very seriously—locate the real elsewhere. They deny reality even to the ideas, asserting that they are only illusions and that if we are to be happy we must rid ourselves of them, including the idea of oneself—a position it is impossible to disagree with. The real is to be located in the All, which is inapprehensible. Others claim that the real is to be found exactly where Plato said it is not to be found, in the material world, to which we respond with our various senses; others say that real is the apprehension; others that the real consists of the mental constructs we make from our sensory apprehensions. Still others claim that the real is the relation between the perception and the phenomenal world it perceives. The real, then, consists of these phenomenal ghosts. Others locate the real in the Divine, or identify God as the only real, or claim that the real is to be found in the unconscious. Still others assert that the real is what the reason produces, or that the will controls the reason and the real is what the will produces. And so on. All of these positions have been argued with the utmost intellectual splendor, but I do not find any of those arguments even faintly convincing.

Rather I ask myself what it is that these varying definitions of the real are trying to locate; and I think that the answer is that they are trying to establish the ultimate control over and justification of human behavior. I suspect that the philosophical speculations on the term "real" do no more than recognize the meaning of the term "really" in such a sentence as, "I really believe that Nixon was a splendid president," a sentence in which "really" does no more than recommend that the responder to the sentence should control his behavior by the assertion.

But if that is all "real" amounts to, why have human beings been so passionately concerned to locate the habitat of the "real"? Aside from seeking for explanation and justification and validation for behavior—a speculative function of which the epistemologically minded seem to be frequently unaware—the answer, I think, lies in the fact that traditionally the real is not talked about without also talking about something called the "mind." The mind has some relation to reality, it is claimed, or sometimes it is reality, or its contents are reality, or the content of reality is the mind, and so on, to include all the permutations that this distressing pair of words has been put through. Now if you ask me to go and find a mind and bring it back to you, I cannot do so. But it does not follow that when people use the word "mind" they are not responding to anything at all. On the contrary. But what is it that the word is a response to? Again, I think the answer is fairly obvious. It is the fact that different individuals can and do respond differently to the same stimulus or stimulus field. In short, the word "mind" is equivalent to "variability of response." What this amounts to is that whatever the real may be or wherever it is located it is not real until it is responded to by human beings. The question now is, How shall we usefully characterize that response?

My own position, I suppose, is that of semiotic phenomenalism, a position which, I hope, has no philosophical respectability. The notion of semiosis I use is not to be confused with that of the currently fashionable French semioticians, whom I regard as mad, bad, and dangerous to know. Rather, it derives from American sources, Peirce, Mead, Morris, with more than a touch of Wittgenstein and Philosophical Analysis. Though I agree with Mead that the meaning of any sign is the response to that sign, that is not the problem I am concerned with here. Rather, I point to Peirce for respectability. Of all the writers on signs I have encountered he is one of the few who recognizes that semiosis involves somebody doing something. Thus he introduces the "interpretant," that is, not the one who does the interpreting of the relation of the sign to object but rather the proposition that results from that interpretation. The point is that he does not stop with that hypostatized pseudo-entity, the mind, but continues on to the result. It has been said that the difficulty of Peirce's position is that the interpretant itself becomes a sign, and so on *ad infinitum*. But I do not see that this is a difficulty; rather, I see it as the condition of semiosis. The object of the sign could not be an object if it were not already a sign. That is, the world turns into sign fields as it moves into an individual's sensory apprehension. We cannot locate a beginning point or foundation for semiosis, because in attempting to do so we are already engaged in semiotic behavior, a condition which we cannot transcend or move outside of. Hence for human beings behavior which is not under genetic control—and there is very little of that— consists of responding to signs by generating signs. Thus I propose that the defining attribute of human behavior is semiotic transformation. The most extreme instance of semiotic transformation is negation, either verbal or nonverbal.

We are now in a better position to understand why we are haunted by such words as "real" and "true" and "verifiable," and so on with the rest of that exasperating family. The conviction, universal in philosophical history, that the real and the mind are inseparable suggests that experience does not become real to us until it is subjected to semiotic transformation. Let me give a couple of examples from an area of behavior of a fairly sensational nature, a tactic which may at least serve to lighten the gloom which has settled over our profession, examples, then, from sexual behavior and pornography.

My first example comes from well-equipped brothels, the widespread use of mirrors on ceilings and walls of bedrooms. What little we know about sexual behavior also indicates that the use of strategically placed mirrors in private homes is not uncommon, and that masturbation in front of mirrors is likewise a very common practice. A mirror offers semiotic transformation in two ways. First, it reverses the sign field, and second, it permits us to see ourselves from a point of view from which without reflection we could not possibly see ourselves. My second example comes from pornographic films made primarily for a heterosexual male audience. In such films more footage is devoted to the presentation of the erect penis than to the female sexual zone. Likewise more footage is devoted to oral sex than to genital sex, for in the former the erection is on view continuously, while in the latter only intermittently. The obvious and banal thing to say is that such footage is an appeal to an unconscious homosexuality, but I do not think that is the case at all. Rather, I propose that even so intimate and intensely sensory experience as sex is not felt to be real until it is semiotically transformed. Even when merchandizing pornography is legally forbidden, it circulates commercially; and of course talk of a pornographic character is constant in what Philip Rieff calls remissive situations. Almost every artist, as soon as he or she learns to draw, will draw some pornographic pictures. Pornographic grafitti are universal. Edmund Gosse longed to see sexual intercourse actually described in detail in a printed novel.

However, semiotic transformation does not start with transformation of a sign field into verbal or nonverbal semiotic objectifications. An earlier stage, though not always present, is subjective, that is, the "mental" transformation into covert verbal signs or nonverbal signs, or images. Prior to that is the transformation into a physiological response, for every stimulus that reaches the brain is converted into a physiological response somewhere in the body. If that response is sufficiently strong it is experienced as an emotion; that is, the physiological response, rising above the threshold of perception, becomes a sign which can be variously interpreted, as either, for example, fear or anger, depending upon the situation. And transformation can be continued in the other direction, from the construction of a semiotic complex, such as a pornographic film, into the manipulation of an existent nonhuman field, the material or natural world.

To give another example, there is in my local state prison a very interesting inmate. While in a mental hospital in California he and a fellow prisoner planned upon release to capture a young woman, rape her, kill her, and eat her. That is exactly what they did. If you are shocked by this, you are either naive about human behavior or pathologically optimistic. A friend of mine, Professor Robert Stewart of my university, a sociologist with whom I work very closely, has suggested that mutilation before, during, or after rape is exactly analogous to scientific behavior. Thus scientific behavior is fundamentally the completion of the process of semiotic transformation by manipulating the material world to produce what is then interpreted as either a predicted or unpredicted consequence, that is, a sign that confirms or disconfirms the verbal proposition that is the prior stage in the total process of semiotic transformation.

Now if we look at my young cannibal from the point of view of semiotic transformation it seems to me reasonable to say that his was a highly creative act—just as the Iranian students were highly creative in their manipulation of the United States embassy and its personnel. My prisoner's life before his creative crime suggests that he interpreted hindrances to his behavior, of which he had experienced many in areas important to him, as deliberate hindrances. This accumulation of interpretations led to a condition of seething resentment. And I use the word "seething" to suggest that the physiological responses to his interpretations brought about powerful emotions which were the driving force behind transformation of that resentment into his creative crime. The point is, rapes involving mutilation are not uncommon; rapes involving murder are considerably less common; and rapes culminating in cannibalism are pretty rare. At least, I hope so.

There is a further point to be derived from this case. Fantasies of rape are not uncommon; and judging by material I have examined at the Kinsey Sex Research Institute, women's fantasies involving sex and the infliction of pain upon men are probably of equal incidence. Such fantasies, or covert semiotic transformations, are not carried out into action; the process of semiotic transformation is complete, cut short by two stages. But like the carrying out of rape, murder, and cannibalism, they involve the violation of a cultural norm. So did at one time the mutilation of cadavers for medical research and surgical training. Powerful cultural sanctions can prevent the consummation of semiotic transformations. From this we may perhaps conclude that the degree of creativity is a function, first, of statistical infrequency, and, second, of cultural violation or vandalism. I propose that creativity is a consequence of behavioral randomness and at the same time a violation of the culturally established controls over randomness. Certainly, studies of scientific and artistic creativity show that neither is a logical development of the existing culture, whether scientific or artistic, but a kind of quantum leap.

Turning now to the second meaning of "creativity," its cultural validation, I propose that the factor of cultural control is equally important. If a semiotic transformation is validated and labeled a significant innovation or an instance of creativity, that validation is possible only if the cultural emergent can be accommodated within existent cultural controls. But that does not mean immediately accommodated. First, it may be pointed out that because of variability of response, minimal innovation is a constant in any category or mode of human behavior. Nobody can learn anything perfectly. Second, though much of evidential value has disappeared, in both science and art there are sufficient records of fruitless instances of process creativity to suggest very strongly that probably the overwhelming mass of process creativity leaves no lasting traces, is not accommodated by the cultural controls, and is forgotten. If judged at all, such instances are judged as error. Third, a great many consequences of process creativity are incapable of being accommodated at the time of their appearance, though virtually identical consequences are subsequently validated, sometimes centuries later. Medieval philosophy produced philosophical emergents which were fruitless but which, as we say, anticipated the emergence of the same or highly similar ideas in this century. Fourth, many process innovations are kept available but not exploited. The cultural controls are sufficiently accommodating to preserve them but not make use of them, for making use of an innovation necessarily involves modifying the cultural controls over innovation. Finally, a few innovations are immediately labeled creative by enough and important enough individuals and are accommodated, and the cultural controls are accordingly modified.

What this amounts to is that the common notion of creativity is hopelessly inadequate because it attempts to explain only validated creativity. Because all behavior is minimally creative, at the least, we cannot restrict the term to any class of completely or partially consummated semiotic transformations. Likewise, the validation of an emergent as creative is unpredictable, uncontrollable, and currently incomprehensible. Although research in the full range of validation and invalidation of the emergent consequences of semiotic transformation would be rewarding, the incompleteness of the historical record makes such research impossible. Only the validation of what a culture has already designated as creative can be studied. The results of such research could be most illuminating, but only if creativity is recognized as the violation of cultural norms, even when the creative emergent is culturally accommodated with little delay. Finally, if an emergent is responded to with full range of response from negative to positive, it is probably a good candidate for validation. The explanation is that there are no cultural instructions on how to respond to it. Hence the response is random within the poles of rejection and acceptance.

# CHAPTER THIRTEEN

# Truth in Art? Why Not?

When one starts puzzling about "truth" it appears to be reasonable to find out what philosophers have had to say about it; philosophy, after all, is dedicated to determining what truth is. But there are and have been a great many philosophers all of whom seem to have somewhat differing notions on the subject, or at least all the major ones. However, to read even cursorily the couple of dozen major philosophers of Western culture, not to speak of those from India and China and the Moslem world, is something few professional philosophers have done. Either they continue what they believe to be some existing philosophical tradition, or they react against that tradition and, with at least the partial aid of some other tradition, endeavor to disprove the tradition they dislike and to carve out some new or more subtle conception of truth. Whatever they do, the position they take and the line they pursue to develop it are rarely based upon more than a casual knowledge of a few philosophers and a detailed study of even fewer. Or if we turn to the history of philosophy, as written by various individuals, we are still in trouble. One philosopher told me that there is no good history of philosophy and cannot be, for a history of philosophy must necessarily be written from a particular point of view. It has been perhaps too unkindly said that John Herman Randall turns everybody into a pragmatist.

Happily there is an alternative, *The Encyclopedia of Philosophy,* published in 1967, written by hundreds of different practicing philosophers. The advantage of such a work is that one is not at the mercy of a particular philosopher with his philosophical point of view. Rather, one encounters Hume, Descartes, Plato, Hegel, Kant in many different articles, each of which tells you something valuable that the others do not. Moreover, the reader encounters dozens and dozens of minor individuals, men who form the background to the major figures, who enable one to understand why the major philosophers are indeed major, and who reveal themselves as the carriers of the philosophical traditions from which the great figures make innovative departures.

Admittedly the scale of the *Encyclopedia* presents a bit of a barrier. It consists of eight volumes, totaling 4,045 pages, not counting the index. About ten percent, at the most, is made up of bibliographies. The volumes are two-columned quartos, each page containing the equivalent of three pages of an ordinary scholarly book. Thus the text consists of at least 11,000 pages of such books, or the equivalent of twenty-two 500-page scholarly works. To find out by reading this mass of material what philosophers have thought of truth is clearly a formidable task. Happily, however, I have been able to read the whole thing, with the exception, I must admit, of perhaps a couple of hundred pages of symbolic logic and mathematics, for which I have no training. Though occasional articles were tiresome, on the whole I found the experience enlightening, often entertaining and pleasant, intellectually highly profitable and even exhilarating.

Yet one's conclusions from such a course of reading are somewhat melancholy. I cannot resist the notion that in the course of 2,500 years of philosophical culture remarkably little has been accomplished, if one considers the vast amount of work and the extraordinary intelligence and learning involved in the philosophical enterprise. And if one sets out on this task in the hope of discovering a really solid comprehension of what truth is, one might as well go to the movies. Nevertheless, a good many modern philosophers claim that in the last fifty or sixty years there has been a philosophical revolution, a very simple one, but shattering. All these centuries, they maintain, philosophy has been mistaken. Philosophy has not been talking about mind, or ideas, or concepts, or thought, or consciousness, or the inner world, or the outer world, and so on, but it has been talking about language, or to be more precise, about words, or, to be even more precise, about verbal behavior, though very few philosophers even today have gotten that far. Above all, for two and a half millennia, philosophers have been *talking*—or doing something more or less equivalent to talking, *writing*. At any rate, whatever they have been doing, they have been *doing* something.

Some philosophers have maintained, then, that the only thing to do is to forget all philosophy that has been produced before this revolution, or continues to be produced in spite of it. Others, more cautious and of a more generous temper, have said that the past needs reinterpreting in the light of the revolution, and can be reinterpreted, and that thus it will be discovered that past philosophy has said a great many very useful things, even though the philosophers who did the saying did not know it.

As for "truth," that word has suffered from the revolution a severe attrition of meaning and usefulness, so severe that one is inclined to be surprised and puzzled that philosophers still use the word at all, though they seem to do so, almost without exception, even if all that unfortunate word can claim for itself is the result of a tautological deduction. Some still talk, for example, about synthetic truths and analytic truths, but others maintain that it is impossible to make a distinction between the two. Others claim that there is something that can be called inductive truth, as opposed to deductive truth, but others maintain with great fervor and impressiveness that though we have a right to claim deductive truth we are completely at a loss in trying to understand either how we arrive at an inductive truth or how to prove it once we have arrived.

In the light of all this it seems advisable to approach the problem from the other end, not from the word "truth" but from considering what people are doing when they use the word. By that I do not mean to attempt to examine what an individual is doing when he says, for example, "What I just told you about the accident is the truth." Obviously his interest is to get his listener to believe him, that is, to get his listener to control his behavior by that statement. That explanation of the use of the term "truth" is good enough as far as it goes, and it goes farther than most philosophers are currently prepared to. It seems obvious, for example, that when a scientist makes a statement with the word "truth" in it, he is doing no more than the man who makes his statement about the accident. The difficulty is that this explanation of the use of "truth" still leaves the "truth-use situation" open to the correspondence theory of truth—that is, a true statement corresponds to something in the nonverbal reality and offers a description of it. Thus from one point of view, the statement in question is a normative statement in that it asserts that the listener *ought* to believe the statement about the accident, yet from another point of view it is a statement that the preceding statements about the accident were true descriptive statements, and that this statement by subsuming those statements is also a descriptive statement.

It would seem, then, that it is necessary to dig deeper into the situation and examine more carefully the situation of uttering a statement with "truth" in it. Given a situation and a response to it, what has happened? Here we must look at the character of response itself. It is generally agreed among most psychologists today that a response to a situation is a transaction. That is, the situation stimuli are fed to the brain, but the brain's responses to those stimuli are not passive. On the contrary, the stimuli are interpreted by the brain. This means that what the stimulus contributes and what the brain contributes cannot be separated. Further, every stimulus that reaches the brain is transmitted to some part of the organism. If the response by that part is so powerful that the speaker becomes aware of it, we call it an emotion. But even if the speaker does not become aware of it, the additional stimulus to the brain is nevertheless present and becomes a factor of the total situation to which the speaker is responding. That is what accounts for the extreme ambiguity of the word "emotion." If the speaker when uttering his statement about the accident speaks in a strained or unusually loud or soft tone of voice, speaks in any way abnormal for his mode of intonation, we are likely to assume that there is an emotional factor in his response and are therefore inclined to disbelieve him or at least to question his veracity and to give him a polygraph test.

At this point it is useful to introduce the notion of the "sign" and semiotic behavior. A sign can be defined, first, as a configuration distinguished from a ground, and, second, as a configuration to which there is an interpreted response. But since all responses are interpreted responses, it follows that to human beings the world consists of signs, or, more cautiously, the world turns into signs as it enters a human's perceptual field. One class of signs to which we respond consists of verbal signs, not merely words but streams of words, for we interpret a stream by our syntactical expectations. If our syntactical interpretations are violated severely enough we cannot respond; we cannot interpret that stream. To the question, "Is that what happened in the accident?" the response is, "What I just told you about the accident is the truth." In this case verbal signs have been responded to by generating verbal signs. But in describing the accident, the speaker responded to nonverbal signs by generating verbal signs. In both cases the stimulus field is subjected to a semiotic transformation, which may or may not have been influenced by a physiological response. Perhaps the effect of the accident was so severe and disorienting a psychophysical shock that the response was vague and fragmentary. But reliable or not, the response was a semiotic transformation, responding to a sign field by generating a sign field.

Clearly the responsive sign field cannot possibly be identical with the stimulus sign field. I look out of the window in front of which I am typing this paper. I see a number of trees and three or four houses, as well as bushes, ground covered with dead leaves, camellia blossoms, and so on. There is no way that by a semiotic transformation I can produce an exact replica of what I am seeing. Moreover, just by generating a verbal stream which uses various nouns, verbs, prepositions, punctuation marks, and so on, I am transforming that semiotic field into one controlled by syntactical and other verbal conventions. Even if I should make a highly detailed drawing it would be subject to the conventions of such drawings, such as perspective, to be found in Western culture.

What this means is that all statements that claim to be true statements are the consequence of semiotic transformation, and in any semiotic transformation we can distinguish three factors: the preservation of the perceptual attributes of the field being responded to; the interference by the brain in receiving the stimuli—an interference which we call mind, or reason, or imagination, and so on; and the conventions of the semiotic modality into which the transformation is made. If, for example, one examines with care one's covert nonverbal images provided by remembering semiotic fields, it becomes apparent that there is a certain unique and personal style to such images; perhaps some category of configurations is always neglected or always distorted in some particular way. Some people remember in color; some do not. The point is that even remembered covert images are the result of semiotic transformations. Obviously the most bizarre transformations, for most people, occur in dreams, which mix up semiotic transformations from any number of widely separated or contiguous interpreted semiotic fields, the details of which are selected and combined in marvelously unpredictable ways.

If this analysis has any weight, it seems obvious that questions about whether a statement is true or not—or a drawing—are pointless, and that statements claiming truth are absolutely empty. It would appear, then, that when we say that a statement is true we are simply saying, "Let's get on with it," the "it" meaning whatever we happen to be doing at the moment, conducting a trial about responsibility for an accident or writing a philosophical treatise. Claims for truth, then, are interactional conveniences, and the attempt to make a distinction between descriptive and normative statements collapses into the single category of normative statements. When we claim a statement to be true, what we are doing is asserting that from this semiotic field we are selecting and transforming certain details or attributes which we propose to be the items appropriate for facilitating the behavior we are currently engaged in, whether the individual is interacting with another or others or only with himself. This does not mean that we should retreat into absolute skepticism, for the notion of skepticism emerged only in response to the realization that claims for absolute and perfect truth were suspect and perhaps without foundation. Skepticism arises only when claims for truth are made. It is a mere by-product of our urgency to continue on the course we are currently pursuing.

When we say, then, that any humanly produced verbal or nonverbal semiotic transformation is true, we are saying that it is appropriate and justifiable to act as *if* a certain set of features in the field being responded to had *not* been subjected to transformation, and as *if* that set were the *only* set of features in that field.

From this point of view works of art are obviously semiotic transformations, more obviously so, indeed, than other kinds of transformation. That obviousness comes from the modes of presenting works of art—on a stage, within a frame, by using rhyme, or by using the sounds of the intonations of linguistic utterance and with these creating what we call music. Another way of saying that semiotic transformations are normative is saying that they are fictive. In art, as opposed to other kinds of verbal and nonverbal discourse (to extend the range of that word beyond language) that fictiveness is announced. Even in spite of that—and this shows "true" is not antithetical to "fictive"—all kinds of claims have been made for the truth of works of art. But what was Aristotle doing when he said that the truth of poetry is at a higher level than the truth of history? He knew perfectly well that poetry is an "invention," even though he seems considerably less aware that his philosophical discourses were also inventions. All he meant, all he could mean, is that the truths of poetry, or the truths derived from poetry by semiotic transformation, can be appropriate instructions for getting on with it in a greater number and range of situations than can the truths in historical discourse or transformationally derived from historical discourse. And that in general is the pattern of claims for the truths of art. So vague is this claim—since it does nothing to specify the kinds of situation such truths can be appropriately and successfully used for generating responses to—that the claim usually amounts to little more than a claim that high value is properly ascribed to the work of art in question, or to the category of art—whether music, or dance, or painting, or poetry, for each of which claims have been made that it is of higher value than any other kind of art.

For example when we say that Shakespeare's *Othello* is a play true

to human nature, we are merely saying that there are certain identifiable modes of human behavior which at times it is appropriate to
respond to by transforming them into such words as "jealousy," "resentment," "revenge," and that when such modes are allowed un-
controlled free play in a situation, they are likely to mess up that
situation very thoroughly and produce highly disagreeable consequences. Therefore the "moral truth" is that we ought to control and
if possible terminate such modes when we distinguish them in ourselves or in others. The fictiveness of *Othello* is not only announced by
the word "tragedy" if one reads it, or by seeing it performed in a theater, but the fictiveness is also to be found in the fact that if the complete history of an actual Othello, Iago, Desdemona, and the rest of
them were observed from beginning to end there would be a great
many other modes of behavior to be observed; and indeed that the
resentment, the revenge, and the jealousy might even be so indiscern-
ible that we would be quite mystified by the murder of Desdemona
and the suicide of Othello. Moreover, a behavioral mode transformed
by one person into "resentment" can easily be transformed by someone else into "a love for justice" or "egalitarianism."

This brings in another characteristic of art which is found in other
discourses as well and which does much to account for our judgment
of the truths of discourses. That characteristic is the intensification of
the devices of the semiotic modalities which are the termination of
the transformational process. A simple example in poetry is onomatopoeia, as in Tennyson's "Elaine the fair, Elaine, the lovable / Elaine
the lily maid of Astolat." By intensification I mean the more frequent
occurrence of a particular device or devices than is found in ordinary
semiotic transformation. For example, everyone uses gestures, but the
dance selects and intensifies the occurrence of certain gestures. Any
gesture can be selected for intensification, just as any art can use any
of the semiotic devices of a particular modality found outside of art.
As a general term for this process of intensification I shall use the word
"rhetoric," for two reasons. First, the classical rhetoricians were concerned with the deliberate intensified use of particular verbal devices,
and second, their concern was the art of persuasion.

The limitation of their thinking about this matter was their belief
that only certain devices were useful for the art of persuasion. In this
I believe they were mistaken. It was the intensification itself that was
persuasive. In all cultures the poet, whatever his poetic modality may
be, is admired. The reason was best put by Oscar Wilde, who called
himself the Lord of Language. If an individual exhibits high rhetorical
competence, mastery over the language which everyone uses, the ten-

dency to believe that he is equally the master of what he purports to be talking about is virtually irresistible. If we wish to resist it, we have to tell ourselves to resist it. The persuasiveness, the "truth" of Rembrandt's portraiture, which is said to exhibit profound insight into personality and character, is merely the result of the fact that he violated the norms of conventional good looks and presented an intensification of those innumerable physiological variations, whether the result of genes, suffering, or age, which everyone, especially as one gets older, exhibits. Whether or not a particular Rembrandt portrait actually gave any information about the human being whose face and costume were being semiotically transformed is something we can scarcely know. My suspicions are aroused by the fact that all his subjects look so benevolent, or if not benevolent, so dignified. I find it hard to believe that he was careful to paint only benevolent and dignified people. That intensification, at any rate, was the rhetoric of Rembrandt's portraiture, very different from the rhetoric of Vandyke's portraits, which are also said to exhibit profound insight into personality. The general rhetoric of portraiture is the rhetoric of uniqueness.

Rhetoric can be found in music. Consider a typical episode in a Bruckner symphony. It begins softly and in the bass, either in the major or the minor. Gradually the themes are presented more insistently, while the general melodic contour climbs steadily towards the treble. More and more orchestral resources are employed, with greater and greater volume. The brasses become more prominent. The level of violence is steadily raised. The mode shifts between major and minor with increasing frequency. Finally the whole marvelous panoply of sound slams into a minor seventh, as if into a brick wall. The orchestra collapses. Deep in the bass one hears the theme again, very softly, or perhaps a new theme, as Bruckner picks up the pieces and gets ready to try all over again. The rhetoric of Bruckner is built around an intensification of total frustration, or hindrance to one's capacity to keep going. That is the explanation for his rhetoric of length, and for the overwhelming effect of the coda of the last movement, when a principal theme is presented in the major, with tremendous orchestral force, and with no hindrance to ongoingness at all.

The peculiar advantage of the artist lies in the freedom of his rhetoric. By that I mean that he can use any semiotic modality. The illustrator to an anatomy textbook is limited in his rhetoric by the purpose which his illustrations are to serve, the maximum clarity in the delineation of physiological details. He must adopt a set of semiotic conventions and use them with complete consistency. But the painter can do anything from painting a flower with the most exquisite detail to covering a vast canvas with red and then introducing a jagged spike of white thrusting up from the bottom edge, in the manner of Clyfford Still. He can do this because fictiveness is announced. For this reason his employment of semiotic devices is theoretically unlimited. The only limitations are the current culturally established conventions for his particular art; even so, he can exhibit his mastery by violating those conventions, just as all those artists who are called great have violated (or transcended, if you wish) the artistic conventions of their time. The lawyer, on the other hand, must select those particular devices which experience has shown to be most effective in the particular kind of case he happens to be engaged upon. The philosopher and the scientist and the historian are limited in the verbal devices they can use. For such discourses we are inclined to grant truth-value if, and only if, we judge their rhetoric to be appropriate to the situation which they are semiotically transforming. The writer of fiction, however, can use anything he thinks he can get away with. The historian has to keep going in the face of the hindrances presented to him by vast collections of documents; the scientist has to keep going in the face of the hindrances presented to him by the results of his experiments; the philosopher in the face of the requirements of logic and the necessity to stabilize his terminology throughout his discourse.

The artist, however, because he has announced the fictiveness of his discourse, knows no such limitations. If, for example, he is a writer whose primary interest is to exemplify a particular philosophy or morality or ideology, there are no restraints on his rhetoric other than the appropriateness of his exemplifications. He can intensify any verbal device he pleases. Consider Dante. His exemplifications of various sins and various virtues are generally considered to be marvelously appropriate, in spite of the fact that for many of his exemplifications scholars have had a terrible time in demonstrating just why they are appropriate. But the sheer virtuosity exhibited in keeping that *terza rima* going convinces the reader that somehow or other they must be appropriate, that both the ideology of Dante and his exemplifications must be "true."

To sum up, rhetoric, whether verbal or nonverbal, that is, the intensification of the devices of a particular modality of semiotic transformation, conveys the sense of mastery, for it is, after all, a true mastery of that semiotic modality, and that semiotic mastery carries with it the conviction that what is said is true. The artist, because he does not conceal the fictiveness of his discourse, has far greater free-

dom in the rhetoric of intensifying semiotic devices, and therefore exhibits a correspondingly greater mastery over his semiotic modality.
Consequently the conviction that he is offering a higher truth than is
possible in any other kind of discourse is overwhelmingly powerful.
As Keats said, whatever is beautiful must be true.

# III

# THEORY OF ART AND CRITICISM

# CHAPTER FOURTEEN

# Psychology and Literature

Distrust, suspicion, and even contempt are common enough between members of the humanistic disciplines and the behavioral sciences. There is justification enough on both sides for such hostility, but it may be that both sides pay too high a price for their complacency. Some years ago I was a member of what was supposed to be an important committee of the Modern Language Association, though events proved otherwise. During nearly three days of meetings the committee members, all English professors, frequently punctuated the discussion with sneers at the behavioral scientists. Ignorant of what psychologists and sociologists have learned about small-group behavior, they were trapped into determining to do something which could not in fact be done and which, in a different form, they had initially rejected, although the first form of the proposal was at least feasible, though probably of no great value. A suggestion that a technique common among behavioral scientists be employed was roundly and contemptuously rejected, although six months later, at a second meeting of the committee, it was again proposed by a member who had initially been the most vociferous in attacking it. As was to be expected, once again it was rejected, and the committee was dismissed, since it had failed to achieve anything.

Behavioral convergence is a common characteristic of small-group behavior, whether or not the convergent behavior is rational or appropriate to the problem being considered. It is one of the reasons why committees and seminars so frequently produce nothing of value and make decisions and arrive at conclusions on inadequate evidence and irrational grounds. If small groups of this sort do arrive at reasonable and appropriate decisions, the explanation is probably that of random effect. That is, the small group in itself does not conduce to rational and appropriate behavior; only the randomly controlled presence of a personality both rational and intelligent can make a group productive. The intimate group of William and Dorothy Wordsworth and Coleridge, with such temporarily attached and distantly associated members as Southey and Lamb, is a good instance. It has been suggested recently that Coleridge did first-class and original work only during the existence of that small group. Otherwise his work was characterized by confusion, obfuscation, and plagiarism.

If this is the case it is not surprising. The Wordsworth-Coleridge small group was an early instance of how the alienated Romantic resolved the problem of alienation: he became a member of a small group of like-minded artists and their hangers-on. To be sure, many of these groups have produced work of value, that is, work subsequently socioculturally validated; but as Murger shows so well, the overwhelming majority of them has produced, and continue to produce, little but the gratification of social support in the form of the convergent behavior of small groups.

This is an example of how students of literature might make profitable use of the conclusions of the behavioral sciences and particularly psychology. There is yet another reason why the hostility of students of literature is proving costly to them. One of the most common rhetorical phenomena of criticism is to justify an interpretation by an explanatory regress to a general statement about human behavior. These are at best intuitively arrived at—that is, like all intuitions, we do not know how we arrive at them—but are more frequently truisms, platitudes, old wives' tales. I have rarely observed any effort to support the probability of such statements by an appeal to the literature of psychology, except to psychoanalysis, a matter to which I shall return.

As an example, probably few words recur more frequently in the rhetoric of criticism than does "creative." Yet how many literary students are familiar with the extensive work done on creativity by psychologists? On the other hand, to turn our attack in the opposite direction, it must be admitted that much of that work is rather dubious. The general way of procedure is to study some particular kind of creativity, such as that of architects. A large and carefully sampled group of architects is asked to identify the creative architects of the country working at the time of the study. These architects now designated by their colleagues as "creative" are then studied, and much of interest is learned. For example, one of the childhood factors often characteristic of the architects so designated was "the experience of frequent moving within single communities, or from community to community, or from country to country, which provided an enrichment of experience, both cultural and personal, but which at the same time contributed to experiences of aloneness, shyness, isolation, and solitariness during childhood and adolescence."[1] But the question that arises here is whether or not McKinnon and his research associates were influenced by the Romantic tradition maintaining that isolation and solitariness, that is, social alienation, are conducive to creativity. Would they have made the observation were it not for that tradition? Is the frequency of such experiences among creative architects of a high or low statistical significance? That is, were it not for that tradition would McKinnon have given that observation an importance ranking with the other childhood-adolescence phenomena he mentions? To put it more bluntly, does a general ignorance of cultural history distort the findings of psychologists? They are aware, of course, of cultural differences among societies, for such information has been made widely available by the closely associated anthropologists, but I find little awareness of cultural history. Further, it will be observed that the creative architects studied are those so designated by other architects. This appears to give the students of creativity their desired objectivity. But does it? Are they not in fact studying those innovative and productive architects who have been labeled by other architects with the honorific term "creative"? Are they not, then, studying the current fashions in the architectural profession of using the word "creative"?

To spell this out, "innovation" is a constant of behavior, but it must be socially validated to be called "creative." I do not deny that McKinnon and Barron have made valid generalizations about creativity, or at least interesting and perhaps useful ones, but at the same time I find that their conclusions are distorted and deprived of some substance because while they were studying creativity among their designated architects they were also studying, though apparently without knowing it, the current mode of creativity-validation among architects at the time of the study. One meaning, though not the only meaning, of "deviant" is innovation that is socioculturally invalidated. Al Capone and others in the 1920s, under the cultural stimulation of prohibition, applied the methods of American nationally organized business to crime, thus innovating what is probably best understood as the criminal counterbusiness. Another meaning of "deviant" is behavior designated as socially invalid. Such a usage conceals the creativity of social "deviants" like Al Capone, who generated what was probably one of the most creative acts of recent American history. Nor can that innovation even be said to be socially invalidated. On the contrary it has been enthusiastically validated by a subculture of respectable size, considerably larger, one would guess, than the subculture of American architects.

As for productivity, in my readings in this field of psychology, I believe I discern a confusion between "creativity" and "productivity." High productivity of an individual member of an occupation, whether poetry or chemistry, is often considered a mark of creativity. But high productivity is frequently productivity within the subculturally recognized paradigms of that occupation. But if "creativity" is used to refer to innovation or, preferably, deviancy from norms, high productivity within the limits of the paradigmatic tradition is mistakenly identified with creativity. (I am using "norm" here in the popular and imprecise sense. A "norm" is a fairly high-level regressive construct, quite complex in character. The imprecise sense seems to be the one most used by behavioral scientists.) It is as if one were to say that Robert Montgomery was as creative as Tennyson. Yet there is little question that psychologists have taken over "creativity" from humanists, particularly literary critics, and have scarcely attempted to remove from it the confusions which have steadily been introduced into the usage of the term for the past several hundred years. Thus it is used to validate literary deviancy but also to validate paradigmatic productivity. This latter usage sheds some light on the individual writer. Since any individual knows about himself in the same way that he knows about others, and since he generates instructions for himself in the same way that he generates instructions for others, he is most usefully regarded as a social dyad, that is, as a small group. He is thus subject to the behavioral convergence of all small groups. Thus arises a puzzle of validation. Should a writer be called creative who continues to write with equal value in a literary paradigm he himself has innovated, or should a writer be called creative if and only if he deviates from the paradigms he himself has innovated? Roughly speaking, the first is the test for creativity which obtained before 1800, the second has obtained since. Finally, "creativity" is most commonly used in neither of these senses but merely as a eulogistic term without attributes other than mere approbation.

"Creativity" is but one of several terms which are common both to students of literature and to psychologists, but I think what is true of this term is probably true of others: a word with multiple meanings in literary rhetoric is taken over into the rhetoric of psychology without having been subjected to semantic analysis. It also works in the other direction. The term "reinforcement" has gradually emanated from psychology and penetrated the general culture. Although I rarely see it in literary criticism, I hear it with increasing frequency from my literary colleagues, and I know that they use it in teaching. This is no doubt laudable, an instance of the serious effort to make use of psychology in the study of literature, just as the psychological study of creativity is a serious effort to use what was believed to have been an important discovery in the criticism of literature and the other arts. Unfortunately, "reinforcement" in psychology itself is as vaguely and imprecisely used as "creativity" is in the rhetoric of discourse that purports to be an appropriate response to works of literature.

Nevertheless the two words have an important function in common. Both are terms of a high-level explanatory regress; that is, both are theoretical terms; both are constructs. Now just as the rhetoric of criticism frequently regresses to general statements about human behavior, sometimes taking its vocabulary from psychology itself, though rarely, so psychology can find exemplifications of its explanatory propositions in literature. I have been fortunate in being able to examine a manuscript, regrettably unpublished, prepared by a psychologist friend of mine—it is possible for humanists and behavioral scientists not only to be friends but even to be intellectual companions—which consisted of a series of propositions of behavioral psychology exemplified by poems. In his *Verbal Behavior*, B. F. Skinner uses poems both to exemplify his propositions and to provide material for analysis. This does not mean much to me, because I do not think that he is a very good scientist, and I am sure that he is a very bad philosopher and moralist. Perhaps the explanation for both of these limitations is that he started out in life to be a writer.

A better example comes again from my own experience. Some twenty-five years ago a nonpsychoanalytically oriented clinical psychiatrist told me that his teacher, a man for whom he had the greatest respect, had instructed him that one could not be a good psychiatrist unless one were thoroughly and richly familiar with the great fiction of nineteenth-century Europe, England, and America. As a still rather naive student of literature I was immensely exhilarated by this splendid validation for my profession—or so I thought. But I was also puzzled. Granted that this was so, why should it be so? I believe that now I can offer an explanation for what still seems to me an interesting proposition, though I am not so naive as I was and certainly far less exhilarated by the study of literature; the notion seems now an insufficient validation.

To use a starting point familiar to students of literature, if one accepts Sir Philip Sidney's justification for poetry as the beginning of a comprehension of what happens in literature, one can say that poetry exemplifies what Sidney called a "truth," but what I would call an explanation, or more precisely an explanatory regress, without worrying, for the present purposes, about whether the explanatory proposition which the work of literature exemplifies is or is not true. (For my own part I do not believe that any explanations are true; or, more precisely, a "true" explanatory proposition is one that has heuristic value only.) Sidney's is also the position of Hegel in his *Philosophy of the Fine Arts.* But I do not believe that either Sidney or Hegel has given an adequate account of the matter, which is considerably more complex. Let us postulate, however, on their models an explanatory-exemplary axis to language. This theory asserts that explanatory statements explain exemplary statements, that exemplary statements exemplify explanatory statements, that in any rhetoric the number of levels between the most exemplary statement and the most explanatory statement is indeterminable, and that movement from exemplification to explanation is an explanatory regress.

　　Now the Hegel-Sidney theory asserts that art is always under the control of explanation, that it always exemplifies an explanation or set of interrelated explanations. But the Romantics discovered what Spenser's allegorical thinking had already shown, as one example among many. Just as it is possible to generate new theoretical, that is, explanatory propositions from a meditation upon such propositions, so it is possible in response for exemplary propositions to generate innovative propositions of the same sort which are not under the control of any existent explanatory propositions. Indeed, under the press of the failure of explanation it frequently happens, and perhaps very commonly with artists, that thinking moves out of the verbal into the nonverbal, that is, into thinking, even problem solving, by generating subjective nonverbal imagery. That seems to be one of the many possible functions of dreaming. Considerable confusion is caused in literary discourse by the failure to distinguish true imagistic thinking from sentences which are not imagistic (though they are called that) but rather highly exemplary. Imagistic and exemplary innovation generated by response to verbal exemplifications was, for complex cultural reasons, not only a discovery of Romanticism but even central to it, the imagistic being translated into exemplary rhetoric. It is the tradition vaguely and inadequately called Symbolism. Before Romanticism a symbol was an exemplification of an existent explanation. With Romanticism literature began to be marked by exemplifications for which there was no existent explanation. One of the central themes of Romanticism, to the present

day, in all the arts has been what might be called "free exemplification." Actually, my statement that Hegel asserts that art is always
under the control of explanation is not strictly true. He does make
such assertions, but it is clear that in his speculations about the origins of art he conceives of it in precisely this way, as free exemplification, or nonexplanatory thinking, which generates explanation.
Indeed, the principles of his *Phenomenology of Mind* and his position
as a fundamental Romantic thinker almost demanded that art be so
conceived.

This discovery of the Romantics provides a partial explanation also
for the enormous expansion of fiction writing in the nineteenth century and particularly the movement of fiction to a much higher cultural level. It further serves to provide a partial explanation for the
increasingly self-conscious "realism" of fiction, a fictional technique
whereby the massive use of exemplary sentences provides a matrix
for the generation of free exemplification. This tradition culminates in
such works as *Billy Budd*, which defies explanation, and *Ulysses*, which
ignores it, governing its generation of exemplary statements by a completely arbitrary schema derived from another work of fiction. Hence
to the student and therapist of the psyche, the psychologist and the
psychiatrist, nineteenth-century fiction offers both training in free exemplary thinking and massive amounts of material which can be used
to generate innovative explanations of behavior. The psychologist can
benefit by adequate use of nineteenth-century fiction and Romantic-
Symbolist poetry, and of earlier fiction and memoirs. (One of the models of much early nineteenth-century fiction is pre-1800 memoirs.)
This use would provide a learning experience that could break down
the paradigmatic experimentation characteristic of academic and professional psychology which is so noninnovative. Material with which
to extend and supplement both his experimentation and his theoretical constructions would also be provided. Probably my friend's
teacher could not explain his interest in nineteenth-century fiction
this way, or perhaps any way, but no doubt he experienced in reading
that fiction a fruitful disorientation.

Thus it can, I believe, be reasonably said that literary criticism ought
to be able to find in psychology explanatory propositions for its justifications and interpretations; it ought to be able to find exemplifications for such propositions both in psychological experimentation
and in literature; and it ought to be able from a knowledge of psychology to generate innovative explanations which will reveal hitherto unobserved aspects of literature and its origins in the individuals
who produce it. And psychology ought to be able to use the theoretical
explanations of literary criticism as directions for innovating scientific

investigation; it ought to be able to find exemplifications for its explanatory propositions in literature as well as psychological experimentation; and it ought to be able to generate theory with the aid of the theoretical propositions of criticism. Psychologist and literary critic, then, each ought to be able to incorporate into his own rhetoric segments of the other's, both to generate and control high-level explanatory regress, or theory, and to generate and control specific investigations into categories of units of study in their respective fields. This kind of disciplinary interaction ought to be happening, but except for a very limited number of studies in both fields, it is not.

The explanation for this is not merely the hostility between humanists and behavioral scientists. That in itself is absurd and unnecessary. Both, after all, are concerned with studying human behavior and the consequences of human behavior. The reason for the hostility may, after all, be mere academic jealousy, a social phenomenon, not an intellectual one, giving further evidence that being a humanist does not make a man either morally or intellectually better, and that the scientific study of the psyche does not make a man more objective, propositions for which there is abundant evidence to be found elsewhere and in both disciplines. There is no intellectual reason why psychology and literary criticism (to use the term in its widest sense as the study of literature, from inspirational evaluation to bibliographic analysis) should not fruitfully interact. The reason that they do not, except for an occasional isolated study, is the theoretical weaknesses of both.

It is hardly necessary to adumbrate at length about the weaknesses of literary theory. Literary criticism engages in evaluation without a theory of evaluation. It does have modes of evaluation, but they are endless and all equally valid, as far as I can determine. It is possible to conclude, as I have, that the least interesting thing possible to say about a literary work is that it is good or bad. Rather, there is no theory of what the literary critic is doing when he engages in evaluation. The critic rarely sees evaluation as a social process which has little to do with the work he is evaluating, but has a great deal to do with the generation of literature subsequent to his evaluation. What happens as the consequence of literary evaluation? This question may belong to sociology, but it seems to me a puzzle that the literary critic should wrestle with, though he rarely does so. Explanation of literary evaluation is ordinarily justification, a rhetorical demonstration that the kind of evaluation that particular critic is doing is the kind he ought to be doing.

Literary criticism engages in hermeneutics, though it does so without a theory of interpretation. The most sophisticated literary criticism is founded on a naive use of such terms as "meaning," "intention," and "mind." Not one of these terms is subjected to analysis, although they are among the most scandalous terms in modern philosophy and psychology. There are, to be sure, various controls over literary hermeneutics, but, like evaluative controls, they are modes, not theories.

A general theory of literary interpretation based on what there is useful in psychology and philosophy—and there is less in both than there should be—has yet to make an appearance.

Literary criticism engages in an explanation of the situations from which a work emerged and into which it enters, that is, the consequences of its emergence. This is traditionally known as "historical criticism." Of the three kinds of literary criticism it is the most mature. It is soundly based, in the sense that the distribution in space and time of the emergence of literary works is structured, not random. On the other hand, that distribution is not yet understood or explained by what scientists and some philosophers of science like to call "laws," though a scientific law is merely a termination of an explanatory regress, a termination which has not yet been overthrown. Thus explanatory criticism has an enormous wealth of information about the emergence of individual works but very few general explanations that can subsume exemplary statements the content of which is the identification of factors of emergence and its consequences. Thus, in another sense, the emergence of literary works is random, in that explanations for such emergence are either feeble or nonexistent.

Finally, literary criticism is further limited by fashion. It turns its attention to and defines as literature, or sometimes with a little more sophistication as "serious literature" or "literature worth studying" or "great literature," those works which are currently validated at a high cultural level.[2] Consequently in all three kinds, literary criticism ascribes universality to attributes of literary works which are culturally localized in time and place. As a further result of this situation "literature" is a field which has no boundaries. Hence the study of literature is even more paradigmatic than are the scientific disciplines—and that is saying a good deal. As a further consequence it is, except for "historical criticism" within its limitations, nonaccumulative and astoundingly repetitious.

It is hardly surprising, therefore, that though an occasional psychologist is ingenious enough to use literature, psychology can find little to use in literary criticism. When the psychologist does attempt to use a bit of critical rhetoric, such as "creativity," he gets into a terrible mess. However, there is no reason for a psychologist to assume a position of intellectual and moral superiority vis-à-vis the literary critic. The weakness of psychology, however, does not at first glance lie in its weakness of theory. Psychology has lots of theories, often elaborately structured, and its field of inquiry is on the whole well bounded, though my own opinion is that the distinctions between psychology, sociology, and anthropology rightfully cause great discomfort. I think August Comte was correct when he defined sociology to include all three, that is, made "sociology" identical with the modern term "behavioral sciences." (I also believe he was right in asserting that even mathematics, astronomy, physics, chemistry, and biology are properly subsumed by "sociology"—a proposition that one finds an occasional psychologist in agreement with.) This uneasiness is reflected in the introduction to *Human Behavior: An Inventory of Scientific Findings* by Bernard Berelson and Gary A. Steiner,[3] a work that lists and discusses 1,045 reasonably reliable generalizations at which behavioral psychology has arrived, plus a group of unnumbered Freudian generalizations, which the authors think should be included for completeness but which they do not consider even reasonably reliable. Nevertheless they think that though their field may be fuzzy at the edges, a characteristic, to be sure, of all disciplines, it is reasonably clear towards the center, though the location of the center is possibly a little unclear. The chapters have the titles of the more or less current areas of psychology: development, perceiving, learning, and so on. But there are also chapters on the family, organizations, the society, and even one on culture; thus the uncertainty of the boundary of psychology is manifest. At any rate it is unquestionably a fascinating book though somewhat miscellaneous in character. The most notable lacuna in the book is its discussion of theory, but that is what the authors designed and what their title indicates.

Quite a different work is *Handbook of General Psychology.*[4] This consists of forty-five chapters by sixty behavioral scientists, and the emphasis is on metatheory and theory and the history of each area of psychological study. Together these two books give a sweeping picture of the current state of psychology; and the *Handbook,* with little that could be said to belong to sociology and anthropology, is more representative of the organization and activity of academic psychology, though there is a paper on humanistic psychology and some serious attention to Freud, particularly in the chapter on psychosomatic medicine. (An interesting aspect of the book is that though there has been for at least a decade a considerable rebellion [usually now known as neobehaviorism] against classical academic psychology from within the ranks of academic psychology, and a seeking of new possibilities in phenomenalism, for example, and field work, rather than laboratory work, it would be almost impossible to guess that from the *Handbook.*)

One rises from these two books with certain distinct impressions. First the amount of work and money poured into psychology in the last fifty years has been staggering. Equally impressive is the ingenuity in designing experiments and the intellectual and scientific rigor which if not always achieved is always attempted. But second, one is equally impressed by the fact that so little has been accomplished in the fulfillment of psychology's program of arriving at solid, verified propositions about human behavior. And equally impressive is the absence of large-scale theory. There are frequent references to the fact that psychology has as yet very little to say about higher-level cognitive activities. Here, then, is one reason why literary criticism can find little in psychology to help it. Psychology has not yet reached those higher-level modes of behavior which are responsible, it would seem, for the production of literature, even literature at a low cultural level.

The recognition that psychology has not yet reached higher-level cognitive activities is usually accompanied by the implication and often the statement that it is, after all, on the way, and that it is only a matter of time before it gets there. I do not think that it will. The belief is that psychology will build from what one author calls mini-theories to a large, inclusive, and solid general theory. These miniature theories are generalizations based upon carefully controlled laboratory experiments. The assumption is that a stimulus may be isolated from a real-life stimulus field and responses to it observed in animal and human behavior under laboratory conditions, conditions in which the stimulus factors may be controlled, in short, a psychologically neutral situation. That a stimulus is the same stimulus when it is isolated from a real-life stimulus field is itself questionable. The nature of the human brain certainly appears to be such that in real-life situations a particular stimulus cannot be identified, since the interpretative response is affected not merely by the (hypothetical) stimulus but by all the stimuli in the perceptual field. Further, the life experiences of the experimental organism affect, as in psychologists themselves, the interpretation of the response. This appears to be true in animals as well as in humans, for in reinforcement experiments on animals, those animals that do not get reinforced are ordinarily removed from the experimental situation as not being good experimental subjects. There is an intellectual charm in this methodology which I find unable to resist, partly because it is so much like the studies of humanists.

A California psychologist named Brunswik has objected that experimental situations are not isomorphic with real-life situations and that on these grounds much psychological experimentation must necessarily produce invalid results.[5] However, experimental situations, whether involving animals (including that strange strain, the laboratory rat, of which the less said the better) or humans, are in fact real-life situations. In experiments involving humans, for example, the psychologist is actually channeling their behavior, policing them, exercising social control. The social control cannot be objected to, since social control is the ineluctable condition of all human interaction, including interaction with oneself. Rather the psychologist does not know he is doing this. His objectivity is thus spurious, and he is as much a "humanist psychologist" as the psychoanalyst.[6]

Another "humanistic" aspect of psychology can be discerned in a different kind of study. Berelson and Steiner (p. 269) present an example of "long-lasting aggressive consequences of extended frustration in childhood." A table is headed "Differences in aggressive behavior in persons having different degrees of childhood frustration." The behavior traits listed are "Rude answering to parents," "Irritated by parents," "Feeling that teachers are unfair," "Carrying grudges," "Frequent quarreling with friends," "Broken engagements." Group 1, the most frustrated, showed an average of 64.0 percent of these behavior traits, while Group 4, the least frustrated, showed an average of 36.2 percent. This difference is impressive, perhaps; it suggests that childhood frustration has a high probability of producing long-lasting adult aggression. The trouble with this is that there is no explanation of why Group 1 had *only* an average of 64.0 percent or why Group 4 emerged with an average *as high as* 36.2 percent. More important, however, is the fact that "aggression" itself is used only in reference to socially invalidated acts. To be successful does not an individual have to manifest "normal aggression"? But that merely means that the aggression is channeled in socially approved ways, not that socially approved aggression is not aggression. Indeed, there are good reasons for believing that *all* behavior is aggressive, since a nonnormative definition of aggression is "manipulation of the environment to the organism's benefit." If human beings misjudge what is beneficial, that is neither here nor there. Clearly, much socially disapproved aggression is highly beneficial to the individual who manifests it. The lesson, if any, of this investigation seems to be that if you want your child to be able to take care of himself, frustrate him when he is young, as indeed all parents have always done. In short, we have here an instance of what is so common in psychology—an explanatory term is taken from ordinary language and used without being subjected to semantic analysis. The result is that what was really happening in this investigation was an exemplification of the transmission of normative judgments of aggression. Once again, the objectivity claimed turns out to be an example of "humanistic" psychology.

This particular investigation, however, is both quite old and obviously naive. A much more sophisticated method of personality study has emerged in multivariate experimental personality study, in which the statistics are far more complex, particularly in the use of factor analysis. Even the definition of personality is reasonably acceptable: "Personality is that which enables us to predict what a person will do in a given, defined situation."[7] The upshot of this kind of study is that personality factors tend to cluster, as in "university professors are highly intelligent, low on dominance, and outgoingness, low on superego strength, high on radicalism, and self-sufficiency" (p. 806). But it is so easy to think of university professors in whom none of these factors seems to be present. Can this be true, possibly, of professors at the University of Illinois, where Cattell is located and Howarth has worked? Such a statement might be useful to a college president in handling his faculty, but only if he recognizes that in any situation involving large numbers of his faculty he will find these traits more frequent than the opposite traits, but, like all statistically based information, what is really offered is a set of numbers to which certain terms and phrases are attached. The predictive quality is applicable, perhaps, to a large population of professors in a major university, but does it apply to Okefenokee A & M? And does it apply even in a major university in all situations? My own experience is that what one encounters in a large faculty meeting is low intelligence, high dominance and outgoingness, high superego strength, low radicalism, and low self-sufficiency. Possibly the explanation is that in such situations only a minority is ever heard from, but there seems to be nothing in multivariate personality assessment that tells one that in some situations the traits of a particular group either are unreliable or must be reversed. Since, moreover, this is a statistically based statement, it cannot be used to predict the behavior of an individual. Furthermore, in all the examples of occupations or such groups as alcoholics, the cluster of personality traits resembles to an astonishing degree the popular stereotype or caricature of such professions or behavior groups. This suggests that those stereotypes help determine the traits, and that in turn leads one to wonder if the clustering might not be a statistically trivial phenomenon and that Cattell has been governed in his response by normative factors not present in the data.

What appears to be going on in multivariate personality study is quite interesting. The naive approach to personality is marked by an effort to create a coherent concept of any individual's personality, including one's own, an effort necessarily made possible only by ignoring incoherent factors. This naive approach remains unquestioned in literary study. The multivariate approach, which attempts to get away from the naive approach, tries to see the personality as an incoherent package, or as it is called, profile, and most interestingly to identify personality traits which are not recognized and categorized in naive personality rhetoric. So far so good. But then to attempt to arrive at generalizations about such categorically disparate groups as airmen, Olympic athletes, farmers, university professors, neurotics, alcoholics, and homosexuals seems to be little more than the effort to make spurious sense out of the data of personality profiles on the model of the unanalyzed naive approach. Would a different shuffling of the profile cards show farmers and professors to be alcoholic homosexuals? Here is an instance of what often happens: psychology appears to offer the student an innovative notion corrective to his theoretical inadequacies, and then withdraws it.

This failure to analyze naively used terms from ordinary language happens with technical psychological terms as well. I can do no better than to quote from one of the two of these sixty psychologists who seem to have some genuine awareness of what psychologists are in fact doing. Professor Benbow F. Ritchie, after analyzing what he calls the "pop-op" definitions of reinforcement of Skinner and others, has the following to say:

> The ideas of reinforcement, of stimulus, of response, of habit, and of drive were never given the kind of careful analysis they require. . . . As a result, all the most interesting and important questions about behavior and learning remained unanswered. The failure to provide these distinctions is, I think, the reason for the distrust of learning theory that in recent years has swept through academic psychology.[8]

We have here the same failure to subject terms to analysis that we have encountered in the discussion of "creativity."

In short, there are a number of dubious matters about experimental psychology, the foundation of psychological theory, or so it is affirmed, and apparently not a few psychologists are deviant enough to question these paradigms. But this dubious foundation of psychological theory is by no means the only trouble. Possibly a symptom, however, of that basic trouble is the increasing popularity of psychometrics and of statistical analysis. Little understanding of the nature of statistics is to be gained from the handbook, but I found an illuminating discussion in *Randomness, Statistics and Emergence,* by Philip McShane, S.J.[9] It is Father McShane's contention that science has two kinds of data, the lawful and the random. By lawful he means, in my terms, that theoretical statements successfully subsume exemplary statements and are themselves subsumed and validated by such terms as "law" and "cause." His theory is that randomness is the subject of statistical investigation, and that an interaction between the random and the lawful is the source of scientific development. Statistics is the means of investigating what the lawful cannot take care of: the random is the residual of the lawful. I find Father McShane singularly convincing in this, though not in everything, and its importance here is that the increasing use of statistics in psychology indicates the lack of success in constructing the lawful, that is, verified theory, and indeed suggests the disintegration of psychological theory, instead of its integration. The increasing importance of statistics in psychology hints, therefore, that there is an increasing flow of the residual. Moreover, the increasing mathematicization of all branches of psychology, made so much easier by the ravishing joys of the computer, has had the effect, I strongly suspect, of deflecting psychologists from the study of human behavior to the study of mathematics. It would be an odd and amusing result if the computer, instead of freeing the psychologist—and members of every discipline susceptible to computer use—limits him to looking for data which can be successfully subjected to computer analysis. I would not question for a moment that the computer is a magnificent invention, but it may, like the excessively rich diet of Americans, lead to obesity.

The questionable aspects of psychological experimentation may be one reason for the increasing flow of the residual. Another is, I believe, the assumption that psychology will build from mini-theories to large-scale theory. This involves the assumption that in the various levels of theory construction—and psychological metatheorists appear to anticipate a good many levels—there is a necessary or immanent or logical relation between levels. Going up is induction; going down is deduction. It is hardly necessary to remind the reader of the terrible beating these terms have taken in the past seventy years. (Indeed, one is a bit startled by the frequency with which these terms are encountered in the *Handbook.*) But if the connections between sentence-as-stimulus and sentence-as-response is a conventional connection—

and it can hardly be otherwise without postulating a metaphysic of immanence, which, to be sure, a great many philosophers now do, though they do not seem to know it—then the connection between levels of an explanatory regress is a conventional level. This means that every level of an explanatory regress has an emergent relation to the level below. And if so, the proposed Walhalla of psychology is threatened with a Götterdämmerung before it is even built. And that, I suspect, is the significance of the increasing popularity of statistics and the increasing refinement of statistics over the past seventy years. Psychologists in general and even Father McShane, I am sorry to say, appear to believe that emergence is an attribute of the natural world. But I do not think that that is the case. Emergence is an attribute of the levels of explanatory regress. We do not move from one level to a higher one by induction or by the immanent logic. We often move by the paradigms of convention to higher levels, but "creative" motion upward is by innovative deviance. Paradigmatic explanatory regression follows a rule of computer technology: "Garbage in; garbage out."

By building up from basic units of behavior, psychology will never construct a theory of human behavior which literature can use. It must begin with a level of explanatory regress that deals with what it calls higher cognitive activity, including its own. And that means it must begin with language, which is not the instrument of higher cognitive activity but is higher cognitive behavior itself. Nor can a theory of language be built up from linguistic units, as Noam Chomsky has already unwittingly demonstrated, having by now proved that what he set out to do cannot be done.[10] The Chomsky approach can never reach the crucial problem in language, the connection between two separable utterances. Since psychology builds its theory on the connection between statements, it must begin by understanding that connection. It is not easy.

Thus psychology can do something with literature itself, but almost nothing with literary theory. Literary criticism, on the other hand, can reach into psychology, into learning theory, into perception theory, into information theory, into interference theory, and so on, and find isolated low-level generalizations which it can use. In fact, the serious study of literature can ignore such isolated generalizations only at its peril, only by complacently maintaining its present theoretical impoverishment. Thus psychology is more useful to literary study than, for the most part, literary criticism is to itself. The ultimate lesson is this: if psychology should succeed in creating a general theory of human behavior, such a theory will subsume the study of literature. Currently, however, literary critics need not feel themselves seriously threatened.

## A Note on Psychoanalysis

Freud was one of the greatest observers, but not, I think, a great theorist. The reason is that he was not observing the unconscious, but rather was interpreting the verbal behavior of disturbed individuals placed in a highly protected situation and encouraged to talk about what in their culture was socially invalid to talk about. His was a single-minded hermeneutic enterprise governed by a metaphysic of instinct which was, historically, an inversion of Romantic Transcendentalism. Since Freud used a term magical in its power to attract early twentieth-century literary critics—symbol—Freudian literary interpretation achieved considerable popularity. Every now and then it experiences a revival if some literary critic or other happens to go through, or at least into, psychoanalysis.

The contention that the psychoanalytic interpretation of literature must be invalid, since one cannot psychoanalyze a dead person, has always caused considerable embarrassment and highly defensive responses among Freudians. The answers offered have never been successful because it was not realized that the structure of the Freudian unconscious was, like Chomsky's deep structure of language, not a revelation of underlying structure but an explanatory regress from verbal behavior. Thus the proper answer to this particular claim of the invalidity of Freudian literary interpretation is that one can make a hermeneutic response to utterances whether the utterer is living or dead, or present or absent. Freudianism is a hermeneutics of one aspect of human behavior, uncoordinated with other aspects, except for the nonverbal thinking of dreams. Since it is not a response to the full range of behavior, it cannot be called a theory of human behavior. The pragmatic defense of psychoanalysis, that it effects cures of cognitively disturbed individuals through psychotherapy, is neither here nor there. What psychotherapeutic technique is not effective for some members of the population of the disturbed? It has always been admitted that psychoanalytic therapy is ineffective with some individuals. One is reminded of animals discarded from experimental psychology because they are poor experimental subjects. It also appears to be the case that cognitive disturbance is usually resolved in about two years whether the disturbed individual experiences therapy or not.

On the other hand Freud was undoubtedly a man of enormous

intelligence, with astounding powers of grasping personality factors, and remarkably gifted in myth construction, myth being a form of discourse that is not fully disengaged from a purely exemplary level of explanation but has not yet reached a coherent explanatory level. His was a kind of intuitive multivariate personality assessment. He thus could grasp the theme or clustering of personality factors which experimental multivariate study, using factor analysis, has likewise arrived at. Recent psychoanalytic theory, following the later Freud's interest in ego psychology, has separated out this element from Freud's writings.

All this is evident in the publications of the most intelligent and certainly the best-informed Freudian critic now writing, Professor Norman N. Holland. His recent book, *Poems in Persons*,[11] contains the following assertion in what he calls, too fiercely, "A Polemical Epilogue." Professor Holland is too kind and generous a man to be very polemical. "Psychoanalytic theory . . . has advanced to become the only psychology capable of a comprehensive view of man that spans the largest social and philosophical issues and the most precise clinical questions, especially people's choices of particular words." The last phase is the giveaway. Thus his own experimentation with responses to poems follows the Freudian models and the Thematic Apperception Test (TAT), itself derived from Freudian theory. He offers his subjects a poem by H. D., the only poet to leave a fairly complete record of her own psychoanalysis, to which he has previously given, with this aid, his own psychoanalytic interpretation. He then instructs his subjects to give any reactions to the poem that happen to occur to them. Not surprisingly, in their responses he discerns a personality theme.

There are two reasons why he should do so. As I have suggested, the construction of a coherent personality theme is the naive, unanalyzed approach to personality. What one does is to make analogical categorizations of apparently dissimilar and unrelated statements by observing the pattern of those statements. A reading of Freud's case histories shows that that is how he proceeded. There is, of course, nothing wrong with this; that is how we always proceed with any set of apparently unrelated stimuli. Freud was merely a genius who did it in a new field and with a new explanatory regress to govern his analogies. But there is a second reason why Professor Holland should have seen what he did. If you place a small group in a closed room, such as a committee room, and let them interact verbally, a group theme will emerge. I have already referred to this as the typical behavior of small groups. An individual as a social dyad is a small group. If as Freud discovered, if as the Rohrschachs and the TAT's discovered, you face any individual with a not evidently structured stimulus field, one for which validated conventions do not already provide instructions for responding, and deprive him of instructions for verbal or other performance, but also demand that he respond verbally, the result will be like that of the small group in the socially isolated committee room. There will be a convergence of behavior. Further, if you place the individual in a series of such situations, the identical theme, to be perceived analogically, will emerge. The explanation is that at an indeterminably early age any individual begins to limit the range of his behavior, and to increase the limitation of that range by the redundancies of his own repeated limitations, redundancies which he responds to by observing his own behavior as a stimulus field. We need not worry about whether this process is "conscious" or "unconscious." The redundancies of his behavior are instructions for further behavior. Repeating the pattern of what Freud did, Professor Holland, not surprisingly, discovered what Freud discovered. Granted, provisionally, that there are personality themes and granted, provisionally, that they are not trivial, the interesting question would be how they are adapted to differing situations and modified and maintained and disintegrated over long periods of time.

However, Professor Holland's claim that this explains the bond between poem and reader cannot be maintained. At best it explains why there is a relation between personality clustering and modes of evaluating poetry, or, for that matter, anything else. I cannot see that Professor Holland has contributed to our comprehension of literary hermeneutics by conducting experiments in which hermeneutic restraints are cast aside.

Finally Professor Holland has insisted that in moving into ego psychology psychoanalysis has matured and has completed the work of Freud. This may be, but I cannot see that the kind of statements that Freudian ego psychologists make about personality differ very strikingly, if at all, from either naive or sophisticated statements about personality made by non-Freudians.

## NOTES

1. Donald W. McKinnon, quoted in Irvin L. Child, *Humanistic Psychology and the Research Tradition: Their Several Virtues* (New York: Wiley, 1973), p. 54.

2. For a nonnormative definition of "high culture" see my "The Arts and the Centers of Power," *Critiques 1971/72* (The Cooper Union School of Art and Architecture, 1972). This essay has also been published in *1972 Proceedings of Conference of College Teachers of English of Texas* 37 (September 1972): 7–18.

Reprinted in my *Romanticism and Behavior* (University of South Carolina Press, 1977).

3. New York: Harcourt, Brace & World, 1964, p. 712.

4. Edited by Benjamin B. Wolman (Englewood Cliffs, N.J.: Prentice-Hall, 1973), p. 1,006.

5. Egon Brunswik, *The Conceptual Framework of Psychology* (Chicago: University of Chicago Press, 1952).

6. I owe this point to Dr. Robert L. Stewart, Professor of Sociology, University of South Carolina.

7. E. Howarth and R. B. Cattell, "The Multivariate Experimental Contribution to Personality Research," *Handbook*, p. 799.

8. Benbow F. Ritchie, "Theories of Learning: A Consumer Report," *Handbook*, p. 458.

9. Dublin: Gill and Macmillan, 1970, p. 268.

10. Considerable help in understanding this has been given me by Dr. Richard Gunter, Professor of Linguistics, University of South Carolina.

11. New York: Norton, 1973, p. 183.

# CHAPTER FIFTEEN

# Perceptual and Semiotic
# Discontinuity in Art

Philosophical aesthetics has always been vitiated by the selection of works of art which the aesthetic theory purports to explain, justify, and validate. An examination of the history of aesthetic theory shows plainly enough that the various aestheticians involved have explained the art validated at the time of writing as at the high cultural level, their own. New theories of aesthetics appear as the fashion for such art changes, an instability controlled by changes in regnant ideologies at the same cultural level. The explanation of art proposed in what follows subsumes all works of art, at all cultural levels, at any time or place. Primitive art, for example, is not significant for this purpose, for the arts of primitive peoples—arts which usually have, by now, an immensely long tradition behind them—are not only currently validated by high culture in the Western canon of art, but also can be safely considered as the products of the highest levels in primitive cultures. Rather, what needs to be subsumed is art at all cultural levels in the advanced cultures, not only kitsch art but all varieties of popular art—pornographic art of the most obvious sort and jokes told in workingmen's bars, as well as flowers grown in spare tires and mailboxes mounted on wagon wheels, and the art of the kitchen. Art invaded the kitchen in the 1930s; by now the kitchen is not infrequently the most elaborate example of interior decoration in the house. Interior decoration from the simplest sort to the most elaborate sort needs to be subsumed, along with Mickey Mouse watches. A theory of art that cannot subsume Disneyland as comfortably as it subsumes the Sistine ceiling is not worth paying attention to, nor is a theory that cannot explain the ubiquity of art.

Such an attempt to subsume all works of art, however, encounters immediately a major difficulty, a question rarely asked. How do we know that a particular object (including verbal objects) was a work of art to the individual who made it and within the culture in which it was generated? This problem is made all the more difficult by the history of modern aesthetic theory. For more than two hundred years the notion of "art" has been culturally established at the higher cultural levels and has even penetrated deep into the culture. That is, the individual responding to a work of art now defines himself as a responder-to-a-work-of-art. That interpretation of his behavior has been learned from comparatively recent culture. "Art" having been established at a high cultural level as a term that ascribes value, and that ascription having penetrated to lower cultural levels, to categorize an object as "art" often does no more than ascribe value to it. Moreover that work-of-art-response has been canonized as "aesthetic response," and such a response, having been learned, can be transferred to any perceptual configuration and to any object whatever. And this in spite of the fact that any clarity about what the "aesthetic response" might be has never been achieved by aesthetics, a philosophical and quasi-philosophical rhetoric which has been the principal barrier to understanding art.

The present theory proposes that a work of art can be identified if a chronologically arranged series of objects of the same function (such as a series of Madonnas or of ashtrays) shows an instability which is not governed by the function of the object in question. Thus the American axe handle was perfected in the course of the eighteenth century and has remained stable ever since. The eighteenth-century instability can be traced to the need to improve the productivity of the woodsman for the sake of clearing the land for agriculture. The instability, then, was not an artistic instability. On the other hand, in the 1930s the traditional placement of the oven on gas stoves—at a convenient height—was changed so that the oven was below the burners. The convenience of using the oven was drastically interfered with, a change easily traceable to the ideological influence of the International Style, or of "Modern Style," as it was called at the time. A work of art cannot be identified in isolation, then, but only as one of a series of functionally identical objects which, as a series, shows nonfunctional stylistic dynamism. Moreover, if we examine a series of objects identified as works of art but generated at successively lower cultural levels, the same phenomenon is observable. Thus the higher the cultural level at which English poetry is written—and European poetry in general—the greater the probability of syntactical distortion. Similarly, a series of functionally identical objects, such as kitchen stoves in the 1930s, shows at higher cultural levels the control of the style of the kind of object by artistic interests. This phenomenon is non-functional stylistic emergence, and the two—emergence and dynamism—are subsumed under the more general term "external discontinuity."

The historical (horizontal) and cultural-level (vertical) dimensions of art are experienced as perceptual discontinuities, that is, as violations of the perceptual expectations for a particular series of functionally identical objects. External discontinuity, however, is less significant than the kinds of perceptual discontinuity found within a work of art, or "internal discontinuities." The evidence for such discontinuities can be most tellingly summed up by recounting an experiment done at Yale by Professor Irvin Child. In his research into artistic valuation he chose hundreds of pairs of works of stylistically similar works of art, and then had the protocols for the superior of each pair determined by a panel of "experts"—art historians, art critics, art instructors, and artists. In one experiment with a boy in early adolescence Professor Child informed the subject as to which was the superior work after each of the boy's determinations of superiority. After a number of his decisions and of protocol judgments the boy said, "Oh, I get it. The best one is always the crummy one." The experts, all from a high cultural level, invariably had selected as superior the object with the greater perceptual disorder. If, for example, one slide of a Persian tile decoration was asymmetrical, and the other symmetrical, the experts invariably chose the former.

The reader may easily perform an experiment which will demonstrate the phenomenon. Select a period of music with which one is unfamiliar—say late seventeenth-century Italian instrumental music—and listen to a number of works in chronological order. Initially all the music will sound very much alike. In time, however, the differences will emerge. What has happened is that the perception averages unfamiliar patterns, and thus builds up expectancies. Once the expectancies are built up, the violations of those expectancies emerge. Or, if one is unfamiliar with *Tristan und Isolde*, at the first hearings the work will be judged stylistically continuous. After a number of hearings, however, the stylistic discontinuity between the first and second acts and between the second and third will outweigh the stylistic continuity.

That mode of perception theory, then, known variously as expectancy theory or psychological set theory, is the first assumption of the explanation of art proposed here. The second, and parallel, assumption is semiotic theory, a complex problem the fundamentals of which, however, are sufficient for the present purposes. As for the first, art exploits the instability of the perceptual determination of configurations. Perception is a determination because no two configurations are precisely identical, but in ordinary behavior the determination of a configuration is transferred to a new configuration if the differences are negligible in the judgment of the individual doing the determining and transferring, a judgment controlled by his interests at the time of the transfer. Thus, when one crosses a street with heavy traffic, the perceptual differences among the various automobiles are negligible, for the interest is getting across safely. On the other hand, a cinema of a simulated street-crossing can bring out the perceptual differences among the configurations of the various moving automobiles and dwell on them. The individual watching the cinema sequence can respond to those configurational differentia, since his interest is not in crossing a street but in responding to a work of art.

The fact that the configurations in either case are automobiles or photographs of automobiles entails the other assumption, the configuration as sign. The notion of "sign" can be resolved into two further propositions. A sign is any configuration distinguished (by a human being and certainly the higher animals) from a ground. And, the meaning of a sign is the response to that sign. For the first, Charles Peirce (1931–1958) said that the world consists of signs, presumably for human beings. For the second, George Herbert Mead (1900) made the point as early as 1900, evidently from a Hegelian background. Thus the transfer of a perceptual determination from one configuration to another is, semiotically, categorization. Further, any sign is a category if the response to it can be judged as a response already in the response repertoire of the responder. Hence, from the semiotic point of view, art exploits categorial instability.

Both perceptual transfer and categorization are accomplished, obviously by analogical judgments, for analogy, in the last analysis, is all we have to think with. Since the perceptual or semiotic construction of an analogy always depends upon ignoring certain attributes of two or more (to an indefinite number) of semiotic configurations, any analogy can be deconstructed by bringing into consideration the neglected attributes. Thus in exploiting configurational and semiotic instability, art exploits analogical instability. To distinguish between the configurational and the semiotic aspects of art I shall usually refer to the formal aspect and to the semantic aspect ("semantic" shifts the emphasis to interpretation).

The instability internal to a work of art—its crumminess, as the boy so perceptively said—can be analyzed into three kinds of instability: implicit, internal, and modal.

An exhaustive description of how each of these appears in the various arts is impossible here, even for those arts which are canonical at the high cultural level—painting, music, sculpture, architecture, poetry, fiction, the informal essay, and dance, and various combinations of these, as theater and opera. A few examples must suffice. In Western diatonic music the implicit patterns of melody are the scale and the triad. (In Schönberg's music and that of his followers the implicit pattern is the chromatic scale.) A violation of either of these patterns of expectancy produces a melody, but, melody having been established, the explicit presentation of these implicit patterns is responded to as melody. Once a melody is presented and, frequently, established by repetition, the melody itself is now violated or "varied." This is internal discontinuity: the presentation of a configuration followed by a configuration sufficiently like the original to justify transfer of configurational determination, but sufficiently different to exploit configurational instability. To the practiced ear, key change is an instance of the third type of discontinuity, modal, but a more obvious example can be found in the shift from a typical first theme in a sonata-allegro movement (loud, upward-moving, fast) to the second theme (softer, downward-moving, slower). Violations of rhythmic patterns are implicit discontinuity; violation of a specific rhythmic pattern is internal discontinuity; shift from one rhythmic pattern to another is modal discontinuity.

In painting, the implicit forms are those patterns which children all over the world make when they start to make signs, whether in the mud with a stick or on the wall with crayons: the line, the x, the cross, the closed line, the circle, the biomorphic configuration, and so on. Rhoda Kellogg (1969) has established the universality of this semiotic phenomenon, and Rudolf Arnheim (1969) has discussed it, though both have confused semiotic behavior with artistic behavior. This again can be easily tested. Project a slide of any painting and then put it out of focus. The higher the cultural level the more the painting will be dominated by a single, now easily observable, implicit configuration, and the greater the violation (that is, the more implicit) of the configuration in the actual painting. The perfect example is Malevich's *White on White*. Most people judge the interior configuration to be square, just as the painting itself is. But in fact the interior form is not square. In addition, the configurations between each edge of the interior form and the edge of the painting imply four triangles, and these are of increasingly distant implication. The painting is unusual in that the implicit form of the interior shape is explicit in the shape of the whole painting. The relation between the two creates an internal discontinuity, while the four implicit triangles create a series of internal discontinuities. Modal discontinuity in painting may be observed in presenting part of the painting brightly lit and another part in shadow. Chiaroscuro introduced a new source of modal discontinuity. But modal discontinuity may also be observed between a foreground filled with many figures and a background of clear blue sky. It is still more easily observed in a series of paintings in the same room or painted as a series, such as Monet's cathedral series; and it is highly important in the narrative panels of Michelangelo's Sistine ceilings.

In poetry is to be found one of the most effective uses of implicit patterns. No expectation is so powerful as syntactic expectation, because none is so enormously redundant in ordinary behavior. The violation of those syntactic expectancies which are implicit in the very act of utterance is so effective that incomprehension of serious violations is extremely common, even among experienced readers when they encounter a new mode of syntactic violation. The first readers of *Ulysses* and *The Waste Land* experienced a fearful semantic disorientation. Indeed, an enormous amount of inaccurate interpretation of poetry, even among professional critics, is the result of the failure to straighten out the syntax into normal order. The famous cruxes of "The Wreck of the Deutschland," for example, disappear is the syntax is exhaustively disentangled. The theory of poetic ambiguity is the mere consequence of incompetence in syntactic disentanglement. Syntax can also be manipulated to produce both internal and modal discontinuity. A sudden shift from, say, distorted syntax to straightforward "prose" syntax and back again produces internal discontinuity. Wordsworth is a master at this. An extensive passage in distorted syntax followed by an extensive passage in normal syntax produces modal discontinuity, for the extension sets up expectancies of continuation.

Rhythmic discontinuity works very much as it does in music. In English poetry the appearance on the page of a poem, unless it is free verse, sets up an expectancy of either double or triple rhythm, that is, for the individual familiar with English poetry. The opening of *Paradise Lost* plays upon this. The stresses of the first line are (x///x/xxxx/), but those of the second line are the implicit form (x/x/x/x/x/). Moreover, since this alternation of stress is an abstraction from the actual four levels of English stress, even a regular pattern is generally implicitly discontinuous. Part of rhythmic expectancy is syllabic expectancy—an expected number of syllables per line. Violation of the syllabic form entails violation of the implicit rhythm. Change of implicit rhythm creates modal discontinuity.

Rhyme is a minor but useful possibility for internal discontinuity. A half-rhyme or no rhyme where expected produces internal discontinuity, and change in rhyme pattern can produce modal discontinuity. More important than rhyme in the arsenal of discontinuity at the disposal of the poet is phrase. In English common meter (iambic pentameter), for example, juncture in a line appears twice, at the end of the line and in the middle. Insofar as the implicit pattern requires a juncture in the middle of the line the result is two asymmetrical stress patterns (x/x/x and /x/x/). Thus the rhythmic inexhaustibility of common meter is in part a consequence of the instability of these two kinds of stress phrase; they are and are not subsumable by a single category. The juncture within the line, in part as a result of this instability, is highly flexible in its position. The formal expectancy is that the mid-line juncture (caesura) appears after five syllables, but that expectancy is frequently violated. The end-line juncture, therefore, is a more powerful expectancy, since it is less frequently violated. In traditional common meter a run-on line is a powerful discontinuity. What happens between junctures is the phrase, and the establishment of a phrase length, and the violation of that expectation is one of poetry's most useful devices for discontinuity. (The same phenomenon, of course, is observable in music.)

It is to be observed, however, that in poetry, since it is a mode of verbalization, perceptual determination begins to be supplemented by semantic categorization as a source for discontinuity. Syntax can hardly be straightened out without a scrupulous semantic interpretation, and phrase length (i.e., juncture) is frequently determined only by semantic responses, as opposed to pure perceptual responses, as in, for example, rhyme. Hence in poetry a new type of modal discontinuity appears, depending upon semantic devices. The most useful term for this is rhetoric, a general definition of which is "a judgment of linguistic overdetermination," that is, a greater frequency of a linguistic pattern than one would expect in ordinary verbal behavior. The CB radios of truck drivers, for example, rapidly generated a striking rhetoric. Any set of semantic patterns can be used to generate a rhetoric if the patterns are sufficiently redundant, such as, for example, metaphor. A more subtle and more purely semantic modal discontinuity is found in a shift of what is usually called point of view, but is probably better understood as a shift in the speaker's self-definition, or self-interpretation. Ordinary interaction depends for its smoothness on stability of self-definition, but poetry can shift within the same poem from, say, a lover defining himself as gratified to, in the next stanza, the same lover defining himself as frustrated and disappointed.

Semantic discontinuity can be most clearly grasped in fiction. A work of fiction presents a "character," that is, a persona, the selective, deceptive, and coherent semantic interpretation of an individual's behavior patterns, best understood as a randomly assembled package of such patterns, each of which is under the control of various social institutions. In ordinary interaction we expect a stabilized persona. That is the implicit form of fiction, in which the presentation of the persona is followed by information which requires us to introduce into that persona attributes incoherent with those already presented. The more central and important a fictional character is, the greater the persona discontinuity. Thus fiction exploits the actual persona instability of ordinary life. This kind of discontinuity can even be exploited in presenting an unstable persona of the narrator, as in *Vanity Fair*.

Internal discontinuity in fiction is primarily achieved by "plot." This device amounts to the presentation of a problem, that is, a semantic incoherence (the murder in the locked room, or the refusal of Johnson's *Dictionary* to Becky Sharp: the subsequent bestowal of it, and Becky's subsequent rejection of it). In ordinary behavior an incoherence of this sort is either resolved as soon as possible or, more frequently, pushed out of the way and the awareness of it suppressed. In fiction the "plot" is the postponement of the problem solution, that is, the maintenance of problem exposure until the end of the fiction, an end which can be postponed as long as the author wishes or his publisher will tolerate. (The butler committed the murder, and the incoherence between Becky's talents and her social aggressiveness is resolved in her achieving respectability through the channeling of her intelligence and willfulness into socially validated behavior.) In tragedy the persona construction of the leading character is destroyed, particularly what persona construction endeavors to stabilize—self-ascription of value. In comedy just the reverse occurs.

Finally modal discontinuity in fiction is accomplished by rhetorical instability. The shift between the narrator and the conversation of the characters is an obvious example, as is the shift between poetry and prose in Shakespeare's tragedies. More subtle is the shift between the high metaphorical rhetoric of one character and the abstract, non-metaphorical rhetoric of a character with whom he is interacting. At the time it was written, no fiction had exploited modal discontinuity so thoroughly and brilliantly as *Ulysses*. The informal essay, lying between poetry and fiction, moves into the field of art because it exploits both personal and rhetorical discontinuity.

The notion of discontinuity in art explains one source of art's power to elicit emotional response. It may first be observed that what we call "emotion" is the physiological response to a perceptual categorization, a response which the brain always produces somewhere in the body. When that response rises above the threshold of perception, we say that the individual is "emotional," since the physiological response is now fed into the brain as a perceptual determination and thus is included in the material from outside the body, that is, perceptual determinations (semiotic categorization) which the brain is currently processing. In ordinary behavior a principal source of emotion is a destabilization of perceptual determination and semiotic categorization, as in the dark one might fall over a coffee table which has never been at that spot before and which one *knows* could not have been moved. Incoherence of determination (categorization), or disorientation is thus an emotional resource which art exploits.

But it is not the only emotional source. Art is said to be "expressive" and often "expressive of emotions." In the first place, there is no emotion without cognition, and in the second, the word "expression" gets aestheticians into exactly the same difficulties that the word "mind" gets philosophers into. Hypostatizing that word, philosophy is faced with the insoluble problem of "other minds"—insoluble because it is a pseudo-problem, as has been increasingly evident ever since the publication of Hegel's *Phenomenology.* The word "mind" merely subsumes observable variability of response. In aesthetics if art is the "expression of an individual's emotions" or even "of an individual's mind," how can other individuals respond to it? That response can be possible only if the "expressive" artistic deposits are conventions, that is, signs. The problem of "individual expressivity" has led to the problem of "artistic communications," another insoluble problem if expressive signs are judged to be unique to the individual generating them.

The way out of this conundrum is to abandon the notions both of expressivity and of communication. Signs may be dichotomized in two ways. The first is the dichotomy between verbal and nonverbal signs. We have no other word for "nonverbal" signs because human behavior is almost entirely under the control of verbal signs. Hence we can talk about nonverbal signs only from within the sphere of verbal signs, and can conceive of them only as negations of nonverbal signs. Whether such signs are natural products or humanly generated is of no importance: since "natural signs" are human determinations and categorizations of configurations not produced by human agency, they are—as signs—generated by human semiosis. (The production of nonverbal signs is often at the present time confused with the production of art, as Arnheim confuses them. If a child making an X with a stick in the mud is making art, then an atomic reactor is art. This does not deny that in the design of the building to contain it and even in placement of objects within the building artistic interests are at work.)

Now one class of nonverbal signs is often designated as uniquely expressive. These are configurations such as verticality, horizontality, color, scale, light, shadow, line, solidity, hollowness, axial depth, pitch in music and linguistic intonations, gesture, volume, speed, vowel euphony and consonantal alliteration in poetry, and so on. Except for color, all of these can be traced to human behavior. It is also apparent that in art they are conventional signs, even though there is no agreement as to what they are signs "of," that is, what categories of human behavior they direct our attention to. Only some aestheticians, for example, think that music is devoid of "meaning," that is, that music has no semantic function or dimension. Practically every one else thinks that music is "meaningful." On the other hand, there is little agreement on how the various signs of music should be verbally categorized. That music is "about" some aspect of human behavior is widely accepted, but what aspect or aspects is the question.

To explain "expressive" signs, then, requires a considerable overhaul of signs. The proposal here begins with the proposition that the most interesting attribute of the human brain is its capacity to produce random responses, a capacity which becomes intensified as one moves up the evolutionary scale. In human evolution verbalization was responsible for an enormous leap in the capacity for randomization of response—for this reason: the distinction between verbal and nonverbal sign response is that nonverbal sign response depends upon a continuity of perceptual determination transfer (response transfer, categorization); verbal sign response, however, is independent of perceptual continuity, the only perceptual continuity being that of sound (or writing or print). Consequently verbal categorization can subsume any two configurations, such as a visual configuration judged to be a fly and a sound configuration judged to be the word "God," and likewise between any two sound configurations categorized as words, such as "tree" and "theory." Since interaction cannot take place without predictability of behavior, or behavioral continuity, the potential and actual randomness of human behavior must be controlled. The best word for subsuming all modes of behavioral control is "culture."

A controlled pattern of behavior, no matter how simple or complex, is best understood by taking a metaphor from the theater: "performance." Culture, then, consists of instructions for performances. Signs that elicit a performance in individuals who have learned the appropriate performance response to that sign or set of signs I call, therefore, "performatory signs," whether signs are verbal or nonverbal, as the arrangement of furniture in a classroom.

The signs usually recognized as "expressive signs," on the other hand, are not easily understood as performatory signs. For one thing, the capacity to elicit emotional response is also an attribute of regulatory signs. If both kinds of signs are conventional, the effectiveness of regulatory signs is connected with the fact that an aspect of that conventionality is their explicability. But it is precisely the inexplicability, in a conventional sense, that is the attribute of "expressive signs," as we have seen. The hypothesis proposed here is that they have to do with *how* a performance is carried out. If we observe the virtually universal sign of rulership—height (daises, thrones, and crowns)—we can have a clue to the character and function of these signs. The clue is stronger if we observe that height is a virtually universal attribute of any social role at the top of an institutional hierarchy. The height appears to regulate some aspects of human behavior. The elevated throne regulates the level of activity directed toward the monarch.

This is best understood by conceiving that activity as unidimensional. The relation of any organism to its environment is its manipulation and exploitation of that environment, the end result of that manipulation being survival or nonsurvival, as the case may be. Hence the most suitable word for behavioral activity that includes the notion of a continuum of levels as an attribute is "aggression." (The distinction between "aggression" and "aggressiveness" is solely a normative or value distinction.) The advantage of "aggression" and "aggressiveness" is that both are used both pejoratively and eulogistically. Since all terms are performatory and hence normative, "aggression" meets the requirement of normative ambiguity. "Passivity" is commonly understood as a negation of "aggression," but an examination of behavior reveals that "passive" behavior is a means of controlling the behavior of an aggressor. It is best understood as seduction, the only alternative to which in behavioral control is, ultimately, force. Further, from the point of view of "aggression," "control" becomes more lucid. Since the individual is a social dyad, responding to his own behavior as he responds to the behavior of others, control over oneself is not different from control over others. The socialization of the infant is training the infant by force and seduction to impose culturally validated controls on himself. In addition, control can be interpreted in one of two ways, either as a hindrance to aggression, or as a guidance to aggression. A hindrance to aggression is judged unacceptable; guidance of aggression is judged acceptable. Hindrance or guidance can be imposed by either oneself or others. The conclusion of this is that "expressive signs" are better understood as "regulatory" signs, since they regulate the level of behavior, that is, of aggression. Thus the second way of dichotomizing signs is into the pair "regulatory" and "performatory."

An historical example will illustrate how the notion of regulatory signs may be applied. The notion that such signs are expressive signs developed from Romantic critical and aesthetic speculation. The Romantic, alienated from his culture, was deprived of the cultural supports for the validation of his persona. It was necessary to find in the persona itself, therefore, a source for the self-ascription of value. Since art was already one of the high culture's value signs, the artist could ascribe value to himself by defining himself as an artist, and the artist become more important than the work of art. The production of a work thus became a source for self-ascription of value. Hence art began to be thought of as self-expression, for the word "self" (central in Romantic thinking) subsumed the processes of self-ascription of value. Moreover, to maintain the level of a self-ascription of value in negation of the culturally validated modes of such value ascription, it was necessary for the artist to raise the level of his aggression. Regulatory signs became increasingly aggressive. In music the signs regulating an increase of the level of aggression are upward pitch-movement of melody, increased volume, increased tempo, increased scale, and increased discontinuity, for discontinuity itself is an aggression against the stabilizing protocols of culture. Thus the last movement of Beethoven's Fifth Symphony instead of offering a reduction of aggression after the higher levels of aggression in the first and second movement, as the eighteenth-century symphony had done, proposed a higher level of aggression than in the preceding movements. Likewise, as cultural controls became increasingly unacceptable, the minor mode became increasingly more important in serious music, as in the minor scherzo of that same symphony. Throughout the nineteenth century the regulatory signs in all the arts became increasingly dominant over performatory signs. In painting this led to abstract art. All this indicates that the direction of external discontinuity is under ideological control.

In the assemblage of a work of art, configurations, regulatory signs, and performatory signs can be independent of each other, or a particular configuration can be all three. An example is a drawing which presents a centrally dominating vertical triangle with a very acute apex (internally discontinuous from other triangles in the drawing); that same configuration can be a regulatory sign (unimpeded aggression), and also a performatory sign (a church steeple). In this case the interpretation would be that unimpeded aggression is reserved for God, a thoroughly Christian notion. As we have seen, this second possibility is particularly important in poetry, in which the discontinuity depends upon syntax, which in turn depends upon appropriate response to performatory signs. Nevertheless, poetry does present pure configurational signs, though not nearly in the abundance of the visual and aural arts. One device of rhetoric is overdetermination of sound: rhyme, vowel euphony, and alliteration. It seems probable that order is valued because it requires a high degree of aggression towards an environmental field if it is to be ordered, that is, predictable and coherent. It is enough to consider the aggression of the primary-grade teacher in training her charges into orderly and predictable interaction with one another and herself. But, since we regard that aggression as desirable and acceptable, we call it guidance of the children rather than impedance of their behavior. Thus, as suggested above, in music a melody that moves downward in pitch and in the minor is a lowering of aggressive level judged as the result of impedance, while a downward-moving melody in the major is judged as the result of guidance. In the dramatic use of music, as part of a dramatic situation without words, as in ballet, or with words as in song and opera, the impedance and the guidance are ascribed to characters. These same semiotic conditions hold in poetry. Rhyme is fundamentally an assurance to poet and listener that the poet is capable of enough aggressive competence towards his language to be trusted in what he says, that is, in the presentation of performatory signs. It can be used dramatically, in that a shift from an unrhymed section of a poem to a rhymed section is an indication of the raising of the level of aggression. If the poem is one which involves a secondary dramatic level—the speaker is addressing someone—then the shift to rhyme is an increase of aggression towards that someone. The content (the performatory signs) is the source for determining whether that aggression is to be interpreted as either impedance of the aggression of the someone or guidance of his aggression. And these considerations apply likewise to vowel euphony and alliteration.

With the aid of these proposals it is now useful to turn back to external discontinuity, both horizontal (historical) and vertical (emergent at cultural levels). As suggested above, to order a situation requires a high level of aggression; but so does the introduction of disorder into an ordered situation. Until the full emergence of the Romantic ideology in the course of the nineteenth century, all modes of art tended to present a high degree of order in the interrelation of the performatory signs, along with either a coherent or an incoherent presentation of regulatory signs (high and low levels of aggression) and anything from a high to a low level of discontinuity. These are variables, then, that operate independently. The Romantic ideology has moved the artist in the direction of performatory disorder, incoherent regulatory signs, and a higher level of discontinuity. This is consistent with what has already been suggested, the increase in aggressive level in Romantic art.

Thus what lies behind historical external discontinuity is the artist's aggressive violation of the stylistic norm of the tradition in which he is working. And the higher the cultural level, the truer this is. Before the nineteenth century the primary mode of aggressiveness was the exploitation of formal discontinuity, and with the Renaissance the increasing level of incoherence in the regulatory signs. (The second is particularly the mark of Mannerism.) Thus the higher the cultural level, the higher the level of the artists' aggression. What lies behind this phenomenon is the continuum from low to high culture, from the acceptance of guidance to the judgment that the guidance of cultural controls is an impedance. That is, the higher the cultural level of the individual, the greater the probability of his aggressive attack upon the culture's ideologies. The history of philosophy is far more unstable than the history of farming.

What makes this cultural vandalism possible can be deduced from the situation in which art response takes place. The higher the cultural level at which it is produced and encountered, the greater the psychic insulation and social protection provided for that encounter. The same insulation and protection are made available for all situations in which the performance requires sustained problem exposure, that is, tolerance of configurational and semiotic instability—the college campus, the library, the office of the corporation executive, the scientist's laboratory, the scholar's study.

Art, then, exploits one of the irresolvable problems of any individual and of any society or culture. On the one hand the level of aggression must be kept high enough so that the individual can successfully (in his judgment) exploit the environment. On the other hand, it must be kept low enough so that the individual can successfully interact with others, the result being the satisfaction of the same interest. That is why adolescents are such a nuisance; they have not yet mastered the protocols of levels of aggression appropriate in the new social situations into which, on emergence from the family, they must enter. They must also establish a higher level of aggression than is permitted in the family situation. Obviously, it is not only art that regulates aggression.

Art exploits performatory signs, regulatory signs, and discontinuity, and it does so in a special kind of situation, one in which nothing is at stake. Because nothing is at stake, because the responder to a work of art can experience an irresponsibility otherwise available only to gods, and because the higher the cultural level the greater the psychic insulation and social protection provided in the art-perceiving situation, he can rehearse semantic interpretation, variability of aggressive level, and toleration of the destabilization of perceptual determination and semiotic categorization. Of these the most important is clearly the toleration of destabilization. Art may profitably be thought of as an abstraction of cultural controls from the existential situations in which they are experienced. Cultural controls are based upon perceptual determination and semiotic categorization; these controls are themselves under the control of verbal behavior; and verbal behavior is under the control of high-level explanations (regressive from the perceptual), best understood, in the broadest possible sense, as ideologies. Ideologies are always to a certain extent inappropriate for any situation to which they are applied and the behavior which they control, for ideologies have always emerged as responses to previous situations. In the fullest sense, therefore, cultural controls are always and inevitably out of phase with any existential situation. They can operate only if the individual suppresses his possible responses to perceptual and semiotic attributes which the currently operating controls cannot subsume, just as a scientist can proceed only by ignoring data which his theory cannot subsume. When that data is so qualitatively and quantitatively different from the successfully subsumed data, the theory (or scientific ideology) is undermined and must be modified. By abstracting controls from existential situations, art enables the individual to contemplate them, to modify them, and to undermine them *with impunity*. And that impunity distinguishes the art situation from other insulated and protected situations.

It has been said over and over that a good work of art is marked by unity and order. As for unity, any perceptual field is unified if the criteria of judgment are loose enough, and none is if they are sufficiently stringent. As for order, it means no more than the confirmation of expectancies, that is, predictability, and in semiotic constructs the presentation of what is judged to be coherence. And as with unity, coherence is a matter of judgment, not of inherent or immanent qualities. If one examines a series of critical discussions of a given work of art, one will find judgments of unity and coherence, and of disunity and incoherence, and both kinds of judgments are equally plausible and equally well argued. If one takes art seriously, one does not bother with such trivialities, just as one does not bother with the absurd ascription to art of semantic autonomy, of a unique and untranslatable meaning. For if one takes art seriously, one recognizes it as an adaptational device for escaping from cultural controls, which are of necessity, and in the long run, maladaptational.

Art exploits the brain's capacity for randomness, without surrendering to it. It is thus the source or preparation or rehearsal for tolerating randomness and sustained problem exposure, that is, perceptual and semiotic discontinuity, for randomness is the source not only for error but also for culturally validated error, which we call, when it is validated, creativity. Art is the human defense against the inadequacy of cultural control, for it is the preparation for the acceptance of perceptual and semiotic instability, an acceptance which is the only road to transcending the limitations of cultural controls. That is why art is ubiquitous, to be found in all cultures and at all cultural levels, and why it must have existed in now decayed organic materials long before the oldest works of art that have survived, the cave paintings of France and Spain. That is why, as I once said to a young Danish critic, the damned stuff is all over the place.

Readers familiar with my book *Man's Rage for Chaos* (1965) will recognize this paper as a summary of that work as well as a considerable modification of it, as, for example, the change from "primary signs" to "regulatory signs." In fifteen years a theory of anything as slippery as art ought to show *some* change. The problem in theory construction is to exploit the inherent instability of theory without surrendering to it and without failing in the other direction, excessive stabilization.

## REFERENCES

Arnheim, R. *Visual Thinking*. Berkeley: University of California Press, 1969.
Kellog, R. *Analyzing Children's Art*. Palo Alto: National Press Books, 1969.
Mead, G. H. "Suggestions Toward a Theory of the Philosophical Disciplines," *Philosophical Review* 9 (1900): 1–17.
Peckham, M. *Man's Rage for Chaos*. Philadelphia: Chilton, 1965.
Peirce, C. S. *Collected Papers of Charles Sanders Peirce*. Cambridge, Mass.: Harvard University Press, 1931–1958.

# CHAPTER SIXTEEN

# "Literature"

## Disjunction and Redundancy

Most definitions of literature emanate from high cultural levels and are most readily subsumed under the category of, in a loose sense, philosophical behavior. The most interesting feature of such definitions is their instability. As new cultural stages emerge, definitions of literature are innovated in response to cultural change—to emerging interests, ideologies, philosophies, issues, and so on. Such efforts at definition are almost invariably normative, a phenomenon that is evident from the changing ascriptions of value granted to particular works. Either the work can be made or it cannot be made, or it is or is not made, to serve the emerging situation. If adaptation is accomplished, a work to which value has traditionally been ascribed will continue to be valued. If not, then the value ascription is withdrawn. At any given time, of course, some individuals, unaware of or resistant to the emergent culture, will continue to make the traditional ascriptions. It is evident that high cultural definitions are unlikely to be more than temporarily satisfying, since their interest is not in defining literature but in comprehending and establishing an emergent culture. To be sure, in the short range, a spurious stability will appear, because, if there is no significant cultural change, the definitions of the most recently emerging culture will tend to stabilize but a new cultural upheaval will force their abandonment.

What is needed is, first, a field definition of literature, a field that will be established non-normatively and will begin by accepting as literature whatever anyone says is literature or some subcategory of literature—poetry, fiction, informal essay, etc. Such a field definition is non-normative and includes within its boundaries not only literary works emanating from a high cultural level but also the infinitely greater bulk of literary discourse found at all other levels: Edna Ferber, Ella Wheeler Wilcox, Edgar Rice Burroughs, pornographic fiction, jokes, limericks, and so on. What would be excluded are works in which verbal behavior is but one of several-to-many semiotic systems—plays, movies, operas, comic books. That the scripts of such works can be considered apart from the other semiotic systems in the original is an interesting point to which it will be useful to return, for it shows that the advantage of a field definition is the blurred character of the boundaries of such definitions.

Nevertheless, though a field definition is useful, "field" remains a metaphor, but "literature" is a category. The question is whether it is a conjunctive or a disjunctive category, whether all works of literature may reasonably be said to have at least one internal attribute in common, or whether this statement may not be reasonably made.[1]

There is little question that virtually all definitions of "literature" assume that it is properly to be regarded as a conjunctive category, that all works of literature, whether a dirty joke or *Paradise Lost*, have in common an immanent and defining attribute; that is, other modes of discourse are without that attribute. Without trying to claim exhaustiveness, I think that most definitions can be boiled down to the following types.

First is the definition based upon the assertion of a common psychological or subjective origin. Thus literature has for some time been defined as a product of, or expression of, the imagination. Since it is easily demonstrated that certain other types of discourse—philosophy, science, history—are equally products of the imagination, this difficulty is countered by saying that literature is a verbal product of the "creative imagination." But this strategy does not seem to help much. Consider Immanuel Wallerstein's appeal to "the empirical evidence" in his recent *The Modern World-System: Capitalist Agriculture and the Origins of the European World-Economy in the Sixteenth Century.* Now the fact of the matter is that if "empirical evidence" means here what it does to, let us say, a physicist, or a chemist, or even a few sociologists, Wallerstein does not have any. What he does have are documents and certain artifacts, such as ploughs, which are by no means self-explanatory. Moreover, his book is not based even upon very much of his own examination of such historical documents but upon the research of others. This is not to denigrate a fine scholar and a book of considerable importance, but rather to point out that, guided by Marx, Wallerstein has certainly produced a discourse marked by what anyone would call a product of the "historical imagination."

But is it "creative"? If "creative" is taken in its most extreme and narrow sense, the mark of discourse which has no correspondence in anything, verbal or nonverbal, outside of the literary discourse in question, then the question remains unanswerable, for we do not know whether Wallerstein's thesis indeed has any relation whatsoever to what really happened. There is no doubt that a good many competent historians will disagree with him entirely. In short, it has proved impossible to confine the term "creative" to any particular mode of behavior.

This leads us to the second type of definition, one based upon content. This usually takes the form of a claim for some kind of semantic autonomy, most frequently appearing in the form of a claim for literature of a unique kind of "truth." When inquiry is made into what this "truth" is, it usually turns out that literature exemplifies some philosophical or moral truth or that it furnishes an ineffable or otherwise unutterable truth. It can be experienced by the individual reader but cannot be communicated. It is reasonably obvious that what is going on here is an effort to ascribe value to literature—and, in practice, only some works of literature, ordinarily a rather small class—by using the highly eulogistic term "truth." It is quite obviously normative and just as obviously the product of a high cultural level, though not the highest. From another point of view, that of the total non-normatively defined "field of literature," the semantic content of literature is infinitely varied. No one semantic function can be said to be a defining attribute of literature. Literature is a semantic field in which anything goes.

The third kind of definition concerns itself with the formal aspect. Literature is said to have unity and coherence (or "aesthetic" unity, a formulation so question-begging that it is not worth discussing). Even if this were so, these cannot be defining attributes, for surely other kinds of discourse may be reasonably said to be marked by the same attributes. Further, any perceptual field (and literature is such, for it consists of discourse perceived either by eye or by ear) is unified and coherent if the criteria are sufficiently loose; and none is if the criteria are sufficiently stringent. Unity and coherence are matters of judgment, a fact easily demonstrated by the enormous amount of disagreement. How many articles have been written and even published on the unity and coherence of *Beowulf*! Nevertheless, a formal definition does have some possibilities. There is little doubt that literature can present a degree of incoherence, of disunity, or incomprehensible relationships to be found in no other kind of discourse. Poetry, for example, can conform to or violate the syntactic norms of the language in which it is written. A fictional character can be thoroughly inconsistent or incoherent. Indeed, consistency of character increases as the importance of the character in the work decreases, and as the cultural level of the work is lowered. Plots can be resolved or left unresolved. Two stanzas of the same poem may be quite contradictory. And so on. This definition is at least promising. If the norms of linguistic behavior are behaviorally maintained, rather than genetically maintained, and such behavioral maintenance certainly seems to be the case, then it can be said that the violations of linguistic norms to be found in literature are socially permitted. This leads in the direction of some kind of sociocultural definition of literature.

A fourth kind of definition, of minor importance but worth mentioning, is the dysfunctional. It is said that there are elements in literature or there are attributes of literature which are superfluous to its semantic function, to what is being said in, or by, the work. "Grace, elegance, charm, power" are words commonly used to designate this superfluous dysfunctional attribute, but the most common term is probably "style." Literature, then, is discourse marked by "style." That this is a normative definition is indicated by the extremely various efforts to state what that "style" amounts to. On the other hand, one often enough hears of some works that they have no style (the fiction of Balzac, for example) but are certainly works of literature. Yet this definition has possibilities, for it is often said that certain nonliterary works, such as those of Buffon, are so marked by literary style that they are "really" works of literature. This is promising, for at least it shows the fuzziness and instability in the boundaries of the field of literature.

No doubt there are other types of definitions of literature, though I can think of no others. At least, however, it seems reasonable to attempt a definition of "literature" as a disjunctive category. This means that works called "literature" do not have any immanent and defining attribute in common. It follows that discourses are categorized as "literature" as a consequence of some sociocultural judgment. This is best understood by considering what has been mentioned before, the instability of the boundaries of the literature field. Certain works, such as Carlyle's *French Revolution,* are no longer read as history but rather as literature. Yet certainly it was first published as history, and as recently as thirty years ago was included in one historian's bibliography as one of the best English histories of that event. Buffon and any number of originally philosophical works are read now as literature. Some time ago a psychologist recommended to me the works of Jung, not because of their scientific or psychological value, which he discounted, but for their splendid imaginative and literary qualities. Schopenhauer and Nietzsche are not infrequently labeled bad philosophy but good literature. Richard Hooker and Sir Thomas Browne are categorized as literature but not as anything now significant in terms of the nonliterary genres in which their works were originally written. A work of literature, then, is such because someone has judged it to be a work of literature.

If we modify the first type of definition (literature as an expression or product of the imagination) to the definition of literature as a fictive discourse as well as a disjunctive category, what has happened to such works becomes obvious. It is asserted that their nonfictiveness is no longer of importance or significance or value but that they can be profitably read as fictive discourses. The definition of whether a discourse is fictive or nonfictive is then a matter of someone's judgment. And indeed the history of science itself is filled with statements originally judged to be nonfictive but now judged to be fictive. This can best be explained by the judgment that all discourse is fictive, that all utterance, all linguistic behavior, is fictive.[2] Discourse is a construct of that which lies outside of language. Culture, in the full, anthropological, sense, consists of directions for a performance, and language is subsumed by culture. Even "descriptive" statements—such as, "There is a mouse in the corner over there"—are in their full form instructions for a performance: "If you look in the corner over there, you will see a mouse—if he's still there." All words which are referential—an inadequate term but one which will have to serve here—are categorial, even proper names, because a proper name categorizes separately perceived configurations. Hence the disagreement on the attributes of bearers of proper names.[3] Moreover, categorial words are not under genetic or perceptual control. Verbalization makes the human construction of the world free or, more precisely, indeterminable. What makes it possible to recategorize a nonliterary work as a literary work is that its fictiveness continues, no matter how it is categorized.

What makes a discourse a work of literature, then, is that it is identified as fictive. Such identifications may be internal: "Once upon a time." They may appear in the title: *Jim James: A Novel.* They may be prefatory: "I heard a good joke the other day." The conventions of fictive identifications are innumerable, but can be uncertain. Is *The Tale of Genji* a novel or a memoir? They may be situational; they may be typographical; they may be tones of voice. Whatever they are and however the announcement of fictiveness is made, that announcement is a cultural convention.[4] Furthermore, since behavior is indeterminable, those conventions can be played with, can be modified.

Thus the script of a theater piece can be read apart from the theatrical situation, and theater pieces may or may not have scripts. In the same way an *exemplum* can be extracted from a sermon and presented as literature.

But if this disjunctive definition of literature as a discourse identified as fictive is accepted, we are bound to ask why such identifications should be made. That is, what are the consequences of such announcements? It is a sentimentality to conceive of language as "communication." Rather language organizes, directs, controls, and modifies behavior. If, because of language, human behavior is indeterminable, then humans are not social animals in the same sense that bees and ants are, or even the higher mammals, much of whose behavior is certainly cultured, or learned, though it is still under perceptual if not full genetic control. And if humans are not social, then interaction, which is economically necessary and ineluctable, must be controlled. The accomplishment, language, which makes human behavior indeterminable is also the instrument which for the most part makes it determinable. Ultimately, however, the sanction for the control language exercises is force. But if force fails, there is no recourse. Consequently the burden of interactional control falls upon language.

Two attributes of human behavior need to be explained, and explained in the same way: deviance from established norms and channeling of behavior within those norms. To the degree any behavior is badly transmitted, to that degree there will be a spread of deviance. But how is behavior maintained? Why is there not far greater deviance than there is? In any society there is, statistically speaking, only very little. (Wealthy societies can tolerate far more than can poor societies.) The answer, I believe, lies in the phenomenon of redundancy, the endless repetition of the same verbal (and nonverbal, under the control of verbal) instructions in various verbal and nonverbal semiotic modes.[5] Without such redundancy, including instructions that individuals give to themselves, behavioral patterns deteriorate, as a language learned in adolescence will deteriorate if it is not continually used. Even frequent but irregular use is not enough to maintain competence. One forgets the dates in a literary field one has ceased to teach and study. Now the literatus is part of this redundancy system, simply because he is a human. Any individual is a precipitate of the indescribably complex control system which is language; with infinitely rare exceptions, his presence or absence, his existence or nonexistence, makes no difference. His behavior is controlled by that system, but because of the brain's capacity for random response, deviance (innovation, creativity, the imagination) is constantly being introduced in, on the whole, minute and statistically insignificant amounts. The decisions the literatus makes, then, are under the control of the linguistic behavior of his culture, and his fictive discourse exemplifies the verbal redundancies of his culture. At the higher cultural level those redundancies are organized into and justified by ideologies. A work of literature is a discourse, the fictiveness of which is announced, and which exemplifies the redundancies and ideologies of the culture in which it originates. From this point of view literature (even orally repeated jokes) is of the highest importance in maintaining behavior by constantly exemplifying verbalizations of a level higher than the work itself, "higher" here meaning "subsuming." The characteristic of the literary situation for the receiver is that he is not required to do anything immediately in response to the instructions received. Literature, then, maintains the redundancies of a society in those situations in which performance, other than attentiveness, is not required. Literature (and the other arts) maintains redundancies during periods of economic disengagement, or periods of disengagement from control by hierarchical institutions such as religious, schooling, and governmental institutions which, however, maintain economic competence. (This is true of other activities as well, such as participation in sports or stamp collecting. Spectator sports, however, fall within the boundaries of art.) The literary conventions of fictiveness are announcements of the suitability of such discourse for periods of economic and institutional disengagement.

But there is a joker here. I have already implied the identification of randomness, deviance, innovation, creativity, imagination. Periods of economic disengagement, obviously, are periods of the greatest tolerance for randomness of behavior, that randomness which is the most striking product of the human brain. The games of children are economically preparatory; they are abstractions of adult interactional patterns. The play of children, in which they discover their own interests, is marked by randomness. Because of this tolerance for randomness, literature is, first of all, a disjunctive category and, second, one that not only maintains behavior but also modifies it. The justification for the teaching of literature is that, by providing exemplifications of a variety of ideologies, it modifies the overall behavior of the student in the direction of flexibility. As situations change, patterns of economically engaged behavior must change. A certain portion of the society, gradually sifted for decisions at a higher socioeconomic level, is trained by the literature of high culture in perceiving the possibilities of alternative modes of behavior and alternative ideologies, and in randomization and innovation. (This does not deny that high-culture literature can be and frequently has been used only for exemplificatory redundancy.) Furthermore, literature, because of its disjunctive character, and because of its potentiality for incoherence, can be used to undermine regnant ideologies. To Pope ("What oft was thought . . ."), literature is properly employed in the modification of the exemplification of ideological redundancies in the direction of clarity and effectiveness. To writers at a high cultural level for nearly the past two hundred years—a time of extraordinarily rapid culture change at all levels of social organization, from the fundamental economic modes of interaction to the construction of the most exacting ideologies—not merely this modification but the undermining of ideological redundancies has been the most valued objective—even, in some instances, to the point of undermining ideological behavior itself.

What is literature? It is a discourse which exploits in periods of economic and institutional disengagement the fictiveness of utterance by announcing that fictiveness, and thus has the capacity to maintain the redundancies of its culture, to modify those redundancies, and to undermine them. Thus it has the capacity to support the economic interactional patterns of its culture, to modify them, and to destroy them.

NOTES

1. See Jerome S. Bruner, *A Study of Thinking* (New York, 1956), p. 159. Bruner takes the category of disjunction from Bertrand Russell's *Introduction to Mathematical Thinking* (1919).

2. In J. L. Austin's terminology, all utterances are "performative," i.e., instructions for behavior. Utterances of which such words as "truth," "real," "descriptive," etc., are predicated are utterances for which the predication is a "performative" instruction that such utterances should control our behavior, or must control our behavior, if the predicator has sufficient power to enforce his predication; cf. the Inquisition and General Amin.

3. The problem of proper names is one of the more notorious of the many failures of philosophy. John R. Searle does a considerably better job than most in his essay "Proper Names and Descriptions," *Encyclopedia of Philosophy.* "We learn to use proper names and we teach others to use proper names only by ostension or description, and both methods connect the name to the object only in virtue of specifying enough characteristics of the object to distinguish it from other objects" (vol. 6, p. 490). He appears to ignore, however, the fact that we encounter what he calls bearers of proper names in a series of situations spread over as much as a lifetime. The characteristics (or attributes) change. John Jones, a gentle man, may become savage, but it is still convenient to call him John Jones. Cobbs Creek may have its course changed and straightened, but it is still Cobbs Creek. The consequence of the institution of

proper names is a stabilization of behavior by stabilizing response. Searle is at least aware of the imprecision of proper names, and sees something of its advantages. Were it not for the instability of the attributes, one of the most powerful devices of fiction would be impossible: the establishment of the attributes of a proper name, the description of some attributes and the ascription of others. This is known, inaccurately, as "character development."

4. This is something children have to learn. Initially, the socialization of children, i.e., bringing them under linguistic control, requires that all statements be accepted by the child as "true," an acceptance traditionally backed up by the force of the parent. The child must subsequently learn that some utterances are "not true," are "made up," are "a story," and that the utterer of a "story" is not "telling a lie" when it is announced that the "story" is indeed "made up," that is, does not require obedience or acceptance as "true." Children very often have a great deal of trouble in learning this distinction and are inclined to believe *Star Trek* to be history.

5. There is no adequate theory of signs available at present. Peirce's distinctions among "icon," "index," and "symbol" are untenable, since one may respond to an "icon" as if it were a "symbol" or an "index." He is in fact talking about modes of response. Morris's notion of "disposition to respond" does not depend upon phenomenal observants. My own position corresponds with G. H. Mead's position that the meaning of a sign is the response to that sign. Unfortunately Mead did little with this idea. But at least, depending upon Hegel, he broke with the tradition that the meaning of a sign is immanent, and also with the very confusing and inadequate notion of "reference." A sign, then, is a configuration for which a response has been conventionalized, but this use of "convention" does not exclude conventionalization within the behavior of a single individual, nor does it exclude the notion that such conventionalization may occur only once. Nor does it exclude error, or what is judged by someone to be an inappropriate response. Irony depends upon the possibility of judgments of inappropriateness. My own discussion of signs in *Man's Rage for Chaos* is highly unsatisfactory, dependent as it is upon Morris. In *Art and Pornography* the theory of signs is vastly improved, but still inadequate. In *Explanation and Power: An Inquiry into the Control of Human Behavior,* the theory of signs is, I believe at the moment, in a reasonably satisfactory condition.

# CHAPTER SEVENTEEN

# Three Notions about Criticism

My three notions are possible answers to three questions, which to me exhaust the possibilities of questions about criticism, although others, no doubt, will not find them equally exhaustive. These questions are (1) What are the kinds of critical statements? (2) What makes criticism possible? and (3) What is the present state of criticism?

I

Resisting the notion that my thinking must be invalid because I am about to introduce another triad, I discern three kinds of critical statements, of which the first is the *interpretational statement*. I begin with this because it is one of the factors frequently involved in the second kind. It is with some relief that I conclude that there are but two kinds of interpretational statements. In the first, the critic endeavors to determine, either from internal factors or from factors external to the composition of the work, what were the interests (or, somewhat more grandiosely, the ideology or ideologies) which governed the decisions responsible for the salient semantic attributes of the work, or at least what the critic judges to be the salient attributes. In the second kind of interpretational statement, the critic uses the work to exemplify his own interests (or ideologies or ideology). Obviously, in the first kind the critic's interests (henceforth, "ideologies" are to be understood) are also involved, for they govern his decisions about the interest of the writer of the work. The difference between the two kinds of interpretational statement is that exposure, in the first kind, to other interests can have an effect upon the critic's own interests, even to the extent of loosening (if not freeing) him from his bondage to them, while the second kind is unlikely to have any such corrective effect. I use the word "corrective" because I regard all ideologies as necessary but also more or less unsatisfactory, and the blind adherence to any ideology or interest as highly damaging both to the individual and to his sociocultural situation.

But this distinction between kinds of interpretational statement cannot be left without some consideration of what makes it possible, and what the effects have been. No utterance controls or determines a response to that utterance. The response is always a determination; the response (a decision, if only metaphorically) involves interpretation, even when the determination is under the severest cultural control, such as torture or the threat of execution. *Hence there is no immanent or necessary connection between any work of literature and any interpretation of the work.* On the contrary, the possibilities of interpreting any work of literature are, if not infinite, at least indefinably great. In the past two hundred years there have been the two interpretational tendencies mentioned above. The first, which is to control possibilities by an effort to determine the interest of the author, has produced increasingly rich and complex interpretations, so that, even if certainty is unattainable, there has been an increasing convergence of interpretation, at least for a number of works to which high value has been traditionally ascribed. The second kind, using the work of literature to exemplify the critic-interpreter's interests, has spread into a delta of interpretational possibilities. The explanation for this is that the last two hundred years have seen the emergence of a great many rival ideologies, each of which has developed its particular role of literary criticism. (If any of these ideologies have not done so, we can safely assume that they probably will.)

The second kind of critical statement consists of *judgments of competence.* These, as I have suggested, can be based upon interpretation. Thus from the interpretation can be derived some general proposition or "truth," philosophical, ethical, historical, sociological, psychological, and so on. Thus we ascribe value to Balzac, say, because of the competence of his "profound sociological insights." On the other hand, we might deny his authorial competence on the grounds of "stylistic" competence. As ideologies change, and as styles change, the ground of judgments of competence changes. John Sparrow once judged what was then "modern poetry" to be simply incompetent; the poets hadn't learned how to write poetry. Free verse was initially judged to be the consequence of incompetence; then judgments of competence in writing free verse were gradually developed. Like interpretational statements judgments of competence can always be countered by drawing upon some rival justification or determination of competence. "My Last Duchess" can be judged prosodically incompetent because one does not notice the presence of the rhymes. (A surprisingly large number of professional students and teachers of literature think that the poem is in blank verse.) But it can also be judged extraordinarily competent for precisely the same attribute: that is, for the "subtlety" of its rhymes. A poem may be judged competent because it is charming, delicate, touching, and straightforward; or it may be judged incompetent in spite of all these attributes because it does not offer an ironical conclusion. Or a poet may be judged less competent because he invariably offers a "mechanical" ironical conclusion (as the common judgments of O. Henry stories illustrate). It seems obvious that judgments of competence, like interpretational statements of the second kind, are traceable to the critic's interests (which we call "biases" when we do not accept them). As with ideologies, the immense delta-spread of styles emerging in the last two hundred years, the result of the ideology that a competent writer must develop a unique style rather than developing competence in an existent style and then modifying it, has brought about an equivalent delta-spread of rationalizations for judgments of competence. As a counter to this, there is a critical tendency to judge that what from one determination of competence is a flaw may indeed have served the writer's interests and therefore be justifiable. Thus what is said to be the crudeness or banality of Balzac's style may be determined to serve the interest of directing the reader's attention to characters, situations, and events; while the marvelous complexity of Proust's style may be determined to be a flaw in that it directs the reader's attention from what Proust is saying—or away from the semantic aspect or content of the novels. The stylistic surface of Swinburne has persuaded a great many readers that he had nothing of interest to say. These (or other readers), if persuaded that Swinburne had indeed something of interest to say, might then determine him to be an incompetent poet. The gnarled and knotted syntax and the "ugly" phonic character of Browning's later poetry has been responsible for the fact that it has been pretty much neglected. On the other hand, both of these stylistic attributes can be judged to be challenges which are richly rewarding when overcome and one penetrates to the interpretation of Swinburne and Browning. Thus their respective styles could be judged not as incompetent but as supremely competent.

What it appears to come down to is that if one values a work of literature, it is not difficult, at least for someone trained and experienced in the rhetoric of literary criticism, to determine either that the ascription of value is justified by the writer's high competence or that, correspondingly, an ascription of negative value can be justified by a determination of the writer's incompetence.

We come then to the third kind of critical statements, *ascriptions of value*. The fact that to the same work can be, and constantly is, ascribed both negative and positive value, justified by a determination that the identical literary attributes can be judged as an indication of either competence or incompetence, suggests that though the same language is used for judgments of competence and judgments of value, the two judgments are quite different in kind, even though judgments of competence can be used to justify and rationalize judgments of value. Let me use an example from my own recent experience. In the first six months of 1979 I had occasion to reread six of the major novels of Dickens, from *Pickwick Papers* to *Little Dorrit*. All six were novels I had once admired and delighted in. But now, in my sixty-fifth year, I found all of them, except *Pickwick Papers*, simply execrable. I can read no more of what I now regard as drivel. With little trouble I can construct a justification for my position. For example, I could say that the novels are marked by Romantic formal strategies but that these strategies are in the service of an Enlightenment ideology. And I could even, perhaps, argue this rationalization at such length and with such a command of the devices of literary critical rhetoric that some readers might take it seriously. But I cannot honestly justify by rationalization a judgment I regard as too easily unjustifiable. If those were Dickens's interests, it is impossible to deny that he was superbly competent in exploiting that ideological incoherence. Thus there is no necessary connection between judgments of competence and judgments, or ascriptions, of value. No matter what justification for my present judgment I construct, it seems clear that my former ascription of value to Dickens's fiction and my present withdrawal of that ascription to the point of detestation are matters of personal history and temperament. That is, I once could use Dickens to serve an interest, but now I cannot. But what is that interest?

I would suggest that ascriptions of value to a literary work, to any work of art, to any being or to any human activity, or to a tree, or to a landscape are all the same kind of behavior. We may call it the "value experience" to distinguish it from the verbal (or verbally justified) ascription of value. Probably the most common term used to verbalize that experience is "beauty," though currently "meaningful" seems to be at least as popular. Central to the value experience is the ascription of value to oneself, evidently learned during the socialization of the child. Parents engage in two quite distinct ascription activities in bringing up children (or at least that is the norm—exceptions may account for sociopaths): on the one hand the child is constantly judged competent or incompetent in the performance of various specific activities; but on the other hand he is given generalized praise for being such a good child, or the nicest little boy in the world. That is, *value is ascribed to him without reference to competence,* and, in the course of his further development and in adulthood, that value continues to be ascribed, maintained, and stabilized by various institutions, membership in which constitutes value ascription: clubs, religions, honorary societies, nations, and so on. Religious rituals, mass, communion, animal or human sacrifice, patriotic celebrations—all those behavioral strategies which anthropologists call the "sacred"—are the most obvious modes of experiencing the self-ascription of value. In secularized cultures such as ours, psychotherapy has assumed the function of restoring and stabilizing the self-ascription of value, at least for a respectably large portion of the population. All psychotherapists work for somebody, and, except for cases involving a physiological abnormality or trauma or lesion, they all appear to work the same way, that is, teaching the patient to ascribe value to himself. For others, those to whom psychotherapy is unacceptable or too expensive, new religions emerge or are revived, such as white witchcraft or Druidism, or are imported from alien cultures, a phenomenon of increasing frequency in our culture during the past 150 years. Now, just as certain perceptual configurations that are displayed by value institutions are signs to the individual of his own value (in childhood, Christmas and birthday presents; in adult life, communion or even the mere listening to a sermon or an invitation from a socially exclusive hostess), so there can be extra-institutional signs to which the individual responds in the same way—that is, as *signs of his own value.* Having learned from institutions to respond to value signs, he can now select them for himself.

In artistic matters for quite some time the capacity to use a work of art to maintain or restore or improve the self-ascription of value has been known as "taste." And that is why it is idle to argue about taste, although, as I have indicated, it is always possible to *justify* a taste; but that is simply because language makes it possible to justify anything. If we say, then, that someone has excellent taste in poetry, for example, we are saying no more than that the individual's poetry value signs have been validated as value signs by the small subculture of those interested in literature of a high cultural level. It is not, then, a question of whether I was right or wrong in ascribing value to Dickens up to fifteen years ago, when I last read one of his novels, or right or wrong in my current inability to do so. Rather, at one time I could use Dickens's novels as value signs (a sign that maintains my own value), but now I cannot. The explanation in my particular case is probably at the present time inaccessible, but a general explanation can be offered. The self-ascription of value subsumes judgments of both competence and incompetence, but there is no inherent or necessary connection between value and competence. Consequently, the self-ascription of value is necessarily unstable. Thus the individual, as his experiences modify his personality, finds it necessary to abandon some value signs and to establish others. His taste in literature changes. Psychotherapy, then, is primarily the socialization and institutionalization of a behavioral process which is a constant norm in the individual's own behavior. That process is essential because, as emotional depression shows—an experience in which there is a striking loss of the self-ascription of value and most commonly a decrease in competence in performing behavior in which the depressed individual had previously been competent—the self-ascription of value is necessary to maintain and improve competence, the coin and barter of interaction.

To return to literary criticism: there appears to be, in any culture, a writer or two whose works have been canonized (a term significantly derived from religious practices). In our culture it is obviously Shakespeare, and very little Shakespeare criticism is devoted to denigration. Almost all of it is aimed at providing further justification, either of competence or interpretation, for the verbal ascription to his works of supreme greatness. To deny that greatness is to bring upon oneself, at least from others, denigration, a withdrawal of value-ascription. Thus, an individual who agrees with you on the ascription of value to a particular work or writer becomes, for you, a value sign. Such agreements are an important, even a central, factor in the totality of behavior in response to works of art, and suggest very strongly that ascribing value to others and receiving such ascriptions are central to the socializing process. A good term for the interactional (or social) arrangements for ascribing value to others and receiving ascriptions of value is "agape system," that is, the system of interactional and intra-actional "love." Ascriptions of value to works of literature, then, can be understood as a factor in a culture's agapic system, or better, as one of the many agapic systems in a culture.

Some words can perhaps profitably be added here concerning the kind of critical statement this essay represents. If criticism is responses to works of literature, then this kind is responses to responses. It can be variously called critical theory, or metacriticism. The history of such metacriticism suggests that it is an activity best subsumed by philosophy or, to more modern tastes such as my own, by the behavioral sciences. I must add, however, and hastily, that I do not consider the behavioral sciences as they are presently practiced to be in much of a position to subsume anything. Thus the possibility that metacriticism properly belongs to the behavioral sciences must, at the moment and for the foreseeable future, remain in the realm of the ideal.[1]

## II

I come then to the second of my questions: What makes criticism possible? One answer to this is simple and obvious; we criticize literature because we criticize everything else. That is, we determine its meaning, we judge its competence, and we ascribe value to it. And we do all three in response to both natural and man-made configurations. It would seem odd, for example, to say that a tree is incompetent, but there is no significant difference between saying that loblolly pines are useless and even dangerous as fireplace wood and saying that a swimmer is performing the breaststroke very poorly. In both cases one is saying that the configuration is useful or not useful for some particular human interest. In the same way, a lumberman can say that a tree is "beautiful," meaning that it will make fine wood for expensive furniture, and a painter can use the same word to mean that it will make a splendid subject for a watercolor. Both are acts of interpretation as well as judgments of competence. Thus one can convert a tree into a value sign by leaving milk and flowers for a dryad living in it.

But all this leaves us where we started: What makes any of these judgments possible? We may begin with a phenomenon that has long puzzled me. If the role is sung by a great artist, such as a Callas, we can be completely involved in the sufferings of Lucia di Lammermoor and nevertheless burst into applause for the singer when she finishes the mad scene. The traditional terms for that involvement, "dramatic illusion" and "the willing suspension of disbelief," are, to me, quite useless, merely pointing at the problem but making no contribution to understanding it and solving it. Evidently in the twinkling of an eye we can shift our modes of apprehension. For the sake of some stability in terminology, I shall call our involvement in Lucia the apprehension of the behavior as an *act,* and our applauding Callas as the apprehension of the same behavior as a *performance.* The almost interchangeable use of "act" and "perform" both in the theater and out of it is an indication that any behavior can be apprehended as either an action or a performance. Indeed, in daily life we are constantly making that discrimination, in, for example, disagreements about whether a particular sequence of behavior was or was not ironical, or sincere, or hypocritical, or whether the individual was or was not lying, or conning us.

The explanation for this duality of apprehension and interpretation is that the protocols of all behaviors, behavioral patterns, and behavioral assemblages are learned as appropriate to particular situations. However, once a behavior is learned, it can be presented in kinds of situations other than those for which the connection between behavior and situation was taught as appropriate. In child culture, though often transmitted by parents, this eternal possibility of human behavior is learned in games of "let's pretend." I shall use "action" for behavior that is in accordance with the protocols appropriate to a given situation, and "performance" for behavior not in accordance with those protocols. If our behavior is inadequately learned, we do not present the appropriate verbal and nonverbal signs; our behavior is error-ridden. But when we lie, our behavior violates the protocols of a situation in which the situational demand is that we tell the truth, and at the same time we present the verbal and nonverbal signs appropriate to a truth-telling situation. However, when we lie, we are judging that it is *not* appropriate for us in that situation to tell the truth. Hence, our behavior as *performance* is insincere and dishonest, but as *action* is sincere and honest. The complement to our judgment is the judgment of the individual with whom we are interacting; that is, he can judge either that we are telling the truth or lying, either that we are acting or performing; if the latter, he can, instead of merely condemning us, propose an explanation (one that may or may not be a justification) for our performance, that is, judge it as sincere. Thus one of the oddities of human behavior, the factor that gives behavior its irresolvable and inconsolable strangeness, is that insincerity, hypocrisy, lying, and conning are always and necessarily sincere and honest.

The theater is a two-level situation. We apprehend Lucia in relation to her situation and judge her behavior as action, and as appropriate or inappropriate, and whether or not inappropriate behavior is action or performance. But we applaud Callas for her behavior as performance of Lucia, as appropriate for the theater situation. As Callas she is sincere; as Lucia she is either sincere or insincere as the case may be. Likewise, we can judge Callas as having a bad night, and her performance as error-ridden; or we can judge that she is having a bad night, even though her performance is without flaws, because her performance is "unconvincing" or she "is just going through the motions." We make the same judgment when we decide that an individual is lying because there is a certain quaver or hesitation in his vocal production or some other failure or error in the presentation of certain nonverbal signs (or even because his behavior is too flawless a performance). In both cases we are responding to what we apprehend as an incoherence in the semiotic assemblage we are being offered. In the actual apprehension of the theatrical performance our interpretation is constantly flickering between apprehending the behavior in relation to the dramatic situation and apprehending it in relation to the theater situation. (In nontheatrical situations this flickering takes the form of doubt; in theatrical situations it tends to appear as doubt about the competence of the performance.) We find a theatrical experience most rewarding when that flickering is eliminated by an apprehension of the behavior solely in relation to the dramatic situation, that is, as action. As an example, on my fourth viewing of Visconti's film *Death in Venice,* my apprehension occasionally, though rarely, flickered because of my judgment that Bogarde's performance was at times a bit exaggerated. But only on my fourth viewing. On the other hand, even on first viewing I was aware that the frames were shot to eliminate certain modern aspects of Venice. For a moment or two I shifted from apprehension of action to apprehension of performance, but only because I know Venice well. In the same way, while listening to an electronically reproduced performance of music, I apprehend the sound as action; but if there is a flaw in the recording technique or a bit of dust on the record or a scratch, I shift to apprehending the sound as performance.

This distinction between action and performance, common to the theater and ordinary nontheatrical experience, this dual possibility of apprehension, is what makes criticism possible. We say of the first appearance of a new department chairman before his faculty that he performed his role very well. The metaphor of the theater is one of the oldest metaphors for talking about behavior, not only in constant use but part of the basic terminology of the behavioral sciences. Nevertheless, when we speak of the "role" of the department chairman we are quite aware that we *are* speaking metaphorically, that what we mean is that his behavior was in accordance with the protocols learned for that kind of behavior in that kind of situation. By using the word "role" we announce that we are engaging in criticism. Because of this distinction between action and performance we may condemn a man for lying, but admire him for lying so well—or we may regret that Tennyson was insincere in concluding *In Memoriam* with an optimism he himself, he said, had never arrived at, and yet admire him for fulfilling the protocols for an elegiac lament. We can apprehend a literary work as either action or performance. If we interpret it as offering some large generalization about the human situation, we may judge it as appropriate or inappropriate to our understanding of the human situation, or to the understanding of the human situation culturally available at the time it was written. If we judge it as competent or incompetent, we are judging it as either error-ridden or insincere, or both, or as sincere but error-ridden. Or we may judge it as corresponding to our taste, that is, as to whether or not we can use it as a value sign. But if it does serve us as a value sign, we are apprehending it as pure action. However, it is of great importance to realize that if we apprehend it from the point of view of taste, and find it incapable of serving us as a value sign, we are also apprehending it as an action, even though we may subsequently rationalize that response by judging it inappropriate in its meaning or incompetent in some way or other. Finally, it would seem to follow from this that to apprehend a work as action is to facilitate our own actions as interpreters and perceivers of competence.

## III

We come finally to my third question: What is the present state of criticism? My answer to that is: Not very satisfactory; even, very unsatisfactory. One factor responsible is an economic factor. I refer to the infamous requirement of publication for tenure and promotion of university and, increasingly, college faculty members. Publish-or-perish should be recognized as a policy of *publish-and-perish,* intellectually and morally. It is a policy responsible for a moral and intellectual corruption unparalleled even in the higher education establishment of this country. The enormous expansion of that establishment, dependent as it has been on the massive exploitation of graduate students for freshman and sophomore instruction, has meant a corresponding decline in the overall or average quality of graduate instruction and a similar decline in the quality of graduate students, many of whom are now themselves giving graduate courses. Two examples are enough to show what has happened.

Throughout the country there has been a proliferation of regional scholarly-critical associations, meeting at least annually, the unavowed purpose of which is to provide opportunities to give papers which are then entered in one's *vita* for promotion and tenure. There has been a similar enormous expansion of journals devoted to the publication of papers written solely for the same purpose. Two results are worth noting. One is that the probability of an important paper or even book being read by someone who can profit from it is increasingly remote; the other is the increase in the rate of expansion of the number of ideologies exemplified in the second kind of interpretational criticism just discussed. And these ideologies are increasingly bizarre. It almost seems that the more bizarre the mode of interpretation one chances upon, the better the chances of publication.

The major explanation, however, lies in the peculiar place of literature (and art in general) as an institution in our culture. In the course of the nineteenth century, as a consequence of the Enlightenment secularization of culture, two novel value institutions emerged, the Nation and Art. Nationalism, emerging from Enlightenment ideology and quantitatively the dominant of the two, turned individual nations into value institutions, so that even religious institutions became subsumed by nations. From Romanticism emerged what came to be known as the Religion of Art. That is, art became for many individuals, perhaps the majority at the higher cultural level, the dominating value institution. In spite of some superficial indications to the contrary, in academic circles and their nonacademic adjuncts (that is, for most writers and critics) literature continues to be a value institution, a source for stabilizing the self-ascription of value. Hence arguments about taste, about which it is pointless to argue; such arguments are not merely analogous to arguments about whether a candidate for sainthood should be canonized or not; both kinds of arguments belong to the same category of behavior. Hence, also, the pietistic tone of most criticism and metacriticism. Most literary critics are to literature as theologians are to religion. The trouble with all this is that an examination of the biographies of individuals of accomplishment, particularly when significantly innovative, is a result not of using every effort to stabilize the self-ascription of value but rather of accepting its inherent instability and exploiting it. Thus there is a vital distinction between accepting a literary work as a value sign because it has been institutionally canonized and independently determining it as a value sign. To argue about whether or not a work should be or has been properly canonized is not to take taste seriously. To take taste seriously is to recognize it as a function of the inherent variability and instability of one's unique personal history and one's interpretation of that history. The value of the institutionalization of literary value signs lies not in their presentation as articles and objects of faith, but solely in their presentation as possible and at best traditionally recommended value signs. Literature, after all, is merely something that some human beings do, the deposit of a particular kind of behavior. But so long as literature is predominantly a value institution, a comprehension of literature's place in human life will continue to be eluded, as well as any rational comprehension of literature itself, including a firmly grounded theory of criticism, and especially, and above all, a firmly grounded theory of interpretation.

### NOTE

1. The foregoing highly condensed discussion of value is given extensive and detailed presentation in my *Explanation and Power: The Control of Human Behavior* (New York: The Seabury Press, 1979).

# CHAPTER EIGHTEEN

# The Problem of Interpretation

There certainly seems to be at the present time something of a crisis in interpretation. The structuralists and the deconstructionists have created even more confusion than did the New Critics, and for some of the same reasons. Hirsch's *Validity in Interpretation* did an excellent job of demolishing the position of semantic autonomy, the notion that poetry has a unique mode of meaning. But his analysis did not go nearly deep enough, and his positive conclusion—that the task is to determine the meaning that was intended in the mind of the poet—turned out to be quite useless. For what do "mind," "meaning," and "intention" mean in this context? I do not know nor does Hirsch know. To be sure he can give a verbal definition or transformed semiotic equivalent of each of these words, but neither the words nor the definitions can tell us what to look for either in the nonverbal phenomenal world or in the poem itself.

One must begin with certain primitives, or assumptions. And the first one I shall use is that no kind of semantic event happens in any kind of literature that does not happen in ordinary verbal interaction. The illusion of semantic autonomy arises merely from cultural parochialism, that is, the failure to observe that the full range of what we call poetry, in all cultures, is semantically so various that any semantically based definition of poetry is untenable. And that illusion also comes from the notion that the kind of poetry one happens to ascribe value to is the only kind that can be properly called truly poetry. Semantic definitions of poetry are no more than that.

From this first assumption I proceed to the next. Any theory of the interpretation of literature is necessarily subsumed by a theory of the interpretation of ordinary, mundane, spoken verbal interaction. But we must dig deeper than this. One cannot stop with words, or verbal behavior, because verbal behavior always takes place in some kind of situational context, and that context obviously plays a part in the act of interpretation. A theory of verbal behavior, therefore, must be subsumed by a more general theory, a theory of signs, or a semiotic theory. And here a further difficulty arises. Signs are said to have something called significance, or meaning. A sign, as the French say, wants to say something. Yet it can scarcely say something unless there is somebody to receive and respond to what it wants to say. Unless there is response on the part of somebody, there is no significance, no meaning. Clearly, a theory of signs must be subsumed by a theory of meaning. And if without response there is no meaning, then meaning can scarcely be immanent. And if it is not immanent, then the meaning is the response.

This is a theory of meaning which I arrived at—or more precisely was backed into—because a search of twentieth-century theories of meaning developed by philosophers and linguists revealed nothing that could withstand analysis—the reason being, from my present point of view, that they were all theories of immanent significance, theories that words and nonverbal signs have meaning, whereas it seemed clearer and clearer to me that the responder to the sign is the member of that dyad who *has* the meaning. That meaning of a sign is the response to the sign is a position George Herbert Mead arrived at in 1900, though he did not do very much with it, or much that turned out to be very satisfactory. This notion that the meaning of any sign, verbal or nonverbal, is the response to that sign gives us our first insight into interpretation, for it is quite obvious that in ordinary verbal interaction one of the most common phenomena of verbal behavior is uncertainty over meaning. All of us have asked thousands of times what is meant by some statement or word or sign. When we shift to literary interpretation, the problem is not, then, why there are different interpretations of the same work, often totally inconsistent with one another. Nor is it enough to say, as most students of the question have said, and as Hirsch tried to say, and failed, that one interpretation is right and others are wrong. We cannot say that because, in fact, we have no criteria of rightness and wrongness in interpretation, nor, as I shall point out later, can we have. Rather, the question is, Why is interpretational variety possible? But if we locate meaning in the response, and reflect upon the endless occasions in which we are uncertain of meaning, that is, uncertain of how we ought to respond, it becomes clear that uncertainty is the very condition of interpretation.

Let me put this in the form of two corollaries to the proposition that meaning is response. The first is that all possible signs are capable of eliciting in a single individual but one response; the second is that any sign is capable of eliciting from an individual any of all possible responses. Clearly, it is only in extreme situations, such as psychosis, that either of these possibilities actually occurs. It follows that there are factors which prevent such extremes, which control response; that is, control meanings. Thus, when we are uncertain of the meaning of some semiotic configuration and request further information so that we might respond, we are asking that our response be controlled by the individual responsible for presenting the semiotic configuration, or—and this is the crux of the matter for literary interpretation—if the generator of the sign configuration is not present, it is necessary for us to seek elsewhere for that control.

For the full importance of this condition, it is useful to begin at the simplest and fundamental level of sign response. A sign, then, is any perceptual configuration to which there is a response. An old but useful experiment is instructive. It has been found that if individuals are presented with a randomly shaped type of configuration, that is, one which cannot be identified as a regular geometric formation, within less than a minute they will identify it. If it is organically shaped, it might be identified as a cloud, or a whale, or an oyster, and so on. Two things are to be noticed in this. First, the time lapse between the presentation and the identification is a period of uncertainty. Second, the uncertainty is followed by the identification. We may say, I think, that two controlling factors are at work. First, the configuration, perceived as a figure against the ground, is perceived as a sign. Second, the experimenters *instructed* the subjects to identify the configuration, a fact which the experimenters themselves evidently failed to take into consideration. Now, unless the subjects had already determined the configuration to be a sign, they could not have identified it. Next, the responses were random within a certain range. That is, each subject identified the sign as a configuration marked by a continuity of perceptual attributes with a configuration previously encountered, such as a cloud. A further factor in the response is to be noticed. In the case of each response there was a transfer of a response, that is, of a meaning from configurations already experienced and identified to the configuration new in experience. Behaviorally, then, categorization is the transfer of response in the individual's repertory to a novel configuration. This leads us to a fuller description of sign response. It is categorization, by means of perceptual attributes. A sign, then, is always categorial: a sign response is subsumed by the explanatory term, analogy; and of highest importance, the identification of the unidentifiable configuration is some individual's analogical *determination* of a categorial meaning.

But something more may be derived from this analysis. Categorization (meaning-response transfer) in semiotic behavior is a judgment that there is a sufficient continuity of perceptual attributes to justify meaning determination. However, the subject who identifies the unidentifiable configuration as a *cloud* might very well deny that there is sufficient continuity of perceptual attributes to justify identifying it as a *whale*. Hence, analogical determination of meaning depends upon ignoring perceptual attributes which cannot be subsumed by the categorization. Thus anyone who insists upon the presence of such unsubsumed attributes can undermine and invalidate the categorization. The lesson of this is what we have already seen on other grounds: meaning determination is inherently unstable.

Now, when we turn from nonverbal signs to verbal signs, that inherent instability is enormously increased, indeed to a degree indefinably great. The reason is that nonverbal categorization depends upon the absolute minimum of continuity of perceptual attribution between any two verbal signs. All that is left is a class of sounds or, in written verbalization, the mere presence of a class of visual configurations. Thus, it would be difficult for me to transfer a response learned from encountering mountain ranges to an encounter with a minnow. All I could do would be to simply respond somehow or other. But, if I am an evolutionist, I can subsume both minnow and mountain range under the same explanatory structure, one of many levels, and terminating in its regress from the perceptual in the word "evolution," and, if a creationist, under an entirely different explanatory structure, terminating in the word "God." Or, as Susan B. Anthony said to a nervous recruit, "Trust in God, dear; *she* will help you." We may subsume under the word "God" any verbally determined attributes we wish, and, as Susan B. Anthony did, change those verbally assigned attributes at will—according to our current interest. But these verbal attributes are, obviously, nothing but verbal categories, since all signs are categorial. It was Susan Anthony's interest in feminism that controlled her re-ascription of subsumed attributes to the word "God." An interest, then, can be defined as the controlling factor in semiotic categorization. Hence, in semiotic response two factors are always at work, categorization, and control of categorization by limiting the range of categorization.

Let us now consider an example of semiotic behavior in which both verbal and nonverbal signs are clearly present and identifiable. I walk into a restaurant and sit down at a table. A waiter approaches. I ask him for a cup of coffee. He goes into the kitchen, returns with the cup of coffee, and places it in front of me. What has been the waiter's semiotic behavior? First, we may note that he has responded to my utterance in a way I judge to be appropriate. Now, obviously he can do so because we both speak the same language. Nor need that fact be considered here. All that can be said upon the subject is that we know that children learn the language of their culture and that we do not know how they do so, although the recent work of Jerome Bruner is promising. On the other hand, since verbal signs are subsumed by the more general term "sign" and since animals, at least the relatively higher ones, engage in learned nonverbal semiotic behavior, I do not think much will be understood of how children learn competence in verbal semiosis until we have understood how they acquire competence in nonverbal semiosis. In any case, I shall turn to purely verbal semiosis in a moment. To return to the waiter, on the basis of what I have already proposed I think what the waiter has done can be described in the following rather formulaic and abstract proposition. The waiter has performed *a perceptual disengagement of an analogically determined recurrent semiotic pattern from an analogically determined series of semiotic matrices.* The pattern he disengages is the request for coffee, a request which can be given in a variety of ways. The waiter responds to all such requests in the same way, analogically determining that each such request is a variant of a single pattern. The matrix is the semiotic configuration of restaurant plus customer plus request. The controlling interest of the waiter, that which controls his interpretation of pattern plus matrix, is his desire to keep his job. But that economic interest is also the matrix for the pattern of restaurant-plus-customer-plus-request. And we can move in the other direction. Suppose the customer says, "I'd like a cup hat of coffee." It is perfectly possible for the waiter to be so confused by this statement that he is unable to respond. In this case, the "hat" is the recurrent pattern, but the matrix, the syntax of the sentence, is, for our waiter, a member of a series which provides insufficient analogical continuity for him to determine how to respond to the sentence. Thus the first level of matrix for a word is the semiotic configuration of syntax in which it appears. Hence a vertical series of superimposed matrices can be indefinitely extended, and a superimposed matrix turns the matrix it subsumes into a pattern.

Let us change the situation. I ask for the coffee, but the waiter says that he's sorry; he can't provide it for me. The reason is that it is exactly 11:00 A.M., and at that precise time all the waiters in the city are going on strike. Here the waiter is controlling his response by a completely different matrix, and his economic control has an opposite effect. Or, he may be indifferent as to whether he keeps his job or not. The control is his passionate devotion to union solidarity. Or let us say he brings the coffee and pours it over my head. Perhaps his accumulated resentment in being in a socially subordinate position—that is, constantly, while on the job, having his normal aggressiveness hindered by accepting the control of others—is the control that leads him to determine that the appropriate response to my request is to pour coffee over me.

From this example we may take several further steps. It is now possible to grasp what we are doing when we raise questions about the interest or the intention of an utterance, that is, as it is ordinarily believed, about the intention of the generator of an utterance. An enormous amount has been written about the word "intention" by philosophers and literary critics. Hirsch's use of intention, mentioned previously, is an instance. The three possible responses of the waiter might be categorized as "normal," "exceptional," and "paranoid." Here a great illusion appears. It is easy enough to see that responses we judge exceptional and paranoid call for interpretation, but it does not occur to us that the normal is equally mysterious. We have here an instance of the great error the psychologists and sociologists of the deviant make. They assume that the normal is given, and that only the deviant needs interpretation, that is, explanation. But as we have seen, all three are alike in that each of the waiter's interpretations is under the control of a vertical series of superimposed patterns and matrices. That is, no explanation of the deviant is valid unless the "normal" is explained in the same way. The interpretative behavior in all three types is under the control of a multi-leveled structure of matrix and pattern. The normal, in short, is not given, is not "natural." The impression we have that it is, is only the result of the high frequency of its occurrence.

Recently there has been considerable interest in what only appears to be a new theory of the criminal personality. It appears that a criminal personality is a criminal personality because he is a criminal personality. This may seem like a return to Gertrude Stein, but I regard it as a great step forward, and I do so because it shifts the theory away from socioeconomic situations which are said to create criminals, but which in fact create ten times as many noncriminals; thus the production of a criminal seems to have no relation to the social or economic class from which the criminal has emerged; and thus, I suspect that the criminal personality needs to be explained in the same way that the academic personality needs to be explained. We are puzzled that some people are criminals. I find it equally puzzling that some people are college teachers, or, let us say, so intensely interested in classical music (an interest regarded by millions of people in this country as hopelessly bizarre) that their interest is inconsistent with their economic welfare, just as the criminal's interest is incoherent with his freedom of action. After all, the only criminals we know anything about are the ones who get caught. I regard this innovative concept of the criminal personality as a step forward because it clears the air, and permits us to ask what the criminal personality's interest might be in being a criminal. It is said that criminality is not normal and needs to be explained. But it is clear that it is normal, particularly when we put cigarette hijacking in the same category as lifting a box of pencils from the department stock room for the use of one's children—a common event in faculty behavior. The difference is that the criminal's interest in criminality is greater than the faculty member's. A dominating interest in criminality, so that it controls virtually all of one's economic life, is like any other interest, a strategy for limiting the range of behavior, a matrix that controls response to a certain category of semiotic configurations.

Now, when a TV thief is brought before the judge and it is determined that the thief has a history of stealing TV sets, we say that it was his intention to steal this particular TV set. We interpret the semiotic pattern of his theft by perceptually disengaging it from a series of analogically determined thefts, that is, from a series of matrices. We are controlling our interpretation by subsuming a pattern and matrix under the word "intention." Clearly, if intention is a psychic event—now in the past—we can never know what it was or even whether or not it existed. We are not talking about anything phenomenally observable. Rather what we are doing is taking the first step in constructing a controlling hierarchy over our interpretation of the theft. When we use the word "intention," therefore, we are limiting our possible responses and setting out to generate what we judge will be an appropriate response. When we say that Dickens's intention in writing *Oliver Twist* was to protest against the treatment of orphans (or whatever intention we choose), all that we are doing is constructing a matrix which will serve to control our interpretation of the text.

The establishment of a literary intention is not a discovery; it is, as in all verbal interaction, the construction of a matrix. In the overwhelming majority of interaction situations, that construction is immediate. When, however, we are uncertain of how we ought to respond, we mediate our response by separating the matrix from the pattern. We pull our hand from a hot stove; that is an immediate response. Mucius Scaevola held his hand in a fire. That is a mediated response.

An example that actually happened will clarify this. Professor Irvin Child of Yale, a psychologist, was interested in artistic evaluation. For the purposes of his investigation he collected a large number of slides of stylistically matched pairs of works of visual art, principally paintings, but also such works as Persian tiles and carpets, and so on. He then asked his protocol group—members of the art department and art history department at Yale—to select the better work in each pair. Interested in exploring the possibility of a relationship between IQ and artistic judgment, he used a number of children as his subjects. With one boy he tried the experiment of informing the child after each judgment whether or not his judgment coincided with that of the "experts." After a dozen or so choices, the boy said, "Oh, I get it. The best one is always the crummy one." He was quite right. Given a choice between symmetrical and asymmetrical Persian tiles, for example, the experts always chose the asymmetrical design. What happened is clear enough. The pairs of paintings were the analogically determined recurrent semiotic patterns. But the instruction to choose the better of each pair left the boy in the realm of uncertainty of response. Clever enough, however, to observe the two contrasting semiotic matrices— the noncrummy and the crummy—he determined on the basis of perceptual continuity that the appropriate response was to pick the crummy one as the better one, "crumminess" being his term for what I have called elsewhere the perceptual discontinuity of works of art.

This insight permits us to take the next step. Just as the meaning of any pattern is not immanent, so the subsumption of any pattern by a matrix is not immanent. That subsumption, it needs to be emphasized, is a matter of determination, and a determination is a judgment that the response generated is an appropriate response. Hence the subsumption of a pattern by a matrix is a judgment of appropriateness. It is for this reason that we cannot speak of a right or wrong response to any utterance; we can only speak of its appropriateness, and moreover only of its appropriateness in the judgment of some actual living individual. In the case of Professor Child's subject, he was "right" only in the sense that his judgment was adjusted to coincide with the judgment of those whom Professor Child had categorized as "experts," individuals whose verbal response to works of art and whose general behavior in connection with works of art was at a high cultural level. Their judgment of appropriateness of evaluation came to control his judgment, simply because Professor Child had told him which of each pair their judgment selected, and because he was clever enough to determine analogically the perceptual continuity among those they had judged the better. Their judgment became, as we have seen, the matrix of his judgments, and his judgments, like theirs, were judgments of appropriateness, for they judged their judgments to be appropriate at the cultural level at which Professor Child instructed them to operate. That is, he did *not* tell them to engage in judgmental performance in a way different from the way they ordinarily performed in making judgments of works of art. Their performance was simply controlled by what to them was a cultural norm.

From this we can go further and arrive at a general definition of culture, in the anthropological sense. Culture is learned behavior, as opposed to genetically controlled behavior. Culture is instructions for performance. Culture is what turns human behavior into performance. The necessity for culture emerges from the fact that the meaning of any sign is not immanent but is response to the sign. However, if human interaction is to take place with any smoothness, as it must for fundamentally economic reasons, meaning must be stabilized. If semiotic behavior, found in animals far lower on the evolutionary scale than the human animal, is adaptive, it is, like any adaptation, also a maladaptation to semiosis. Culture stabilizes performance, that is, it stabilizes responses to signs. What we think of as a normal response is merely one which cultural controls have highly stabilized. But even so, as I have pointed out, we are constantly experiencing uncertainty and asking for further instructions, that is, more limiting controls over our responses, over our "meanings." Thus the effort, such as Hirsch's, to establish a theory of validity in interpretation on theoretical grounds must necessarily fail, must necessarily end with such an empty formula as "determining the meaning that was intended in the mind of the author"; for what is "mind" but a word that subsumes variability of response? Hirsch's effort is merely an example of what our profession is primarily engaged in, the stabilization of the interpretation of certain canonical or culturally sacred texts. But it is also equally obvious that with the emergence of the New Criticism and the untenable doctrine of the semiotic autonomy of literature, that stabilization has ceased to be the task of at least many of the most active publishing members of our profession. What has been going on for several decades is the spread of interpretational deviance, following the principle that I proposed in my book on pornography, that to the degree that any behavior pattern is badly transmitted, to that degree there will be a spread of that pattern into a delta of deviancy. We have seen why that has been possible, and the explanation may be put in this form. *Any analogically determined series of semiotic matrices can be used to control the interpretation of any analogically determined recurrent semiotic pattern.* That is, any work of literature can be interpreted any way you want to. By that I mean, what controls the interpreter's interest, his way of limiting his response to a work of literature, can be any cultural control, highly stabilized or highly innovative. When a Romantic ideology controlled the acting of Charles Kean, he turned Shylock from a comic into a tragic character. If there is doubt and uncertainty about the appropriate interpretational response, if, because of cultural change at the high ideological level, interpretation becomes destabilized, then, if it is not restabilized, the spread of interpretation into a delta of deviance will necessarily take place, as it has been taking place for the past forty years. The delta has become wider and wider. And by "high" I mean separated and deeply regressive from the perceptual configuration by a multi-layered vertical series of pattern-matrix subsumptions.

I am not concerned here with why this should have happened. From one point of view there is nothing odd about it. The history of interpretation is a history of reinterpretations of canonical texts, as in St. Augustine's Christian interpretations of classical mythology, as in typology, as in the medieval fourfold method of interpretation, as in Blake's reinterpretation of Milton, or Coleridge's of Shakespeare. But from another point of view it is very odd. By that I mean that there has long been established, for nearly four hundred years, a model for the interpretation of literature. And that model is the norm of interpretational behavior; that is, when I ask the waiter for a cup of coffee, he does not refuse, he does not pour it on my head, but he brings it to me. My claim is the *interpretation in the presence of the generator of an utterance and judged by him to be appropriate is the proper model for the interpretation of an utterance in the absence of the generator of that utterance.* If in the presence of the speaker you are uncertain of the appropriate response, you can ask for further instructions. You mediate your response by those instructions. In his absence you mediate your response by constructing as best you can what you judge to have been the matrix that controlled the generation of the utterance. If a friend whom I am about to visit phones me and asks me to pick up a pack of cigarettes for him on the way to his house, without specifying what kind of cigarettes, I mediate my response by remembering that he always smokes filtered Chesterfields. When I arrive, he might say, "Oh, thank you for remembering what I always smoke." Or he might say, "Damn it, I wanted unfiltered Pall Malls. I've changed my brand and I forgot to tell you." Thus in face-to-face verbal interaction mediation can change uncertainty to certainty, but in distant interaction the inherent uncertainty can never be resolved.

Another example of the inherent instability of matrix selection can be found in our responses to theatrical performances. I refer, of course, to the notion of "theatrical illusion," a problem which Coleridge did not solve but merely restated in his "willing suspension of disbelief." When an opera singer concludes an aria on a high note, with chest thrust out, arms at the side, one foot forward, the body turned away from the center of the house, the audience bursts into applause. Or in the midst of a performance, one can suddenly realize that a lamp on the stage is just like Aunt Minnie's. Or my realization while watching the film of *Who's Afraid of Virginia Woolf* that George's library contained *two* sets of the Heritage Press edition of Gibbon, a minor carelessness by the set decorator. In a theater piece there are two matrices possible. The semiotic information before us—gesture, speech, costume, props, etc.—can be interpretationally controlled by the matrix of "an action" or by the matrix of "a performance." If we are, for example, not very interested in the action, we can easily find ourselves employing the matrix of performance. When the opera singer assumes her end-of-an-aria stance, she is presenting a sign to the audience that they should respond to her not as a character in an action, but as a singer in a performance. And obviously, the shift of matrix from action to performance happens constantly in ordinary life, as when, for example, we decide that someone is lying; or when we say that someone is putting on a good act, we are pointing out that he is engaged in a performance. Indeed, if the distinction between action and performance matrices and the instability of that distinction were not inherent in human interpretational behavior, the theater could never have come into existence.

The model for the interpretation of literature I proposed above is what Frank Kermode in his interesting book *The Classic* has called historical-philological interpretation. He asserts that it really got under way in the early seventeenth century, but to my mind it got under way in the interpretation of nonliterary historical documents in the early fifteenth. At that time several Florentine historians claimed that the medieval negation of the value of the historical figure Cicero was an error. That negation had been based on his opposition to Augustus and the establishment of the empire. But since the Roman Empire had been established by the will of God to provide secular support and an arm of force for the Christian church, Cicero was certainly to be condemned. The new historians, however, claimed that Cicero could not be blamed for his opposition to Augustus, because, living before Christianity, and having been brought up in the ideal of the Republic, he could not possibly know what God's purpose was in establishing the Empire. He was not, then, a bad man, but a good man.

At about the same time and in the same place a radical change was introduced into painting—perspective. Mountains and trees were no longer emblems of mountains and trees without consideration of the scale of the human beings acting in the foreground. Rather, the background was constructed as it might have been seen at the time of the event by an individual standing at a particular fixed spot. What was common to both of these radical changes—that in historiography and that in painting—was the effort to place the historical event in a situation in which it might have taken place. The questions now were, What was the semiotic matrix of Cicero? What was the semiotic matrix of the episode in the saint's legend? Shortly, the old medieval device of presenting two or more episodes of the same legend within a single emblematic landscape was abandoned, and for the same reason. There emerged what might be called situational thinking. Within two hundred years there had appeared the basic theory of modern science, inaccurately and inadequately called inductive as opposed to deductive reasoning. Rather, the basis of modern science was the decision to ascribe truth value to a proposition not because it was asserted to be coherent with the propositions from which it was derived, but if, and only if, it was judged to be a set of directions for so manipulating nonverbal configurations, and if and only if the consequence of that manipulation could be appropriately interpreted as confirming the proposition in question. That is, what emerged was the experimental method, which simply amounts to asking what happens to this configurational complex, subsumed by a verbal description, when it is placed in a nonverbal situation and subjected to various nonverbal manipulations. The most interesting thing about all this is that such experimental or testing behavior is the norm of human behavior. When a Neolithic farmer told his son that to plow bottomlands one needed a special plow and several oxen, he was being scientific, especially if he said, "If you don't believe it, try it with the plow you use on the uplands and with only one ox." The basic scientific sentence is, "If you do so and so, then such and such will happen." And that sentence is the basic sentence of all our instructions for interacting with the nonverbal, for it is the only way the inadequacy of the verbal instructions, or scientific theory, can be uncovered, located, and corrected. It seems clear to me that the historical-philological interpretation of literature is, like science, based upon the norm of interpretation, and that both are culturally convergent, emerging from the matrix of situational thinking.

Moreover for a long time, for science until the late nineteenth century, and for historical-philological interpretation still, it was assumed that both could arrive at certainty. However, as I have pointed out, interpretation at a distance is inherently uncertain. And as for science, scientific experimentation always produces more data than the directing theory can subsume and data of a kind it cannot subsume at all. As Ludwig Boltzmann demonstrated eighty years ago, scientific theory is a verbal construct, and the tremendous advance of science in the past eighty years has been the result of the recognition and exploitation of the inherent instability of scientific theory, that is, its inherent uncertainty. Likewise the uncertainty inherent in historical-philological interpretation at a distance is responsible for the endlessness of historical-philological research, the endlessness of its effort to construct the situation or matrix which controlled the generation of the literary text in question.

Nevertheless, though the use of the term "research" is justifiable for both scientific behavioral and historical interpretation, there are profound differences. The first is that science gets outside of the verbal, but historical-philological interpretation, as the second term shows, does not. Yet this difference, though great, is not so great as first appears. In my formulation of the fundamental scientific decision I quite deliberately and carefully wrote, "if and only if the consequence of that manipulation could be *appropriately interpreted* as confirming the proposition in question." That is, as I indicated at the beginning of this essay, to human beings the perceptual configurations of the world are signs. This is the basic reason, not fully realized by Boltzmann, but begun to be realized by Mead, for the inherent uncertainty of science. Even so, science has put men on the moon. That's pretty certain. Just as the ability to cross the street and not get run over is also pretty certain. Even so, though our reconstructions of the cultural matrices of the past can never have the certainty of putting men on the moon, they remain, if we read the reconstructions generated in the seventeenth century, pretty impressive.

The second difference is of considerably greater importance. It has been realized for some time that successful scientific theory construction depends upon the principles of parsimony and elegance. From what I have proposed so far, it is not difficult to understand why this should be so. Once again it is a matter of interpretation. Parsimony simply means that, in scientific theory construction, the theoretical vocabulary should be kept to the minimum absolutely necessary. Only thus can meanings be stabilized. For the same reason elegance is desirable, for elegance simply means the least possible number of relations among the basic terms of the vocabulary of the theory. Obviously, both are instruments of behavioral control in generating responses to scientific theory. But the student of literature is faced with an entirely different problem. Extravagance of vocabulary and inelegance, or shagginess, of possible relations among the terms of that vocabulary is the characteristic of literature, and the higher the cultural level at which the literature is generated the more true this is. When, in order to generate an experiment, a scientist responds to a scientific theory by interpreting it to make it applicable to his projected behavior, he is controlled, if the theory is properly constructed, by parsimony and elegance. But the student of literature, engaged in interpreting a literary work, has no such built-in guiding controls. Not coherence but incoherence is the semantic character of literature, an instance of the same phenomenon that Professor Child's young subject observed when he said, "The best ones are always the crummy ones." Not semantic continuity but discontinuity is the character of literary art. For example, the more important the character in a work of fiction, the more frequently the reader has to change the attributes which the proper name of that character subsumes. It follows that for a complex work of literature, though not necessarily for all works, such as a limerick, the author himself is under the control of a variety of shifting matrices. The lesson of this is that no single matrix can be unsuccessfully used to control the interpretation of a work of literature of even slight complexity, of one that exhibits neither parsimony nor elegance. Again, the higher the cultural level the truer this is.

For example, consider the long-standing debate as to whether Satan is or is not the hero of *Paradise Lost*. On the one hand, using Christian theology as the appropriate matrix, one must conclude that he is not the hero. On the other hand, as Christopher Hill has recently claimed, when one considers Milton's intense interest in and approval of rebellion against established authority, Satan is a heroic figure, that is, a figure whose example is to be imitated in great actions. Yet, if we recognize the inherent shagginess of works of literature, the inherent inelegance and semantic extravagance, it seems reasonable to claim that he is made heroic at the beginning so that the discontinuity of his deterioration and degradation can be semantically effective. The first matrix controls our interpretation to say that Satan is not justifiable; the second controls our interpretation to say that he is. The third uses a matrix that subsumes far more works of literature and of art than either of the others. It is more general, and if accepted, it clearly subsumes the second interpretation without denying that Milton found grandiose rebellion very attractive, for it assumes the probability of semantic incoherence in literature. To repeat, to ask what Milton's intention was is merely to ask, "What is the appropriate way to generate a response?"

I should like to conclude by giving two examples of historical-philological interpretation, both dealing with works that have caused more interpretational contention than all but a few major works of English literature, *The Rime of the Ancient Mariner* and the tragedies of Shakespeare.

For the *Ancient Mariner* I begin by observing three recurrent semiotic patterns which I judge to be justifiably subsumed by a single category: the shooting of the albatross, the madness of the hermit when he hears the Mariner's confession, and the keeping of the wedding guest from the wedding, in order to hear the story that drove the hermit mad. All three of these I see as a violation of community, the community of bird and man in sharing the same food, the community of re-entrance into the community after sin, and the interruption of a basic ritual of community. In looking for a matrix to justify this categorization I observe that Coleridge was interested in social organization all his life, and that in his late years, in his reinterpretation of the trinity, he identified the holy spirit with community. I interpret the poem, then, as concerned with the theme of alienation from community, a matrix that subsumes, I think, the Nightmare Life-in-Death, a phrase first used in Coleridge's 1817 revision, when, perhaps, he had begun to understand his own poem, or at least decided the reader needed a clue. Further, I interpret the blessing of the snakes and the dropping of the cross of guilt into the sea as a reversal of cultural values, turning the snake, a traditional emblem of evil, into an emblem of good. I feel further justified in using the matrix of alienation and cultural reversal by subsuming that matrix under the more general matrix of Romantic alienation, a widespread series of semiotic recurrences throughout literature and culture in the past 180 years, but, of course, a series analogically determined. With these as controlling categories, I then interpret the last part of the poem, the part usually neglected by interpreters, that is, the saving of the Mariner by the spirits of the natural world, as a justification for his alienation. Thus, I conclude, when he wrote the poem, Coleridge judged alienation to be both necessary and justifiable, in spite of the fact that it was the

occasion of suffering both for the alienated individual and the culture
from which he had separated himself. And since he had been freed
from the sign of the guilt of his alienation, he had passed the first stage
of alienation, the conviction of guilt. He was on the way to the kind
of cultural violation to be found in his redefinition of the trinity and
his proposal of the theory of the clerisy—that is to his transcendental
psychologization of Christianity and his denial of the validity of current social arrangement, both moving in the direction of an attempt
to reestablish a theoretical and pragmatic basis for a restored community.

To propose a theory of Shakespearean tragedy, especially for one
whose dominating interest is nineteenth-century culture, is to take a
terrible risk, but if we are not to take intellectual risks in this profession, I do not know why we are the most pampered group in the
country. I begin, then, by observing a recurrence which many have
observed, the extinction of a royal family or ruling individual or
group, and the establishment of a new dynasty or new ruler. This
recurrence puzzles me. It makes me uncertain how to interpret it, and
I look for further cultural instructions. But since I am interested in
historical-philological interpretation, they must be instructions more
or less contemporaneous with Shakespeare. On reading Burton's
*Anatomy of Melancholy,* or in modern terms his analysis of neurosis and
psychosis, I come across the statement that the cause of melancholy
is socio-moral infection, and that this infection is analogous with the
disturbances in the heavens, such as those that herald the fall of
princes, and with the plague, that is, with infection in the microcosm
and in the macrocosm. I consider that plague has been endemic in
Europe for some hundreds of years, that it was judged to be a visitation
of divine punishment, or else something spread by Satan or men in
league with Satan. And I learn from a scholar of Renaissance English
literature that socio-moral infection is a commonplace in the sermons
and moral writings of the period. Turning once again to the tragedies
I observe that the ruling family or ruler is infected with a moral illness
which spreads throughout his family, and that the presence of this
infectious moral failing is often mentioned in the early exposition of
the play, such as Hamlet's claim that there is something rotten in the
state of Denmark, and by "state" he certainly seems to mean, I conclude from other recurrences of that semiotic pattern, the ruling establishment. Health cannot be restored to the state until the moral
infection has spread through the royal family and wiped it out, or until
the individual ruler is himself destroyed, as in *Coriolanus* and *Othello,*
which gives a clear example of the mechanics of moral infection. Iago

transmits his infection to Othello, and both are members of the ruling establishment of Cyprus.

Two things I readily admit. First, though I find this interpretation of Shakespearean tragedy (and perhaps of comedy) quite convincing, I find also that it deprives Shakespeare's tragedies of much of their interest. But then I examine my own assumption, my own controlling matrix, and it seems obvious that as a product of the cultural developments of the last few hundred years I am interested in interpreting the plays from the point of view of character, character as destiny, to employ a famous phrase. Like all interpreters of the Shakespearean tragedies I have run across, I perceive the causes for events to emanate from individuals. But supposing I take a more modern position, one which I share with B. F. Skinner, with whom I share very little. It is a position which arouses for most people great antipathy. The position, briefly, is that behavior is under the control of situation, and that the most that can be said for individual character is that the individual organism transforms the semiotic material of the situation by generating signs. (What I share with Skinner, of course, is only the first "that" clause in the preceding sentence.) Thus it follows that if a situation changes, most individuals who have been responding in roughly the same way will respond to the change by changing their behavior in roughly the same way. It seems to me probable that the Elizabethans, with their notions of order and disorder, and of social health and disease, were responding to this readily observable phenomenon. A situation, then, consists of cultural instructions controlling the behavior of individuals in that situation. If the cultural instructions are changed, most of the individuals will respond in the same way. Hence their transformations of that situation will increase the redundancy of the new cultural instructions, and thus increase the probability that the individuals in the situation will respond in the same way to the new instructions. Socio-moral infection, then, is a metaphor for a readily observed behavioral phenomenon, as is the Elizabethan metaphor of the body for the phenomenon of interaction as controlling and modifying behavior. Our interest in "character as destiny" has concealed from us what the Elizabethans, I think, were responding to more concretely and intelligently. Such a matrix for the semiotic data of the Shakespearean tragedies makes more sense out of them, I think, than does the traditional matrix of "character." That moral infection matrix subsumes more data in the plays than the traditional characterological matrix, and it provides an explanation of why the tragedies maintain their appeal, in spite of the failure in agreement of generations of characterological interpretation. "Character" too is metaphor, and for understanding individuals in both life and fiction a very deceptive one.

The second point I would admit is that I would not claim for a moment that this interpretation successfully subsumes *all* of the semiotic data in a Shakespearean tragedy. Far from it. These works are loose, baggy monsters, very shaggy, very incoherent. Hamlet retains his theatrical vitality because he is perhaps the most incoherent character ever put on stage, and therefore, perhaps, the most convincing. We are as personalities incoherent, but only the greatest writers have the wit to say so.

To conclude, then, my position is that since literature only selects and intensifies, and makes more incoherent, according to its cultural level, the semantic functions of ordinary face-to-face verbal interaction, the most appropriate model for the interpretation of literature is the model offered by interpretation in such interaction. I think that the *historical-philological,* or *situational,* interpretation of literature has almost as solid a theoretical base as does science, the difference, of course, being that literary interpretation does not move out of the realm of verbal signs, and though the interpretation of the nonliterary arts does, it does not move beyond the realm of man-produced signs, or man-arranged signs, as in gardens. Science is more solid because it interprets signs not produced by man, that is, natural signs. But it is not certain, because a scientific theory is true only until it is abandoned for what is judged to be a better one. As for the current fashion of deviant interpretation—that is, interpretation interested not in what controlled the generation of the work of literature, but only in using the work to exemplify an interest of the interpreter—it is not, I think, a serious rival to historical-philological interpretation, or even a serious alternative. Rather, it is governed by an ideology of which the practitioners are themselves unaware, and which, as a cultural phenomenon, I am very interested in interpreting and explaining. But that is another story.

# CHAPTER NINETEEN

# Literature and Behavior

I have been asked to address myself to a statement I recently made on the nature of criticism: "metacriticism properly belongs to the behavioral sciences." Lest I be misunderstood, let me also add a qualification I made in that same essay: "I do not consider the behavioral sciences as they are presently practiced to be in much of a position to subsume anything"; and "the possibility that metacriticism belongs to the behavioral sciences must, at the moment and for the foreseeable future, remain in the realm of the ideal." But to show that I am trying to be fair, let me also add that I think that the study of philosophy, "metaphilosophy," also belongs to the behavioral sciences. Indeed, my position is very much that of Auguste Comte, who proposed that eventually all the sciences would be subsumed by what he called "sociology," a term which, for him, subsumes everything that we call the behavioral sciences and philosophy as well. In fact the position that the study of anything cannot transcend the human condition, including the study of the human condition, is met with increasing frequency. Thus the notion of scientific objectivity must, it is felt, be abandoned. For me, though no doubt many philosophers would tell me that I am wrong, that position is implicit in Kant and very nearly explicit in Hegel. But since Comte's ideal has certainly not emerged, the best we can do, if we wish to consider the place of literature and the study of literature in human behavior, is to observe as well as we can what writers and critics are doing in their situations, and what those situations seem to be, and how they are related to other situations.

Actually, for me, the necessity for studying literature and criticism and metacriticism from the behavioral point of view is so obvious that I find it extremely difficult to argue the position. Human beings do things, and among the things they do is literature, and talk about literature, and talk about talk about literature. Why? And how are these odd kinds of behavior possible? Yet it is apparent that most teachers and critics and scholars of literature find my position exceedingly bizarre, while I, on the other hand, find it equally bizarre that they seem so helpless in explaining and justifying what they do. Perceptive and conscience-stricken teachers find their activity continuously eroded by wondering if what they do is of any value, while the rest seem, so far as I can make out, to fall back on the notion that literature transmits the great human values. They are supported, it seems, by a kind of a piety that certainly appears to have some analogy to religion, vague as that analogy might be.

I think it is not unfair to say that the prevailing opinion is that literature occupies a position so discontinuous from other modes of human behavior and particularly of verbal behavior that equally discontinuous modes of responding to it and discussing it are necessary, and that such modes must be developed from an analysis of literature in itself, without reference to other modes of verbal or nonverbal behavior, with the sole exception that the same claim is made for the nonverbal arts. Thus claims are made that literature presents a unique kind of truth, inaccessible to any other modes of stating truths, whatever a "truth" may be. Or that the analysis of literature requires a kind of analysis of internal relations not required of other modes of discourse. Or that it needs an analysis that totally destroys its meaning, while that process presumably cannot be applied to other modes of discourse, or at least that it would be inappropriate and even pointless to do so. Or that it gives a unique insight into the human mind, or into the unconscious, or into human culture and its history. And so on. All of these notions can be subsumed under the more general notion that literature has a unique value in human life, a value which cannot be stated, but can only be asserted and experienced. Or it is asserted that the value is demonstrated by claiming that the "true" work of literature—which means in practice any work that theoreticians happen to like, for whatever reasons—is of the highest significance because it expresses and reveals the creative imagination.

Clearly if I wish to sustain my position that literature is not discontinuous from other verbal behavior, and that not only is it continuous with all verbal behavior and through verbal behavior with the rest of human behavior, but that it is subsumed by verbal behavior, itself subsumed by the rest of human behavior, and must be studied from the point of view of those subsumptions, I must dispose of the notion that it is discontinuous and not so subsumable. Unfortunately I feel as helpless in doing so as an evolutionist confronting a creationist—and for much the same reason. For the literary pietist, literature is redemptive, a term clearly that needs some explaining.

We all know that the notion that poetry is divinely inspired is very ancient, with its classic location in Plato, though he may have meant that it must be divinely inspired because it makes so little sense. At any rate the notion did not arrive at its full bloom until Romanticism, which made, to me, the unfortunate and theoretically disastrous decision to separate poetry from rhetoric. Hegel placed the arts, including literature, at nearly the apex of the hierarchy of the spirit, that is, in more modest terms, culture, or learned behavior. Religion he placed higher than the arts, and philosophy higher than religion. The impulse, to be sure, to judge the philosopher as the redeemer of mankind was not unique to Hegel; it is by no means uncommon in the history of philosophy. Hegel, however, did make an important distinction, even though he was not sure of it and even, it would seem, preferred not to accept it. I mean the distinction between the redemptive and the redemptionistic. Without for the moment considering why and how human beings are continuously concerned with their own value, I ask only that the notion be accepted, and the corresponding notion that the sense of one's own value is inherently unstable. A redemptionistic ideology, then, such as religion or a historical philosophy which promises in the future, either near or distant, an ideal social life, is an ideology that proposes that in some other form of self-conscious existence, either above the earth or inside it, or on it, we will experience eternally, as often as not, a relief from that inherent instability. Whether we are to go to heaven or hell or to some dreary Greek Hades or the Buddhistic Western Paradise, or whether mankind is destined for some condition of social perfection, the problem will be resolved. The redemptive, on the other hand, is merely the notion that one factor in the inherent instability of one's own value is the experience of that value, and it is the frank acknowledgment that we are constantly seeking such experiences for the simple reason that they keep us going.

The confusion between the redemptive and the redemptionistic was clarified by Hegel, but in such a way that it confused even him. On the one hand he believed that the history of man moves in the direction of freedom, by which he meant the increasing self-consciousness of the spirit, but that the goal of absolute freedom can never be reached, that the process, therefore, is endless. But he also affirmed that the historical process does have a goal and that that goal is the absolute freedom of the absolute and completed self-consciousness of the spirit. And he asserted that in spite of the fact that he knew perfectly well that the *Phenomenology* permitted no such conclusions, and said so. Of these two possibilities the cultural redundancy of Western Europe, insofar as Hegel was understood at all, selected the second, the redemptionistic, as it was only a secularized form of the overwhelmingly predominant and culturally redundant redemption-ism of Christianity and did little more than repeat the secularized op-timistic redemptionism of the Enlightenment. To be sure, there was a pessimistic strain in the complex weave of Enlightenment thinking. However, pessimism, I think, must be recognized as a form of re-demptionism. The human enterprise will end in disaster but at least the problem of value will be resolved. Schopenhauer was only the reverse of Hegelian redemptionism, just as, according to Hegel, the Kantian categorial imperative was only the reverse of the revolution-ary terror. During the 1830s and the 1840s the general thrust of Eu-ropean thinking was in the direction of Hegelian redemptionism. Marx is but one of innumerable examples.

In the 1840s, however, there was a reverse. The emergent position abandoned all modes of religious and social and historical redemp-tionism. By the end of the century all that remained as a source of value was art, the embodiment of the creative imagination. Observe how that word "creative" continues covertly the notion of the di-vinely inspired poet. In *Parsifal* Wagner presented the reason per-fectly: "Only the self-redeemed is truly redeemed." That is, only the individual in isolation, in social and cultural withdrawal, can by means of the aesthetic experience enter a transcendent realm of value. Such a transcendent experience assures the individual that only his experiences of value are real, and that his experiences of loss of value, of denigration and self-denigration, are illusions. This notion was fre-quently embodied in the notion of "style," for art was considered to be the unique appearance of style, and style was of the highest sig-nificance because it is metaphysically neutral. Hence aestheticism, or as I prefer to call it, stylism, became a secular redemptionism. Since then the only emergent redemptionism is the sexual as found in D. H. Lawrence, Wilhelm Reich, and *Playboy.* From this has emerged the notion—I have often encountered it—that all art is erotic, a peculiar mish-mash in which the ingredient of Freudianism is obvious.

The semantic theory of stylism was Symbolism. "A poem should not mean but be." That is, as the director of the Junior Great Books Program has informed us, a work of literature is applicable to an endless series of actual situations. In more sophisticated form this belief appears in the belief that the meaning of a poem cannot be limited. The meaning, or the interpretation, is important only to the degree it gives you access to the being of a poem, to the redemptionistic realm of stabilized value, and that any meaning or interpretation you ascribe to the poem is justified if it makes the experience of that access possible. This position is what I shall now call literary redemptionism. The present virtually complete failure in emergent academic literary culture to establish a theory of interpretation results from a redemptionistic position, not from a consideration of meaning in ordinary or nonliterary utterance. The striking and important consequence is the theory that literature is discontinuous from and not to be subsumed by verbal behavior, in turn subsumed by nonverbal behavior.

With the position of literary redemptionism it is impossible to argue, just as it is impossible to argue with a racist, or a social redemptionist, or a true believer of any religion, or a nationalist, or a philosophical redemptionist, convinced that philosophy is the way to establish the conditions of truth, or a believer in masculine superiority or a believer in feminine superiority. Their investment in the interest-bearing certificates of their value ideology is too great, and the interest rate is too high, for them to be susceptible to any argument. I know this from personal experience, for I was brought up and educated and trained in the culture of literary redemptionism; and it was only about twenty-five years ago that I began to have doubts. Indeed, it is even unkind to attempt to disabuse literary redemptionists of what I regard as their consoling illusion; at least it would be unkind to a great many of them, for deprived of that, they would have virtually no stable source of value left. Even my book of 1965, *Man's Rage for Chaos*, was an attempt to *prove* the value of art on the grounds of adaptation of organism to environment. In defense let me point out that the book ended with the suggestion that art and literature are terrible nuisances, and that if one is very old and very wise and very lucky one can get along without them. Alas, I am not yet old enough or wise enough or lucky enough for that happy result. Besides, talking and writing about such nuisances is how I make a living, and the economic advantages in commitment to a redemptionist ideology are very great indeed, and not only for Billy Graham and the Bob Jones University.

So the only thing to do is to go around literary redemptionism, to forget it, and to begin with human behavior itself, to assume heuristically the continuity between literary behavior and the rest of human behavior. One could begin almost anywhere, but I shall begin with the question I have been discussing. Is the ascription of value to literature continuous with the ascription of value to anything else, and in particular is it continuous with the ascription of value to oneself?

One central function of child-rearing is pretty obvious. The aim of the process of acculturation is to make the child sooner or later economically independent of the family of origin, or of a surrogate family. (In undeveloped societies the aim is to make the child economically contributory to the family.) To put it this way puts the emphasis upon training the child to be reasonably competent in the innumerable modes of learned behavior we call, in the anthropological sense, culture, from suckling to earning the Ph.D. Obviously in this process it is necessary to instruct the child in his degree of competence, and beyond that to train him to judge his own competence in any behavioral pattern. To accomplish it, it is economically parsimonious to have general or subsuming signs that the child is indeed being competent in a steadily increasing variety of behavioral patterns. The most obvious nonverbal signs are signs of love, while the most obvious verbal signs are "good" and "bad." Thus the child enters into the immense redundancy of agape or social love, that is, value ascription. Other signs of value ascription are presents on birthdays and holidays, and on unanticipated and, to the child, randomly selected occasions. As he moves out of the immediate family circle into interaction with his peers, child culture brings still more signs of value, the radiating centers of innumerable children's games. Extrafamilial value institutions are entered into, such as clubs or gangs, admission to which is a sign of value. From these develop not only the clubs of grownups, such as the Masons with their elaborate value ritual and rich set of value signs, but even more important, membership in a religious institution.

All churches and temples are as elaborate and as richly decorated as the community can afford, and ordinarily even more than it can afford. (The extreme simplicity of Puritan churches is a mere negation of this universal redundancy, to be classed with other modes of rebellious cultural vandalism.) The amount of economic value that is locked into religious buildings and their decoration should tell us, I think, what is going on. The ritual of communion alone is enough to reveal that the divine (i.e., the nonverbal and verbal signs that purport to represent and establish the divine) is the highest level in the regress of value judgments from judgments of competence. And for our purposes it is sufficient to point out that for most people the most splendid art and literature they encounter is that of their religion. The use of art as a value sign begins with clothes and toys and goes on to the Sistine ceiling.

But there is an incoherence in this system of establishing the ascription of value by means of various kinds of institutions, each with its defining insignia, that is, of maintaining competence by an immense redundancy of agape signs. One is that the individual child must learn not only to ascribe value to others but also to himself. He must become competent in the self-ascription of value. But he must also become competent in judging his own incompetencies, and competent in doing this without destroying his own self-ascription of value, of himself as a value sign, as part of the agapic redundancy systems. From this incoherence arises the inherent instability of the self-ascription of value. Is one or is one not a sign of one's own value?

From this incoherence emerges a new enterprise, the innovation of value signs. A culture as a whole innovates value signs as the economy develops, for the reason that value is a bottomless abyss. And the individual does the same, for the individual is the surd-like deposit of his cultural milieu.

Historically, as societies become more complex and richer, religious buildings and governmental centers (often the two are the same) are the most conspicuous and the richest sites for using works of art as value signs. It is not surprising, then, that as the individual develops his own economy, he invests it in the value signs of works of art. He imitates in his home as best he can the artistic richness of religious and government buildings. If he is a subordinate governmental center himself, he has the means, through taxation or skimming off taxation, to surround himself with works of art. And so on, down through the various economic levels, to the point at which only a few flowers, natural value signs, are available. The individual, then, ascribes value to a work of art to the degree it is effective to him as a sign of his own value. It is not surprising, therefore, that as European culture became secularized, art and literature became important sources of the individual's value, and at high cultural levels complex demands about responding to works of art became the norm, for the transcendence of religion continued into artistic and literary redemptionism. It is necessary to remember, however, that to a given individual anything can be a value sign, that there are any number of categories of value signs besides works of art, and that for probably the bulk of any modern population to use a work of art and one's competence in responding to it as a primary sign of one's own value is simply bizarre, or, more likely, incomprehensible.

If, then, there is a continuity between ascribing value to works of literature and the general behavior of ascribing value, if the ascription of value to works of art can be understood as no more than one redundancy in the vast complex of maintaining competence by means of the agape systems, the way is perhaps a little more open to accepting the subsumption of literary behavior to verbal behavior and behavior in general.

The first question to be encountered is, What is literature? If we can arrive at some conclusions about that it might then be possible to consider that possible continuity, or that literature derives from and is not independent of other verbal behavior; to consider, that is, what makes literature possible. Now we all know what literature is until we start asking ourselves what it is. And when we do that we do what we always do when we ask what any category is. We set about assigning to that category a set of attributes such that if the object or configuration in question can be said to be characterized by those attributes, then it is properly subsumed by that category. I put it this way because we do not ordinarily take the trouble to spell out the conditions of categorization unless we are in some uncertainty as to what the object is, that is, how it *ought* to be categorized. Now I certainly would not deny that literature is a category, since my position is that all terms are categorial, including proper names. But the question is, What kind of category is it? Only a cursory acquaintance with either theoretical or practical criticism instructs us in short order that that is a question on which there is a great deal of uncertainty and disagreement, sometimes violent. For 150 years or so it was insisted by all but a few that the poetry of Alexander Pope is not poetry at all, but only verse. On the other hand, Carlyle's *French Revolution* was once categorized as history, but is now categorized as literature. We can all think of endless examples of this phenomenon of judgment. Further investigation shows that judgments about whether a work is truly a work of literature or not are invariably in the interests of some higher-level or subsuming interest, which for the sake of brevity I will call an ideological interest. There is one kind of category which I believe to be very useful here. It is the disjunctive category which subsumes a collection of objects or discourses or whatever which have no attributes in common except that for some purpose or other it is useful to subsume them under the same category. "Literature," I believe, is a disjunctive category. To put it bluntly, a discourse is a work of literature if you say it is. And you can say it is a work of literature if you want to, for once you have learned from canonical works and from education how to respond to a recognized work of literature, you can so respond to any discourse.

To this the obvious answer is that literature is fictive. Now this is quite true, but is fictiveness a defining attribute of literature? When we think of scientific laws that have turned out to be fictions, or histories that have had the same thing happen to them, it would seem that fictiveness is not a defining attribute. But perhaps it is too much to ask that the category of literature have a defining attribute. Perhaps it is enough to say that it is a field with ill-defined and rather vague boundaries, that there are transitional discourses that lie between literature and nonliterature, and that, as long as we are reasonably confident about the attributes of the clearly belonging members of the category, we need not worry about what lies on the outskirts. And this is the way we ordinarily go about literary affairs. The interesting fact is, however, that what lies on the ill-defined and vague borders can be successfully categorized as either literature or nonliterature. This possibility suggests two explanations: one, that the realm of nonfictiveness includes literature, and the other that nonliterature is also fictive.

For the first position there is some evidence in the claims that literature presents truths, either directly or implicitly. I do not mean an otherwise inaccessible truth, such as the kind of truth claims for literature made by literary redemptionists, but ordinary statements, often, of course, very general in nature, such as "Most people are [or are not] in the last analysis morally decent." And there is not the slightest doubt that a great deal of literature presents, either directly or by exemplification or both, precisely this kind of truth. Thus what is fictive in literature is the exemplification of a truth, nor would it be difficult to show that the writing of a work of literature, like the writing of a work of philosophy, or political science, or history, or psychology, or anything else, is under the control of an ideology, or sometimes ideologies, even incoherent ones. Thus the detective story is under the control of the ideology, or mythology, or "philosophical truth" of causality. This leads us to the second position, that all discourse is fictive. This can be approached from two directions. One is that when we use the word "truth," what we are saying is that the statement for which truth is claimed ought to control our behavior. Thus, all statements, including general scientific laws, are normative. But are they also fictive? To this I reply, Yes. My reason is that man is a semiotic animal; his fundamental mode of behavior, on which all other modes of behavior rest or from which all are derived, is semiotic transformation. As the world comes into the individual's perceptual fields, it turns into signs. And I define a sign as a configuration distinguished from its ground and responded to. I put it this way because to say a sign is a configuration to which there is a conventionalized response makes it exceedingly difficult to account for unpredictable responses and innovative responses. The individual responds to a sign field by generating a sign field, whether it is a single word, like "ouch," the Sistine ceiling, or Hegel's *Phenomenology*. Such a generated sign field is necessarily a semiotic construct. Consequently it appears to me that claims that unequivocally true statements are possible are quite indefensible and, to demythologize such claims, are a factor in behavioral control. To put my point somewhat differently, philosophical skepticism has arisen only because philosophical claims to arrive at truth cannot be substantiated. On these grounds I would say that all utterance is fictive, as well as normative. What distinguishes literature from other fictive discourse, all other discourse, is that the fictiveness is announced, by some formula ("once upon a time"), or by typographic dress, or by tone of voice in oral literature, or "I heard a good story the other day" for orally transmitted jokes. It is for this reason that it is possible to announce to oneself that any discourse is literature, just as Meyer Abrams, quite fruitlessly I think, decided that Hegel's *Phenomenology* is best understood as a *Bildungsroman*.

Still, there is another sense of the word fictive which needs to be explored. No one fancies that the events of *Vanity Fair* really happened. Carlyle's *French Revolution*, however, is based upon documents which claim that the events offered in those documents really did happen. On the other hand, does anyone imagine that the events in Wordsworth's *Prelude* did not happen, no matter how he interpreted them? Or to take another example, a mixed example, the events of the Revolution of 1848 presented by Flaubert's *Sentimental Education* really did happen, were learned by Flaubert from various documents (since he was not in Paris at the time) and are attested to by plenty of other documents. In this restricted sense the novel presents both fictive events and historical events. The conclusion appears to be that literature may or may not be fictive, in the narrow sense of "invented" or "imagined." It would appear that in literature the fictionality of statements is a matter of indifference. In a work of literature anything can happen.

A word also needs to be said about the relation of fictionality to ordinary behavior. What is its source? A common answer, and perhaps the usual answer, is that it takes its origin from our capacity to fantasize; but that answer leaves us with the problem of the source of fantasy. The most common answer to this is that fantasy emerges from remembering, both conscious and unconscious. Here a difficulty encountered by the relatively new discipline of narratology is pertinent. The problem in narratology is the source of the sequencing of events, related either causally or some other way. But remembering, however, is by no means narrational or sequential but random, or, more mildly, associational. But fantasy has a directional or narrational character. Furthermore, under fantasy should be properly subsumed not only fantasies about what cannot happen, though we certainly would like it to or in darker moods are afraid that it might, but also fantasies about what can happen. When I plan to drive to a shopping mall and buy something in a department of a department store, I ordinarily experience a covert nonverbal sequential and narrational series of images of my route by car and foot to the area of my desired purchase. Or I may make a list of what I need at the grocery store. That is, I engage in planning. Planning, on the whole, seems to me a much neglected factor in human behavior, our attention being ordinarily focused on the putative "causes" of our behavior. However we may account for the way we plan, it is clearly planning that is the immediate control over what we do. Hence I propose that fantasizing has its source in what is much more important in what we do, planning, and that planning, since it is narrational and sequential and ordinarily causal in structure, is the source of fictionality. Thus there is no discontinuity between planning an errand and writing a novel, since planning is the structuring of remembering.

Both Professor Barbara Herrnstein Smith and I have arrived independently at similar conclusions. She has written in her excellent *On the Margins of Discourse* of the kind of situation which is characterized by permissiveness of constructed discourses, distinguishing it from ordinary situations of "the marketplace," situations in which the primary interests for the speaker or writer are economic and controlling. With this position I entirely agree, though I would add—exploitative. The way I put it is that the literary situation is one in which both reader and writer are not directly under the control of economic institutions, or government, or education, such as the family, or religious. Oddly enough the probability of the adequacy of this definition of the literary situation is improved in that in a great many countries and cultures the writer and the reader are both under stringent control by governmental, educational, or religious institutions. To us such control seems aberrant and a failure in human freedom. To authoritarian countries and cultures our position no doubt seems aberrant. Indeed in modern times such governments and intellectuals in such countries have often enough said so. In advanced societies freedom from censorship is both recent and rare, and becoming rarer. No one can deny the fact that a great many popular writers, like Harold Robbins, are directly under the control of literature as an economic institution. Nevertheless, the very fact that the literary situation can be permissive is enough for the present argument, as is the fact that the writer is usually free, even in authoritarian cultures, to write material which has no relation to the exemplification of enforced ideologies. Thus the majority of nineteenth-century Russian opera libretti were derived from fairy stories.

I would propose, then, a distinction between institutional discourse and literary discourse. However, this does not mean that there is any discontinuity between the two simply because there is a tendency in literary discourse to intensify cultural permissiveness. Actual literary discourse ranges all the way from a discourse so tightly controlled that it is indistinguishable from or at least continuous with institutional discourse to total permissiveness, such as that so marvelously and absurdly exploited by Gertrude Stein—or for that matter your favorite pornographer. Thus in the matter of fictiveness there is a continuity between ordinary verbal behavior and the verbal behavior of literature. This does not mean, of course, that there are no cultural conventions which control both the range and degree of literary permissiveness. For us historical discourse must not include speeches or dialogue, unless they are quoted from a document for which immediacy and accuracy are claimed. But Classical historical writing had no such convention, at least as far as speeches were concerned. The distinction between epic and history was not the sharp one we make. But such cultural conventions are no different in kind from the cultural conventions which control the writing of military correspondence or scientific reports. Nor are they different from the cultural conventions of nonverbal behavior, such as which fork to use or whether or not infants are to be breast-fed in public. The conventionality of literary norms is continuous with the conventionality that governs and controls all of human behavior and is not to be understood apart from such ordinary conventionality. The reasonable conclusion from all this is that any statement that begins, "Literature is . . ." or "Poetry is . . ." should either be ignored or studied as a cultural phenomenon of some interest, with a view to discovering the ideology that controls it.

I shall turn, then, to the next problem in which I believe it to be fruitful to subsume literary behavior under various modalities of ordinary behavior. I have proposed that what marks literature is that the fictiveness of the discourse is announced, and that the individual reader can categorize any discourse as literature if he so desires. He can respond to a scientific report exactly as he responds to a novella by Henry James, and more than once I have run across the claim that the dialogues of Plato are most fruitfully categorized as philosophical fiction, rather like the novels of Aldous Huxley. Plato, then, offers not a rigorous search for truth but an entertainment of ideas. What makes such an announcement of fictiveness and such a recategorization of discourse possible? The problem can be put in several ways. How is it that the work of literature can offer you entertainment and amusement, which you can take seriously or not as it pleases you, or in order to give you something to do when you are not under the control of institutions? At least it can offer this amusement to those individuals who like and are interested in verbal entertainment. I have proposed elsewhere that an interest is a behavioral strategy that restricts the range of behavior and thus provides a defense against the randomness made possible by semiotic behavior and almost infinitely more possible by verbal behavior. Hence only a minority of any population prefers to spend most of its noninstitutional time in verbal amusement, a point that is worth remembering when we lament that more students do not elect literature courses. But it also seems to be the case that most people like to spend some of their free time in verbal amusement, though proportionally fewer today when so many other varieties of amusement are available. Only literary redemptionists think the world would be a better place if, as I. A. Richards put it, everybody learned to be good readers of poetry. To be interested in literature is no different in kind of behavior from being interested in repairing carburetors or in robbing banks. Still, the question remains as to what makes it possible to suspend for literary purposes the normal conventions of institutional discourse.

Another way of putting the problem is to consider why it is that truth value is not immediately ascribed to all utterances. Why do we not assume that all statements, all utterances, are true? That is, what makes it possible for us to determine that some statements ought to control our behavior and that other statements ought not to, and how is it that we can make the distinction? When I consider this question I like to think of the sixteenth-century Puritans who said that it was morally evil to go to the theater or read fiction because in doing so you encountered only lies. Sir Philip Sidney was a poet and found this offensive. In rebuttal he climbed upon the highest horse he could find and claimed that poetry presents higher truths than does history. The best I can make of this is that a truth that is announced as a lie is a higher truth than a truth which is announced as a truth. With that I turn my back on Sir Philip and return to the much more interesting Puritans. For indeed literature is a lie, or rather it can or cannot be. When Elizabeth Browning wrote her *Sonnets from the Portuguese* and addressed them to her husband she certainly did not think she was lying about the love for him stated in the poems. Rather, what she was saying seems to be something like, "I can say 'I love you' in the rhetorical conventions of English love poetry with greater precision, fullness, and emotional intensity than I can utter the same sentiments when we are both worrying about when funds are going to arrive from England or whether or not I am going to have another miscarriage." Or she could have been saying to herself, "I have ceased loving Robert, but since I am stuck in Italy and my father is behaving very disagreeably, I don't want him to know it." The *Sonnets from the Portuguese* could have been boldfaced prevarications. It is not a question of whether literature is sincere or insincere. It can be either. Nor is it necessary that we decide one way or the other. We can say that whether or not a given work is sincere is of the first importance, or we can say that the question of sincerity in literature is completely irrelevant. Both positions have been hotly argued, and no doubt will continue to be argued just as heatedly. What the argument means is that the literary situation of the reader is as permissive as that of the writer. But to this matter, that of interpretation, I shall return.

To make the distinction between true and untrue statements, as I have defined them, is something children learn and must learn at a very early age. To understand what is at issue we must consider the learning of any behavioral action. No behavioral action is learned in isolation from and/or without reference to a situation in which the action in question is the appropriate action. To learn an action is to learn, then, the protocols of a situation. Further, that learning is eventually, if not immediately, learned in terms of categories or kinds of actions and situations. "We don't go up the down staircase. We go up the up staircase." Eventually the child learns that no two members of a situational category are precisely the same and that therefore the action appropriate to that situation, itself a category of action, must be subtly or grossly modified. From this it is but a step to learning that an action may be performed in a situation to which that action is inappropriate. The child learns the game of "let's pretend," but having learned that, it can learn, when questioned about some offence the commission of which offers the promise of punishment and threatens immediate loss of value, to say that it did not commit the offense when in fact it did. In the judgment of the mother the appropriate response to her question is an admission of guilt; in the judgment of the child, the appropriate response is an affirmation of innocence. To distinguish such behavior from action I shall call it performance.

The interesting Puritans, then, were making an almost valid point when they objected to the lies of plays and stories. But they omitted an important factor in the situation. This can be understood by considering the white lie. Someone lies and then subsequently says, "Yes, I was lying, but I did so for a morally justified purpose." The speaker to whose utterance the response was a lie judges one set of protocols to be appropriate to the situation; the liar judges quite a different set of protocols to be appropriate because he judges the normal protocols to be inappropriate. Now on learning of the total situation we can either disapprove of the white lie on the grounds that one should never lie, or approve of it, on the grounds offered in justification. What is involved is the perception of a two-tiered situation. The protocols as judged by the white liar are hierarchically superior to the protocols as judged by the original speaker. In the theater we have precisely the same situation. We can be horrified by seeing a murder on the stage, and then applaud the actor for having performed the murder so convincingly. In the opera situation we can be deeply involved in responding to the aria in which the heroine laments the suffering the situation of the drama has forced upon her, and the next moment applaud her for the beauty of her singing, appropriate to the theater. Likewise in the theory of acting there has long been an argument as to whether the actor should feel the emotion presented by various verbal and nonverbal signs, or whether he should simply be masterful in presenting those signs. It is not possible that that argument will ever be settled one way or the other. What both actor and audience have in common is the permanent possibility of judging the situation from the awareness of either level. The characteristic audience response is one of flickering from one perception to the other, but most people tend to judge a play successful if they are responding to the performance as action, that is, perceiving the appropriateness or inappropriateness of the behavior in relation only to the situation of the play. They are, as we often say, carried away. On the other hand, many critics—and this is often said to be the proper pursuit of criticism—judge the behavior solely according to the protocols of the theater situation. Music criticism brings out this distinction quite sharply. Critics tend to have a particular style of judgment. One may say that he was moved by the pianist's performance, and then justify his decision of excellence by discussing the pianist's technical competence, his mastery of the protocols of playing the piano; or he might say that he was moved in spite of certain technical lapses. Another critic may be totally uninterested in whether he is moved or not, or may even be suspicious of being moved, and discuss solely the technical competence. This goes back to the question of value ascription of works of art. In any case, the judgment of competence always follows the value

ascription and is most fruitfully considered as a justification or rationalization of the ascription of positive or negative value. And of course
the same conditions hold true of responses to and criticism of works
of literature.

But at this point a distinction needs to be made in the use of the
word "performance." We can say of a political speaker that his performance was superb and he was absolutely sincere; or we can say
that his performance was superb but he was lying through his teeth.
The distinction can be brought out if we say that his performance was
superb but that it was *only* a performance. Thus in one sense of performance we are responding to the mastery or competence of the protocols appropriate to the situation, and in the other sense we are
responding to the situation as two-leveled. When we say that we
know someone is lying, what we are saying is that the liar judges the
situation to be two-leveled and we judge that he is making that judgment. Now clearly literature is a performance in the second sense. Or
is it? Performance, in the sense of distinction between action and performance, is what makes literature possible, but the uncertainty as to
whether the author is sincere or not, that is, as to whether or not the
work is an action, is a constant. It is not enough to say that we know
it to be a performance because in the kind of situation which the work
presents or implies the verbal behavior is not that of ordinary situations. True enough, but we can say that of a political speech or of a
scientific report or an analysis of the economy. Literature has its conventionalized rhetorics, but there are also conventionalized rhetorics
for any interactional situation, including interaction with oneself. For
some people whether a literary work is an action or a performance is
a matter of indifference; for some it is a matter of vital importance.

For example, suppose I receive from my nephew a birthday card
with a typical bit of greeting card poetry. I can say that the competence
of the poem is at a low level, but that the poem is not a performance
on the part of my nephew but an action, even though he did not write
it himself. But I can say this only because I already have reason to
believe on other grounds that my nephew is genuinely fond of me.
Or that he wants to be my heir and the poem is only a performance.
This brings up two eternal difficulties in the fact that we can both act
and perform. One is the famous James-Lange theory. If we engage in
a performance often enough and long enough, our behavior will have
a tendency to shift from performance to action. The corresponding
difficulty is that we are constantly engaged in judging whether a behavior we are put in a position of responding to is an action or a performance. Some of you may very well be saying to yourselves,

"Peckham is putting on a pretty good performance, but it's only a performance. I don't really think he believes a word of what he is saying." Others of you may be saying to yourselves, "Peckham really believes what he is saying, but he is not saying it very well. I can only half understand what the devil he is trying to assert." In short, the fact that we can both act and perform is responsible for the inconsolable duplicity of human behavior. It is why lying, hypocrisy, deception, cheating, conning are possible—and literature.

If performance, then, is what makes literature possible, there is no discontinuity between literature and the rest of human behavior, verbal and nonverbal. However, even if verbal conventionality, or rhetoric, is not a defining attribute of literature, is there no defining attribute, no attribute which justifies us in saying that literature is in some way discontinuous from the rest of verbal behavior? I think the answer is Yes, with qualifications. I have maintained for a good many years that art, including literature, is characterized by perceptual-categorial discontinuity. My position is that literature, like the other arts, offers the violation of expectancy, or the failure of predictability; and requires, for adequate response, a toleration of uncertainty in categorization, or sustained problem exposure. Let me give a few examples from literature to show what I am talking about. In poetry there is a violation of a preestablished rhythmic pattern, and of a newly established rhythmic pattern; the violation of an established rhyme scheme; the violation of the pattern of an established stanza structure; the violation of an established caesural position. In lyric poetry, in the formal essay, in fiction, there is the violation of a rhetoric which implies a stable and coherent persona or narrative voice or speaker; in both prose and poetry there is the violation of syntactical rules. In both poetry and literary prose there is the violation of established rhetorical modes. What we call character development is the violation of the established attributes which the narrative has implied for a proper name. Plot is the presentation of a problem the solution to which is postponed as long as the writer desires, and which he further postpones by the introduction of subordinate plots, which may or may not be related to the main plot, or may be only thematically related. But once again, is this kind of violation of expectancies unique to literature?

The answer can be illustrated from certain detective novels, in which the professional police detective quickly arrives at the wrong solution, but the more patient, more intelligent, and better educated amateur detective, ordinarily from a higher cultural level, arrives much later at the correct solution. Thus problem exposure in institutionally controlled situations tends to be extremely limited and even when permitted is under the control of the behavioral protocols of that institution. Sustained problem exposure and violation of the institution's protocols are ordinarily to be found only at the highest hierarchical levels of that institution. Moreover, the individuals permitted that kind of behavior are protected psychically with quiet offices, socially by secretaries and aides who limit access, and economically by high salaries. This last is particularly important, because it is essential for such risk-taking personnel to know that if they fail and are dismissed they will still be at a high income level. The sustained problem exposure of both writer of literature and reader, then, is not discontinuous from other verbal behavior, especially since the kind of sustained problem exposure characteristic of the highest level of institutional behavior is almost entirely verbal. Literature, then, is marked by an intensification of perceptual-categorial discontinuity, and the higher the cultural level at which the work is written, the greater the intensification. But clearly that intensification is an aspect of the permissiveness of the literary situation, not a defining attribute which makes literature discontinuous from the rest of behavior.

We come, then, to the last question but one which I wish to explore. Why is the literary situation a permissive situation? To answer this, I return to the learning of actions, and to the point that an action is a category of an action, and the situational protocols learned as part of the action are the protocols of a category of situations; and therefore any emergent situation requires modification of both action and protocols. That is what we mean by behavioral adaptation. For several reasons any behavior, action or performance, is always to a certain extent inadequate and inappropriate to it. The first reason is that behavior is learned, and learning is always imperfect relative to what ought to be learned. The second is that we can never identify and respond to all the factors in a situation which have a bearing upon it and on our action. And the third is that we must act, must keep going, must get on with it. However, the discontinuous character of the literary situation, for both writer and reader, is by no means so compelling. I am speaking, of course, for the normal reader and writer. Professional readers, who read in order to get material for giving a lecture or running a discussion group, are under the control of an institution. Professional writers are under the control of what I have mentioned before, economic literary institutions. Ordinarily the permissiveness of the literary situation permits not only the absence of compulsion, but also the leisurely exploration of factors pertinent to the reading and writing situation, and correction and improvement of our learning in order to respond with some adequacy to literature. The adaptational purpose of the literary situation now becomes, I think, relatively clear. What the permissiveness of the literary situation permits is what ordinary situations do not permit—training in sustained problem exposure and in the tolerance of categorial instability, which in turn involve improved competence in verbal behavior and modification and correction of the cultural norms of verbal behavior. For this last one example will suffice. I have suggested that literature exemplifies an ideology, itself a mode of verbal behavior. But because of the permissiveness of the literary situation a work of literature can reveal by means of exemplification the inadequacy of any ideology. That is why any newly installed authoritarian regime either gets complete control of writers, and through educational systems of readers, or imprisons and executes them. Moreover, there is another factor which the permissiveness of the literary situation makes possible, and that factor is the nature of meaning. My position is that meaning is not immanent, that the meaning of an utterance is a response to that utterance, or, to state the proposition with greater precision and to account for the selective factor in response, meaning is the determination of what is judged to be an appropriate response to an utterance.

This brings me to the final point I would make about the continuity of literary verbal behavior with the rest of behavior, both verbal and nonverbal, the question of interpretation. At the present time the problem of interpretation is increasingly polarized. At one pole are those who insist that the task of the interpreter of a work of literature is to determine the one possible meaning of the work. At the other pole are those who insist that it is the character of literature that it is capable of an endless variety of interpretations and that new interpretations ought to be innovated. As for the first position, it is clearly impossible. If perfect and final interpretation is the goal, then it can be approached only asymptotically. But even the notion of an "asymptotic approach" is suspect, for it implies that it is possible for us to know whether or not we are approaching a final and certain interpretation. And this is not possible, for reasons to be examined in a moment. The objection to the other position is that reinterpretation is not a defining attribute of reading literature. Here again there is continuity with the rest of verbal behavior. The simple state of affairs is that a culture is constantly reinterpreting any document or discourse which is highly valued within that culture, particularly if that document is granted a role in behavioral control. This would seem to exclude literature, were it not for the fact that literature frequently exemplifies those controlling documents. One has only to think of reinterpretations of the Bible, or of the Constitution, or of scientific theories, or of philosophical and theological treatises and essays—in short any document which is granted authority in settling any kind of argument, religious, moral, political, critical, and so on. Innovative and emergent reinterpretation is actually a norm in verbal behavior. Any major cultural redirection or innovation brings about all kinds of reinterpretation. Marxism and Freudianism are obvious examples, and I have already spoken of the impact of aesthetic redemptionism as it appears in Symbolism upon the interpretation of poetry. In the matter of interpretation, then, the permissiveness of the literary situation is continuous with the permissiveness in situations under institutional control.

It would appear that the claim for total permissiveness in the interpretation of literature on the ground of its discontinuity from nonliterary verbal situations is without foundation. What is needed, obviously, is a theory of interpretation. Without attempting here to propose one, since I have done so elsewhere, it will be enough for the present purposes to point out, on the basis of what I have said so far, that in ordinary verbal interaction there are two norms of interpretation. Since meaning is not immanent but is a determination by an individual, and since there is therefore no theoretical limit to the interpretation of any utterance, the effort in all interpretation is to set up limits to interpretation. This is the case whether the interpretation is rigorously controlled with the heuristic aim of arriving at a final and perfect interpretation or whether it is performed under the control of a total permissiveness. In fact, it would seem that the latter is more likely to set up rigid rules for interpreting than the former. The explanation for this can be found by examining the conditions of the two norms of interpretation. One norm proceeds by directing its attention to the situation in which the utterance in question emerged. Note that I used the past tense, "emerged," not "emerges." When I reply to an utterance, that utterance is no longer in existence. My reply is historical, whether the utterance has ceased to exist only a moment ago or two thousand years ago. To be sure, an utterance may be recorded in a document, but as utterance it no longer exists. In either case, if I am uncertain about how to respond—and uncertainty is the fundamental condition of semiotic response, for reasons already given—I attempt to derive from the situation in which the utterance emerged limits to my interpretation. This kind of interpretation is ordinarily known as intentional interpretation. But "intention" is a word like "truth." When we tell ourselves to look for the intention we are only telling ourselves to set up limits to our interpretation derived from our analysis of the situation in which the utterance emerged. "Intention" merely says that we are uncertain, and that if we are to get on with the job we have to do something about that uncertainty by considering the situation. The error is to suppose that intentional interpretation can ever be complete, perfect, and final. Yet it can be richer than it ever is.

For help at this point it is useful to turn to the philosophy of science, which emerged at about the same time that philological-historical scholarship did, and from the same cultural situation. The scientist, guided and controlled by a theoretical construct, generates by means of experimentation a set of data, from which, both controlled by his theory and with the aim of improving it, he selects a subset of data. That subset operates a feedback which he *interprets* as confirming or disconfirming his theory or modifying it. Further, in his experimentation he necessarily generates more data than he can use and data of a kind he cannot use at all. The historical scholar, seeking control over interpretation, generates from documents and artifacts (such as nonverbal works of art) surviving accidentally from the situation in which his text emerged, sets of data which he uses to control his interpretation of the text, his initial interpretation of which is structurally analogous, and even identical, with a scientific theory. Again, like the scientist, he must perforce select a subset of his data and use it to confirm, disconfirm, or modify his interpretational theory. The apparent difference is that the natural scientist is responding to data which are not man-made. But his apparent difference is of less significance than it appears to be. All perception is interpretation, and the scientist is as much an interpreter of his data as is the literary historian, and his interpretation is just as much under cultural control. From this analogy or identity between the natural scientist and the literary historian a further lesson of great importance may be drawn. A science becomes more satisfactory and adequate to a larger range of sets and subsets of data not by arriving at "true laws of the universe" but by exploiting the inherent instability of scientific theory. Late in the nineteenth century the realization of this condition of scientific development led directly to the explosion of science in the twentieth. Thus it is not only the case that the literary historian cannot arrive at a final interpretation; it is also the case that he can make his interpretation more adequate and satisfactory by exploiting the inherent instability of his interpretation of a text. And, as we look back over the development of literary historiography during the past five-and-a-half centuries, we can see that that is exactly what has happened, even though the practitioners of the discipline did not know it. And in that they were just like scientists of the past and even most scientists of lesser rank today. We cannot "know" the "true and perfect and final interpretation" of *Macbeth*, any more than a scientist can "know" "natural laws," but we can interpret with greater adequacy, satisfactoriness, and richness more of the verbal data of that text than Alexander Pope could.

The other norm of interpretation extracts the work from its situation of emergence; but it does not interpret it nonsituationally. Rather it places the work in a different situation. I shall call one norm genetic interpretation, and the other norm antigenetic interpretation.

Antigenetic interpretation uses the work of literature to exemplify an ideology. Deconstructionalism, for example, exemplifies the Romantic ideology of the analytic dismantlement of the superstructure of Western culture. Antigenetic interpretation has always been practiced. It is one way of preserving the canonicity of valued literary works, just as it is one way of preserving the canonicity of any culturally valued and authoritative document. The interesting thing about it is that it is more rigid in setting up its limitations than genetic interpretation. Once an utterance has been removed from its situation there are no limits to its interpretation. It must be put into a situation other than that from which it emerged. Rigid and inflexible limits have to be set up or interpretation assumes the character of schizophrenic discourse, sliding by analogy and metaphor from one mode of interpretation to another, without any control except the personal limitations of the interpreter. Genetic interpretation, however, has a built-in flexibility, because the situation is inexhaustible and interpretation proceeds by exploiting its inherent instability and its power to generate fresh situational data, not only from other literary texts but also from the full range of texts and artifacts available to the cultural historian. Consequently antigenetic interpretation can gain flexibility only by modifying the controlling ideology, or by abandoning it for another. Hence it is particularly open to ideological or intellectual fashion, as the history of criticism in the past fifty years makes very clear. Indeed, it would seem that the rate of change in antigenetic interpretation is going up, as indeed is to be expected. Thus it would appear that the interpretation of literature, whether genetic or antigenetic, is continuous with all interpretational behavior.

Am I in a position, then, to say that I have now proved that the study of literature is properly approached by considering it as a mode of behavior continuous with nonliterary modes of behavior? Not at all, for the word "proof" is no more than an instruction to terminate analysis and exemplification of the proposition in question. Like "truth," like "intention," like all utterances, "proof" is a normative term, telling us what we ought to do. Any proof can always be questioned. Rather, I believe my position makes it possible to examine usefully a number of hitherto intractable literary problems. Parsimony and fruitfulness are essential for any theory construction. I have endeavored to present reasons for thinking that to consider literary behavior as subsumed by verbal behavior and verbal behavior by the rest of behavior has the advantages of both parsimony and fruitfulness.

# Title and Name Index

# Subject Index

UNIVERSITY PRESS OF NEW ENGLAND publishes books under its own imprint and is the publisher for Brandeis University Press, Brown University Press, Dartmouth College, Middlebury College Press, University of New Hampshire, University of Rhode Island, Tufts University, University of Vermont, Wesleyan University Press, and Salzburg Seminar.

ABOUT THE AUTHOR

Morse Peckham was professor emeritus at the University of South Carolina. A recognized authority of European Romanticism, Peckham published numerous books on a wide range of topics, including *Man's Rage for Chaos: Biology, Behavior, and the Arts; The Birth of Romanticism, 1790–1815*; and *Explanation and Power.* His most recent book, *The Romantic Virtuoso,* was published in 1995 by Wesleyan.

Library of Congress Cataloging-in-Publication Data

Peckham, Morse.
    Romanticism and ideology / Morse Peckham.
      p.  cm.
    Includes index.
    ISBN 0–8195–6285–8 (pbk.)
      1. Romanticism.  2. Ideology and literature.  3. Criticism.
    I. Title.
    PN603.P393   1995
    809'.9145—dc20                   94–45308